Crowdsourcing the Law

Crowdsourcing the Law

Trying Sexual Assault on Social Media

Francine Banner

LEXINGTON BOOKS
Lanham • Boulder • New York • London

Published by Lexington Books
An imprint of The Rowman & Littlefield Publishing Group, Inc.
4501 Forbes Boulevard, Suite 200, Lanham, Maryland 20706
www.rowman.com

6 Tinworth Street, London SE11 5AL

British Library Cataloguing in Publication Information Available

Library of Congress Cataloging-in-Publication Data Available

ISBN 9781498550949 (cloth : alk. paper)
ISBN 9781498550956 (electronic)

∞™ The paper used in this publication meets the minimum requirements of American National Standard for Information Sciences Permanence of Paper for Printed Library Materials, ANSI/NISO Z39.48-1992.

For my parents, who believed Anita Hill.

Contents

Acknowledgements

First and foremost, thank you to Nicholas Paron for the careful work in researching and editing this manuscript. Nick, this book is infinitely richer because of your painstaking research and the thought-provoking questions that came up during our conversations. Thanks, also, to Jocquan Mooney for your attentive and culturally sensitive editing of the manuscript, and to Becca Rhode, who guided this project through its final stages. I also want to offer special thanks to my friends and colleagues, in particular, Gray Cavender. Gray, you have become a trusted advisor, mentor, and friend, and your support means more than you know.

This project was developed under the auspices of several grants and workshops. I want to acknowledge CEW+, the University of Michigan Center for the Education of Women, for providing research funding pursuant to a Riecker Undergraduate Research Grant, as well as the UM-Dearborn Office of Research and Sponsored Programs, which provided generous funds toward copyediting and indexing. I also want to thank the participants in the From Scolds to Trolls: The Silencing of Visible and Audible Women conference held at Lancaster University in 2015, especially Jamie Abrams, who has provided thoughtful comments and suggestions at many different stages.

Most importantly, I want to recognize those nearest to my heart, my students and my family. When I left corporate law, I could not have imaged I would have the opportunity to teach about topics I love across so many disciplines and environments. Every class I teach is a new adventure, and each group of students challenges my worldview—sometimes just a little bit, often a lot.

Lastly, to my wife, my daughter, my mother, and my mother-in-law, you are the strongest, bravest, and most creative women I know. You are my role models, and this book could not exist without you.

This book is adapted and reprinted in part with permission from *Hon est Victim Scripting in the Twitterverse. 22* William & Mary Journal of Women & the Law 495 (2016).

Introduction

In May 2017 Bill Cosby was tried on three counts of aggravated indecent assault. The jury hung, and the proceeding resulted in a mistrial. Just one year later, Cosby was retried. This time, the jury voted unanimously to convict.

What changed from the first Cosby trial to the second? Factually, nothing.[1] For alleged victims and perpetrators of sexual assault, however, 2018 was a different world. In January 2017, amid abundant criticism, Donald J. Trump was sworn in as the forty-fifth president of the United States. The election inspired waves of social media campaigns. Previously silent masses tweeted #NotOkay. Ultimately, the #MeToo and #TimesUp social movements attracted hundreds of millions of participants around the world.

During the second Cosby trial, the judge took pains to explain that these social movements were excluded from the courtroom. He carefully questioned would-be jurors as to whether they had heard of #MeToo, disqualifying those who admitted their knowledge of the movement might impact their ability to remain impartial.[2] Jurors themselves discounted any impact these campaigns might have had on their decision-making, referencing instead the impact of legal-sounding criteria, such as evidence and credibility.[3]

Bill Cosby, however, was not just convicted in a bricks-and-mortar courtroom. He arrived at the Montgomery County courthouse having faced a drawn-out trial in the court of public opinion, his jury comprised of millions of Americans newly obsessed with dry procedural doctrines, such as statutes of limitations, and "woke" to the power of social media to effect legal change. Of 120 potential jurors in the second trial, only one claimed not to have heard at least something about the new, global conversation about gender, power, privilege, and consent.[4] After Cosby was convicted, celebrity attorney Gloria Allred proclaimed from the court house steps that the outcome meant that women would be believed, "not only on #MeToo but in a court of law."[5]

One way to study history is through conjunctures, snapshots of social relations at particular moments in time.[6] During some of these moments, authority remains unquestioned as people stick to the status quo. But during others—during moments of crisis, conflict, or dissent—spaces are opened up where power structures are made visible and definitions are open to change, out of which, ultimately, the trajectory of history may be altered.[7] Not every historical moment is up for grabs but, legally speaking, this one is. The verdict in the 2018 Cosby case is a sign that we are in a moment of crisis that may presage a shift in the institution of law itself.

Every day, millions take to social media[8] to post, pin, snap, and tweet about a host of topics, from wedding planning to parenting to recipes. They also offer opinions about emerging sexual assault allegations against a growing list of perpetrators from seemingly every corner of art, sport, and industry. Debates that just a few years ago would have taken place in real life have been relocated online; commenters are eager to share their thoughts on guilt or innocence with legions of virtual strangers.

Crowdsourcing—accessing and mobilizing the resources of the masses—is the newest model of activism and industry.[9] For entrepreneurs, the crowdsourcing model is an expedient and inexpensive way to identify and harness talent and to distribute risk. For activists, it is a means to motivate and to enfranchise. The unparalleled ability to mobilize the masses today is changing the character of social institutions ranging from education to religion to healthcare. Researchers even comment that, thanks to genealogy and DNA testing sites, "citizen scientists" are changing the ways in which we imagine the family itself.[10]

Like other institutions, law is not immune to the influence of the crowdsourcing model. Today, more than 60 percent of adults in the United States use social media, accessing platforms like Reddit, Facebook, Twitter, and YouTube.[11] Six in ten of these people use social media for access to news.[12] Engaging these online social network systems as archival sites, this book offers a "history of the present," situating contemporary debates about issues surrounding sexual assault cases—Cosby, Weinstein, Nassar, Turner—in the context of the history of rape law in the United States.[13] The methodology is best described as interpretive analysis,[14] focusing on the ways in which a collective legal consciousness about sexual assault is being constituted across varied online conversations—comments, GIFs, memes, and tweets.

Unquestionably, social media are playing an increasing role in influencing legislation. In 2016, a victim impact statement criticizing the six-month sentence received by Stanford swimmer Brock Turner for sexually assaulting an unconscious young woman went viral.[15] The next year, as a result of public outcry, California added mandatory minimum sentences for sexual assaults and broadened its definition of rape.[16] In June 2018, a landmark event occurred with the recall of judge Aaron Persky, who presided over the Brock Turner case. The petition to recall the judge had been circulated on social media and signed by more than a million people.[17] Persky was the first California judge in eighty-six years to be recalled before finishing his term.[18]

What does this ability to instantaneously access and mobilize public opinion mean for law, an institution whose essence and authority historically have been attributed to its antidemocratic principles and the protections it affords against a tyrannical majority? This important question is at the heart of this project.

THE NEW WATER COOLER

President Trump's election and first years in office attest that social media may be the new street corner or, perhaps, the new soapbox. In 2016, social network service Twitter appeared to be on its way out and then—deus ex machina—the Trump campaign emerged, igniting the service as a medium not only for political one-upmanship but for promoting national policies and engaging in international diplomacy.[19] Today, Twitter is one of seemingly countless social network sites[20] to which users gravitate to share opinions on a variety of topics and to forge connections with like-minded others.

The 2016 U.S. presidential election was widely described as a "referendum on gender," with candidates accusing one another of, at worst, sexual assault and, at least, complicity. In the midst of a contest steeped in appallingly sexist rhetoric, possibly the most jaw-dropping moment occurred when a several-years-old tape was released of then-candidate Trump stating,

> You know, I'm automatically attracted to beautiful—I just start kissing them. It's like a magnet. Just kiss. I don't even wait. And when you're a star, they let you do it. You can do anything. . . . Grab 'em by the pussy. You can do anything.[21]

In response to the tape, some suggested the candidate was a self-confessed sexual predator. Others, including the candidate, dismissed the comments as "locker-room talk," just typical hyperbole to which the candidate was prone. Further, some argued, even if true, this conduct only amounted to "groping"—not a "real" crime like sexual assault.[22] Polls taken around the election offer an entirely different, and perhaps more troubling, hypothesis—that voters may have *both* agreed that Trump's conduct met the legal criteria for sexual assault *and* decided that, in the scheme of things, such conduct should not disqualify a person from holding the highest public office in the United States.[23] After all, some voters reasoned, candidate Clinton's husband also had been accused of engaging in sexual violence, and Hillary Clinton herself was accused of covering up those crimes.[24]

Today, real-life ideological boundaries have been solidified to the point where it has become exceedingly challenging to converse across political, social, racial, and economic borders, particularly about "sensitive" topics like sexual assault. Despite substantial growth in public awareness about topics such as acquaintance rape, "slut" shaming, and rape culture, as a society, we remain hopelessly confused about which behaviors are criminal and which are, to borrow comic Amy Schumer's categorization, not criminal but also "not cool."[25] There is no one definition of sexual assault that applies across all fifty states today.[26] To complicate matters further, many of us may have experienced "gray area" behaviors, as witnesses, as targets of violence, or as perpetrators.

While the general public may feel uncomfortable discussing sexual assault with neighbors or coworkers, the popularity of Twitter, Snapchat, and a host of other social media platforms suggests that we are not shy about expressing our opinions online. Every day, over two billion people participate on social network sites.[27] Twitter, comment sites, and YouTube provide not only platforms for disseminating one's own opinions but a low-stakes space in which to establish connections with similarly minded strangers. If our opinions aren't accepted on one site, we can head to another.

Nils Christie once described the practice of lawyering as "stealing" conflicts from ordinary people.[28] As lawyers reframe disputes in a way that is recognized under law—sorting legally cognizable claims from merely emotional ones, culling "relevant" evidence, and defining one party as the "winner" and another as "loser"—important facts, sometimes the facts most important to the plaintiff or victim,[29] may be excluded from the courtroom. Christie wrote,

> [I]t is difficult to stage what we might call a political debate in the court. When the victim is small and the offender big—in size or power—how blameworthy then is the crime? And what about the opposite case, the small thief and the big house-owner? If the offender is well educated, ought he then to suffer more, or maybe less, for his sins? Or if he is black, or if he is young, or if the other party is an insurance company, or if his wife has just left him, or if his factory will break down if he has to go to jail, or if his daughter will lose her fiancé, or if he was drunk, or if he was sad, or if he was mad? There is no end to it.[30]

This critique gets at the heart of the objective of a criminal trial, which is not to ascertain the truth but to determine whether there is guilt beyond a reasonable doubt. The defense and the state sugarcoat facts, largely ignore victims, and encourage one-dimensional representations of perpetrators. Parties to legal cases may find it immensely dissatisfying to have what to them is the most important aspect of their narrative suppressed in the compressed and highly regulated environment of the courtroom. Within the stringent parameters of the law

> the big loser is us—to the extent that society is us. . . . It is a loss of opportunities for a continuous discussion of what represents the law of the land. How wrong was the thief, how right was the victim?[31]

In the court of public opinion, there are no such strictures. All evidence of guilt and all defenses can be considered regardless of seemingly arcane procedural considerations. In the physical courtroom, the judge is a gatekeeper, balancing whether evidence against the accused may be admitted based on the calculation of its probative value versus its possible prejudice to the defendant. Online there is no hearsay exclusion, no Daubert rule governing what constitutes "expert" knowledge, and no rule 702 prohibiting cross-examination of victims' character.[32]

In the case of recent accusations against comedian Bill Cosby, just one story on gossip site TMZ garnered three thousand five hundred comments.[33] A Fox News article about Cosby's conviction drew more than eleven thousand responses.[34] The law is not an abstract and distant entity insulated from public opinion but rather is being molded through these conversations that occur online every day. As Richard Delgado describes, "We participate in creating what we see in the very act of describing it."[35]

When people respond to a newly posted video clip on YouTube or comment on a recent gossip or news item, an opportunity arises—a conjuncture—in which law as an institution is open to critique, revision, and reform. While protests continue to be effected in "traditional" ways—marches, signs, phone calls to legislators—political change today is just as likely to be inspired through more novel avenues, such as memes or viral challenges. Social media also serve as a conduit for amplifying more established means of change-making, offering the ability to rapidly take an issue from local to global by setting up a GoFundMe site or moving a petition online to change.org.

Until recently, social media largely were disregarded as fields of study, dismissed as sites of "throwaway" speech unworthy of scholarly attention. Scholars shied from the type of granular, qualitative research in which this book engages, confronted by an abundance of hateful rhetoric, an information overload, and a lack of valid, generalizable data. However, to not explore the copious conversations taking place on social media is to risk missing the analysis of an entire cultural moment. As opportunities to engage with one another via social media have risen, so too have possibilities for everyday people to participate in creating law.

ARMCHAIR EXPERTS

As a practical matter, today, we are all experts in at least some aspects of legal studies. Sites like Nolo.com and LegalZoom.com functionally enable us to be our own attorneys, handling property disputes, drafting wills, and resolving petty conflicts without the expense or hassle of retaining counsel. Many local courts now offer virtual sites where litigants can manage dockets, pay fines, and even enter pleas, eliminating the need for physical courtrooms, judges, and attorneys entirely.[36]

Over the past thirty years, the public has honed its criminal legal expertise by consuming an increasingly steady diet of fictional, procedural docudramas like *CSI: Crime Scene Investigation* and cornball reenactments orchestrated by Judges Wapner, Judy, and Joe Brown. Today, "true crime" is the rage, thanks to myriad podcasts and binge-worthy documentaries like *Serial*, *Dirty John*, and *Making a Murderer*. Legal dramas have been transformed from the purely fictional—*Perry Mason*, *Columbo*, *Ally McBeal*—to shows "ripped from" real-life headlines—the *Law & Order* and *CSI* franchises—to simulacra of the real—*The Jinx*, *The Keepers*, *The Act* and many, many more.

In 1987, Arnold Schwarzenegger starred in *The Running Man*. Set in an imaginary, dystopian universe of the 2017 United States, the film features a *Survivor*-like game show to which viewers tune in each week to vote whether criminals should be pardoned or executed.[37] Around the time the film was released, *America's Most Wanted* kicked off a juggernaut fictional, legal entertainment half-hour program that was increasingly intertwined with real-life legal processes.

Since the 1980s, shows like *America's Most Wanted*, *COPS*, and *To Catch a Predator* have provided costs savings for television networks while performing an important public service, educating people about legal procedures and processes while assisting government agencies in crime control functions. *America's Most Wanted* was embraced by the Federal Bureau of Investigation as an opportunity to "build a national community of informants; the FBI website in turn promote[d] the television program on its official Most Wanted list."[38] Mariska Hargitay, best known for playing fictional Detective Olivia Benson for twenty seasons on *Law & Order: Special Victims Unit*, has leveraged her role on the show to testify before the U.S. House of Representatives and to launch, through her foundation, a nationwide advocacy campaign to fund rape kit testing reform.[39] In a particularly surreal development, after sixteen seasons on reality television, Kim Kardashian recently announced that she was going to become a lawyer, leveraging her status as a household name to work to free the unjustly incarcerated.[40] At this point it is unclear if Kardashian's attempts to join the California bar stem from the star's social justice commitment or her desire to introduce a new plot line.

The cost-effectiveness of "reality" programming, coupled with the rise of online subscription services like Netflix, Hulu, and Amazon, mean that the public is receiving more "true" or "real" legal information than ever before.[41] We are not just passive consumers of this legally oriented mass media. As *The Running Man* predicted, we are able to weigh in not just on who should remain on a tropical island or who should get the golden ticket but whether people should get married, if they are entitled to plastic surgery, and—more and more frequently—whether they are guilty of violent crime. After *Making a Murderer* aired on Netflix, garnering twenty million viewers in just the first week of the series, a viewer started a petition to free one of the show's protagonists, Steven Avery, on online site change.org. Today, there are more than half a million signatories urging reconsideration of Avery's conviction.[42] In February 2019, Avery won an appeal, one of only two cases in history in which a Wisconsin appellate court remanded a pending post-conviction case to allow introduction of new evidence.[43] The airing of another Netflix show, *The Keepers,* focusing on the unsolved murder of Catholic sister Catherine Cesnik, led to the development of a Facebook page that has well over one hundred thousand followers.[44] As a result of lobbying by that online group, the Maryland legislature recently voted to extend the state's statute of limitations for sexual assault victims to sue their abusers.[45] Social media discussions regarding the case have inspired other potential survivors to come forward with allegations of abuse by parties profiled in the series.[46]

The public today unquestionably has more access than ever to legal information and has a growing ability to mobilize based on that information. However, does access to information equate to understanding? So far, most research says no.

Viewing television shows and movies about the justice system does influence public attitudes toward law and crime, but this may or may not inure to the benefit of those actually involved in the legal system.[47] Manderson describes how, in 2006, General Patrick Finnegan, then Dean at West Point, met with the producers of the drama series *24* to discuss his concerns that the show was "influencing the thinking and training of U.S. Army officers."[48] The general cited a report by an advisory panel to the intelligence community concluding: "Prime time television is not just entertainment. It is 'adult education.'"[49] The type of education the officers were receiving, however, was not only dubious but concerning, encouraging expediency over due process, lone-wolf actions, and brutal interrogation tactics.[50]

Richard Sherwin describes the conversations about law that take place in popular culture as the intertwining of "real law" and "folk law," arguing that what the average person recognizes as "commonsense" legal knowledge is based in both fictional and nonfictional claims.[51] A prime example of this is the so-called *CSI* effect, the theory that viewing crime shows impacts jurors' expectations for now-disputed evidence and procedure in real-life trials.[52] "Folk law," however, is a benign descriptor for what is taking place today. More apt is Lawrence Friedman's characterization of the discussion of law in popular culture as a reflection in a "fun house mirror," replete with potentially insidious distortions and disinformation.[53]

Shows like *CSI* or *Criminal Minds* are not harmless guilty pleasures. These shows not only perpetuate myths about the availability of DNA evidence and the speed at which such evidence can be analyzed, more significantly, they tend to ignore potentially boring legal "technicalities," like the exclusionary rule, protecting defendants from being convicted on illegally obtained evidence, or the Brady rule, requiring prosecutors to turn over exculpatory evidence.[54] In their obsession with catching the "bad guys," they instruct viewers that crimes "arise from bad thinking and action and not from social circumstances or systemic issues."[55]

Documentaries like *Making a Murderer* do highlight procedural issues, such as police misconduct or false confessions; however, they risk entrenching a different, perhaps equally problematic mindset among viewers. Because such media are presented as "reality," consumers might be tempted to confuse them as portraying the "truth." *Making a Murderer* has been critiqued as heavily skewing toward the defendants' perspectives, omitting, for example, Steven Avery's previous involvement with physical and sexual violence.[56] Other "true" crime shows—*COPS*, *Lockdown*, *Snapped*—narrowly circumscribe what is displayed to favor the state, for example, beginning a story at arrest, the least favorable time frame for a suspect or defendant.

Cheryl I. Harris captures the impact of our growing consumption of law-focused media:

> [T]he paradoxical result is that visibility is heightened but our vision is obscured: We see more, but understand less. . . . The law becomes less a system of formally expressed rules by which reasoned decisions are reached . . . than . . . [a framework of] social control through which certain beliefs and images are privileged, legitimated and ratified and myths are given power.[57]

The coupling of today's "reality" crime and legal dramas, daytime courtroom shows, documentaries, legal commentary, and podcasts with the newfound ability to influence law on social media can educate the public and can inspire civic participation in inventive and exciting—but also potentially insidious—ways. This is particularly true in the context of sexual assault, which more than any other crime has been haunted by mythologies informed by gender, race, and socioeconomic status.

SOCIAL MEDIA AND RAPE MYTHS

A disturbingly large chunk of criminal law is founded on incomplete, reactionary, or wholly fallacious assumptions about human behavior; legislation often is passed based on research that is, at best, incomplete and, at worst, nonexistent.[58] We laugh at the ridiculous claims of yore that witches float or that those with "criminal tendencies" have strong jaws and protruding skulls, but to mock now-debunked criminal justice theories overlooks the extent to which—to a striking degree—our current legal system continues to be reactive, rooted in myths and moral panics. In the 1980s, for example, lawmakers promoted the images of the "crack baby" and "crack mom," stereotypes that not only turned out to be untrue but promoted racist societal beliefs that contributed to the disparate incarceration of Black men.[59] We are continuing to reckon with the impact of the juvenile "superpredator" scare during the same era, which led thousands of juveniles to be charged as adults, facing life without parole in state and federal systems.[60] In the 1990s, societal fears of child abductions led to the creation of sex offender registries, which the majority of criminal justice scholars argue are not only unnecessarily punitive and stigmatizing but also largely ineffective.[61] The list of misguided legislative decisions goes on and on. Sexual assault law, however, is the only area of criminal law where the foundational fallacies are so pervasive and harmful that they have been given a label: the rape myth.

Today, most of us probably are at least aware of the existence of rape myths—stereotypical and insidious beliefs about sexual assault that shape both black-letter law and public opinion about events, victims, and perpetrators. Some, like victim blaming, function as self-preservation, dispositional explanations creating an artificial distance between the victim and the general public by promoting the idea that survivors are personally responsible for an assault based on what they wore or where they went. Another self-protective myth is that the "typical" rape occurs when a stranger leaps out of the bushes at night rather than between beloved family members, colleagues, or friends.

Other rape myths function to maintain race-based, gendered, ableist, heteronormative, or otherwise privileged hierarchies, for example, the misguided idea that Black[62] men are more likely to rape than white men, that gay men are more likely than straight men to be "predatory,"[63] that only pretty women are victims, or that men cannot be victims at all. For centuries, the justice system treated these assumptions not as myths but as commonsense truths, meaning that rape law historically functioned to exclude countless deserving victims. The common law itself provided a very narrow definition of and severe punishment for the crime of rape.[64]

As Melissa Murray highlights, rape law historically was not about achieving justice for victims or protecting society. Rather criminalizing or not criminalizing sexual behavior has been an expedient vehicle for policing social relations, effecting discrimination, and enforcing social control. "Rape law constructed white women as wives and mothers, whose legal and social identities were mediated through and protected by their husbands. Together, rape law and the death penalty operated to protect white women because they were their husbands' possessions and the vessels for bringing forth the next generation."[65] A 1923 article in the *Michigan Law Review* detailed a husband's rights to consortium with his wife at common law: "In addition to his complete control over her property, he was entitled to her custody, her services, and her conjugal affection; any interference with those rights . . . gave rise to a right of action by the husband, based on the injury done to 'his interest in her.'"[66]

Numerous categories of persons—married women raped by their husbands, sex workers, LGBTQ+ persons, prisoners, and others—were not even considered under the law, dismissed as "unrapeable" because sexual access to their bodies was presumed. For centuries, Black women were excluded from legal recourse entirely, systematically raped as an integral part of upholding the terrorist system of slavery and later subjected to the roaming hands of employers as domestic workers.[67] As Fannie Lou Hamer famously opined, "a Black woman's body [was] never hers alone."[68] Both the extent of sexual violence against Black women and Black women's advocacy against such violence have largely been excluded from stories of feminism and of the civil rights movement.[69] In the United States, rape law also has had a Draconian impact on Black men, who have been wrongfully prosecuted for sexual assault in alarming numbers and who have faced extralegal consequences for presumed minor sexual transgressions like whistling at a white woman.[70]

Social movements like #MeToo provide a crisis moment, an opening for challenging fictions about sexual assault, but they also may operate as a tool for reinventing and reentrenching them. In the past, myths were oral traditions shared among the public in order to explain phenomena, an attempt to lessen fears by imposing a logical structure on events that otherwise seemed random and terrifying. Today, participants on social media are engaging in virtual myth creation, discussion of high-profile sexual assault cases serving to challenge or to confirm the validity of our own "commonsense" beliefs. Just as social media can be a vehicle for inciting social change, platforms like Twitter, YouTube, or news comment sites are also fertile grounds for making and reinforcing myths. Sexual assault law, more than any other type of law, is at risk of being influenced by conversations on social media, because rape law is built on stereotypes and fictions.

The study of social media is also particularly relevant to exploration of sexual assault law because rape is a crime for which justice often has been sought outside of formal legal institutional structures. The narrow parameters of common law rape statutes, coupled with courtroom processes excluding all but the most ideal victims, have made it unlikely that justice will be delivered in a bricks-and-mortar courtroom. Historically, even victims who did meet the stringent criteria for victimhood under common law rape statutes were unlikely to pursue legal remedies.

Collective outrage at and vindication of the theft of female purity is romanticized in fictional works from *Romeo and Juliet* to *West Side Story*. These narratives highlight that, unlike "simple" assaults or property crimes, which are deemed to happen to individuals, the crime of rape largely continues to be viewed as impacting not only the victim but her community.[71] This means rape, above other crimes, has been accompanied by a unique accountability—and often stigma—for survivors. Procedurally, female victims of sexual assault did not speak for themselves in the legal system but were spoken for by males—brothers, fathers, and husbands.[72] Under the doctrine of coverture, categorizing married women as under their husbands' legal protection, rape was perceived not as a crime against a survivor's bodily autonomy but rather the infliction of economic and reputational damage on a family or group. Across the globe, rape persists as an effective weapon of war because of this powerful and pervasive idea that the crime dishonors not only the person but the collective.[73] A shocking number of victims of sexual assault in many societies today continue to "disappear," shamed by what is deemed an irretrievable loss of honor.[74] As the community's honor is regained by avenging a woman's rape, the survivor herself becomes invisible.

In the United States, the sexual assault laws of today are much different than the rape laws of forty years ago. Since the 1990s there have been revolutionary changes across all fifty states. Among the significant accomplishments of the women's movement are the introduction of "rape shield" laws prohibiting attacks on an accuser's character, the gradation of crimes and penalties into degrees, and the abolishing of the problematic Hale instruction, a vestige of the 1700s that required judges to warn jurors about accusers' capacity to lie.[75] More recent changes to law include the extensions of numerous statutes of limitations and, in some localities, the imposition of affirmative consent requirements.[76]

Carol Smart warns, however, that the extensive changes to rape law being advanced by the women's movement risk being "Pyrrhic" unless greater societal issues also are addressed.[77] Today, although laws on the books have undergone radical change, neither rates of reporting sexual assault nor rates of conviction of perpetrators have radically increased as a result of legal reforms.[78] A recent FBI report identifies sexual assault as the second least solved crime in the United States, with a clearance rate of only 32 percent.[79] Recent revelations about the predatory behavior of Bill Cosby, Larry Nassar, and numerous others suggest that serial rapists have been operating for decades without consequence or accountability, despite the evolution of procedures designed to encourage reporting and facilitate prosecution. Examining how law is engaged in conversations on social media helps make inroads in exploring this disconnect, analyzing the ways in which sexual assault law on the books both contributes to and diverges from commonly held beliefs about and understandings of sexual assault. It can also help us begin to answer the vital question of whether the #MeToo movement indeed might break the wheel, at long last destabilizing the corrupt and exclusionary power structure that the law has so long supported.

HORIZONTAL CONVERSATIONS

How does one study social media? This project does so by approaching online archival sites, using methods that are engaged by legal scholars to explore legal consciousness in physical locations.[80] Susan Silbey characterizes legal consciousness scholarship as exploring and explaining the "gap" that exists between "law on the books and law in action."[81] As Halliday and Morgan put it, "[t]o study legal consciousness is to study the taken-for-granted and not-immediately-noticeable: the background assumptions about legality which structure and inform everyday thoughts and actions."[82]

Particularly influential in this project is the work of Peggy Levitt and Sally Merry, who introduce the idea of vernacularization to explain how complex, global legal concepts are presented to and, importantly, adapted within local contexts.[83] As legal pronouncements are disseminated from the top, vernacularizers—in social media terms, influencers—steer the conversation on the ground, translating and adapting complex concepts for the lay public, editing how much and what type of information reaches those on the streets. As David M. Engel highlights, the process of incorporating law into society is one of negotiation and compromise. As everyday people talk about legal concepts, ideals, biases, and assumptions are injected so that law in everyday life is not identical to law "on the books."

The idea of vernacularization is reflected in a statement by actor and political junkie Alec Baldwin, who tweeted in 2017 that evening talk shows were today's grand juries, and not very good ones.[84] Although intended to be humorous, his tweet rings true. Although law does have a *vertical* or top-down influence, the institution really is shaped by what Engel refers to as *horizontal* discourse, the conversations taking place within and across local—and virtual—sites.[85] As a methodological approach, "[t]he horizontal perspective does not place any particular conceptual framework in the foreground, but through observation . . . asks what discourses are found in particular fields of everyday life and only then considers the origins of key concepts, ideas, and beliefs that it discovers."[86]

Silbey explains that the gap between law on the books and law in everyday life is "useful to the powerful, because its persistence provides an alibi for the particular form that the gap takes."[87] It is within this space between law on the books and law "in action," for example, that rape myths are able to flourish. Each day, across social media, millions of "commonsense" opinions are offered about sexual assault cases, focusing on issues ranging from the veracity of alleged victims, to the guilt of the accused, to the fairness of the process. Presented as "evidence," these opinions all too frequently promote the continuation of unequal power relationships and protect the status quo.[88]

Just a few years or even months ago, we might have been tempted to dismiss social media as a racist, sexist, misogynist wasteland devoid of meaningful discourse. However, as recent judicial decisions involving the president's immigration-related tweets attest, just because comments are brief or crass does not mean that commenters are eschewing conversations about law.[89] In 2018, more than fifty courts considered whether binding contracts had been formed or intent shown by use of emoji.[90] The acceptance of tweets and emoji as legally significant is just the tip of the iceberg. Law on the ground is being constituted whenever everyday people battle over contested meanings. This is not happening in the courtroom, the classroom, or the break room. It is happening online.

To explore legal consciousness about sexual assault, this book adopts a case study approach that focuses on recent accusations against some long-standing household names—Bill Cosby, Donald Trump—and some more recently cast into the spotlight—Harvey Weinstein, Brock Turner, Larry Nassar, and Brett Kavanaugh. Because so few sexual assault cases actually reach conviction—and in an era in which, on average, more than 95 percent of criminal cases are settled via plea bargain[91]—examining the extensive public discussion of these allegations taking place online provides a unique and important lens into the real-life operation of sexual assault law today.

These highly publicized cases—and the parties thereto—are important because they provide an impetus and space for the public to discuss and debate contested social issues, to assess the state of our values and norms, and to consider where the boundaries between law and morality should lie going forward.[92] When sexual assault allegations are brought against celebrities—or when individuals are transformed into unwilling celebrities by sexual assault allegations—these are political trials. They are events that inspire the public to ask "[W]as justice done?" or perhaps to question the legal process as a whole.[93] Shoshana Felman describes how well-publicized criminal trials come to symbolize a collective "legal memory."[94] The name O. J. Simpson today, for example, is less likely to invoke a referential image of a former NFL player than a particular point of view on race relations, or an overarching feeling that the justice system delivered justice or inequity. With recent hearings still raw in the public imagination, the name Brett Kavanaugh already invokes less an image of the man himself than a general feeling that the system is biased or fair, largely depending on one's political leanings.

In the context of discussions about sexual assault—and by extension sexual relationships more generally—the bodies of public figures like Kavanaugh, Turner, and Weinstein become flashpoints for societal concerns, anxieties, and desires.[95] Monica Lewinsky recently wrote of the post-traumatic stress disorder she experienced after the politicization of her affair with President Clinton that her personal illness was "a microcosm of a larger, national [trauma]."[96] She describes the attention she received as part of Kenneth Starr's investigation of Clinton in visceral terms, including herself among observer and observed: "We watched the wholesale dissection of a young, unknown woman . . . who, due to legal quarantine, was unable to speak out on her own behalf."[97]

In the 1980s, feminists proclaimed, "My body is a battleground," the refrain signaling the extent to which women's personal sexual histories become sites for public debate about birth control, abortion, reproductive technologies, and sexual freedom. In the context of discussions about sexual assault, social media are sites in which the very bodies of parties to sexual assault cases similarly become battlegrounds as debates about intimate personal details are transformed into *political* discourse, critiques of individuals intimately connected to larger anxieties about race, gender, class, and power. For all of those involved in sexual assault cases—the accusers and perpetrators, but increasingly the attorneys, judges, and jurors—the personal is political.

As the merits of accusations and defenses and the validity of courtroom verdicts are debated among online commenters, social media become micro-courtrooms where incidents are reenacted, victims' veracity and perpetrators' responsibility are evaluated, and, often, the law itself is reimagined.

TYRANNY OF THE MAJORITY

Since its inception, U.S. law has been reactive to public opinion, with law and society forming a feedback loop.[98] Distinct from other historical conjunctures, however, today the power of "the people" to effect legal change is at an all-time high. And, importantly, overall respect for law and for the legal profession may be at a nadir. Although lawyers recently have reclaimed a positive spotlight for activities like representing undocumented migrants or separated parents and children, the profession is still recovering from the "tort reform movement" of the 1980s and 1990s which effected a powerful and successful smear campaign against civil law, constructing plaintiffs as greedy manipulators, plaintiffs' lawyers as smarmy "ambulance chasers," and the courts as a biased engine for rewarding the unworthy.[99]

In the criminal context, we may finally be correcting course from a lengthy period of backlash against the rights-expanding Warren court, a period during which judges and courts were constructed as biased and fickle, and judicial discretion framed as negative.[100] Nonprofit organizations like Cop Watch and Black Lives Matter have expanded public awareness about how not only courts but law enforcement historically have functioned to uphold a racist status quo. Books like Michelle Alexander's *The New Jim Crow* have raised consciousness about the systemic failures of the corrections system, connecting the dots between the racist and sexist history of the law and mass incarceration.[101] The significant popularity of specialty courts and movements toward alternative sentencing might indicate that judges again are seen as providing a voice of reason in the face of system-wide failures of justice.

Just when the idea of judicial discretion seemed to be on the verge of rehabilitation, however, thanks to crowdsourcing, mandatory minimum sentences are back on the table and individualized sentencing called into question.[102] It is heartening the extent to which conversations about recent sexual assault allegations against seemingly privileged defendants, like Brock Turner and Harvey Weinstein, on social media question the ways in which racial and socioeconomic inequalities impact criminal sentencing. It is less heartening that, rather than advocating for reducing sentences for poor or nonwhite defendants, commenters tend to advocate for extending criminal sentences, eliminating probation and parole, or otherwise expanding the net of the criminal justice system.[103]

Virtual conversations not only critique the participants in the legal system today, they question the institution of law itself. Over the past decade, we have witnessed a wholesale failure of public institutions to respond adequately to survivors of sexual assault; massive sexual assault scandals have tainted almost every venerated U.S. institution—churches, the military, prestigious colleges and universities. In the best case, these institutions blatantly failed to respond to repeated allegations of sexual assault. In the worst—and more common—scenario, these institutions marshaled resources to protect bad actors and endorsed rape cultures that sanctioned criminal behavior.

Lon Fuller proposed eight conditions that any law should meet to be a "good" law. Among these are that the law must be clear and intelligible, free of contradictions, constant, and administered in a manner consistent with its meaning.[104] The closer laws come to meeting Fuller's conditions, the more trust people will have in a given legal system. If the failure of sexual assault laws to meet these conditions is not made clear by the staggering rates of sexual assault reported across all branches of the U.S. armed forces, it certainly is visible with the revelation of chronic and systematic abuse of more than 150 young women by official team physician Larry Nassar, victims who included nearly the entire 2012 Gold Medal Olympic Gymnastics team—known as America's "fierce five"—or with ongoing convictions implicating predators in higher and higher echelons of the Catholic church.[105] As rampant sexual abuse continued across revered institutions, over a quarter of a million rape kits sat untested, allowing serial rapists to remain free.[106]

Donald Black famously proposed that law as an institution is at its strongest when other societal institutions—education, the family, religious organizations—are at their weakest. It is less clear what transpires when law itself appears to be breaking down. Concerns about political motivation and partisanship overshadow every level of the judicial process. The chief justice of the Supreme Court himself recently felt the need to reassert the independence, and therefore competence, of the judiciary, asserting, "We do not have Obama judges or Trump judges, Bush judges or Clinton judges."[107]

For centuries, legal scholars have insisted that the greatest value of law lies in these antidemocratic principles. When Alexis de Tocqueville toured the United States during the mid-1800s, he described the independence of the American judicial system as a crown jewel of our democracy.[108] The rule of law, judicial appointment processes, and doctrines like stare decisis are proclaimed to be bulwarks against the tyranny of the majority. But there is no roadmap for what happens when the institution of law itself is revealed to be so tragically flawed. As Juliet Williams observes, "[I]in the face of the catastrophic failure of the legal system to care for and deliver justice to victims of sexual violence, it is hardly surprising that the court of public opinion has emerged as a proxy for formal adjudication."[109]

As social networks increasingly become forums for decision-making, the historical rationales for limiting the influence of public opinion on law are amplified. Boyd et al. caution that it is important not to mistake the availability of online social networks for the presence of actual *networking*. Psychologists point out that online comments often exhibit "disinhibition," meaning that online we tend to be much worse people than we are face-to-face.[110] Factors such as geographical distance, the availability of anonymous identities, an absence of immediately responsive social cues, and a lack of proximate social consequences mean that we tend to say things online that we would never dare to—and may not even want to—say in person.[111] Social media offer an important venue for marginalized voices but, at the same time, a platform for outliers whose fringe views likely would be filtered out of in-person conversations.[112]

The collective tone-deafness in the virtual world is compounded by our persistent, human desire to form allegiances and social groups, even with virtual strangers. The internet has revealed a dangerous tendency toward political polarization, confirmation bias driving people to seek out viewpoints consonant with their own.[113] Comment sections on the web have become "magnets" for racists, misogynists, and trolls, a disturbing phenomenon that has caused many news sources to severely limit access or to eliminate such sections entirely.[114]

Hughey and Daniels describe how the structure of social media both "constrain and enable" racist, sexist, and homophobic discourse.[115] Online sites encourage users to aim for brevity—many set character limits and provide specific formats for posting. Although not subject to the stringent character limitations of Twitter, online comments also tend to be brief by necessity, with those that are too long receiving responses like DNR (did not read) or CSB (cool story, bro).

In an environment where being concise is essential and anonymity common, communicating one's own position and making connections with others often are accomplished via coded language and metaphor. Jack Dorsey, Twitter's founder and CEO, describes how "bird chirps sound meaningless to us, but meaning is applied by other birds."[116] His statement elucidates that, within the linguistic constraints of the Twitter service, once 140 and now 280 characters, connections to other users are established in shorthand via mechanisms like hashtags.

In a universe that depends on brevity, engaging recognizable, often race- and gender-based tropes provides a way for online commenters to quickly classify and order social relationships, as well as to articulate their own political and socioeconomic position vis-à-vis other users. Terms like "gold digger," "slut," or "bitch" are not merely derogatory but reaffirm the speaker's own superior social, economic, and moral standing.[117] On social media, what might have been isolated, lingering, or nascent biased views can be compounded and reinforced in the context of group dynamics that facilitate the displacement of responsibility for any particular point of view away from individuals and onto a group as a whole.[118] Research by the Center for Media Engagement supports this phenomenon, describing that comments that engage terms that are partisan or uncivil are more likely to be recommended, "retweeted," or "favorited" than those that are congenial.[119]

Patricia Hill Collins offers that dominant groups often come to define themselves by reference to the other, a group "makes itself through imagining itself as everything the Other is not."[120] Comments like "I'm not saying she's a slut, but" or "We all know that women are" are appealing because they accomplish two things at once—reducing personal accountability for prejudice and reinforcing the authoritative viewpoint of what we perceive to be the dominant group. As these comments multiply, moral responsibility is increasingly diffused and group dynamics work to encourage dehumanization and victim blaming.[121] In other words, the "gap" between sexual assault laws as written and public understanding of those laws has a tendency to be filled by discourse condemning the least empowered.

Rather than identifying the internet as colonized by sexists, homophobes, and racists, Celia Ridgeway describes online environments as replete with ordinary people who would not behave in these ways in their day-to-day activities.[122] Maureen Linker, similarly, refers to online conversations as a "release valve," allowing people to voice beliefs they may feel discouraged or thwarted from expressing in everyday conversations.[123] Linker observes that, in our rapidly changing world, many of us may "lack the language for thinking and reasoning about social issues in more complex and intersectional ways," causing conversations to default to using "reductive categories" in regard to controversial issues such as gender, socioeconomic class, or race.[124] If one is "working through" some racist, homophobic, or sexist views, the internet is an easy way to test the waters, enabling the sharing of one's views with an online public rather than voicing those views to colleagues or IRL (in real life) friends who may be less accepting.[125] Joseph Reagle notes of online comment sections that, although there is a reason they are at the bottom of the internet ("there is a lot of dreck down there"), "in sifting through the comments, we can learn much about ourselves and the ways that other people seek to exploit the value of our social selves."[126]

The tendency of social media to reinforce socially conservative points of view and to encourage expressing those points of view in the least civil way means that women, and especially young women, have been particular targets for online bullies, doxers, and trolls, with the rape and death threats suffered by outspoken women like game designer Anita Sarkeesian and writer Moira Donegan more the norm than the exception.[127] Haque writes of the experiences young women face online,

> We once glorified Twitter as a great global town square . . . But I've never been to a town square where people can shove, push, taunt, bully, shout, harass, threaten, stalk, creep, and mob you . . . for eavesdropping on a conversation that they weren't a part of . . . to alleviate their own existential rage . . . at their shattered dreams . . . and you can't even call a cop.[128]

If comments are not directly targeted at women, then women are still likely to encounter "ambient sexism," a consistent operation of male privilege in online discourse.[129]

As will be obvious to any Facebook or Twitter user, although the democratic promise of the internet may be limitless, social media have expanded the capacity of the public to share misogynist, racist, sexist, and all manner of "-ist" opinions. Although the effect is often to exclude women from the public sphere, both genders engage in online trolling of women pretty equally, reinforcing this hypothesis that the internet is a site in which we can all try new identities on for size.[130]

As a law student, I had the privilege of studying constitutional law with First Amendment scholars Larry Sager and Chris Eisgruber. The lasting refrain I retained from the duo was that "[t]he remedy for bad speech is more speech." As Ruthann Robson notes, today, social media have "largely replaced leaflets distributed on the corner as a source of information that will be used in making 'decisions which affect the welfare of community and nation.'"[131] Justice Alito labels social media sites the "21st century equivalent of public streets and parks."[132] Does the traditional approach to "bad speech"—dependent on one's capacity to drown out another speaker on the street corner—still hold true in the paradoxically confined and seemingly limitless arena of the internet, a place where it often seems like a tyrannical majority holds sway, emboldened by anonymity and empowered by a sudden ability to mobilize that knowledge, rapidly and deliberately, toward social change? Or, is the common refrain that "words can never hurt me" an obsolete adage that rightfully is disappearing with our deepening understanding that some speakers are imbued with louder and more authoritative voices than others?

Researchers today highlight the tangible harms inhering in exposure to hostile and demeaning words and environments.[133] Mary Anne Franks labels the First Amendment a "free speech fraternity," weighted toward upholding a white male dominated status quo and poised to inflict real harm on those who don't conform.[134] What happens when social media imbue what used to be called "mere words" with more power to influence law than ever before?

ETHICS AND METHODS

More than 65 percent of adults who are online and more than 75 percent of young people online are using some type of social network system to communicate.[135] So-called big data or metadata relating to the use of social network systems can reveal all sorts of information, from market trends to voting patterns. Such data can be extremely useful to the criminal justice system; for example, Hardaker et al. worked with the British government to analyze hundreds of thousands of tweets in order to determine the general geographic location of and hours in which people were most likely to tweet rape threats. The government then could use this data to make inferences about type of employment and socioeconomic status of those most likely to commit abuse in the online environment.[136]

While big data can reveal larger trends about crimes like cyber bullying, there is not yet an algorithm that can detect when users engage coded language, irony, nuance, and metaphor. We can quantify how many times a commenter mentions Bill Cosby, for example, but not necessarily capture the spirit of what was said about the celebrity or identify whether the comment was made in seriousness or in jest. As Hughey and Daniels, who engage in qualitative discourse analysis of racism in online comments, observe, "racist language has . . . changed form to become more subtle," the metaphors and coded speech used to signal racist perspectives may not be made visible via quantitative methodology or even with engagement of a qualitative method that involves counting, such as ethnographic content analysis.[137]

To capture the complex ways in which legal definitions and crime categories emerge over time, it is essential to engage qualitative research methods like discourse analysis. As Marwick identifies, it is by identifying a relatively small sample of comments to analyze that one can begin to identify power relationships.[138] When one moves from studying social media as big data to a more local level, however, new and complex concerns arise. Online commenting policies often require that users link their profiles to verifiable information, such as personal emails or Facebook accounts. Efforts to sift out hate speech and offensive comments may deter some people from participating in the virtual public sphere or coerce them to sacrifice privacy for the privilege of public participation.[139] Even when there is an option for anonymity, a striking number of accounts on social networks like Twitter or Reddit are linked to personal Facebook or Instagram accounts, perhaps unwittingly offering information not only about users themselves but family members, coworkers, and friends.

In our surveillance society it might seem ridiculous to suggest that comments and tweets are subject to privacy constraints. The very idea of social network systems like Twitter and Instagram is to collect "retweets" and "likes." Tweets even are used to conduct international politics. As Marwick and boyd point out, profiles on social media often are "constructed with a hyper-aware self-consciousness, as users [know] that misspellings, cultural references, and even time stamps [are] likely to be scrutinized by potential suitors."[140] The taglines for Twitter and YouTube claim, respectively, "You Are What You Tweet" and "Broadcast Yourself!"

Nonetheless, although online commenters may feel comfortable sharing their information with a community—even a community of people they mostly haven't met in real life—many people may perceive the idea that their information might appear as a topic of analysis in a scholarly journal as "horrifying, or at a minimum surprising."[141] Further, users' expectations of privacy are not uniform across social networking sites (SNS). Variations in mission statements, privacy settings, and intended audience may impact the level of caution that must be employed by researchers across diverse media. Hughey and Daniels describe the internet as

> a third space betwixt and between the public and private spheres. It allows for intimate discursive interaction and the formation of an "imagined community" between users who may entertain the notion that they are conversing in the private "backstage," when, in fact, their comments are on a public "frontstage" for all to read.[142]

To comply with the requirements of the Institutional Review Board at the University of Michigan–Dearborn, the tweets and comments analyzed herein have not been identified by "handle," alias, or user name. Any comments discussed have been accessed from sites publicly available for searching without a log-in. Although they would provide rich discussions about law, comments from Facebook—which cannot be searched without an account and that users may be more likely to identify as "private"—were not collected or analyzed. The tweets examined as part of this project were collected via Twitter's publicly searchable database, not by logging in to the author's Twitter account. Quoted comments and tweets are presented as originally posted without alteration or correction of spelling, grammar, and the like; however, unless they are attributable to a public figure, they are not identified by handle or user name.

Because this book discusses comments that are not only racist, sexist, and homophobic but also potentially threatening, the manuscript de-identifies comments as well as the platforms on which they were made. The research for this book was conducted by visiting hundreds of sites across the internet, from newspapers to blogs to video broadcast sites. These platforms are treated as sociological research sites, utilized as an ethnographer might do. Websites related to newspapers like *USA Today*, the *New York Times*, or the *Washington Post* with readerships of one million or more are described as "major papers" or "papers of general interest." Sites like TMZ or People Magazine are labeled "gossip sites." Jezebel, Babe.net, and Bustle are identified as feminist sites or sites dedicated to young women's interests. Fox News and Breitbart are described as conservative news outlets.[143]

What might seem like an abundance of caution results from the particular historical moment in which this book is being written. Several recent social media research projects have been critiqued for lack of attention to human subjects' concerns. In 2012, for example, researchers from Cornell University drew criticism after collaborating with Facebook to manipulate nearly seven hundred thousand users' newsfeeds in order to explore how an influx of positive or negative posts would impact users' moods.[144] More recently, political consulting firm Cambridge Analytica was shut down after data for more than eighty-seven million Facebook users was shared with the Trump campaign, potentially influencing the results of the 2016 U.S. presidential election.[145] As a result of the data harvesting, thousands of people signaled their outrage at the invasion of privacy by participating in the #DeleteFacebook campaign.[146] The concerns voiced about Facebook's data collection by writer Alexandra Kleeman are apt for researchers studying social media. Kleeman writes that, although she herself maintains a public blog where she shares personal information, "the idea that my data could be used for purposes that I expressly don't want, that freaks me out."[147]

Because of the thorny issues implicit in studying social media, it is tempting as a researcher to avoid the topic entirely. However, as Reagle observes, there is a lot to be learned by sifting through the "bottom of the internet."[148] The reward from the project is not the ability to make broad, generalizable conclusions as a sociologist might do but, as a legal scholar, to take a deep dive into a particular historical moment. To not study social media is to miss describing a watershed moment, not only for alleged victims and perpetrators of sexual assault but for social movements, technology, and law.

BEWARE THE BOTS

In addition to privacy concerns, another significant issue for those studying social media is the extent to which tweets and comments are subject to manipulation. The term "troll" emerged in the 1990s to describe online commenters who, like vessels attempting to catch fish with baited lines, send ostensibly sincere messages that derail conversations by attracting predictable, angry responses, or "flames."[149] Rather than simple disruption, the goal of contemporary trolls is often not just to derail conversation but to persuade commenters to a particular point of view, leading to the ubiquitous caution "don't feed the trolls."[150]

In 2018, trolling has shifted from the province of lone actors to "farms," billion-dollar enterprises organized by governments to influence other states' behaviors by influencing the citizens of those states.[151] Privately owned and state-sponsored organizations now assume false identities online in order to actively disseminate propaganda to sway public opinion in particular political directions.[152] It is likely that efforts by troll farms are having a massive effect on political contests worldwide, from the 2016 U.S. presidential election to the Brexit vote in the United Kingdom.[153]

Today, in addition to trolls, perhaps 15 to 20 percent of participants on social network sites may be bots, automated responses that mimic human communication.[154] Waves of bots have been identified across the internet in response to political contests and significant events such as acts of terrorism, mass shootings, or whether it is appropriate to kneel for the national anthem.[155] Functioning like agent provocateurs do in physical settings, automated bots serve to amplify particular, often contentious, political messages and to inspire partisan dissent.[156] The purpose of the "arguetron" bot, created by Sarah Nyberg, for example, is to engage in lengthy arguments regarding social issues, including feminism and transgender rights. Nyberg found that most online arguments were, in fact, "content agnostic"—identical replies from the bot served to fuel anger across any social context.[157]

Although the idea that some—or even many—of the comments and tweets analyzed herein might be posted by trolls or could be the work of automated bots seems concerning, in fact, an ubiquitous presence of bots and trolls in online conversations about sexual assault strengthens the argument that discussions about high-profile sexual assault cases are not gossip or distractions but part of larger political discussions. For decades, Catharine MacKinnon and other feminist scholars have argued that sexual assault is not a "women's issue" but a human rights concern, and that conversations about sexual violence should not be segmented from conversations about political and economic issues. It would not be surprising to find automated propaganda among the comments analyzed here because, as the book argues, there are significant political interests in conversations about sexual assault.

A related and equally pressing concern impacting the validity of research on social media is the private ownership of social media sites. As the Cambridge Analytica scandal made abundantly clear, corporations often deliberately and strategically withhold details regarding what information they collect about users and how it is collected.[158] The profit-seeking nature of these corporations means that functionalities, privacy settings, and algorithms for information sharing evolve seemingly overnight and are unlikely to be widely shared with the general public.[159] Boyd and Ellison note that "[S]cholars face a unique challenge in trying to investigate this rapidly moving phenomenon, as they struggle to understand people's practices while the very systems through which they are enacted shift."[160] Companies such as Twitter or news organizations also have a clear interest in manipulating content. Although advertised as public forums, online comment sites and other social network platforms, in fact, are heavily regulated, increasingly moderated to censor offensive and hateful speech.[161] In addition, the desire of individual users to create a monetized "brand" on social media likely inspires significant self-censorship before the send button even is pressed.[162] The risk is that comments are impacted not only by corporatization but by co-optation of income-driven "influencers."

If there are bots, trolls, and influencers among the authors of the comments analyzed here, such a presence serves to emphasize in just how precarious a position law finds itself today. Sexual assault law is currently in a moment of crisis in which meanings of consent, due process, and punishment are being navigated and negotiated. What voices are most persuasive in these negotiations are important questions that frame this project.

THE ROADMAP

This book is divided into three parts, each of which centers on a different theme. Part 1 explores how the online public discursively constructs victims, focusing on three case studies that can be extrapolated to explore greater concepts.

The first chapter concerns *Commonwealth v. William Henry Cosby, Jr.*, the only criminal case to emerge from more than forty allegations of sexual assault against the comedian, exploring some of the comments about alleged victims that one is most likely to encounter online. The chapter identifies the ubiquity of victim-blaming comments situating accusers into particular categories based on status—"slut," "ho," "bitch"—which operate to discipline and to exclude.[163] Connecting these comments to larger rape myths, the chapter examines the idea of the "casting couch," a place where, in the view of many online commenters, the lines between "real rape" and lecherous conduct are less than clear. Beyond describing conversations about Cosby's alleged victims, the chapter asks what these distasteful comments might signify about the public's legal knowledge of sexual assault laws and our views about the capacity of law to afford justice in sexual assault cases.

Chapter 2 shifts from discussing a criminal case to a civil suit, *Kinsman v. Winston*. Exploring accusations against quarterback Jameis Winston by fellow student at Florida State University, Erica Kinsman, the chapter delves more deeply into one, pervasive image that frequently appears in online legal discussions about sexual assault accusers—that of the "gold digger." This chapter explores the history of the term, arguing that, more than merely insulting, the label gold digger is a shorthand way to convey a powerful message about who is and is not deserving of justice.

Chapter 3 focuses on another high-profile case, that of unfounded allegations of gang rape made by a student under the pseudonym Jackie at the University of Virginia against fraternity Phi Kappa Psi. After the allegations were reported in *Rolling Stone*, the revelation of their falsehood led to multimillion-dollar lawsuits against the magazine, the reporter, and the accuser, a set of events known across the internet by #UVAHoax. The chapter explores how, of all rape mythologies operating today, the myth of the false claim has come to be the most insidious. This chapter explores the history of the treatment of women as liars in the context of sexual assault cases, revealing some similarities between online characterizations of Jackie, the UVA freshman, and Hillary Clinton, the 2016 presidential candidate, both facing angry refrains of "Lock Her Up!"

Part 2 of the book shifts the lens from victims to perpetrators. Chapter 4 engages a historical case revived in recent years—that of Emmett Till—to address the complex intertwining of rape and race and the tangible impacts false claims have had on nonwhite defendants. The chapter explores how the largely unsettled history of corrupt and prejudiced rape prosecutions continues to inform today's debates about due process. The chapter also examines how the feminist movement and conservative politicians have been uneasy partners in calling for harsher penalties and longer sentences for sexual assault that may, if inadvertently, result in continued erosions of due process for the least enfranchised.

Chapter 5 further explores social media discussions about perpetrators, using recent convictions of USA gymnastics team doctor Larry Nassar and Stanford student Brock Turner as a springboard to discuss public opinion about perpetrators and punishment. While chapter 4 explores how Black men have suffered particular harms based on the classic myth of "real rape," this chapter examines a potential shift in the public imagination of the "typical" rapist from historical images of "menacing" Black men to Brock Turner, whose image is now featured in a criminal justice textbook under the heading "rape."[164] The chapter explores the ways in which these renewed images of the rapist do and do not reflect reality, questioning whether they challenge or reinforce rape myths. Although much of the attention of feminist analysis has been on treatment of victims, this chapter highlights that perpetrators, too, face specific expectations in the court of public opinion.

Part 3 of the book and its last chapter looks toward the future, examining the recent #MeToo and #TimesUp campaigns, their promise and their peril. Chapter 6 considers who is included and excluded in #MeToo, the rising impact of Title IX in the university setting—a place in which many sexual assault claims arise, and new frontiers—are we moving away from the law entirely in addressing these matters? This final part of the book also explores the smoke and mirrors of bots and trolls. What if some or all of the comments evaluated herein were generated by artificial intelligence or communicated by users situated in a governmental building in Russia or North Korea? Such a discovery might make this book less valid as a study of public legal consciousness; however, it would lend even more support to the argument that discussions about sexual assault are political discussions. When an online commenter dismisses a sexual assault accuser as a "slut" or a "gold digger," characterizes a perpetrator as a "saint" or a "perv," or accuses a lawyer of being a "feminazi," these are political statements that have the potential to disrupt power relationships in a venerated U.S. institution at a critical historical moment.

In early 2018, Steve Bannon, former chief strategist for the Trump administration and head of conservative news site Breitbart.com, made the prediction that "10,000 years of recorded history" were "coming to a close," that an anti-patriarchy movement, signified by #MeToo and #TimesUp, was effecting a role reversal in which women would now be the ones in charge.[165] Whether or not Bannon's dramatic, gendered prediction is accurate, we do seem to be in the midst of a "culture war" during which existing power relationships are being questioned and challenged. In this crisis moment for sexual assault law, social media have the potential to reinforce and reinscribe harmful and exclusionary tropes and stereotypes, but they also have the capacity to function as a powerful imaginary in which existing institutions and structures can be critiqued and where new forms of interaction with the legal system can not only be envisioned but brought to fruition.

Underneath what at first might be dismissed as hate speech, victim blaming, or "throwaway" discourse comments on social media have the potential to effect seismic changes in sexual assault law, both civil and criminal, substantive and procedural. The capacity of social media for widespread organization at lightning speed is changing the rules of the adversarial game. In fact, as the #MeToo movement attests, cataclysmic change may already have begun.

Crafting a history of the legal present highlights the extent to which rape law is grounded in deeply held beliefs, tropes, and stereotypes that are exceedingly troubling.[166] While looking backward, however, the book also looks forward, exploring the uncharted territory of social media, and asking how new mediums and methods of communication are impacting our legal future.

NOTES

1. Disparate outcomes in the two Cosby trials can be explained by numerous factors, such as the presence of different presiding judges, distinct juries, or new counsel, all of which were true in the instant case. Jen Kirby, "Bill Cosby's Retrial May Be the First Real Test of the Power of #MeToo," *Vox*, April 9, 2018, https://www.vox.com/2018/4/9/17139824/bill-cosby-retrial-sex-assault-metoo.

2. Graham Bowley, "Potential Cosby Jurors Are Asked about #MeToo Bias," *New York Times*, April 2, 2018, https://www.nytimes.com/2018/04/02/arts/television/bill-cosby-trial-jury-selection.html.

3. Graham Bowley and Matthew Haag, "Cosby Jury Says Accuser's Credibility, Not #MeToo, Led to Guilty Verdict," *New York Times*, April 30, 2018, https://www.nytimes.com/2018/04/30/arts/television/cosby-juror-interview-gma.html.

4. Bowley, "Potential Cosby Jurors."

5. Sasha Savitsky and Leora Arnowitz, "Cosby Guilty: Jury Rules Comedian Sexually Assaulted Andrea Constand," Fox News, April 26, 2018, http://www.foxnews.com/entertainment/2018/04/26/cosby-guilty-jury-rules-comedian-sexually-assaulted-andrea-constand.html.

6. Fernand Braudel observed that, as one studies history, "[a]s a practical matter, one should look for 'cultural conjunctures'—one must establish initial contact with those periods that provide most illumination." Ananda Abeysekara, *Colors of the Robe: Religion, Identity, and Difference* (Columbia: University of South Carolina Press, 2002), 4, n. 10, citing Fernand Braudel, in *On History* (Chicago: University of Chicago Press, 1980), 207.

7. This book engages the term crisis to mean, as Jamie Abrams offers, "a 'turning point' or a 'decisive change' on a systemic political level, as compared to an individual level." Jamie Abrams, "The #MeToo Movement: An Invitation for Feminist Critique of Rape Crisis Framing" (Paper No. 2018-5, University of Louisville Legal Research Paper Series, April 6, 2018), 766. See also Abeysekara, *Colors*, 4, n. 10.

8. Merriam-Webster defines social media as "forms of electronic communication . . . through which users create online communities to share information, ideas, personal messages, and other content." The distinction between social media and social networks, as well as their role as both platform and community, is discussed in the book. "Social Media," Merriam-Webster.com, August 17, 2018, https://www.merriam-webster.com/dictionary/social%20media.

9. Michael Houlihan and Bonnie Harvey, "How Crowdsourcing Is Shaping the Future of Everything," Entrepreneur.com, January 13, 2018, https://www.entrepreneur.com/article/307438.

10. Kim Martineau, "Crowdsourced Family Tree Yields New Insights about Humanity," *Columbia News*, March 1, 2018, https://news.columbia.edu/news/crowdsourced-family-tree-yields-new-insights-about-humanity.

11. Jeffrey Gottfried and Elisa Shearer, "News Use across Social Media Platforms 2016," Pew Research Center, May 26, 2016, http://www.journalism.org/2016/05/26/news-use-across-social-media-platforms-2016/.

12. Gottfried and Shearer, "News Use."

13. David Garland, "What Is a 'History of the Present'? On Foucault's Genealogies and Their Critical Preconditions," *Punishment & Society* 16, no. 4 (2014): 367, 372. Although she does not explicitly engage genealogy as a method, Mary Beard provides a similar history of the present in her recent book, drawing connections between the mythical silencing of Odysseus's wife, Penelope, to the contemporary silencing of senator Elizabeth Warren. Mary Beard, *Women and Power: A Manifesto* (New York: Liveright, 2017).

14. Informing the methodological approach taken here is Cramer's recent work on celebrity embodiment. Renée Ann Cramer, *Pregnant with the Stars: Watching and Wanting the Celebrity Baby Bump* (Palo Alto: Stanford University Press, 2015).

15. Katie J.M. Baker, "Here's the Powerful Letter the Stanford Victim Read to Her Attacker," BuzzFeedNews.com, June 3, 2016, https://www.buzzfeednews.com/article/katiejmbaker/heres-the-powerful-letter-the-stanford-victim-read-to-her-ra.

16. AB 2888 eliminates probation as an option for offenders whose victims are intoxicated or unconscious, while AB 701 expands the state's definition of rape beyond the use or threat of physical force. Matt Ford, "How Brock Turner Changed California's Rape Laws," *Atlantic*, October 1, 2016, https://www.theatlantic.com/news/archive/2016/10/california-law-brock-turner/502562/.

17. German Lopez, "Voters Recall Judge Who Sentenced Brock Turner to 6 Months in Jail for Sexual Assault," *Vox*, June 6, 2018, https://www.vox.com/policy-and-politics/2018/6/6/17433576/judge-aaron-persky-recall-brock-turner-results.

18. Tracey Kaplan, "Recall Aftermath: Will the Removal of Judge Aaron Persky Prompt a New Legal Battle?," *Mercury News*, June 6, 2018, https://www.mercurynews.com/2018/06/06/judge-persky/.

19. "This status has helped improve the company's fortunes. Daily usage is up a healthy 12% year over year, and Twitter reported its first-ever quarterly profit in February, capping a 12-month period during which its stock doubled." Austin Carr and Harry McCracken, "'Did We Create This Monster?' How Twitter Turned Toxic," Fast Company, April 4, 2018, https://www.fastcompany.com/40547818/did-we-create-this-monster-how-twitter-turned-toxic; Nolan D. McCaskill, "Trump Credits Social Media for his Election," Politico.com, October 20, 2017, https://www.politico.com/story/2017/10/20/trump-social-media-election-244009; Joshua Toplosky, "The End of Twitter," *New Yorker*, January 29, 2016, https://www.newyorker.com/tech/elements/the-end-of-twitter.

20. This book uses boyd and Ellison's definition of "social network sites" as "web-based services that allow individuals to (1) construct a public or semi-public profile within a bounded system, (2) articulate a list of other users with whom they share a connection, and (3) view and traverse their list of connections made by others within the system." danah m. boyd and Nicole B. Ellison, "Social Network Sites: Definition, History, and Scholarship," *Journal of Computer-Mediated Communication* 13, no. 1 (2007): 210–30.

21. Mark Makela, "Transcript: Donald Trump's Taped Comments about Women," *New York Times*, October 8, 2016, https://www.nytimes.com/2016/10/08/us/donald-trump-tape-transcript.html.

22. Matt Wilstein, "TBT: When Mark Halperin Dismissed Sexual Assault Allegations against Trump," *Daily Beast*, October 26, 2017, https://www.thedailybeast.com/when-mark-halperin-dismissed-sexual-assault-allegations-against-trump.

23. According to a 2016 *Washington Post* report, nearly 70 percent of voters believed that the candidate had "probably" made unwanted sexual advances; however one in five claimed they would vote for him in any case. Alia E. Dastagir, "Some Say One False Report Could Cripple the #MeToo Movement. Is Progress That Fragile?," *USA Today*, December 8, 2017, https://www.usatoday.com/story/news/2017/12/08/analysis-movement-metoo-but-heres-why-were-still-talking-believewomen/923156001/.

24. Josh Gerstein, "Meet the Four Clinton Accusers Who Joined Trump," Politico.com, October 9, 2016, https://www.politico.com/story/2016/10/clinton-accusers-donald-trump-debate-229444.

25. Kaiser, "Amy Schumer on Her 'Friend' Aziz Ansari: It's Not a Crime, But It's Not Cool," *Celebitchy*, February 1, 2018, http://www.celebitchy.com/565075/amy_schumer_on_her_friend_aziz_ansari_its_not_a_crime_but_its_not_cool/.

26. For example, while many jurisdictions criminalize digital penetration, some penalize the crime to a lesser degree than penetration with a penis, and some jurisdictions do not criminalize digital penetration at all except as "indecent contact." Carol E. Tracy and Charlene Whitman, "Rape and Sexual Assault in the Legal System," *AEquitas Women's Law Project* (2013): 19; Corey Rayburn Yung, "Rape Law Fundamentals," *Yale Journal of Law and Feminism* 27, no. 1 (2015): 16.

27. In 2017, 81 percent of the U.S. population used some form of social media. "Percentage of U.S. Population with a Social Media Profile from 2008 to 2018," Statista.com, August 17, 2018, https://www.statista.com/statistics/273476/percentage-of-us-population-with-a-social-network-profile/.

28. Nils Christie, "Conflicts as Property," *British Journal of Criminology* 1, no. 17 (1977): 4.

29. This book engages the terms victim and survivor interchangeably, with the understanding that, with regard to both societal and self-identification, these terms can be very different. Chapter 1 discusses some of the distinctions between the labels "victim" and "survivor" in both social and legal context.

30. Christie, "Conflicts," 8.

31. Christie, "Conflicts," 8.

32. Federal Rule of Evidence 412(a) provides that "[t]he following evidence is not admissible in a civil or criminal proceeding involving alleged sexual misconduct: (1) evidence offered to prove that a victim engaged in other sexual behavior; or (2) evidence offered to prove a victim's sexual predisposition." The majority of states also have adopted similar rules. The Daubert rule is provided in Fed. R. Evid. 702.

33. "Polaroid of Robed Bill Cosby before Alleged Dickinson Rape," TMZ, November 21, 2014, http://www.tmz.com/2014/11/21/janice-dickinson-bill-cosby-rape-robe-pictures/?adid=TMZ_Search_Results.

34. Savitsky and Arnowitz, "Cosby Guilty."

35. Richard Delgado, "Storytelling for Oppositionists and Others: A Plea for Narrative," *Michigan Law Review* 87, no. 8 (1989): 2416.

36. Online case resolution systems increasingly are being developed by courts to facilitate resolution of civil matters and minor criminal disputes. Maximilian A. Bulinski and J. J. Prescott, "Online Case Resolution Systems: Enhancing Access, Fairness, Accuracy, and Efficiency," *Michigan Journal of Race and Law* 21, no. 2 (2016): 205–248.

37. *The Running Man*, directed by Paul Michael Glaser (Los Angeles: TriStar Pictures, 1987).

38. Ouellette describes how the 1980s daytime show *The Peoples Court* originally was pitched as a "hybrid game show and legal aid experiment" that would educate the public via allowing them to weigh in on real disputes. Ouellette, "Real Justice," 160.

39. Casey Cipriani, "Marisa Hargitay's Rape Kit Documentary Came to Life Because of Olivia Benson—Yes, Really," Bustle, April 13, 2018, https://www.bustle.com/p/mariska-hargitays-rape-kit-documentary-came-to-life-because-of-olivia-benson-yes-really-8778963.

40. Alyssa Bailey, "Kim Kardashian is Studying to Become a Lawyer and Plans to Take the Bar in 2022," *Elle*, April 10, 2019, https://www.elle.com/culture/celebrities/a27101447/kim-kardashian-studying-to-become-lawyer/.

41. Laurie Ouellette, "Real Justice: Law and Order on Reality Television," chapter 4 in *Imagining Legality: Where Law Meets Popular Culture*, ed. Austin Sarat (Birmingham: University of Alabama Press, 2014), 154.

42. Amelia McDonnell-Parry, "*Making a Murderer* One Year Later: Everything You Need to Know," *Rolling Stone*, December 16, 2016, http://www.rollingstone.com/culture/news/making-a-murderer-one-year-later-everything-to-know-w455262.

43. NBC15 Staff, "*Making a Murderer*'s Steven Avery Wins Appeal," WMTV-NBC15, February 27, 2019, https://www.nbc15.com/content/news/Making-a-Murders-Steven-Avery-wins-appeal-506452641.html.

44. Maggie Panos, "7 Important Things That Happened after the Events in *The Keepers*," Popsugar.com, July 28, 2017, https://www.popsugar.com/entertainment/Keepers-Update-43576120.

45. Panos, "7 Important Things."

46. Emma Kerr, "The Latest Assault Victim since *The Keepers* Comes Forward with New Sexual Abuse Story," Oxygen.com, February 8, 2018, https://www.oxygen.com/crime-time/the-latest-assault-victim-since-the-keepers-comes-forward-with-new-sexual-abuse-story.

47. Robson et al. observe that, while only a small minority of people actually have stepped into a courtroom, most have experienced court procedures on TV. Thus, when people serve as jurors, their expectations of processes like cross-examination and deliberation already have been shaped by media to which they have been exposed. Peter Robson, Guy Osborn, and Steve Greenfield, "The Impact of Film and Television on Perceptions of Law and Justice: Towards a Realisable Methodology," chapter 46 in *Law, Culture and Visual Studies*, eds. Anne Wagner and Richard K. Sherwin (New York: Springer, 2014), 1020.

48. Desmond Manderson, "Trust Us Justice: *24*, Popular Culture, and the Law," chapter 1 in *Imagining Legality: Where Law Meets Popular Culture*, ed. Austin Sarat (Birmingham: University of Alabama Press, 2014), 38.

49. Manderson, "Trust Us," 38.

50. Manderson, "Trust Us," 38.

51. Richard K. Sherwin, "Introductory Essay," in *Popular Culture and Law*, ed. Richard K. Sherwin (Aldershot, England: Ashgate, 2006), xiii.

52. Christina O. Spiesel, "Trial by Ordeal: CSI and the Rule of Law," chapter 37 in *Law, Culture and Visual Studies*, eds. Wagner and Sherwin, 830.

53. Lawrence M. Friedman, "Popular Legal Culture: Law, Lawyers, and Popular Culture," chapter 1 in *Popular Culture and Law*, ed. Sherwin, 7.

54. Spiesel, "Trial by Ordeal," 830.

55. Spiesel, "Trial by Ordeal," 842.

56. Kathryn Schulz, "Dead Certainty," *New Yorker*, January 25, 2016, https://www.newyorker.com/magazine/2016/01/25/dead-certainty; Daniel Victor, "'*Making a Murderer*' Left Out Crucial Facts, Prosecutor Says," *New York Times*, January 5, 2016, https://www.nytimes.com/2016/01/05/arts/television/ken-kratz-making-a-murderer.html?_r=0.

57. Cheryl I. Harris, "Myths of Race and Gender in the Trials of O. J. Simpson and Susan Smith—Spectacles of Our Times," *Washburn Law Journal* 35 (1996): 226.

58. David Garland, "On the Concept of Moral Panic," *Crime, Media, Culture: An International Journal* 4, no. 1 (2008): 10; Stanley Cohen, *Folk Devils and Moral Panics: The Creation of the Mods and Rockers* (London: Oxford University Press, 1972); David Altheide, *Terrorism and the Politics of Fear* (Lanham, MD: AltaMira Press, 2006).

59. Doris Marie Provine, *Unequal Under Law: Race in the War on Drugs* (Chicago: University of Chicago Press, 2007).

60. Clyde Haberman, "When Youth Violence Spurred 'Superpredator' Fear," *New York Times*, April 6, 2014, https://www.nytimes.com/2014/04/07/us/politics/killing-on-bus-recalis-superpredator-threat-of-90s.html.

61. Corey Rayburn Yung, "One of These Laws Is Not Like the Others: Why the Federal Sex Offender Registration and Notification Act Raises New Constitutional Questions," *Harvard Journal on Legislation* 46 (2009): 372–73 (discussing the enactment of New Jersey's "Megan's Law" following the rape and murder of Megan Kanka in 1994); Daniel P. Mears, *American Criminal Justice Policy: An Evaluation Approach to Increasing Accountability and Effectiveness* (New York: Cambridge University Press, 2011), 81, 85.

62. Throughout the book, a conscious decision has been made to capitalize Black when used to describe a particular racial group and no to do so in the case of white descriptors. Although some social justice advocates argue on behalf of capitalizing references to both racial groups, and others advocate for using lowercase letters, I am persuaded by Lori L. Tharps's argument that African Americans as a group "are indeed a people, a race, a tribe." In engaging the designation, the book attempts to acknowledge the ways in which, based on skin color alone, both individuals and law as an institution have impacted a particular class or group of persons. I have chosen not to capitalize white because, although there are cases in which white persons experience discrimination, the impact largely is on individuals and not felt as a group or community. Further, the racist "alt-right" movement's attempts to identify white persons as a category suffering unique harms cuts against advances to social justice. Karen Yin, "Capitalizing for Equality," *Conscious Style Guide*, February 22, 2017, https://consciousstyleguide.com/capitalizing-for-equality/.

63. In earlier work, I have described how Pentagon surveys of service members prior to the repeal of the "Don't Ask, Don't Tell" policy engaged stereotypes of gay men as sexually predatory, asking several questions relating to fears about sharing bath facilities or open showers with gay or lesbian colleagues. Francine Banner, "'It's Not All Flowers and Daisies': Masculinity, Heteronormativity and the Obscuring of Lesbian Identity in the Repeal of 'Don't Ask, Don't Tell,'" *Yale Journal of Law and Feminism* 24, no. 1 (2012): 73.

64. Common law defined rape as unlawful intercourse by a man against a woman who is not his wife by force or threat and against her will.

65. Melissa Murray, "Inequality's Frontiers," *Yale Law Journal Forum* 122, February 21, 2013, https://www.yalelawjournal.org/forum/inequalitys-frontiers#footnote12.

66. Beginning in the mid-1800s, numerous states passed Married Women's Property Acts, providing that women could at last sue in their own names in U.S. courts and retain the proceeds from such suits. Legal scholars then began to debate whether this meant that men could continue to sue for diminution of their wives' value. Evans Holbrook, "Change in the Meaning of Consortium," *Michigan Law Review* 22 (1923): 2, 6.

67. Angela P. Harris, "Race and Essentialism in Feminist Legal Theory," *Stanford Law Review* 42 (1989–1990).

68. Danielle L. McGuire, *At the Dark End of the Street: Black Women, Rape, and Resistance—A New History of the Civil Rights Movement from Rosa Parks to the Rise of Black Power* (New York: Random House, 2011), xix.

69. McGuire, "*At the Dark End of the Street*," xix.

70. "Lynching in America: Confronting the Legacy of Racial Terror," Equal Justice Initiative, https://lynchinginamerica.eji.org.

71. Claudia Card, "Rape as a Weapon of War," *Hypatia* 11, no. 4 (1996): 5–18; Anat Berko and Edna Erez, "Gender, Palestinian Women, and Terrorism: Women's Liberation or Oppression?," *Studies in Conflict and Terrorism* 30, no. 6 (2007): 493–519.

72. Garfield Tenzer describes how, historically, sex with an underage girl was criminalized based on the theory that a loss of virginity decreased her value as a bride. Further, the crime provided the ability of fathers to retaliate against the man who diminished this economic value. Leslie Y. Garfield Tenzer, "#MeToo, Statutory Rape Laws and the Persistence of Gender Stereotypes" (Paper, Pace University School of Law, February 8, 2018), 4, available at SSRN: https://ssrn.com/abstract=3120348 or http://dx.doi.org/10.2139/ssrn.3120348.

73. Card, "Rape as a Weapon"; Berko and Erez, "Gender, Palestinian Women."

74. Berko and Erez, "Gender, Palestinian Women."

75. Although the specific wording differed by jurisdiction, the basic content of the Hale Instruction as engaged by judges in the United States is that rape is "a very easy charge to make but a difficult one to rebut." Gilbert Geis, "Lord Hale, Witches, and Rape," *British Journal of Law and Society* 5, no. 1 (Summer 1978): 42.

76. Countries, including Spain and France, and several U.S. states are considering enacting affirmative consent provisions, requiring that alleged perpetrators demonstrate that the other party explicitly, verbally agreed to sexual contact. Many states, similarly, are considering extending statutes of limitations relating to sexual assault. Rebecca Beitsch, "#MeToo Movement Has Lawmakers Talking about Consent," *Huffington Post,* January 24, 2018, https://www.huffingtonpost.com/entry/metoo-movement-has-lawmakers-talking-about-consent_us_5a6758dfe4b06bd14be5067f; Marina Pitofsky, "In Spain, Sexual Assault Legislation Says 'Yes Means Yes,'" *USA Today,* July 18, 2018, https://www.usatoday.com/story/news/world/2018/07/18/spain-sexual-assault-legislation-yes-means-yes/796773002/; Katarina Bergehed, "Sex without Consent Is Rape. Sweden's Move to Recognize That Means Fewer Women Will Have to Say #MeToo," *Time,* May 23, 2018, http://time.com/5288303/sweden-affirmative-consent-rape-law/.

77. Carol Smart, *Feminism and the Power of Law* (London: Routledge, 1989), 49.

78. Rose Corrigan, *Up Against a Wall: Rape Reform and the Failure of Success* (New York: New York University Press, 2014), 3; Ethan Czuy Levine, "Sexual Scripts and Criminal Statutes: Gender Restrictions, Spousal Allowances, and Victim Accountability after Rape Law Reform," *Violence Against Women* 23, no. 3 (2017): 324; Rayburn Yung, "Rape Law Fundamentals," 16.

79. Jim Mustian and Michael R. Sisak, "Despite #MeToo, Rape Cases Still Confound Police," *US News,* December 28, 2018, https://www.usnews.com/news/best-states/michigan/articles/2018-12-27/despite-metoo-rape-cases-still-confound-police.

80. See, for example, David M. Engel, "The Oven Bird's Song: Insiders, Outsiders, and Personal Injuries in an American Community," *Law and Society Review* 18, no. 4 (1984): 551–82; Patricia Ewick and Susan S. Silbey, *The Common Place of Law: Stories from Everyday Life* (Chicago: University of Chicago Press, 1998); Peggy Levitt and Sally Merry, "Vernacularization on the Ground: Local Uses of Global Women's Rights in Peru, China, India and the United States," *Global Networks* 9, no. 4 (2009): 441–61.

81. Susan S. Silbey, "After Legal Consciousness,"*Annual Review of Law and Social Science* 1 (2005): 360, 361.

82. Simon Halliday and Bronwen Morgan, "I Fought the Law and the Law Won? Legal Consciousness and the Critical Imagination," *Current Legal Problems* 66 (2013): 2.

83. Levitt and Merry, "Vernacularization," 443–44. Lauren Edelman engages a similar theory—*legal endogeneity*—to study the processes by which corporations engage and adapt antidiscrimination principles and, importantly, how these now corporatized principles find their way into the language of the courts. Lauren B. Edelman, *Working Law: Courts, Corporations, and Symbolic Civil Rights* (Chicago: University of Chicago Press, 2016).

84. Laura Bradley, "Alec Baldwin Complains John Oliver Has Turned Talk Shows into 'Grand Juries,'" *Vanity Fair,* December 6, 2017, https://www.vanityfair.com/hollywood/2017/12/alec-baldwin-john-oliver-stephen-colbert-talk-shows-grand-juries.

85. David M. Engel describes "horizontal" perspectives on law as exploring "rights consciousness as it actually manifests itself in everyday interactions within a social arena, stratum, network, or community." The idea is to explore "systems of meaning" familiar to ordinary people. David M. Engel, "Vertical and Horizontal Perspectives on Rights Consciousness," *Indiana Journal of Global Legal Studies* 19, no. 2 (2012): 426. Haltom and McCann engage this idea of horizontal discourse in their powerful study of the influence and interactions of mass media with the tort reform movement. William Haltom and Michael McCann, *Distorting the Law: Politics, Media, and the Litigation Crisis* (Chicago: University of Chicago Press, 2004).

86. Engel, "Vertical and Horizontal Perspectives," 426.

87. Silbey, "After Legal Consciousness," 360, 361.

88. Silbey, "After Legal Consciousness," 360, 361.

89. Joseph P. Williams, "Courts Considered Trump's Twitter in Ruling," *US News and World Report,* June 12, 2017, https://www.usnews.com/news/national-news/articles/2017-06-12/donald-trumps-statements-on-twitter-cited-in-courts-decision-to-

upholds-block-on-travel-ban; Richard Wolf, "As Trump Travel Ban (Finally) Reaches Supreme Court, His Talk and Tweets are Center Stage," *USA Today*, April 24, 2018, https://www.usatoday.com/story/news/politics/2018/04/24/trump-travel-ban-supreme-court-campaign-promises-tweets/543952002/.

90. Dami Lee, "Emoji Are Showing Up in Court Cases Exponentially, and Courts Aren't Prepared," *The Verge*, February 18, 2019, https://www.theverge.com/2019/2/18/18225231/emoji-emoticon-court-case-reference.

91. Bureau of Justice Statistics, Criminal Cases, https://www.bjs.gov/index.cfm?ty=tp&tid=23.

92. Friedman, "Popular Legal Culture," 5, 7.

93. Friedman, "Popular Legal Culture," 3; Harris, "Myths of Race and Gender," 227.

94. Shoshana Felman describes how, while factually distinguishable, criminal events often evoke similar emotions and responses. Shoshana Felman, *The Juridical Unconscious: Trials and Traumas in the Twentieth Century* (Cambridge: Harvard University Press, 2002).

95. Cramer, "Pregnant with the Stars," 13.

96. Monica Lewinsky, "Emerging from 'the House of Gaslight' in the Age of #MeToo," *Vanity Fair*, February 25, 2018, https://www.vanityfair.com/news/2018/02/monica-lewinsky-in-the-age-of-metoo.

97. Lewinsky, "Emerging."

98. See, for example, Steven E. Barkan, *Law and Society: An Introduction* (New York: Pearson, 2008) (noting that law is "firmly embedded in society").

99. Haltom and McCann, *Distorting*, 113.

100. The Federal Sentencing Guidelines, for example, were a bipartisan effort to reduce judicial, but not prosecutorial, discretion. Provine, *Unequal*, 124.

101. Michelle Alexander, *The New Jim Crow: Mass Incarceration in the Age of Colorblindness* (New York: New Press, 2012).

102. Bridgette Dunlap, "How California's New Rape Law Could Be a Step Backward," *Rolling Stone*, September 1, 2016, https://www.rollingstone.com/culture/culture-news/how-californias-new-rape-law-could-be-a-step-backward-250347/.

103. Michael Vitiello, "Brock Turner: Sorting Through the Noise," *University of the Pacific Law Review* 49, no. 3 (2018): 634.

104. Lon L. Fuller, *The Morality of Law*, revised edition (New Haven, CT: Yale University Press, 1969).

105. At the time of writing of this book, the most senior Catholic clergyman to have been convicted of sexual abuse is George Pell, former finance minister to Pope Francis and, horrifically, author of the first diocesan protocol for investigating child sexual abuse. Mike James, "George Pell, Once Australia's Most Senior Catholic, Sentenced to 6 Years for Child Sex Abuse," *USA Today*, March 12, 2019, https://www.usatoday.com/story/news/world/2019/03/12/catholic-church-george-pell-six-years-child-sex-case/3146864002/.

106. Alanna Vagianos, "The Rape Kit Backlog Shows Exactly How We Regard Women in This Country," *Huffington Post*, April 13, 2018, https://www.huffingtonpost.com/entry/the-rape-kit-backlog-shows-exactly-how-we-regard-women-in-this-country_us_5acfb5e1e4b016a07e9a8c65.

107. Chief Justice Roberts's words immediately were countered in a tweet from the executive branch emphasizing that the Ninth Circuit Court of Appeals was indeed a bunch of "Obama judges." Robert Barnes, "Rebuking Trump's Criticism of 'Obama Judge,' Chief Justice Roberts Defends Judiciary as 'Independent,'" *The Washington Post*, November 21, 2018, https://www.washingtonpost.com/politics/rebuking-trumps-criticism-of-obama-judge-chief-justice-roberts-defends-judiciary-as-independent/2018/11/21/6383c7b2-edb7-11e8-96d4-0d23f2aaad09_story.html?utm_term=.6724fa63bfd2.

108. Alexis de Tocqueville, "Chapter VI: Judicial Power in the United States," *Democracy in America* (1831), https://www.marxists.org/reference/archive/de-tocqueville/democracy-america/ch06.htm.

109. Dagastir, "Some Say One False Report."

110. Jesse Fox, Carlos Cruz, and Ji Young Lee, "Perpetuating Online Sexism Offline: Anonymity, Interactivity, and the Effects of Sexist Hashtags on Social Media," *Computers in Human Behavior* 52 (2015): 437–38.

111. Fox et al., "Perpetuating Online Sexism"; Joseph M. Reagle Jr., *Reading the Comments: Likers, Haters, and Manipulators at the Bottom of the Web* (Boston: Massachusetts Institute of Technology Press, 2015), 94.

112. Brandon Baker, "Penn Professors Mull President Trump's Effect on Political Communications," *Penn Today*, August 9, 2018, https://penntoday.upenn.edu/news/penn-professors-mull-president-trumps-effect-political-communications.

113. Cass R. Sunstein, *#Republic: Divided Democracy in the Age of Social Media* (Princeton: Princeton University Press, 2017).

114. Mary Elizabeth Williams, "'Don't Read the Comments': The Trolls, Racists and Abusers Won—Reasonable Online Feedback Is a Thing of the Distant Past," Salon.com, September 11, 2015, https://www.salon.com/2015/09/11/dont_read_the_comments_the_trolls_racists_and_abusers_won_reasonable_online_feedback_is_a_thing_of_the_distant_past/.

115. Matthew W. Hughey and Jessie Daniels, "Racist Comments at Online News Sites: A Methodological Dilemma for Discourse Analysis," *Media, Culture & Society* 35, no. 3 (2013): 334.

116. Richard Rogers, "Debanalizing Twitter: The Transformation of an Object of Study," foreword in *Twitter and Society*, eds. Katrin Weller, Axel Bruns, Jean Burgess, Merja Mahrt, and Cornelius Puschmann (New York: Peter Lang AG, 2013), xii.

117. Patricia Hill Collins, *Black Feminist Thought: Knowledge, Consciousness, and the Politics of Empowerment* (New York: Routledge, 2000), 69; Cecilia L. Ridgeway, *Framed by Gender: How Gender Inequality Persists in the Modern World* (London: Oxford University Press, 2011), 4; Elizabeth A. Armstrong, Laura T. Hamilton, Elizabeth M. Armstrong, and J. Lotus Seeley, "'Good Girls': Gender, Social Class, and Slut Discourse on Campus," *Social Psychology Quarterly* 77, no. 2 (2014): 100, 102.

118. Nicola Henry and Anastasia Powell, "Embodied Harms: Gender, Shame, and Technology-Facilitated Sexual Violence," *Violence Against Women* 21, no. 6 (2015): 769–70.

119. Ashley Muddiman and Natalie (Talia) Jomini Stroud, "10 Things We Learned by Analyzing 9 Million Comments from *The New York Times*," University of Texas at Austin Center for Media Engagement, June 21, 2016, https://mediaengagement.org/research/10-things-we-learned-by-analyzing-9-million-comments-from-the-new-york-times/.

120. Collins, *Black Feminist Thought*, 225–26.

121. Henry and Powell, "Embodied Harms," 769.

122. Cecilia L. Ridgeway, *Framed by Gender: How Gender Inequality Persists in the Modern World* (London: Oxford University Press, 2011).

123. Maureen Linker, "Considering Online News Comments: Are We Really so Irrational and Hate Filled?," *Social Epistemology Review and Reply Collective* 3, no. 12 (2014): 9.

124. Linker, *Considering Online News*, 10.

125. Ridgeway observes that, "when people at sites of social change come together to construct some . . . new type of relationship . . . the cultural beliefs . . . that are activated in the background are more traditional than the innovative circumstances they confront." Ridgeway, *Framed*, 159. Similarly, Hardaker and McGlashan describe that online "[u]sers can invent and explore identities that they would struggle to enact convincingly, if at all, offline." Claire Hardaker and Mark McGlashan, "'Real Men Don't Hate Women': Twitter Rape Threats and Group Identity," *Journal of Pragmatics* 91 (2016): 82.

126. Reagle, *Reading the Comments*, 3.

127. Anna North, "What Happened to the Creator of the 'Shitty Media Men' List Shows Why the List was Needed," *Vox*, January 11, 2018, https://www.vox.com/2018/

1/11/16878316/shitty-media-men-list-katie-roiphe-moira-donegan; Michael Salter, "Justice and Revenge in Online Counter-Publics: Emerging Responses to Sexual Violence in the Age of Social Media," *Crime, Media, Culture* 9, no. 3 (2013): 225, 234; Jessica Megarry, "Online Incivility or Sexual Harassment? Conceptualising Women's Experiences in the Digital Age," *Women's Studies International Forum* 47 (2014): 46, 49–50; Fox et al., "Perpetuating Online Sexism," 436.

128. Umair Haque, "Why Twitter's Dying (and What You Can Learn from It)," HuffPost (blog), October 28, 2015, http://www.huffingtonpost.com/umair-haque/why-twitters-dying-learn-from-it_b_8401542.html. As discussed in later chapters, the lack of "policing" the internet may be perceived differently by young women of color, who are less likely to feel safe in nonvirtual spaces.

129. Fox et al., "Perpetuating Online Sexism," 436.

130. An analysis of Twitter conducted by U.K. think tank Demos over a three-week period recently found that half of those disseminating aggressive, sexist messages identified in profiles as female. Catriona Harvey-Jenner, "The Number of Women Who Troll Online Will SHOCK You," *Cosmopolitan*, May 26, 2016, https://www.cosmopolitan.com/uk/reports/news/a43626/women-half-online-trolls/.

131. Ronald K. L. Collins, "FAN 200 (First Amendment News) Ruthann Robson, 'The Cyber Company Town,'" *Concurring Opinions*, September 20, 2018, https://concurringopinions.com/archives/2018/09/fan-200-first-amendment-news-ruthann-robson-the-cyber-company-town.html.

132. Collins, Ruthann Robson, citing Packingham v. North Carolina, 582 U.S. (2017) at 10.

133. Henry and Powell, "Embodied Harms," 768.

134. Ronald K. L. Collins, "FAN 200 (First Amendment News) Mary Anne Franks, 'The Free Speech Fraternity,'" *Concurring Opinions*, September 20, 2018, https://concurringopinions.com/archives/2018/09/fan-200-first-amendment-news-mary-anne-franks-the-free-speech-fraternity.html.

135. J. D. Lieberman, D. Koetzle, and M. Sakiyama, "Police Departments' Use of Facebook: Patterns and Policy Issues," *Criminology and Penology* 16, no. 4 (2013): 442.

136. Hardaker and McGlashan, "Real Men Don't Hate."

137. Hughey and Daniels, "Racist Comments," 336.

138. Alice Marwick, "Ethnographic and Qualitative Research on Twitter," in *Twitter and Society*, eds. Katrin Weller, Axel Bruns, Jean Burgess, Merja Mahrt, and Cornelius Puschmann (New York: Peter Lang AG, 2013), 109–122.

139. Hughey and Daniels, "Racist Comments," 336.

140. Alice Marwick and danah boyd, "I Tweet Honestly, I Tweet Passionately: Twitter Users, Context Collapse, and the Imagined Audience," *New Media and Society* 13(1) (2011): 114–33.

141. Lauren Solberg, "Data Mining on Facebook: A Free Space for Researchers or an IRB Nightmare?," *University of Illinois Journal of Law, Technology & Policy* 2 (2010): 311.

142. Hughey and Daniels, "Racist Comments," 336; Benedict Anderson, *Imagined Communities: Reflections on the Origin and Spread of Nationalism* (London: Verso, 1991).

143. Emily Wolfinger provides an excellent discussion of the ethical concerns regarding analyzing online comments and of the methods various researchers have engaged to address such concerns. Emily Wolfinger, "'But It's Already Public, Right?': The Ethics of Using Online Data," *Data Driven Journalism*, November 25, 2016, http://datadrivenjournalism.net/news_and_analysis/but_its_already_public_right_the_ethics_of_using_online_data.

144. Kashmir Hill, "Facebook Manipulated 689,003 Users' Emotions for Science," Forbes.com, June 28, 2014, http://www.forbes.com/sites/kashmirhill/2014/06/28/facebook-manipulated-689003-users-emotions-for-science/#2bfad356704d.

145. Alvin Chang, "The Facebook and Cambridge Analytica Scandal, Explained with a Simple Diagram," *Vox*, May 2, 2018, https://www.vox.com/policy-and-politics/2018/3/23/17151916/facebook-cambridge-analytica-trump-diagram.

146. Tiffany Hsu, "For Many Facebook Users, a 'Last Straw' That Led Them to Quit," *New York Times*, March 21, 2018, https://www.nytimes.com/2018/03/21/technology/users-abandon-facebook.html.
147. Hsu, "For Many Facebook Users."
148. Reagle, *Reading the Comments*, 94.
149. Reagle, *Reading the Comments*, 94, 95.
150. Reagle, *Reading the Comments*, 95, 96.
151. Dave Lee, "The Tactics of a Russian Troll Farm," BBC News, February 16, 2018.
152. Lee, "Tactics."
153. Lee, "Tactics."
154. Researchers estimate that one in four tweets includes automated information or is generated by an automated source. According to one 2015 study, nearly 70 percent of "fans" following singer Taylor Swift are bots. Many sites ostensibly maintained by celebrities themselves also have automated components. Fiona J. McEvoy, "Social Bots Are Ruining the Internet for the Rest of Us," *Venture Beat*, December 5, 2017, https://venturebeat.com/2017/12/05/social-bots-are-ruining-the-internet-for-the-rest-of-us/; Chris Baraniuk, "How Twitter Bots Help Fuel Political Feuds," *Scientific American*, March 27, 2018, https://www.scientificamerican.com/article/how-twitter-bots-help-fuel-political-feuds/.
155. Baraniuk, "How Twitter Bots Help"; Sheera Frenkel and Daisuke Wakabayashi, "After Florida School Shooting, Russian 'Bot' Army Pounced," *New York Times*, February 19, 2018, https://www.nytimes.com/2018/02/19/technology/russian-bots-school-shooting.html?action=click&module=Top%20Stories&pgtype=Homepage.
156. Baraniuk, "How Twitter Bots Help."
157. Madison Malone Kircher, "Internet Trolls Can't Stop Arguing with Sarah Nyberg's Twitter Bot," *New York Magazine*, October 7, 2016, http://nymag.com/selectall/2016/10/sarah-nybergs-arguing-twitter-bot-exposes-trolls.html.
158. Francine Banner, "Methodological Approaches to Studying Crime and Popular Culture in New Media," in *The Oxford Encyclopedia of Crime, Media, and Popular Culture*, ed. Gray Cavender (New York: Oxford University Press, 2017), http://criminology.oxfordre.com/view/10.1093/acrefore/9780190264079.001.0001/acrefore-9780190264079-e-171.
159. Banner, "Methodological Approaches."
160. boyd and Ellison, "Social Network Sites," 152.
161. Muddiman and Jomini Stroud, "10 Things We Learned."
162. Sarah Pulliam Bailey, "How the Mom Internet Became a Spotless, Sponsored Void," Outlook, *Washington Post*, January 26, 2018, https://www.washingtonpost.com/outlook/how-the-mom-internet-became-a-spotless-sponsored-void/2018/01/26/072b46ac-01d6-11e8-bb03-722769454f82_story.html?noredirect=on&utm_term=.30fc20519b17.
163. Ridgeway, *Framed*; Megarry, "Online Incivility."
164. Allison Sundell, "Brock Turner's Mug Shot Next to Definition of Rape in Textbook," *USA Today*, September 14, 2017, https://www.usatoday.com/story/news/nation/2017/09/14/brock-turners-mug-shot-next-definition-rape-textbook/666857001/.
165. Maya Oppenheim, "Steve Bannon Warns Trump the 'Anti-Patriarchy Movement' Will Be Bigger than the Tea Party," *Independent*, February 12, 2018, http://www.independent.co.uk/news/world/americas/us-politics/steve-bannon-trump-tea-party-anti-patriarchy-movement-times-up-bloomberg-breitbart-news-a8206426.html.
166. David Garland describes genealogical projects as beginning with a scholarly "puzzlement or discomfiture about practices or institutions that others take for granted." Garland, "What is a 'History?,'" 372, 379.

I

The Survivors

ONE

The Casting Couch

Commonwealth v. William Henry Cosby, Jr.

Andrea Constand met Bill Cosby in 2002 in the context of her job as director of operations for Temple University.[1] Cosby developed what he described as a mentoring relationship with the thirty-year-old professional "inviting her to my house, talking to her about personal situations dealing with her life, growth, education."[2] In 2004, during one of these visits to Cosby's home, Constand complained of a headache. In response, Cosby gave her some blue pills.[3] Constand reports that she took the pills, then "fad[ed] in and out of consciousness," waking up "with her sweater bunched up around her and her bra undone."[4] Constand said she'd been assaulted; Cosby claimed the encounter was consensual. Constand reported the incident to the police but the state declined to prosecute.[5] She then joined several other plaintiffs in a civil suit that ultimately settled for more than $3 million.[6] Legally speaking, it seemed like the end of the road.

Then, eight years later, comedian Hannibal Buress called Bill Cosby a rapist during a stand-up routine.[7] Buress's comments opened the floodgates; more than sixty women came forward publicly voicing narratives that were strikingly similar to Andrea Constand's. In 2015, in the context of a hotly contested election for district attorney in Montgomery County, Pennsylvania, the investigation into Constand's allegations was reopened.[8] By 2017, the state determined there was probable cause to proceed with a criminal trial. Due to evidentiary issues and statutes of limitations, Constand's was the sole criminal case the celebrity was likely to face. In the shadow of a highly contentious presidential election, the trial seemed like a litmus test for America's tolerance for sexual misconduct.

In June 2017, a mistrial was declared in the first Cosby trial. The celebrity announced he would embark on a town hall–style speaking tour to educate unsuspecting young men about sexual assault laws.[9] The state announced its intention to retry him.

A sense of déjà vu pervaded April 2018, as Cosby once again walked up the stairs between the Ionic columns of the Montgomery County courthouse. This time, however, the outcome was strikingly different. After a two-week trial, Bill Cosby was convicted of three counts of aggravated indecent assault. In September of that year, he was sentenced to serve three to ten years in state prison.[10]

There are many plausible explanations for the contrasting verdicts in the Cosby trials. Criminal proceedings are live events. Disparate outcomes can be explained by the presence of different presiding judges, distinct juries, or new counsel, all of which were true in the instant case. However, it is probable that Bill Cosby's fortunes were influenced as much by events that took place outside the courtroom as within it.

In 2017, a seismic change occurred when, in response to emerging accusations of sexual assault against producer Harvey Weinstein, actor Alyssa Milano tweeted #MeToo. In the course of a day, the hashtagged status, borrowed from activist Tarana Burke, was tweeted and posted on Facebook twelve million times.[11] As discussed in part 3 of this book, the #MeToo movement has been a game changer, making visible how extensive and oppressive sexual assault and harassment are not only in U.S. society but around the globe. For Bill Cosby, the social movement was nothing but bad news.

During the first trial, a key procedural argument concerned whether accusers besides Andrea Constand should be permitted to testify. The state sought to introduce testimony from other accusers to show that Cosby had a "signature"—a unique pattern of behavior—that involved using his fame to secure women's trust, then incapacitating and assaulting them.[12] The defense countered that this was not a calling card but a cliché. The state was describing behavior so common, the defense argued, that—even if Bill Cosby had done all of these things—they were not unique enough to be a signature.[13] Cosby's attorney categorized what took place between Cosby and Constand as regrettable but not criminal, elaborating,

> How many women and men have been willing to offer up their bodies on a casting couch? Have been willing to exchange sex for favors? Have had remorse after doing so and then accused someone who they believed they could get monetary gain out of and sell a story?[14]

In any criminal trial, the overarching, evidentiary rule is that the probative value of any piece of evidence must outweigh its potential negative impact on the defendant. In making this calculation, the judge, in 2017, appeared to accept the defense's arguments that the ubiquity of coercive sexual encounters between powerful older men and young women weighed against their tendency to indicate serial predation.

Remarkably, in 2017, even the sheer number of accusers was spun into a positive argument for the defense. While the state argued that multiple accusations reinforced the celebrity's guilt, Cosby's attorneys argued that the spate of women coming forward merely suggested his status as a "wealthy target."[15] Attorneys accused fellow lawyer Gloria Allred of "parad[ing] accusers in the media," describing a predatory "barrage" of new accusers claiming, "Me, too."[16] The defense's closing argument took up just six minutes, largely focusing on accusers' thirst for media coverage.[17] The strategy was successful in convincing two jurors to find reasonable doubt.

In 2018, the state tried a different strategy. This time, they argued that the prohibition against introducing prejudicial evidence of prior acts should be overcome by the "doctrine of chances," the mathematical probability that had Cosby engaged similarly with others, he also would have done so with Andrea Constand.[18] For the argument to work, the other accusers' claims did not have to be proven in court but they needed to be credible. This time, the judge found that they were. Five accusers besides Constand were permitted to testify at the second trial.[19]

The success of the rather obscure doctrine of chances argument attests to the state's ingenuity and creativity, but it also suggests the impact of a nascent groundswell of legal change. By 2018, the words "me too" had taken on a different meaning. In the first Cosby trial, the pervasive specter of the "casting couch" weighed in favor of the defense. If so many older male Hollywood power players were pressuring young women for sexual favors, the reasoning went, then such behavior could not be the unique imprimatur of a serial predator.

Just eleven months later, thanks to the #MeToo social movement, the casting couch was starting to look like a strikingly different place. Rather than, as Cosby's attorneys attested, a place where young women were "offering" their bodies in a business transaction, the casting couch now appeared to be a hunting ground. Like Pinocchio at Pleasure Island, we were realizing that what appeared to be a harmless playground for "boys who will be boys" in fact was a long-standing cover for criminal behavior.

For everyday people, defining what acts are criminal, or deviant, and which are merely immoral is an important way to reinforce societal boundaries and to provide reassurance about what is "normal" behavior.[20] Via judicial decisions, legislative decrees, and discretionary enforcement, behaviors regularly flow across the boundary between moral harm to criminal and back again. We are witnessing contemporary negotiations of these boundaries in the context of issues like legalization of marijuana and enforcement of immigration policy where, at least normatively, law on the books may not resemble law as envisioned by the public. These negotiations are not apolitical; at any given time, some stakeholders will have an interest in upholding legal hegemony, while others will have a strong interest in challenging it.[21]

The Cosby trials highlight that we are living at a conjuncture in which sexual assault laws are being renegotiated, both on the books and, importantly, in everyday conversation. Like many discussed in this book, Andrea Constand's allegations sit at the fulcrum of sexual assault law, involving a situation that would not have qualified as criminal under the narrow common law definition of rape but, as Cosby's conviction and sentencing attest, are criminal today.[22]

Although Cosby's actions are defined as criminal "on the books"; however, as Silbey, Engel, and others describe, law in everyday life may tell a different story. Exploring social media discussions about the Cosby trials can provide a lens into the negotiation between immoral and criminal as it is occurring right now relating to sexual assault. When celebrities are accused, or when persons accused become reluctant celebrities, their trials become political trials, what Friedman refers to as "didactic theater."[23] Celebrity bodies become sites onto which society's desires and anxieties are projected, a focus for the discussion of issues outside of "polite" public debate.[24] On social media, Cosby and his accusers become battlegrounds for debating a range of anxiety-provoking topics. Through these debates about the bodies of persons we grow the body of law.

Cosby's trial and retrial are "spectacles," events that involve bigger things "than the individual guilt or innocence of the defendant."[25] The trials opened up opportunities for online discussions about gender, power, race, and rape that we might be reluctant to have around the water cooler. In examining these conversations, we can see whether law in society is in fact the "folk" imaginings of Sherwin's conception or whether law in the public mind is more like the "funhouse mirror" envisaged by Thomas Friedman. We can begin to think about whether online forums are—or even have the potential to be—the public parks and street corners once idealistically envisioned by free speech advocates.

THE CASTING COUCH

When the mistrial in the Cosby case was announced in May 2017, all of the major news outlets published articles announcing the result. Online readers commented more than two thousand times on just one article published by the *New York Times*, and another two thousand comments were made on the *Washington Post* site. A similar article on Breitbart.com garnered another thousand comments.

Deconstructing the results of Election 2016, researchers proclaimed the existence of a "media bubble"—the tendency of liberal and conservative voters to seek out like-minded commenters rather than conversing across political borders.[26] The Clinton campaign, in particular, complained of a Breitbart effect, attributing the candidate's loss largely to conservative voters being pummeled with misogynist rhetoric in siloed environments.[27] But, amid allegations of partisanship, when it comes to discussion of sexual assault, conversations across liberal and conservative sites tend to be disturbingly similar.[28]

Right after the Cosby mistrial, a major newspaper with a readership of over three million ran an editorial advocating extending statutes of limitations for sexual assault in the wake of the inability to prosecute many of the claims against the celebrity.[29] In response, a commenter asks, incredulously, how two people can "hook up" and then twenty years later a woman can claim it was a "sex crime." Another reader describes whatever took place between Cosby and Constand as part of the "free love movement."

On another major news site, a reader similarly complains that "[i]mproper behavior" should not constitute a "criminal case," while another categorizes Constand's allegations as resulting from "bad decisions." Chiming in, a post argues that Cosby is guilty, but only of "manipulation" and "lechery." A commenter on yet another popular news site says that what Cosby did was "creepy, but not illegal."

On an iconic conservative site, one finds similar sentiments. One reader remarks that Cosby "did it, but we have to put it into context. He did not go grab innocents off the street, rape them and leave them bloody (or dead) in an alley."

Categorizations that what Cosby did was creepy or immoral but something less than illegal are common across the internet, where his encounter with Constand is repeatedly described as a "fondling case," a "bad date," a "hook up," a "mistake." A poster on a conservative news site remarks that "using drugs with women for sex . . . isn't rape." On a mainstream news site, a reader similarly decries, "[G]et[ting] touchy feely with a guy, it's called flirting. When a man does the same, it's called unwanted sexual contact—sexual assault." The commenter complains that Cosby's conduct was "normal human sexuality. No rape, no crime."

The internet is replete with comments asking why Cosby's accusers had no bruises, or why they didn't go to doctors or hospitals. As one commenter on a conservative site notes, rapists are "not known to be gentle." A similar post follows up that "real rape is . . . brutal, sadistic, [and] can be proven beyond a shadow of a doubt." Posts across the internet support this point of view, describing that rape "causes injury and sometimes even death" and "leaves devastating injuries." Coupled with this expectation that accusers exhibit physical injury is the belief that victims should fight back to the utmost; one news reader advises, "If being abused, slap the predator in the face."

Like Cosby's defense team, many online commenters argue that the clichéd nature of Cosby's behavior weighs against its criminality. A commenter on a major newspaper's site notes that it is not unusual for "tipsy" women to have sex with someone they never would have been intimate with if sober. Another agrees that "everyone was doing this. . . . Back in the Day, popping pills and having Sex was the thing to do."

At the time of the assault, Andrea Constand was a twenty-nine-year-old business executive employed by a well-regarded U.S. university. Her relationship with Cosby was longstanding, collegial, and professional. In comments across social network sites, however, over and over again Constand is transformed into a wide-eyed, would-be starlet, the location of the attack from Cosby's home—a place Constand had visited many times—into a "hotel," and Constand's experiences with Cosby into a cautionary tale.

News readers offer "lessons for women" based in the Cosby trial, including that they ought to be aware that there are "debts you may owe a rich and powerful older married man who offers to 'help' you, a young and beautiful woman with your career." A fellow commenter agrees that "[w]omen need to take better care of themselves. Bars and hotel rooms are not a place for advancing careers and establishing serious relationships," while another entreats, "Not excusing rapists—but nobody should be stupid. Take care of yourself do not make it easy to be victimized." Comments on a third popular news site warn that a "young pretty girl" needs to not make "questionable decision[s]," such as "walk[ing] down dark alleys, hitchhik[ing], or find[ing] yourself alone with older men who want to 'help.'"

On a prominent conservative news site, a commenter offers a numbered list of words of wisdom "speaking as a woman," including "don't go to hotel rooms with strangers—it implies something" and "don't do drugs . . . with strangers—you're exposing yourself [to] all kinds of bad things." After all, in the "real world" women need to be more sensible.

In various ways, these comments reflect the idea of the casting couch, a metaphor used to describe the location of dubious sexual encounters dating back to the 1920s and 1930s when Broadway producers, the Shubert brothers, were notorious for keeping a salon where they entertained would-be chorus girls.[30] The brothers' proclivities—and their office—became iconic; "casting couch" signifying a place where, depending on one's point of view, powerful men could coerce or exploit vulnerable young women, or an attractive young woman might barter sexual favors for a chance at fame.[31] Although commenters may not specifically use the term, the idea of the casting couch pervades online discussions about Bill Cosby—and other prominent celebrities like Harvey Weinstein—and is suggested via the ubiquity of words like "starlet," "fame," "career," and "power."

Before delving into the implications of the casting couch for both accusers and alleged perpetrators, it is important to question why the casting couch metaphor is relevant to Constand's accusations at all. Constand was not a striving young actor but a business executive. The attack took place not in a Hollywood hotel room but at Cosby's home in Pennsylvania, a place both parties admitted Constand had visited many times in a professional capacity. The persistent reenvisioning across the internet of a meeting between business colleagues into an encounter between a "tipsy" young girl and a "powerful" older man suggests not just the pervasiveness of the casting couch trope, but the continuing power of rape myths in shaping discourse about sexual assault. Where a gap or confusion exists between law on the books and law in action, that space is often filled by "commonsense" knowledge. Our commonsense knowledge about rape is shaped by myths that often reinforce existing power structures and dynamics.

One of the most influential works of scholarship to address rape myths is Susan Estrich's *Real Rape*. A law professor, Estrich intersperses discussion of law with a personal narrative of her own assault, a "stranger rape" that took place in a Boston parking lot in the middle of the day.[32] Relating her experiences with law enforcement, Estrich illustrates the ways in which the rape prosecutions of the 1970s were haunted by the myth of stranger rape—the idea that "real" sexual assaults include only those, rare, violent instances where a stranger—stereotypically an African American male—leaps from the bushes to attack a—stereotypically vulnerable, virginal, young white—female.[33] Inherent in the paradigm are the assumptions that the perpetrator is an evil monster, the victim is passive, and the crime is "always traumatizing."[34]

Social media discussion of Cosby's trials provide insight into the contemporary operation of rape myths, as online commenters negotiate the boundaries of what is and is not really rape—not just according to the law, but according to society.

THE "DATE RAPE" DILEMMA

At Cosby's second trial, the very first person to testify was not an accuser but a forensic psychiatrist, Barbara Ziv, whose role was to educate the jury about rape myths, including debunking the powerful myth that most rapes are stranger rapes.[35] The prosecution's unusual choice to foreground Ziv's testimony emphasizes the extent to which such myths overshadowed the struggle to determine Cosby's guilt or innocence, influencing conversations about nearly every aspect of the accusations.[36]

Ziv highlighted that more than 60 percent of reported sexual assaults do not implicate a stranger but involve a known assailant, often a family member or friend.[37] Further, she observed, rape does not always—and in fact does not often—result in significant and lasting *physical* harm.

Thanks to feminist advocates, contemporary sexual assault laws reflect many of these realities of rape. All states now criminalize a breadth of conduct, from vaginal penetration and sodomy to intentional touching for the purposes of sexual gratification or even sex by deception.[38] The degree of the offense is enhanced when the perpetrator wields a weapon, or if the victim is not conscious or able to consent.[39] After years of exclusion, marital rape is now a crime.[40] Procedurally, the law and the courts have moved away from harmful and unrealistic expectations that victims should have "fought back to the utmost" or should have run away rather than submit to an attacker.[41]

Superficially, at least, these legal reforms have entered the public discourse. It would be challenging to find many adults in the United States today who are not at least aware that rape sometimes happens among acquaintances, or that impaired persons cannot legally consent. To keep abreast of new developments in sexual assault law, we can tune into *Law & Order: Special Victims Unit*, a show with more than seven million viewers that is *entirely about* one crime.[42]

There remains, however, a significant disparity between the statutory law that has been crafted after years of feminist revisions and law is being envisioned and applied in the public imaginary.[43] Faced with what they see as a "gray area" situation—sometimes labeled a "he said, she said" scenario—a typical response by commenters is to exchange opinions about whether the event qualifies as what one person calls "clear cut rape." Not infrequently, a "straw man" argument is raised comparing and contrasting the facts of the given case to what a poster believes to be a more straightforward, hypothetical situation, for example, comparing Constand's lack of bruises to injuries of other more deserving victims "bloody (or dead) in an alley."

The negotiations taking place among online commenters reinforce that the versions of law crafted by legislators or pronounced by judges are not necessarily the understandings of law that become part of public consciousness. The process of vernacularizing law in local context is connected to power relations and value judgments. Lauren Edelman describes, for example, how federal antidiscrimination principles are translated by corporate compliance professionals. When a law like Title VII protecting employees from workplace discrimination is passed, courts or legislators discuss the law as protecting "rights" or prohibiting discrimination. When compliance professionals describe that law to employees, however, it might be categorized as furthering "diversity" or "inclusivity."[44] This is not the simplification of a complex legal idea but a strategic reframing of concrete legal claims or rights into more amorphous corporate objectives. In the corporate interest, Edelman argues, what would have been cognizable legal claims are being transformed into interpersonal conflicts.[45]

Similarly, Sarah Moore suggests that the idea of acquaintance rape advanced by feminist advocates—that sexual assaults are most likely to be committed by our parents, neighbors, teachers, and best friends—is not the idea that has been ingrained in the public imagination.[46] While initially the term "date rape" was used to describe sexual violence occurring in the midst of ongoing intimate relationships among trusted friends, family members, or coworkers, the term now is more likely to bring to mind an event where, rather than unwanted sex occurring in the course of a long-term relationship, a threatening stranger either has administered a drug or taken advantage of a victim he barely knows.[47] A mock juror study by Ellison and Munro supports Moore's argument. When confronted by hypothetical scenarios involving assault by a stranger, participants in the researchers' study "considered it entirely possible that a woman in this situation would simply 'freeze' and remain 'paralyzed' throughout the assault." However,

> [i]n the context of an acquaintance rape . . . jurors were typically committed to the idea that a woman would do her utmost to avoid an assault by issuing strong verbal protests and fighting back. . . . As an extension of this, therefore, jurors also typically expected that a genuine victim of acquaintance rape would have sustained (or inflicted) bodily injuries consistent with the application of substantial force and strenuous physical resistance.[48]

Women's magazines like *Cosmopolitan* and *Elle* bolster the oxymoronic reframing of acquaintance rape as a crime most likely to be committed by people we barely know, often suggesting apps to prevent "date rape," such as Kitestring, which notifies emergency contacts about your location and signals when they should check up on you, or Safety Siren, a virtual rape whistle.[49] Although strikingly few sexual assaults involve involuntary intoxication or drugs, a closet industry of self-help websites have arisen offering assistance to bar-goers in spotting "date rape" drugs such as Rohypnol ("roofies") and gamma-hydroxybutyric acid ("GHB").[50] Today, an undergrad might head to college armed not only with mace but a straw or coaster that changes color when exposed to GHB or nail polish that can detect a roofie. She is less apt to be prepared for her most likely attacker, that nice guy with whom she has been working for months on a class project.

The categorization of self-protective tools and applications as "preventing" rape is, of course, misleading. Applying most criminological theories, what such apps likely do is protect one potential victim by inspiring the would-be perpetrator to target less tech-savvy others. The increasing availability of these tools also risks setting up yet another situation in which, after an assault, the question may become not, *Why did the perpetrator do it?* but, *Why did the victim not use the app?* A survivor describes, "I have a real problem with the [term] 'date' rape drug, because there's no date. GHB is a weapon."[51]

Although some invoke language that is clearly misogynist or derogatory, the way many online commenters talk about sexual assault suggests that they, as Ridgeway and Linker opine, may be ordinary people who legitimately are struggling with defining the boundaries between what constitutes criminal and merely immoral behavior. A commenter on a popular conservative news site conveys a misunderstanding of contemporary sexual assault laws, noting that they are in favor of convicting Cosby but only of a lesser—and nonexistent—charge of "date rape." A poster on the site of a newspaper often deemed liberal-leaning similarly admits confusion over "terminology." The commenter asks, "Is there a difference between 'sexual assault' and 'rape'? Why don't they call it rape, if that's what is being suggested?" The media exacerbate this confusion, eschewing the use of real—and often boring or confusing legal terms—for more salacious, headline-grabbing descriptors.

A few jurors were interviewed after the first Cosby trial. They reported that, while they found Constand a credible witness, when they retired to deliberate, they were unable to agree whether the words used in the criminal statute under which Cosby was charged—"unconscious," "reckless," and "lack of knowledge"—really applied to the events Constand recounted.[52] Jurors asked the judge to explain what it meant to have a "reasonable doubt" that a crime occurred.[53] As one reporter describes, the jurors were incapable of "matching the visceral intensity of . . . testimony with the bloodless language of the law."[54] Though most believed Constand's narrative was *true* and that Cosby's behavior was *wrong*, jurors struggled to situate what she experienced within the criminal legal category of sexual assault. Similar negotiations are taking place in the court of public opinion.

BUT WHERE ARE THE BRUISES?

Many online comments not only reinforce the myth that "real rape" is a violent act by a stranger, they also assume that any "real" sexual assault will result in traumatic and lasting injury. These public impressions not only reflect "folk" knowledge gleaned from years of exposure to crime-oriented television shows, websites, and podcasts, they reflect ideas that are deeply embedded in the law itself.

In 1977 the Supreme Court decided *Coker v. Georgia*, in which the court held that the death penalty was an unconstitutional, disproportional punishment for the crime of rape. Dissenting from the majority, Chief Justice Burger observed that death was in fact a proportional punishment because rape is "inherently one of the most egregiously brutal acts one human being can inflict upon another," a crime which

> inevitably causes serious psychological as well as physical harm. . . . The long-range effect upon the victim's life and health is likely to be irreparable. . . . Rape is not a mere physical attack—it is destructive of the human personality. The remainder of the victim's life may be

> gravely affected, and this in turn may have a serious detrimental effect upon her husband and any children she may have.[55]

During the recent sentencing of USA Gymnastics team doctor Larry Nassar, more than forty years after *Coker*, comments by judge Rosemarie Aquilina echo Justice Burger's view, observing that compared to other crimes, "[r]ape is an exceedingly difficult crime to 'survive.'"[56]

This idea that "real" sexual assault causes "irreparable" trauma persists in online comments insisting that real victims exhibit physical bruising or require visits to the hospital, and those noting that that rape is always "brutal" and "sadistic." In an amicus brief in *Coker*, ACLU (American Civil Liberties Union) women's rights advocates led by Ruth Bader Ginsburg fought against this conception of rape as forever "ruining" female victims.[57] The brief argued that not all persons experience harm the same way; a person's personality, capacity for resilience, social capital, and overall life circumstances impact their reaction to and ability to recover from a traumatic incident.[58] This is true for rape, Ginsburg argued, as it is for other crimes. Yet, as Jamie Abrams describes, sexual assault has been a crime constructed around "crisis."[59]

The words of Samantha Geimer, the alleged victim of film director Roman Polanski who fled the United States after having been indicted for statutory rape in 1978, are relevant.[60] For more than ten years, Los Angeles prosecutors have attempted to renew charges against Polanski; all along Geimer has advocated for dropping the case.

Geimer observes, "I'm fine. . . . You don't have to fall apart to show that what happened to you was wrong."[61]

Many of Bill Cosby's alleged victims—including Andrea Constand herself—describe having experienced profound psychological and emotional harms after their experiences with the celebrity. However, the outward appearances of the accusers—largely strong, successful, confident women—may not comport with the powerful belief that, to be "real," rape must cause irreparable, and visible, trauma. A criticism of the #MeToo movement has been the drive to combat rape by publicizing the extent of victims' suffering rather than redirecting attention to the harms inflicted by perpetrators.[62] Even if survivors personally are suffering in the aftermath of assault, they may not want to share—or feel able to share—their trauma with the public at large.

Like the jurors interviewed after the first Cosby trial, many people on social media are unsure how to situate the real-life story of what happened to Andrea Constand into the language and framework of the law. Comments minimizing Cosby's behavior as "lechery" or a "bad date," or insisting that victims who are telling the truth display significant physical injury and emotional trauma, show just how pervasive rape myths continue to be.

The casting couch mythology impacts not only victims but alleged perpetrators. In arguing that Cosby's actions cannot be criminal because everyone was doing "it" or by identifying his coercive behavior as a result of "normal human sexuality," commenters pathologize sexual assault as an aberrant act committed by perverts and monsters as opposed to a harm more likely to be inflicted by the girl or boy—or business colleague—next door. In "Riding the Bull at Gilley's," Diana Scully and Joseph Marolla critique this societal resistance to apply usual criminological theories, such as Black's theory of self-help, to the study of sexual assault.[63] Instead, our collective preference is for explanations that treat rape as an exceptional crime, victims as indelibly broken, and rapists as far outside the norms of human behavior.

As Black observed, it is by defining some persons, behaviors, and acts as deviant that we situate ourselves as "normal."[64] However, the argument, made by both online commenters and the Cosby defense team, that a behavior cannot possibly be a crime if "everyone" is doing it is at once logically unsound and self-protective, distinguishing "good" people from pathological "others." Kate Harding describes how what we often talk about as "gray" areas in regard to rape are often not gray at all but involve clear-cut cases of nonconsent.[65] Most of the accusations against Cosby involve alleged assaults against unconscious or barely conscious victims, emphasized by numerous memes across the internet alleging that the celebrity has a "sleeping beauty fetish," superimposing Cosby's face on Prince Charming's body as he leans in for a non-consensual kiss.[66] However, by broadening the category of what is not rape, we expand the range of "normal"—read: "safe, noncriminal behaviors."

The sociological concept of rape culture—the theory that a society's or institution's beliefs and values can promote environments conducive to sexual assault—operates to combat this dichotomous distinction, highlighting the ways in which behaviors we might accept as normal or usual—catcalling or locker-room talk, for example—in fact may promote habits and practices that encourage criminal behavior. While the idea of rape culture increasingly is entering the public consciousness, social media comments and memes suggest that society is reluctant to recognize that it is precisely those practices we have long viewed as innocuous or harmless which in fact contribute to more significant social harms. Coming to terms with sexual assault means revisiting our foundational beliefs, even in fairytales.

In reframing a possibly criminal encounter as having taken place on the casting couch, we protect our own, tenuous moral standing, transforming a potentially exploitative event into a purely transactional one, a rapist into a relatively harmless letch, and the accuser herself into something less than an "ideal victim." The casting couch is haunted by the same, rhetorical question that troubles the bricks-and-mortar courtroom:

What was a nice girl doing in a place like that? By just asking the question, we condemn the victim.

CONTRIBUTORY NEGLIGENCE

The casting couch is not a nice place for alleged perpetrators, whose behavior is described as coercive, "lecherous," "pervy," or "creepy." However, again and again, online comments assert that, while the accused may have "taken advantage" of a situation, the real problem lies with the accuser, a young woman who should not have put herself in there in the first place.

Considering Andrea Constand's testimony that she had taken a pill from Bill Cosby for a migraine, a commenter on a liberal news site observes that she should not have "endangered her own well-being by taking drugs or alcohol from a celebrity that impressed her." A tweet puts it less elegantly, referring to Constand as a "stupid clown" for "put[ting] pills in her mouth." In response to an article on Cosby published in a major news outlet, a commenter queries, "Why would a woman take pills offered to her without knowing what they were?"

In the views of many, Constand was not the target of a predator but rather was beset by the tragic combination of ambition and stupidity. As one post on a conservative site warns,

> Hollywood is a dangerous place. Look at all of the dead stars. Dead kids. Victimized kids, young women and young men are the norm. You have to know what you're getting into. If you're naive, you're going to get burned.

Over and over again, Constand and fellow accusers are referred to as "stupid," "silly," "trendy," "naïve," and "young." Although the assault allegedly took place at Cosby's home, cautionary tales about dangerous locations abound. A conservative news reader commenting on reports of the Cosby mistrial observes, "[I]f I walk alone drunk on the South Side of Chicago . . . with a huge chain and a Rolex, I shouldn't be surprised if I get robbed," while another remarks

> If the beach has signs that say "no swimming—sharks in the water" are you at fault for getting eaten? YES. Sharks are animals [illegible], there are people who are animals. If you foolishly give them the opportunity . . . then yes, it is your own fault.

Making the metaphor explicit,

> [W]hen women go to a married man's home, or the playboy mansion . . . they know the score . . . [I]f you choose to go, it also implies consent.

Comments along these lines persist after Cosby's conviction. In response to a story on a conservative news site announcing the guilty verdict, a poster ironically provides, "Yes, and we all should be able to walk down the street at midnight by ourselves—in the crime-ridden areas of Chicago, Memphis, St. Louis, New Orleans, etc.—with no fear of being shot, mugged, robbed and/or killed. Just don't put yourself in those situations." Another major news reader goes so far as to suggest that women should travel with "[c]haperones . . . to protect [them] from poor judgement and . . . celebrity idolization."

Despite Andrea Constand's age at the time of the incident—nearly thirty—and her prior interactions with Cosby in her capacity as a business professional, the version of Constand discursively constructed in online comments is of a naïve, fame-seeking starlet who fell into the grasp of an influential older man. As the collective focus shifts onto the accuser, the actions of the accused become less significant. Ultimately, the perpetrator's responsibility is reduced in proportion to the victim's lack of judgment. As a commenter on a major news site observes, "We all know he's guilty, but how guilty?"

In tort law, the doctrine of contributory negligence historically operated to prohibit civil plaintiffs from recovery if they were somehow at fault for the injury they suffered.[67] Now rejected in the majority of jurisdictions, the outcome of contributory negligence was that, no matter how bad the conduct, the defendant was absolved of responsibility when an injured party acted irresponsibly. The idea of contributory negligence largely is eschewed by criminal law. It defeats the goals of holding perpetrators accountable and of making society safer. On both retributive and deterrent principles, a killer should be guilty of first-degree murder whether the person they plotted to poison was a fellow drug dealer or a pious nun.

Comments implying that alleged victims of sexual assault should not have been wearing a nice watch, walking at night in a "bad neighborhood," or "swimming with sharks" rely on this idea of contributory negligence to absolve Cosby of responsibility. They exhibit a willingness to let a perpetrator—even a "shark"—off the hook if his target acted irresponsibly.

The irony, of course, is that a wealthy person's criminal complaint for robbery would certainly be taken seriously, even if the robbery occurred in a "bad" neighborhood. In fact, practices such as "stop-and-frisk" and "hot spot" policing mean that we are *more* likely to arrest residents of impoverished locations. Why, then, does blame-shifting happen so easily when we're talking about sexual assault?

One answer lies in sexual assault law's specific, gendered history of exclusion. For nearly three hundred years—from the 1700s in Britain until the introduction of rape shield laws in the United States in the 1970s and 1980s—any white male defendant who raised a consent defense was entitled to introduce evidence of the sexual experience of the complainant, and the probative value of such evidence was routinely deemed to outweigh its prejudicial effect.[68] Equating any increase in an accuser's sexual experience with a decline in the veracity of her claim, courts applied what was known as the "law of human nature," assuming that "one who ha[d] already started on the road to prostitution would be less reluctant [sexually] . . . than another who yet remain[ed] at her home of innocence."[69] Chapter 4 discusses how the operation of these stereotypes was influenced by race, with significantly less focus on white women's sexual behavior in cases involving African American defendants and more focus on women's sexuality in the case of Black female accusers of white men.[70]

Assumptions linking a female's chastity to her truthfulness not only permeated rape trials but, more significantly, they impacted who was seen as worthy of the law's protection in the first place. Until after the Civil War, throughout the south the rape of Black women was not considered criminal but rather was encouraged as part of the slavery system; myths abounded characterizing Black women as sexually voracious partners. These myths were politically deployed to obscure the harms of the institution of slavery and to insulate white slave owners from moral critique.[71] Angela Harris writes that, for years, "[r]ape . . . was something that only happened to white women; what happened to black women was simply life."[72] Other groups or "types" of persons—married women, sex workers—historically also have faced exclusion from the law premised on "commonsense" ideas that sexual experience was a proxy for sexual consent. As Lowen describes,

> The ugly truth is that . . . women who engage in "unchaste" behavior were not deemed "worthy" of society's protections. Women who engage in pre- or extra-marital sex have been perpetually viewed as at least somewhat culpable when they are sexually violated. Likewise, women who drink, party, or post provocative pictures of themselves online are often blamed for their own assaults.[73]

With the advent of the women's movement, advocates and scholars began to question this conflation of past sexual behaviors with likelihood to lie. However, these assumptions have not been erased from American law and procedure. For example, the reduction of a murder charge to voluntary manslaughter historically has depended on the fact finder offering evidence of "adequate provocation" by the victim, classically, a woman who drove her husband into a murderous rage by committing adultery.[74] Although discovery of a spouse in flagrante no longer is a criterion for voluntary manslaughter, the "heat of passion" as a justification for killing persists.[75]

Both the letter of rape law and the procedural spirit in which it has been applied provide endless examples of the operation of implicit, and often explicit, biases which serve to shift the assessment of guilt away from the actions of the perpetrator and onto the character of the accuser. Historical examples of procedural blame-shifting in rape prosecutions, examined more fully in chapter 3, include corroboration requirements, demands that victims show resistance to the utmost, and the Hale instruction, which until the 1990s demanded or permitted that judges instruct jurors that rape victims were more likely to lie than victims of other violent crimes.[76] Janzen refers to these procedural and substantive requirements collectively as the "inverted process" of a rape trial.[77] Similarly, Deborah Tuerkheimer characterizes the "recurring tropes of disbelief" that overshadow rape complainants as fostering a "credibility discount," where claims of sexual assault are likely to be met with skepticism.[78]

Annie Clark, one of the protagonists in the documentary *The Hunting Ground*, says she was told by a university administrator that "rape is like a football game," where she should think back on what she could have done differently to have avoided the crime.[79] Similarly, Emily Doe, the victim in the Brock Turner case describes,

> I had forensic evidence, sober un-biased witnesses, a slurred voice mail, police at the scene. I had everything, and I was still told it was not a slam dunk. I thought, if this is what having it good looks like, what other hells are survivors living? I'm barely getting through this but I am being told I'm the lucky one, some sort of VIP. It was like being checked into a hotel room for a year with stained sheets, rancid water, and a bucket with an attendant saying, "No this is great! Most rooms don't even have a bucket."[80]

These descriptions emphasize the supposition that the most effective way to determine the accused's responsibility for a crime is by closely examining the behavior of the accuser. Were this assessment applied in the case of a mugging, the police and court would need to inquire of the alleged victim not only where they were when the crime took place but also the depth of their pocket, the size and shape of their wallet, and whether they wore a wallet chain.

Chastity was of the utmost importance in rape trials because, historically and even today in some cultures, a woman's virginity was the best determinant of her value. Until recently, rape was not viewed as a crime against autonomy but one against property, continuing an assignment of hierarchies of economic value to women's bodies that originated before feudal times. Not only did Anglo-Saxon customs form the historical basis for British and then American law, the U.S. states imposed an additional, unique system of treating bodies as property—rape was freely exploited against Black women as part of the routine, state-supported system of terror and rape law was utilized to confine and constrain the activities of Black men.[81] The treatment of rape as a crime against property is evidenced by the marital rape exception, which assumed that marital vows signified a wife's contractual duty to submit to her husband's will and desire.[82] Women's legal status as possessions was further supported by the coverture doctrine, barring married women from owning property, entering into contracts, or bringing legal actions in their own name.[83] In violating the chastity of a married woman, a perpetrator harmed not—or not only—the woman herself but her husband. For unmarried girls, the harm was ascribed not to the daughter but to her father, who might not be able to "give her away" in marriage. The higher the premium placed on female chastity, the more important it has been to control women's sexual behavior.

Historically, virility and sexual experience have been prized for men while, for women, the pursuit of sexual experience has been equated with a loss of honor, not only for oneself but for family and community. These contrasting, gendered points of view mean that the primary responsibility for regulating male behavior has often fallen not on the shoulders of men but of women.[84] It is unsurprising then, that social media narratives treat it as natural for men to be "sharks" and unnatural for women to seek out sexual experiences, or to frequent places where such experiences are likely to take place.

Today, most of us understand that abundant characterizations of Andrea Constand as "stupid," "silly," or "naïve" fit into what we commonly understand as victim-blaming, a wrongful attribution of responsibility for a crime to its target rather than to the perpetrator. However, although we may be able to recite the textbook definition of victim-blaming—and even know that it is wrong—it is much more difficult to avoid victim-blaming in practice.

It's not our fault. We have a natural tendency to prefer "one-cause," dispositional rationales for crime rather examining more complex, situational factors because dispositional explanations mean that crime is less likely to happen to us.[85] When I lived in Brooklyn in my twenties, a young woman of a similar age was murdered on the front steps of our brownstone. Understandably unsettled, I asked the detectives who came to investigate the crime what they thought had occurred. When the detectives told me she and her boyfriend had a fight, I recall feeling immense relief. I did not stop to think about the likelihood that intimate partner violence—a crime one in three women experience—could happen to me. By attributing crime to dispositional rationales we maintain the illusory and self-protective belief that "good things happen to good people and bad things happen to bad people."[86]

While many commenters seem to believe that Constand suffered some harm at the hands of Bill Cosby, they also view the perpetrator's responsibility for inflicting that harm as mitigated by Constand's contributory negligence, that is, her poor decision to visit him alone in the first place. As one reader of a mainstream news site explains, "I do believe [Constand] was a victim of a crime but I also believe she helped render a 'hung jury' verdict." By all accounts, Andrea Constand is a successful and confident business professional but, in the public's imagination, Constand is a "stupid," silly girl, who wore an inappropriate outfit, drank too much, and dared to travel alone at night.

In online comments one also sees echoes of Ellison and Munro's mock juror study, where participants had a difficult time comprehending why victims of acquaintance rape did not fight back to the utmost. While jurors in the study tended to accept the stories of stranger rape at face value, when victims were described as knowing their attackers, jurors "questioned whether the complainant had 'done enough to say no' in simply telling the defendant to 'stop.'"[87] They identified behaviors such as "offering/accepting a lift, inviting a person into one's home, remaining in one another's company for a prolonged period, paying/receiving compliments, engaging in alcohol consumption, [or] sharing a goodnight kiss" as "indirectly communicating the willingness of one or both parties to engage in intercourse."[88] The researchers emphasize that

> [e]ven in situations in which the complainant claimed to have frozen in fear, and so was wholly unresponsive during intercourse, many jurors accepted that the defendant could have reasonably believed that she was consenting on the basis of her prior conduct; and her inertia during the incident was insufficient in their minds to countermand those earlier, positive signals.[89]

In online conversations about the two Cosby trials, one can clearly see the influence of legal terms on everyday language, many developed via decades of lobbying by the women's movement. "Date rape" and "victim-blaming" have become part of the vernacular. However, at the same time one can also witness the continuing negotiation that is taking place regarding the meanings of such terms. As a commenter to a conservative site observes of comments about Constand, "It's not victim-blaming, it's common sense. But common sense is now being called 'victim-blaming.'"

ACTUAL VICTIMS

Comments on the Cosby cases emphasize that the online public, like real-life jurors, favors "ideal victims." We gravitate toward stories about weak and blameless "little old ladies" who are targeted by "big and bad," unknown offenders.[90] This ideal victim stereotype influences every stage of the process of a rape trial—from the way police react to the initial reporting of an incident through its resolution in the civil or criminal justice system. As any *Law & Order: SVU* viewer can attest, police and prosecutors prefer victims who report promptly, tell a straightforward story, dress modestly, and were stone cold sober at the time of the attack. Harding jokes that, even after seventeen seasons, the male detectives on *SVU*, and Ice-T, in particular, still meet the rape cases that come into the squad room with "total confusion," playing the victim-blaming-everyman to Mariska Hargitay's sage and experienced Lieutenant Benson.[91]

Thanks to efforts by the victims's rights movement, the past thirty years have seen a concerted effort by professionals across the criminal justice system to mitigate against the impression, offered by Christie, that the law is "stealing" parties' claims.[92] There are more and more inroads being made toward incorporating the opinions, thoughts, and ideas of victims into what is largely a process between the defendant and the state.[93] However, as Jill Lepore observes, not all victims' voices are treated as equally deserving—jurors tend to sympathize with those with whom they identify.[94] Lepore describes Justice Thurgood Marshall's rationale for excluding victim impact evidence in felony cases, offered in *Booth v. Maryland*, now overruled by *Tennessee v. Payne*. Marshall explains that the reception of a victim's statement during a criminal trial often depends on "the eloquence with which family members express their grief and the status of the victim in the community."[95] Today, white victims are twice as likely as Black victims to make victim-impact statements.[96]

With recognition of deserving—what Christie calls "authorized"—victimhood, there is often compensation or other benefits. Hundreds of millions of dollars have been donated to assist victims of mass shootings and survivors of terrorism like the Boston Marathon bombing.[97] For "genuine" victims we will not only pay medical bills but contribute to expenses such as food, rent, or psychological counseling. Once ideal victim status is afforded, people are generous. We understand and appreciate the toll that traumatic experiences exact on all facets of life. However, as is discussed more in connection with "false" claims in chapter 3, if one is discovered to have been "playing the victim," attempting to secure benefit above and beyond the harm one has suffered, the consequences can be harsh.

Kristin Bumiller connects our expectations of victims to the idea of the martyr, "a living creature sacrificed to a deity or offered in performance of a religious rite."[98] She points out that the most recognizable victims in Western society—Socrates, Jesus—were both wrongfully persecuted and met "tragic ends."[99] The closer one comes to martyrdom, the more likely one is to be deemed deserving of justice. Both the formal legal process and the public prefer that those who have experienced crime behave as much like martyrs as possible.[100]

An antonym for ideal is *actual*. Actual people are unpredictable and, as Ice-T seems to learn in every episode of *SVU*, those who have experienced trauma are even less so. Crime victims' narratives are often confused, chronologically disconnected, or use less-than-clear terminology to describe what they have experienced.[101] Sexual assault survivors may exhibit disruptions to behavior and cognitive functioning that impact their ability to bring a criminal case, affecting stages from reporting the crime to identifying the perpetrator.[102] Some mass media, like *Law & Order: SVU*, do attempt to educate the public that the conduct of sexual assault victims can be unpredictable, the stories they tell often disconnected or nonlinear. However, attempts at educating the public about how real victims behave come up against a wall of powerful ideal victim mythologies.

In the view of social media commenters, there are two ways in which Andrea Constand was not an ideal victim. The first, evident in the categorizations of Constand discussed above, is that she was hopelessly naïve, "stupid," or "trendy." Drawn into a dangerous situation based on "idolization," Constand is deemed to be unworthy of obtaining justice because her behavior was negligent, deviating from what "reasonable" people—we—would have done in a similar situation.

In the eyes of others, however, Constand is far from innocent or negligent. In the public imagination, there is another type of woman who visits the infamous casting couch. This person is not a feckless young girl but a manipulative fame-seeker, a "slut" who seeks the attentions of a famous man in order to advance her career and, scorned, now seeks to frame the wealthy celebrity. As a commenter on a major news site notes of Constand and her fellow accusers: "These women wanted something from Cosby and were willing to trade their bodies for it." Like their naïve counterparts, these manipulative fame-seekers also are undeserving of justice.

VICTIMHOOD CHIC

On a prominent conservative site, a reader proclaims, "Sorry girls!!! You cash the check, you become a PROSTITUTE, and the rape thingy goes out the window!!!" Another questions, "Who is more honest, the woman who charges up front for sex, or the woman looking for a pay day for sex years later?"

After Cosby's conviction, a news reader critiques that Constand is "out for money not justice. They call it prostitution." Still another observes that "[i]n Kardashian America, victimhood chic is all the rage." A reader of a gossip site cautions "[w]omen using PU$$Y as currency" is "a bad deal. The opportunitie$ are only as good as your current screen test." Another complains, "[w]hen you are a groupie you know what to expect. All these accusers are *just that and nothing more*." And, after yet another allegation against Cosby is revealed on a weekly entertainment magazine program, a commenter asks, "Anyone else here trying to jump on this bandwagon and ride it to richville?"

Similar comments are easy to find on the internet. A conservative news reader queries, incredulously, "Are you SERIOUSLY attempting to push forward the hypotheses that these WOMEN looking to up their casting couch careers were somehow NAIVE and DIDN'T KNOW what was going on with a married MAN[?]" Another reader describes how "real rape" compares to what they see as a new crime category:

> This is "Feminist rape." She willingly went with him, willingly took the drugs, willingly went along with all of it. A year later she realized he wasn't gonna make her a star, so she decided it was rape, and now, thirteen years later, everyone is just supposed to take her word for it.

Janice Dickinson, one of the most famous of Cosby's accusers, faced a steady criticism of "fame-seeking" when, in 2014, she came forward with claims against the comedian. Twitter users complain that the actor (and model) is "fame hungry," "thirsty," and a "fame whore." A tweet refers to sex with the celebrity as "a devil's bargain: Rape 4 Fame."[103] Celebrity gossip readers are aghast that "the public is expected to give a tramp of such magnitude any credibility."

A significant feature of the contemporary legal system is the celebrity attorney. One of the most recognizable of these is Gloria Allred, known for representing some of the accusers of Bill Cosby and numerous plaintiffs in Title IX cases relating to campus sexual assaults. On a conservative news site Allred is described as "sick predator" who "uses her law license to round up false accusers, degrade them by making them play the role of 'victims' all so that she can cash in at a 40% contingency fee plus expenses." Another post labels her "a serial victim maker."

These comments emphasize that today, "victim" is not just a legal term but a social status that has a particular meaning. Allred is, of course, literally a "victim maker"; the task of every plaintiff's attorney is to make a "victim" of their client, shaping a story about a social wrong into a recognizable legal claim. The comments above, however, suggest that being a victim is about more than attaining a legal status; playing the victim can be parlayed into "jackpot justice" and undeserved financial gain.

We are living in the era of the "Insta-model." Reality series like *Botched*, *Intervention*, the *Real Housewives* franchise, *Teen Mom*, *Hoarders*, and *My 600-Lb Life* demonstrate that characteristics and life events that might a few, short years ago have been treated as embarrassing or shameful can now be translated into a particular, if limited, sort of fame. The public routinely is confronted with news of the release of "sex tapes," and tasked to assess whether such tapes are part of a consensual public relations maneuver or "revenge pornography," a criminal violation of privacy.[104] We are conditioned to think that from victimhood comes celebrity.

Historically, sexual assault laws have been more exclusive than inclusive, rendering many more people outside the realm of their protection than within. Even today, the populations most likely to encounter sexual violence are those least likely to be taken seriously when reporting it.[105]

The allegation that an accuser is a "prostitute" is effective because it draws upon this long history of legal exclusion. When an online commenter remarks that a "tramp" or a "slut" is not credible, this is not merely an offhand comment; it evokes centuries of law that explicitly tied female victims' veracity to assessments of their chastity.

Notably, as the public negotiates who is and is not deserving of justice, there are some survivors who come closer to Christie's ideal victim paradigm. One might compare and contrast the social media construction of the Cosby accusers with the 160 women who, in January 2018, gave testimony against former USA Gymnastics team doctor Larry Nassar in a Michigan state court. During Nassar's sentencing, Judge Aquilina praised the profound bravery of these accusers, telling one that

> [t]he military has not yet come up with fiber as strong as you, . . . Mattel ought to make toys so that little girls can look at you and say, "I want to be her." Thank you so much for being here, and for your strength.[106]

Nassar's survivors received a standing ovation as they were honored for "bravery that transcends sports" with the Arthur Ashe Courage Award at the 2018 ESPYS.[107]

There are notable similarities between the accusations against Cosby and those against Nassar. Each case involved an older "advisor" abusing his power against accusers, some of whom were very young at the time of the alleged abuse. In both cases there were lengthy delays by at least some victims in coming forward, a lack of demonstrable physical injuries, and ongoing contact between victim and alleged perpetrator after the alleged assaults. While many of Nassar's victims were children at the time of the abuse, others, like Cosby's alleged victims, were teen- or college-aged women when the abuse first took place.

The internet is flooded with comments praising the athletes who accused Nassar for their bravery in speaking out. They are widely—and deservedly—described as "warriors," "icons," "superheroes."[108] Actor Natalie Portman appeared on *Saturday Night Live* wearing a T-shirt bearing the Judge Aquilina's name; a popular meme portrays the fact finder as Wonder Woman.[109]

Comments from and about the Nassar accusers reflect that in recent years there has been a strong movement to reframe victims as survivors. While, as discussed above, the term victim suggests a vulnerable, unempowered nonagent, the word "survivor" describes a person who has lived through an experience but not let it define her. A survivor is in control of her social and legal destiny. Amanda Thomashow seemed to describe the iconic version of a survivor during the Nassar sentencing, describing how she and her fellow accusers "will rise as an army of female warriors who will never let . . . another man drunk off of power get away with such evil again."[110]

The public is captivated by narratives like those shared by the Nassar accusers and by "Emily Doe," named one of *Glamour* magazine's 2016 Women of the Year for her bravery in sharing a victim-impact statement describing her assault by Brock Turner.[111] *Time Magazine* named the actors who spoke out about Harvey Weinstein's predation—nicknamed the "Silence Breakers"—2017's Persons of the Year based on the "revolution of refusal" their actions in speaking out have inspired.[112]

Despite what initially seems to be a revolution in perception of victims, on social media, the status of "survivor" is not one that is easily conveyed. In the eyes of the public, the Cosby accusers decidedly are not survivors. In fact, among more than ten thousand comments on articles covering the Cosby mistrial and conviction on major news sites, the word *survivor* appears not even once.

The persistent use of the term *victims* to refer to Cosby's accusers could merely be a reflection of the legal terminology. However, it is likely there is a more significant rhetorical distinction at work. In the collective imaginary, Andrea Constand and other accusers are not an army of "warriors." They are not confident, resourceful agents like the Nassar accusers, but largely are perceived as malingering, exaggerating the harm they have suffered, "playing the victim."

This distinction between the Cosby and Nassar accusers can be explained by applying Christie's ideal victim paradigm. Not only are the Nassar accusers student athletes and future Olympians—upstanding citizens who appear to have been overpowered by a "monstrous predator" while going about highly respectable tasks[113]—but women's gymnastics, despite requiring superhuman strength, is a sport that encourages athletes to cultivate an appearance of youthful fragility; even mature competitors often appearing in bedazzled leotards and hair bows.[114]

Gymnasts Megan Nichols and Christine Harrison, both of whom who read impact statements during Nassar's sentencing, were fifteen at the time they were first assaulted by the doctor. Cosby accuser Judy Huth also was fifteen when Cosby allegedly assaulted her.[115] However, while the athletes' assaults took place in a trusted doctor's office, Huth allegedly was assaulted at the Playboy Mansion. While Nichols and Harrison are revered as heroes, in the eyes of many members of the public, Huth is labeled "just" one more aspiring actress who visited the casting couch.[116] As one comment responding to news of Huth's ongoing civil suit queries, "What was a 15 year old doing at the playboy mansion in the first place???"[117]

Notably, in late 2017, when gymnast McKayla Maroney stepped forward as one of the first to accuse Nassar of inappropriate conduct, commenters on a popular gossip site treated her claims with suspicion. Maroney had received some negative press for her behavior during the 2016 Olympics, her expression while another gymnast competed labeled unsportsmanlike and attention-seeking.[118] She had gained more recent notoriety for posing in scanty outfits on Instagram.[119] In reaction to her claims of having been assaulted, "OHHHHH PLEASE," wrote one commenter, "Aged out of Gymnastics/Failed modeling career/Failed singing career/Hey lets just make up some absolute garbage Lie to get some more attention." Some critiqued poor parental supervision, suggesting that, like the Cosby accusers, Maroney might somehow be an accomplice to her own assault. Others signaled their opinions of Maroney's veracity with "#bandwagon."

Gradually, however, other accusers came forward, eventually comprising nearly all members of the 2012 Olympic gymnastics squad. From a potential accomplice, Maroney was discursively transformed into one of a mass of brave survivors and thus, a legitimate victim.

Of course, being identified as a survivor comes with its own constraints and pressures. Monica Thompson identifies a "victim-survivor paradox":

> In order to speak about the trauma of rape one must assume a victim identity. Being a victim maximizes the possibility that the awfulness of rape can be appreciated. But adopting a victim identity also runs the risk of being pitied, not viewed as a survivor and regarded as weak.[120]

No one person is always brave or completely helpless. Whether a person is a victim or a survivor is contextual. As Ubell observes, "[t]here is something in between the ideas of victim and survivor that is both, and yet neither. It is a liminal space that is difficult to label with any precision."[121] But there is no space for liminality—for gray areas—in the court of public opinion.

GET THE "PIG" OFF THE STREETS!

A particularly damning aspect of the accusations against Bill Cosby is that so many accusers took years, sometimes decades, to speak out. For many on social media, the length of time in reporting is a deal breaker; accusers' failure to immediately report to law enforcement is interpreted as suggestive of less-than-wholesome motivations. On a well-known gossip site, a typical post inquires, "Why did they run to the media instead of going to the emergency room to collect evidence to prove Cosby assaulted them?" One of two thousand comments to a story about Cosby's conviction on a major news outlet exclaims, concisely, "Thirty years ago? C'mon!" Another post advises, "Report the crime immediately. . . . People rising from the ashes from ten years ago don't cut it." The lag in time in reporting accusations for some is a "setup," a "railroad," and a "can of worms." In the case of the Cosby accusers, the lack of prompt reporting not only casts doubt on the truthfulness of accusations, it raises questions about victims' character.

Using the Cosby example as a cautionary tale, a major news reader remarks, "So they don't get a conviction. At least her claim was recorded and thus can help someone in the future." On a conservative site, a similar sentiment: "I am a victim of a similar assault . . . as difficult as it was . . . I reported the assault . . . to help prevent future victims!" A post explains why victims must speak up immediately,

> As painful as it might be to testify, the victim has that social responsibility. Otherwise, the victim may share some responsibility for the suffering of the subsequent victim. Almost like quarantining the Ebola victim to protect others.

Rather than seeking formal legal remedies, a different post recommends that women "pursue healing through societal remedies; writing, speaking and counseling other victims. By helping other victims, they will find closure."

There is a term, the "dark figure" of crime, that describes all those offenses that are legally actionable but were not reported to law enforcement. Shaped like a Pac-Man eating a pie slice of reported crimes, the sheer number of crimes that go unreported highlights that the U.S. criminal justice system is more often bypassed than engaged. Interviews with complainants and would-be complainants provide ample reasons why people are more likely to "lump it" than to involve the police in a given scenario, including fear, cost, or lack of recognition that one is a victim.[122] Across all types of cases, objectives in pursuing charges are complex and ambivalent: "a party may file criminal charges intending only to have another person removed from the home . . . [or] may resort to seeking redress through the criminal system because of the dearth of restorative justice practices and the expense of civil legal assistance."[123] Victims of crime may choose to drop charges once they fully understand the consequences of a criminal proceeding for themselves and for the perpetrator.[124] The reluctance to involve law enforcement in interpersonal disputes is magnified in areas where the public is less likely to have positive police-citizen interactions—undocumented immigrants and minority communities disproportionately experience adversarial police-citizen encounters.

Further, most people who report crime do not have a single motivation in doing so. After an accident with a drunk driver, for example, a person might both want to see the driver punished *and* make sure they are compensated sufficiently to purchase a nice, new car. After a break-in, a tenant might desire to have a robber "put away" and also hold accountable the landlord who put off fixing a broken window or a locksmith who installed a faulty lock.[125]

As described earlier, the rationale for not reporting crime is exacerbated in the context of sexual assault. Numerous research studies show that, just as sexual assault victims don't always demonstrate physical harms, it is also not likely that they will immediately report incidents to the authorities. The myriad reasons why victims of sexual assault do not report experiences to law enforcement are well documented, including fear of stigma, post traumatic stress, and a general reluctance to become involved with the criminal justice system. Lens et al. describe that, despite rhetoric emphasizing the cathartic power of telling one's story, in fact, victims who choose to deliver an impact statement report higher levels of anxiety, PTSD, or anger than those who eschew the process.[126]

Importantly, victims themselves are not immune to rape myths. Those who have experienced a sexual assault may not—or at least not at first—view themselves as victims. Research studies of college students conducted by Mary Koss in the 1980s and repeated by Bonnie Fisher and her colleagues in the early 2000s find that many women who have experienced incidents meeting the legal criteria for sexual assault dismiss incidents as "errors in judgment, bad sex, or mistakes," especially if drinking or drugs were involved.[127] This self-doubt about potential personal responsibility for or complicity in events may mean that stories do not always unfold logically or completely.[128] Deb Waterhouse-Watson describes an unfortunate cycle in which fear of disbelief dissuades women from pressing criminal charges, and that the lack of pursuit of charges adds to the widespread assumption that women lie about sexual assaults.[129]

Survivors who do acknowledge having been victimized also may logically assess that sexual assault remains exceedingly difficult to prosecute. This was likely true for many Cosby accusers whose experiences took place before terms like *victim-blaming* and *acquaintance rape* had entered the vernacular, and before offenses like digital penetration formally were criminalized. The assumption that victims should have reported sooner also reflects a lack of awareness of statutes of limitations, some of which carried a deadline for reporting sexual offenses of as little as three months after the offense.[130]

Despite these challenges, and despite growing awareness of the trauma potentially resulting from sexual assault, the court of public opinion continues to place a unique burden to report on the shoulders of survivors. For social media commenters, a complainant who exhibits anything but the purest of motives may be disqualified from ideal or authorized victimhood. The only acceptable motivation in reporting the crime is one that stems from selflessness and societal goodwill: getting the "pig" off the streets or perhaps other socially embedded remedies, such as speaking out about trauma to inspire other survivors.

The freedom with which people express expectations about what Cosby's accusers should and should not have done after an assault reflects the extent to which women historically have not spoken for themselves in the legal context. Mary Beard describes how, historically, women have been deliberately excluded from the sphere of political speech.[131] She recounts the Greek legend of Philomela, princess of Athens, whose brother-in-law, after raping her, cuts out her tongue. Unable to report her crime to authorities, she sings as a nightingale or, in other tellings, weaves the story of her rape into a tapestry. Philomela is indeed "speaking" about her assault—chirping, weaving—but not in terms formally recognized in the context of formal, male-dominated public discourse.[132]

The criminal justice process has long operated to silence the voices of sexual assault complainants via the imposition of procedural hurdles and discretionary assessments of who is and is not a "good victim." The nightingale in mythology is an apt metaphor for the isolation a victim experiences when testifying in a criminal trial. As Ubell describes,

> All eyes are on her as she reveals the intimate details of her victimization. Courtroom rituals do not allow for her to have a trusted individual beside her for support. She must remain in this incredibly vulnerable physical position until she is give[n] permission to leave the witness stand. Thus, it is evident that there is a profound power differential in the courtroom that crushes that victim's voice and does not allow her to tell her story in her own words.[133]

Taslitz compares the situation of sexual assault complainants to Ariel in the fairytale, *The Little Mermaid*. Just as Ariel surrendered her voice to join the human world, if a case goes to trial, victims of sexual assault surrender the privilege of speaking for themselves.[134]

In light of a troubled history that expects victims to quietly and stalwartly endure as martyrs and to conform to regimented expectations of the legal system, the Cosby accusers stand out. Many do not present as having experienced *visible, lasting* physical injury, and some do not seem to have been marred—at least not ostensibly—by crippling emotional trauma.

In the view of social media, victims like Andrea Constand also have not acted in the public interest in reporting their experiences as soon as possible. As one social media commenter puts it, sexual assault is a public health crisis, like the Ebola virus. In not speaking out immediately, Cosby's accusers are deemed to have been complicit in causing others harm.

The combination of these factors frequently results in the judgment of the court of public opinion that accusers are merely "playing the victim," seeking to capitalize on what should be a traumatic experience to achieve an underserved personal gain.

CONCLUSION

Many comments on social media do indeed reflect the offensive, misogynist speech at the "bottom of the internet," but they also provide a lens into how public opinion about law is being shaped in the #MeToo era. In exploring social media discussions of the Cosby accusations, one can see an active negotiation of the boundaries of criminal behavior, attempting to sort out "real rape" from something less or different—a bad date or lechery. Online comments eerily echo Bill Cosby's own characterization of his engagement with Andrea Constand, which he described during a 2005 deposition,

> I don't hear her say anything. And I don't feel her say anything. And so I continue and I go into the area that is somewhere between permission and rejection. I am not stopped.[135]

Even when a victim is unconscious, accountability for the perpetrator's actions squarely sits on her shoulders.

Law as an institution draws its strength from its foundation in unbiased facts, supported by doctrines, procedures, and practices designed to maintain legitimacy and inspire public trust. In reality, however, the U.S. system of law has been built up by continually maintaining systematic biases, restrictive covenants, Jim Crow and anti-gay ordinances, and explicit gender discrimination. For centuries, courts have taken judicial notice of commonsense "facts" in sexual assault cases to support suppositions, for example, that legitimate victims fight back to the utmost or that their lives irreparably will be ruined by the experience of rape. These biases, long inhered in the physical courtroom, not only pervade but may be amplified in the virtual court of public opinion.

Beyond misogynist discourse, online comments about accusations against Bill Cosby reveal that, like legal scholars and practitioners, members of the public are reckoning with the "gray areas" of sexual assault law. When social media commenters engage terms like "date rape," they use it to distance "bad hookups" from real rapes, or to distinguish "regrettable" sexual encounters, "flirting," or "fondling" from the types of behaviors they imagine criminal laws are intended to encompass.

A refrain among comments to the Cosby case is that many of us have "been there." Women "get tipsy" and have sex with people with whom they might otherwise not have. Men get intoxicated and are more assertive than they may have been while sober. For some, to view Cosby as a rapist comes dangerously close to admitting that they have raped. To recognize accusers as survivors requires that we reexamine what we classified as unfortunate mistakes, perhaps for the first time envisioning ourselves as victims.

The dual spectacles of the Cosby trial and retrial, situated squarely in the context of the #MeToo movement, provide a unique lens into the negotiation of sexual assault law during this moment of crisis.[136] The movement presents an opportunity for a radical increase in public understanding about not only the extent and range of behaviors that constitute sexual assault but the ways in which sexual assault fits into the larger scheme of patriarchy and rape culture. In any moment of crisis, however, there are as many voices seeking to entrench harmful stereotypes as there are advocating for reform.

NOTES

1. Jeff Truesdell and Nicole Weisensee Egan, "Who is Andrea Constand, Bill Cosby's Accuser?," People.com, June 13, 2017, https://www.imdb.com/news/ni61172968.
2. Truesdell and Egan, "Who is Andrea Constand?"
3. Truesdell and Egan, "Who is Andrea Constand?"
4. Jeremy Roebuck and Laura McCrystal, "Cosby Accuser Constand Remains an Enigma," *Philad elphia Inquirer*, January 3, 2016, http://www.philly.com/philly/news/20160103_Cosby_accuser_Constand_remains_an_enigma.html.
5. Truesdell and Egan, "Who is Andrea Constand?"
6. Stacy Brown, "Bill Cosby Paid Andrea Constand $3.5M in 2006 Settlement," *Page Six*, March 10, 2018, https://pagesix.com/2018/03/10/bill-cosby-paid-andrea-constand-3-5m-in-2006-settlement/.
7. Tre'vell Anderson, "Hannibal Buress: The Comic Who Kindled the Cosby Firestorm," *Los Angeles Times*, December 31, 2015, http://beta.latimes.com/entertainment/tv/showtracker/la-et-st-hannibal-buress-cosby-joke-20151231-story.html.
8. Nicole Weisensee Egan, "Bill Cosby Accuser Andrea Constand Threatens to Withdraw from Criminal Investigation," People.com, October 27, 2015, https://people.com/crime/bill-cosby-accuser-andrea-constand-threatens-to-withdraw-from-investigation/.
9. Geoff Edgers, "Bill Cosby's 'Far from Finished' Tour Pushes On. But Will It Be His Last?," *Washington Post*, March 24, 2015, https://www.washingtonpost.com/entertainment/bill-cosbys-far-from-finished-tour-pushes-on-will-it-be-his-last/2015/03/24/d665bee4-cf1f-11e4-8a46-b1dc9be5a8ff_story.html?utm_term=.00b04ea08d2e.
10. Laura Benshoff, "Bill Cosby Sentenced to at Least 3 Years in State Prison for Sexual Assault," NPR, September 25, 2018, https://www.npr.org/2018/09/25/651065803/bill-cosby-sentenced-to-at-least-3-years-in-state-prison.
11. Margaret Renkl, "The Raw Power of #MeToo," Opinion, *New York Times*, October 19, 2017, https://www.nytimes.com/2017/10/19/opinion/the-raw-power-of-metoo.html.
12. Associated Press, "Shouting Matches Break Out at Cosby Hearing," *USA Today*, December 13, 2016, https://www.usatoday.com/story/life/people/2016/12/13/cosby-judge-to-weigh-potential-testimony-of-13-other-women/95366650/.
13. Associated Press, "Bill Cosby Trial: Only 2 Accusers Can Testify, Judge Rules," *Times-Picayune*, February 24, 2017, https://www.nola.com/crime/index.ssf/2017/02/bill_cosby_trial_accuser_testi.html.
14. Associated Press, "Cosby Lawyers Say Prosecutors Using 'Casting Couch' Cliché," VOA News, November 1, 2016, https://www.voanews.com/a/bill-cosby-sexual-assault-trial-lawyers-prosecutors-casting-couch-cliche/3574708.html.
15. Associated Press, "Bill Cosby Trial."
16. Associated Press, "Bill Cosby Trial."
17. Associated Press, "Bill Cosby's Defense Gives Closing Argument," DW.com, December 6, 2017, https://www.dw.com/en/bill-cosbys-defense-gives-closing-argument/a-39219996.
18. Prosecutors argued under the doctrine of chances that the more often Cosby allegedly engaged in aggressive sexual behavior with other women, the more likely he would have done the same with Constand. Importantly, it just had to be shown that these allegations of behavior with others *could* have been true, not that they happened beyond a reasonable doubt. Madison Pauly, "Why the 'Doctrine of Chances' Means Bill Cosby's Trial Will Be Different This Time," *Mother Jones*, April 5, 2018, https://www.motherjones.com/media/2018/04/why-the-doctrine-of-chances-means-bill-cos-

bys-trial-will-be-different-this-time/; Mark Dent, "Bill Cosby to Face Multiple Accusers in Upcoming Sexual Assault Trial," *Deadline*, March 15, 2018, https://deadline.com/2018/03/bill-cosby-andrea-constand-judge-multiple-accusers-to-testify-in-constand-trial-1202338879/.

19. Dent, "Bill Cosby to Face Multiple."

20. Kai Erickson, *Wayward Puritans: A Study in the Sociology of Deviance* (New Haven: Yale University Press, 2004); Donald Black, "Crime as Social Control," *American Sociological Review* 48, no. 1 (1983): 34–45; Harold Garfinkel, "Conditions of Successful Degradation Ceremonies," *American Journal of Sociology* 61, no. 5 (1956): 420–24.

21. See, for example, Engel, "Oven Bird's Song"; Susan Silbey, "After Legal Consciousness," 323–68.

22. Bill Cosby was charged under Pennsylvania's "Aggravated indecent assault" statute, which provides that it is a second-degree felony if a person penetrates another person's body "without the complainant's consent" or when "the complainant is unconscious or . . . unaware that the penetration is occurring." 18 Pa. Criminal Code §3125 (2010) (Aggravated Indecent Assault).

23. Lawrence M. Friedman, *The Big Trial: Law as Public Spectacle* (Lawrence: University Press of Kansas, 2015).

24. Cramer, *Pregnant with the Stars*, 14.

25. Harris, "Myths of Race and Gender," 227.

26. Yochai Benkler, Robert Faris, Hal Roberts, and Ethan Zuckerman, "Study: Breitbart-Led Right-Wing Media Ecosystem Altered Broader Media Agenda,"*Columbia Journalism Review*, March 3, 2017, https://www.cjr.org/analysis/breitbart-media-trump-harvard-study.php; Sunstein, "#Republic."

27. Susan Bordo, *The Destruction of Hillary Clinton* (Brooklyn, NY: Melville House, 2017).

28. Francine Banner and Nicholas Paron. "'Hell Hath No Fury . . .': Gendered Reactions to the Cosby Mistrial across Liberal and Conservative News Media Sites." In Debbie Ging and Eugenia Siapera (Eds.), *Gender Hate Online: Understanding the New Anti-Feminism*, chapter 8 (in press).

29. Melinda Henneberger, "Bill Cosby Mistrial Shows Sexual Assault Laws Must Change," Opinion, *USA Today*, June 17, 2017, https://www.usatoday.com/story/opinion/2017/06/17/bill-cosby-mistrial-sexual-assault-laws-must-change-melinda-henneberger-column/102824708/.

30. Ben Zimmer, "'Casting Couch': The Origins of a Pernicious Hollywood Cliché," *Atlantic*, October 16, 2017, https://www.theatlantic.com/entertainment/archive/2017/10/casting-couch-the-origins-of-a-pernicious-hollywood-cliche/543000/.

31. Steven Zeitchik, "Prosecutors Say Bill Cosby Engaged in a Pattern of Sexually Abusive Behavior," *Los Angeles Times*, December 13, 2016, http://www.latimes.com/nation/la-na-bill-cosby-accusers-20161213-story.html.

32. Susan Estrich, *Real Rape* (Cambridge: Harvard University Press, 1988).

33. Estrich, *Real Rape*.

34. Alletta Brenner, "Resisting Simple Dichotomies: Critiquing Narratives of Victims, Perpetrators, and Harm in Feminist Theories of Rape," *Harvard Journal of Law and Gender* 36 (2013): 505.

35. Lily News, "The Bill Cosby Trial Touches on Common Rape Myths," April 23, 2018, https://www.thelily.com/the-bill-cosby-trial-touches-on-common-rape-myths/.

36. Martha R. Burt, "Cultural Myths and Supports for Rape," *Journal of Personality and Social Psychology* 38, no. 2 (1980): 217–30.

37. The Bureau of Justice Statistics found that from 2005–2010, "78% of sexual violence involved an offender who was a family member, intimate partner, friend, or acquaintance." Michael G. Planty, Lynn Langton, Christopher Krebs, Marcus Berzofsky, and Hope Smiley-McDonald, *Female Victims of Sexual Violence 1994–2010*, Bureau of Justice Statistics (2013), https://www.bjs.gov/index.cfm?ty=pbdetail&iid=4594.

38. Tracy and Whitman, "Rape and Sexual Assault."

39. Tracy and Whitman, "Rape and Sexual Assault."

40. Tracy and Whitman, "Rape and Sexual Assault."

41. Jeannie Suk, "'The Look in His Eyes': The Story of Rusk and Rape Reform," chapter 5 in *Criminal Law Stories*, eds. Robert Weisberg and Donna Coker (New York: Foundation Press, 2012).

42. Lisa M. Cuklanz and Sujata Moorti, "Television's 'New' Feminism: Prime-Time Representations of Women and Victimization," *Critical Studies in Media Communication* 23, no. 4 (2006): 303.

43. Susan Silbey characterizes the work of scholars of legal consciousness as exploring this "gap." Silbey, "After Legal Consciousness," 324.

44. Levitt and Merry, "Vernacularization"; Edelman, *Working Law*.

45. Importantly, Edelman argues, these terms then reenter the legal system via litigation involving diversity and inclusion policies. Edelman, *Working Law*.

46. "[B]etween 1990 and 1992 the number of US newspaper reports that featured the phrase 'date rape' doubled, and remained at this level until the middle of the decade." Sarah E. H. Moore, "Tracing the Life of a Crime Category: The Shifting Meaning of 'Date Rape,'" *Feminist Media Studies* 11 (2011): 456.

47. Moore, "Tracing the Life," 459. Levine supports this assessment, describing that jurors' decision-making in acquaintance rape cases reflects cultural beliefs more strongly than adherence to legal statutes. Levine, "Sexual Scripts," 325.

48. Louise Ellison and Vanessa E. Munro, "A Stranger in the Bushes, or an Elephant in the Room? Critical Reflections upon Received Rape Myth Wisdom in the Context of a Mock Jury Study," *New Criminal Law Review: An International and Interdisciplinary Journal* 13, no. 4 (2010): 790.

49. Lauren Panariello, "Apps that Help Prevent Rape," *Cosmopolitan*, August 22, 2012, https://www.cosmopolitan.com/lifestyle/advice/g2170/apps-that-help-prevent-rape/; Natalie Matthews, "This New App Could've Prevented My Friend's Rape," *Elle*, April 17, 2014, https://www.elle.com/culture/tech/a10/kitestring-app-safety-apps-women/.

50. See, for example, WebMD, "Date Rape Drugs," https://www.webmd.com/mental-health/addiction/date-rape-drugs. The definition of "date rape" in Urban Dictionary also encompasses these contradictions, defining the term as "a fast growing phenomenon in Pubs and Nightclubs. The essential idea is that you spike a target's drink with a sedative drug, usually GHB or Rohypnol, and wait for them to become affected and semi-unconscious." Yet, the entry describes, "Due to the nature of the crime, in up to 80% of date rapes the victim knows the rapist well." The Dreamer's Club, "Date Rape," *Urban Dictionary*, February 18, 2005, https://www.urbandictionary.com/define.php?term=date%20rape; see also Karen G. Weiss and Corey J. Colyer, "Roofies, Mickies and Cautionary Tales: Examining the Persistence of the 'Date-Rape Drug' Crime Narrative," *Deviant Behavior* 31, no. 4 (2010): 348–79.

51. Andrea Fox, "5 Gadgets That Alert Drinkers to Date Rape Drugs," EfficientGov.com, May 22, 2017, https://efficientgov.com/blog/2017/05/22/5-date-rape-drug-detectors/.

52. Graham Bowley and Sophie Wodzak, "What Divided the Cosby Jurors? Words, for One Thing," *New York Times*, June 30, 2017, https://www.nytimes.com/2017/06/30/arts/television/bill-cosby-jurors-mistrial-wording-unconscious.html?_r=0.

53. A similar confusion arose during the August 2018 trial of Paul Manafort, when the jury requested additional clarification from the judge regarding the term "reasonable doubt." Richard Wolf, "Manafort Trial: Why 'Reasonable Doubt' is Hard to Define in Courtrooms," *USA Today*, August 17, 2018, https://www.usatoday.com/story/news/politics/2018/08/17/reasonable-doubt-standard-manafort-trial-difficult-define/1017821002/.

54. Bowley and Wodzak, "What Divided the Cosby Jurors?"

55. *Coker v. Georgia*, 433 U.S. 584 (1977).

56. Scott Cacciola, "Victims in Larry Nassar Abuse Case Find a Fierce Advocate: The Judge," *New York Times*, January 23, 2018, https://www.nytimes.com/2018/01/23/sports/larry-nassar-rosemarie-aquilina-judge.html.

57. Murray, "Inequality's Frontiers."
58. Murray, "Inequality's Frontiers."
59. Abrams, "The #MeToo Movement," 784 (describing that years after an offense, the "urgency to report" inherent in crisis language may serve to undermine legal reforms. Crisis language also may influence how victims are perceived since they are not expected to appear calm and collected in the face of what we understand as a "crisis").
60. Michael Cieply, "Samantha Geimer, Victim in Roman Polanski Sex Case, Strongly Defends Him Inside and Outside of Court," Deadline.com, June 9, 2017, http://deadline.com/2017/06/samantha-geimer-roman-polanski-victim-defends-director-hearing-1202109259/.
61. Cieply, "Samantha Geimer."
62. Aisha Harris, "She Founded #MeToo. Now She Wants to Move Past the Trauma," *The New York Times*, October 15, 2018, https://www.nytimes.com/2018/10/15/arts/tarana-burke-metoo-anniversary.html; Heather Jo Flores, "I Refuse to Post 'Me Too' as My Facebook Status. How About Men Post 'I Ignored It and I Won't Anymore' Instead?," *Independent*, October 17, 2017, https://www.independent.co.uk/voices/harvey-weinstein-facebook-me-too-sexual-assault-abuse-men-should-post-too-a8004631.html.
63. Diana Scully and Joseph Marolla, "'Riding the Bull at Gilley's': Convicted Rapists Describe the Rewards of Rape," *Social Problems* 32, no. 3 (1985): 253.
64. Black, "Crime as Social Control," 34.
65. Kate Harding, "Gray Matters: How Rape in Pop Culture Became a Matter of Opinion," *Bitch*, August 2, 2018, https://www.bitchmedia.org/article/rape-in-pop-culture-became-matter-of-opinion.
66. Memes circulated superimposing Bill Cosby's photograph on screenshots of Disney's "Sleeping Beauty" also have significant racial overtones, discussed further in chapter 4. Kilgorus Circus Maximus, "Bill Cosby: Sleeping Beauty," July 17, 2015, https://kilgoriuscircusmaximus.wordpress.com/tag/bill-cosby/.
67. This doctrine has widely been replaced with the doctrine of comparative negligence, which permits plaintiffs found to be partially at fault to still recover in part for their injuries. The-Injury-Lawyer-Directory.com, "Contributory Negligence vs. Comparative Negligence," https://the-injury-lawyer-directory.com/contributory-negligence-vs-comparative-negligence/.
68. Jennifer Wiggins, "Rape, Racism, and the Law," *Harvard Women's Law Journal* 6 (1983): 127; James J. Wesolowski, "Indicia of Consent? A Proposal for Change to the Common Law Rule Admitting Evidence of Rape Victim's Character for Chastity," *Loyola University Chicago Law Journal* 7 (1976): 118.
69. Wesolowski, "Indicia of Consent?," 123.
70. Wiggins, "Rape, Racism," 127.
71. Wiggins, "Rape, Racism," 121; Brenner, "Resisting Simple Dichotomies," 510.
72. Harris, "Race and Essentialism."
73. Kim Loewen, "Rejecting the Purity Myth: Reforming Rape Shield Laws in the Age of Social Media," *UCLA Women's Law Journal* 22, no. 2 (2015): 154.
74. Cynthia Lee, *Murder and the Reasonable Man: Passion and Fear in the Criminal Justice System* (New York: New York University Press, 2007).
75. After a 2018 mass shooting in Texas, for example, many media outlets carried stories bearing headlines announcing that one of the victims previously had spurned the killer's advances. Molly Hennessey-Fiske, Matt Pearce, and Jenny Jarvie, "Texas School Shooter Killed Girl Who Turned Down His Advances and Embarrassed Him in Class, Her Mother Says," *Los Angeles Times*, May 20, 2018, http://www.latimes.com/nation/la-na-texas-shooter-20180519-story.html#.
76. Sydney Janzen, "Amending Rape Shield Laws: Outdated Statutes Fail to Protect Victims on Social Media," *John Marshall Law Review* 48, no. 4 (2015): 1087–118.
77. Janzen, "Amending," 1090.
78. Deborah Tuerkheimer, "Incredible Women: Sexual Violence and the Credibility Discount," *University of Pennsylvania Law Review* 166 (2017): 9, 16.

79. Blake Neff, "CNN's New Rape Documentary Relies on Myths, Not Facts," *Daily Caller*, March 19, 2015, http://dailycaller.com/2015/03/19/cnns-new-rape-documentary-relies-on-myths-not-facts/.

80. Anonymous, "Stanford Sexual Assault Case Survivor Emily Doe Speaks Out," *Glamour*, November 1, 2016, https://www.glamour.com/story/women-of-the-year-emily-doe.

81. Harris, "Race and Essentialism."

82. Maria Pracher, "The Marital Rape Exemption: A Violation of a Woman's Right of Privacy," *Golden Gate University Law Review* 11, no. 3 (1981): 728.

83. Pracher, "The Marital Rape Exception," 728.

84. Brenner, "Resisting Simple Dichotomies," 510.

85. Martha Chamallas, *The Measure of Injury: Race, Gender, and Tort Law* (New York: New York University Press, 2010), 125 (describing how if a bad thing happens to us, we tend to blame situational factors; if it happens to someone else, we search for explanations based on character).

86. Renae Franiuk, Jennifer L. Seefelt, Sandy L. Cepress, and Joseph A. Vandello, "Prevalence and Effects of Rape Myths in Print Journalism," *Violence Against Women* 14, no. 3 (2008): 290.

87. Ellison and Munro, 791–92.

88. Ellison and Munro, 791–92.

89. Ellison and Munro, 791–92.

90. Nils Christie, "The Ideal Victim," in *From Crime Policy to Victim Policy*, ed. E. A. Fattah (London: Palgrave Macmillan, 1986), 17–30.

91. Harding, "Rape in Pop Culture."

92. Christie, "Conflicts," 4.

93. *Payne v. Tennessee*, 501 U.S. 808 (1991).

94. Jill Lepore, "The Rise of the Victims'-Rights Movement," *New Yorker*, May 21, 2018, https://www.newyorker.com/magazine/2018/05/21/the-rise-of-the-victims-rights-movement.

95. Lepore, "Rise of the Victims'-Rights Movement."

96. Lepore, "Rise of the Victims'-Rights Movement." Abrams similarly critiques that the "crisis framing" of sexual assault is classist in its assumption that victims "already occup[y] a degree of security in housing, healthcare, economics, and relationships," Abrams, "The #MeToo Movement," 784.

97. Julia Hutton, "Compensating for Mass Murder," *Atlantic*, April 2, 2015, https://www.theatlantic.com/business/archive/2015/04/compensating-for-mass-murder/389174/.

98. Kristin Bumiller, *The Civil Rights Society: The Social Construction of Victims* (Baltimore: Johns Hopkins University Press, 1992), 58.

99. Bumiller, *Civil Rights Society*, 58.

100. Erin Sheley, "Victim Impact Statements and Expressive Punishment in the Age of Social Media," *Wake Forest Law Review* 52 (2017): 157, suggesting that victim impact statements (VIS) are a more "authentic" expression of experiences of crime compared to the media representations to which the public are generally exposed.

101. Sheley, "Victim Impact Statements."

102. Ann Wolbert Burgess and Lynda Lytle Holmstrom, "Rape Trauma Syndrome," *American Journal of Psychiatry*, February 12, 2015, https://ajp.psychiatryonline.org/doi/abs/10.1176/ajp.131.9.981.

103. Eriq Gardner, "Janice Dickinson Scores Huge Appellate Wins in Bill Cosby Defamation Case," *Hollywood Reporter*, November 21, 2017, https://www.hollywoodreporter.com/thr-esq/janice-dickinson-scores-huge-appellate-wins-bill-cosby-defamation-case-1060782.

104. Debates as to whether tapes of celebrities engaged in consensual publicity of sexual activity or whether such tapes were an unlawful invasion of privacy have occurred in numerous contexts including Pamela Anderson, Kim Kardashian, Paris

Hilton, and, recently, Blac Chyna. Each of the aforementioned women argue that their images have been distributed against their will.

105. World Health Organization, "Addressing Violence against Sex Workers," 24, http://www.who.int/hiv/pub/sti/sex_worker_implementation/swit_chpt2.pdf.

106. Cacciola, "Victims in Larry Nassar Abuse Case."

107. Amy Held, "More Than 140 'Sister Survivors' of Larry Nassar Abuse Are Honored at ESPYS," National Public Radio, July 19, 2018, https://www.npr.org/2018/07/19/630440282/more-than-140-sister-survivors-of-larry-nassar-abuse-are-honored-at-espys.

108. Lindsey Adler, "Aly Raisman Is Ready to Burn It All Down," Deadspin.com, January 19, 2018, https://deadspin.com/aly-raisman-is-ready-to-burn-it-all-down-1822234455.

109. Laura Trabka, "Natalie Portman Gives Shout-Out to Ingham County Judge Aquilina on 'Saturday Night Live,'" *Lansing State Journal*, February 5, 2018, https://www.lansingstatejournal.com/story/entertainment/2018/02/05/natalie-portman-judge-aquilina/306358002/.

110. Julie Mack, "At Nassar Hearing, Victims Evolve Into Outspoken Sisterhood of Survivors," MLive, January 22, 2018, https://www.mlive.com/news/2018/01/day_4_of_nassar_hearing_jordyn.html.

111. Susan Miller, "Stanford Sex Assault Survivor Named a Woman of the Year," *USA Today*, November 2, 2016, https://www.usatoday.com/story/news/nation/2016/11/01/stanford-sex-assault-survivor-named-woman-year/93145144/.

112. Stephanie Zacharek, Eliana Dockterman, and Haley Sweetland Edwards, "The Silence Breakers," *Time*, December 2017, http://time.com/time-person-of-the-year-2017-silence-breakers/.

113. Christie, "Ideal Victim," 24.

114. Joan Ryan, *Little Girls in Pretty Boxes: The Making and Breaking of Elite Gymnasts and Figure Skaters* (New York: Grand Central, 1996).

115. Kyle Kim, Christina Littlefield, and Melissa Etehad, "Bill Cosby: A 50-Year Chronicle of Accusations and Accomplishments," *Los Angeles Times*, June 17, 2017, http://www.latimes.com/entertainment/la-et-bill-cosby-timeline-htmlstory.html.

116. The criminal trial relating to Huth's allegations against Cosby is set to take place in October 2019. Dominic Patten, "Imprisoned Bill Cosby Gets 2019 Trial Date for 1974 Playboy Mansion Assault Case," Deadline.com, November 13, 2018, https://deadline.com/2018/11/bill-cosby-playboy-mansion-assault-trial-date-los-angeles-judy-huth-1202501230/.

117. Huth's civil suit against Cosby is slated for trial in October 2019. Dominic Patton, "Imprisoned Bill Cosby Gets 2019 Trial Date for 1974 Playboy Mansion Assault Case," Deadline.com, November 13, 2018, https://deadline.com/2018/11/bill-cosby-playboy-mansion-assault-trial-date-los-angeles-judy-huth-1202501230/.

118. Jaclyn Hendricks, "The Side of McKayla Maroney You Haven't Seen Before," *New York Post*, May 15, 2017, https://nypost.com/2017/05/15/the-side-of-mckayla-maroney-you-havent-seen-before/.

119. Hendricks, "The Side of McKayla."

120. Monica Thompson, "Life after Rape: A Chance to Speak?, *Sexual and Relationship Therapy* 15, no. 4 (2000): 325–43.

121. Rose Mary Lynn Ubell, "Myths and Misogyny: The Legal Response to Sexual Assault" (Melanie Randall, Supervisor, Western University Master of Studies in Law Research Papers Repository 4, January 2018), vi.

122. As Felstiner et al. classically note, "[d]isputing is a complicated process involving ambiguous behavior, faulty recall, uncertain norms, conflicting objectives, inconsistent values, and complex institutions." William L. F. Felstiner, Richard L. Abel, and Austin Sarat, "The Emergence and Transformation of Disputes: Naming, Blaming, Claiming," *Law and Society Review* 15, no. 3/4 (1980–1981): 638.

123. Kimberly Thomas, "Interpersonal Power in the Criminal System," *American Criminal Law Review* 50 (2013): 270.

124. Thomas, "Interpersonal Power," 270.

125. Phoebe Morgan finds that civil plaintiffs similarly are motivated by intertwined desires, including not only the hope of profit but also the assertion of dignity and self-worth. Phoebe A. Morgan, "Risking Relationships: Understanding the Litigation Choices of Sexually Harassed Women," *Law and Society Review* 33 (1999): 67–68.

126. Kim M. E. Lens, Anthony Pemberton, Karen Brans, Johen Braeken, Stephen Bogaerts, and Esmah Lahlah, "Delivering A Victim Impact Statement: Emotionally Effective or Counter-Productive?," *European Journal of Criminology* 12 (2015), 20.

127. Koss et al., "The Scope of Rape"; Bonnie S. Fisher, Leah E. Daigle, and Francis T. Cullen, *Unsafe in the Ivory Tower: The Sexual Victimization of College Women* (Los Angeles: Sage, 2010), 2.

128. For example, Fisher et al. found that, among female college students who experienced but did not report incidents meeting the legal definition of rape, a significant portion characterized such incidents as a "miscommunication" or a "seduction," Fisher et al., *Unsafe in the Ivory Tower,* 134.

129. Deb Waterhouse-Watson, "(Un)Reasonable Doubt: A 'Narrative Immunity' for Footballers against Sexual Assault Allegations," *M/C Journal* 14, no. 11 (2011), http://www.journal .media-culture.org.au/index.php/mcjournal/article/viewArticle/337.

130. Michelle J. Anderson, "Campus Sexual Assault Adjudication and Resistance to Reform," *Yale Law Journal* 125 (2016): 1947. (Anderson cites Model Penal Code Section 213.6[4] reading "*Prompt Complaint*. No prosecution may be instituted or maintained under this Article [for sexual offenses] unless the alleged offense was brought to the notice of public authority within [3] months of its occurrence," Model Penal Code § 213.6[4] [Am. Law Inst. 1962].)

131. Beard, *Women and Power*.

132. Beard, *Women and Power*. Of note here is Susan Glaspell's play, *Trifles*, addressing the ways in which female victims (and perpetrators) may speak differently than men. See Susan Glaspell, Trifles, in *Literature: A World of Writing*, ed. David L. Pike and Ana M. Acosta (New York: Pearson Longman, 2011), 139–45.

133. Ubell, "Myths and Misogyny," 59–60.

134. Andrew E. Taslitz, *Rape and the Culture of the Courtroom* (New York: New York University Press, 1999), 20–21.

135. Associated Press, "Read Excerpts from Bill Cosby's 2005–2006 Quaalude Deposition," *Los Angeles Times*, May 23, 2016, http://www.latimes.com/local/lanow/la-me-ln-bill-cosby-quaalude-deposition-excerpts-20160523-snap-story.html.

136. Barkan, *Law and Society*.

TWO

Gold Diggers

Erica Kinsman v. Jameis Winston

In December 2012, Florida State University student Erica Kinsman met fellow student and football team quarterback Jameis Winston and two of his teammates at a popular bar near campus. After drinking with the trio, Kinsman accompanied the three to Winston's apartment. While there, Kinsman claims she was led to a bedroom by Winston, where he sexually assaulted her. Winston counters that the pair had consensual sex.[1] Kinsman reported the assault to the Tampa Police Department; however, no charges were filed. Law enforcement did not interview Winston nor potential witnesses.[2] The alleged incident became public in 2013 when Kinsman spoke to the press on the night before Winston was slated to receive the Heisman Trophy.[3]

Kinsman's allegations spawned a complex maze of legal proceedings. In 2014, Florida State University held a disciplinary hearing during which Winston was cleared of all charges. The next year, Kinsman filed a civil suit against the quarterback and the university, alleging that FSU violated Title IX by "deliberate[ly] conceal[ing] . . . student-on-student sexual harassment to protect the football program."[4] Winston quickly countersued for defamation of character.[5] In 2016, FSU settled the suit with Kinsman, the terms of the settlement including a cash payment and a commitment by the university to five years of sexual assault awareness programs.[6] Later in 2016, Kinsman settled with Winston pursuant to undisclosed terms.[7] While the lawsuits were pending, Kinsman appeared in a documentary, *The Hunting Ground*, which profiles the winding road of her accusations against Winston and the university.

Chapter 1 began exploring the ways in which sexual assault victims are being discursively constructed on social media. In particular, the chapter interrogated how the myths of "real rape" and the "ideal victim" inform the public's verdicts as to who is and is not entitled to justice. This chapter continues to investigate how myths about sexual assault impact access to justice by more closely examining just one of the multitude of transgressions that serve to de-authorize victims in the eyes of social media commenters: the filing of a civil suit.

I AIN'T SAYIN' SHE A . . .

In 2015, a popular gossip site broke the story that a new lawsuit seeking damages for injuries resulting from sexual assault had been filed against Jameis Winston, the promising quarterback leading the FSU Seminoles to a record-breaking winning season.[8] In characterizing the suit as "new," reporters engaged in a legal sleight of hand, suggesting that there had been previous civil litigation against the athlete when, in fact, what had transpired was a bungled criminal investigation and a Title IX proceeding at the university. Rather than waste time on legal nuances, the TMZ article instead announced that Kinsman's lawsuit was being filed against the promising athlete "even though he's already been cleared twice."[9]

Some comments—many with racist overtones—suggested that Winston was guilty. Others critiqued what seemed to be a shoddy investigation conducted by Florida law enforcement. The vast majority, however, focused their attention on Winston's accuser, Erica Kinsman. Responses to news of the lawsuit include: "[T]his girl knows how to follow the money"; "[T]his groupie is not going win"; "She just wants a big pay day. Maybe even a made for TV movie"; and "It's all about the money." As one commenter notes, "Rape is rape but her actions that night were all gimme gimme gimme."

When a major news outlet featured an article announcing the settlement of Kinsman's and Winston's suit and countersuit, some quoted Kanye West's lyrics, "Now I ain't saying she a gold digger." Just a few of the hundreds of tweets about Kinsman accompanied by #golddigger, include,

- This girl who's suing Winston . . . just wants to cash in;
- So, it's confirmed that Jameis Winston's accuser is a gold digger, right?
- Golddiggin' like crazy! And
- Gimme a break #liar #golddigger #witchhunt.

On a sports-related news site, a commenter similarly notes, "Look a money grab is what this is. Good for her. She made millions for one nights worth performance."

These social media comments about Erica Kinsman closely resemble those about Cosby's accusers, holding Kinsman accountable for what commenters identify as contributory negligence in causing her assault. Kinsman is condemned for meeting Winston in a bar, for drinking heavily with fellow (male) students, and for accompanying the men to Winston's apartment. The undergraduate is criticized, too, for having self-identified prior to the alleged assault as a "cleat chaser," someone who closely followed the careers of, and attempted to date, celebrity athletes on campus.[10]

In the eyes of many commenters, Kinsman's accusations are even more suspicious due to their timing. News of her lawsuit was revealed during what was a historic winning season for the Seminoles and a celebratory time for Winston himself. Tweets proclaim, "[T]he girl waited till Jameis Winston was the hottest name in college football to try and pull a rape case" and "How convenient 2 weeks before #NFLDraft #GoldDigger Jameis Winston sued by accuser." They note that the accuser's "timing is impeccable"—"Funny how this [story] keeps showing up during football season." Kinsman herself is described as a "scandalous money-seeking whore" who waited to have her press conference on the "day before Heisman."

As discussed in the previous chapter, inherent in sexual assault trials is an "inverted" process of blame-shifting, the guilt of the perpetrator assessed by scrutinizing the behavior of the victim.[11] Historically, this inverted process has focused on an accuser's chastity, on what she wore, whether she fought back, and how she behaved leading up to an alleged rape. Similar to comments about the Cosby accusers, remarks about Erica Kinsman tend toward dispositional explanations for crime, the idea that, simply by putting herself in a dangerous situation—by "cleat chasing"—Kinsman "implied consent" to whatever actions followed.

While we may be likely to recognize overt victim blaming in, for example, critiques of what an alleged victim was wearing, it is more challenging to recognize rape myths when they appear in the form of "commonsense" metaphors like the casting couch. This chapter takes on another latent rape myth disguised as common sense—that a survivor's credibility is impacted by the filing of a civil suit.

CONTROLLING IMAGES

The pejorative terms used across the internet to describe sexual assault complainants are endless—"bitches," "sluts," "hoes," "prostitutes," "groupies"—but there is perhaps none more recognizable than that of the "gold digger," a character that appears in numerous memes, comments, and even in court documents..

Like the casting couch discussed in chapter 1, gold digger is not a novel term. In its very first issue in 1953, *Playboy* magazine featured an article that warned its male audience ominously, "The modern gold digger is . . . after you[!]"[12] The article, about women's access to court-awarded child support, mourned the carefree days when "wives were faithful and alimony was reserved for the little floozies who periodically married and divorced millionaire playboys," noting that now "alimony has gone democratic and any man can get hit."[13] "Even if your wife is a 'trollop' or a 'spendthrift,'" the article continued, "the judge grants 'the little missus' a healthy stipend for future escapades and extravagancies."

While the label itself did not yet exist, the foundation for the idea of the gold digger was being laid two hundred years earlier, enshrined in the personal writings of Lord Matthew Hale, a judge whose dubious caution about victims' lack of truthfulness—known as the Hale instruction—became a routine jury instruction in U.S. rape trials for centuries. Married twice, Lord Hale was tormented by his first wife, with whom he had ten children.[14] After remarrying the judge advised his children that "an idle or expensive wife is most times an ill bargain, though she bring a great portion."[15] In Lord Leigh's case, Hale opined that a husband could confine a wife to the home if she threatened to spend too much because,

> [women] make it their business to paint or patch their faces, to curl their locks, and to ferret out the newest and costliest fashions. . . . [T]hey must have choice diet provided for them. . . . [They] sit in a rubbe [cleaned] parlour till Dinner. . . . After they go either to a Ball or to cards. . . . They spend their parent's or husband's money or estate on costly clothes, new fashions, and changeable entertainments. . . . Their house is their prison and they are never at rest [in] it, unless they have gallants and splendid company to enter.[16]

Centuries later Kanye West's chart-topping single echoes many of these same sentiments, riffing on "commonsense" categorizations of women as lazy, irresponsible consumers. *Playboy Magazine* has folded and the Hale instruction been abolished, but the "gold digger" persists as a powerful controlling image, suggesting a particular category of woman who is willing to lie, manipulate, and deceive to achieve financial gain. When commenters label a rape accuser a gold digger, they are applying a long-accepted script[17] that identifies a claimant as one of a category; on Twitter, "[B]itches just hoes that do anything for money."

Social media characterizations of Erica Kinsman as a "gold digger" engage what Patricia Hill Collins calls "controlling images," characterizations that historically have been deployed to constrain and delimit women's agency. Collins discusses how such images, in particular, have been used to control women of color, tropes like "bitch," "mammy," "jezebel" defining appropriate boundaries of behavior and punishing any women who step out of them.[18] Use of these terms turns real people into stock characters, invoking a stereotype that "make[s] racism, sexism, poverty, and other forms of social injustice appear to be natural, normal, and inevitable parts of everyday life."[19]

Ann Cammett traces how, in the context of the contemporary criminal justice system, narrative representations of the "welfare queen" and the "deadbeat dad" are not merely insults but operate to promote specific, political objectives. She describes that

> the social construction of poor Black single mothers deemed them the agents of their own misfortune due to their unmarried status—assumed to indicate loose morals, hypersexuality, and presumed laziness—framed as reliance on public assistance rather than work.[20]

Similarly, #golddigger draws on a stereotype that describes women's behavior as immoral and hypersexual.

Sandlin et al. argue that what may appear to be commonsense characterizations of women as flighty or irresponsible consumers in fact are connected to women's status as primary domestic caregivers.[21] We tend to "construct consumption as feminine," impulsive, and "excessive" in contrast to men's spending, which is more likely to be described as measured and rational.[22] Persistent memes categorizing "shopping" as a woman's favorite hobby, for example, highlight a tendency for men to be constructed as necessarily policing women's irresponsibility with money.

In reality, however, women shop not just for enjoyment but because they are the persons in charge of "home economics."[23] Kanye West's exemplary gold digger, for example, does not just carry a fancy handbag, she persuades the narrator to feed her kids.[24]

Joanna Bourke describes how, historically, accusations that women are exploiting their sexuality often are tied to larger political issues, such as immigration. In 1830s England, for example, there was a rampant—and false—rumor that Irish women were making rape accusations to blackmail eligible young men into marriage, their efforts often promoted by scheming mothers.[25] Bourke cites a 1913 medical article noting that young girls making rape accusations "lie as easily as morphine fiends."[26]

When situated in historical context, the term "gold digger" is not merely a dismissive insult but a politicized framing that dismisses women's labor as less valuable than men's, devalues women's roles in organizing their households, and casts doubt on women's veracity. In other words, for online commenters seeking to establish social connections and assert their own, superior status, gold digger accomplishes a trifecta.

The image of the gold digger is not only gendered, it conveys ideas about socioeconomic status, race, and class. A related term that more recently has entered the vernacular is "THOT," an acronym used across social media to signify "that ho out/over there" or "thirsty hoes out/over there."[27] Numerous tweets describe Erica Kinsman: "This thot who fucked Jameis Winston . . . wants some money"; "Jameis Winston didn't do anything wrong to the Thot. She is mad because he didn't wife her up!"; and "Jameis Winston almost got swindled by a thot."

As Collins identifies, controlling images are stereotypes based not only in gender but in social class and ethnicity, the trope of the jezebel, for example, tying into myths about Black women's sexual appetites that were created to justify sexual access to African American women's bodies by white men.[28] Today, the term "thirsty" refers to a particular sort of person, a "striver" who is attempting to become famous or to improve her socioeconomic circumstances in any way possible. In the THOT imaginary, which is remarkably fleshed out across social media sites such as Pinterest and Reddit, memes abound reinforcing this theme. The favorite foods of the "typical" THOT, for example, include affordable and easy to prepare options—Hot Pockets, Pizza Rolls, and Cheetos.[29] Like gold diggers, THOTs are not elites but outsiders attempting to relocate resources and improve their social status, if not by unlawful than at least by immoral means. Like #golddigger, #THOT is reductive, displacing the subject from her individualized characteristics and discussing her not as an individual but as a member of a disfavored group or category.

Derogatory terms about female sexuality do not usually describe actual sexual behaviors. Rather, they are engaged to effect control over women as a category, to enforce segregation, and to "draw moral boundaries" between social classes.[30] For example, Elizabeth Armstrong's research shows that wealthy, female students are more likely to label less economically well-off counterparts as "trashy" or "slutty" than the reverse, even though data show that it is wealthier women who are more likely to engage in nonmonogamous behaviors. In labeling some women "sluts," students are able to define their own (superior) moral boundaries and higher socioeconomic status. These terms are often as likely to be engaged by women as men, reflecting that they are less likely to be deployed as descriptors of actual behavior than mechanisms of social control.[31]

In the world of online comments, where being concise is not only privileged but often necessary, engaging a label like "gold digger" or "THOT" accomplishes a twofold objective: it distinguishes the (higher-status) commenter from the (lower-status) accuser, and it transforms the accuser from a full-fledged person into an interchangeable member of a dubious category. As terms like victim blaming and rape culture have been vernacularized, rape myths are shifting from engaging overt to more subtle forms of sexism. A comment that women like to shop seems harmless, but in fact relays gendered assumptions that both delimit women's behavior and cast aspersions on their character.[32] As we know from centuries of rape trials, once the accuser's character is cast into doubt, the perpetrator is more likely to be vindicated.

SUGAR DADDIES AND SUGAR BABIES

#Golddigger appears pervasively in tweets about Janay Palmer Rice, who in 2016 was videotaped by a hotel security camera being brutally beaten by her then fiancé, NFL player Ray Rice.[33] Having decided to marry rather than prosecute her attacker, Palmer has the dubious honor of being labeled the most egregious of the gold diggers. Numerous tweets decry, "Only a gold digger would marry their abuser"; "Janay Rice is a fucking gold digger who's on the come up"; "She married her meal ticket. Gold digger." One comment labels her "the golddigger of the millennium." A tweet jokes, "Ray and Janay Rice are the ideal 'relationship goals' couple. he KO's her, Ravens give him a settlement of $3.5 mill, he buys her a purse."[34]

The perception that a woman would tolerate or even engineer a vicious beating in order to obtain an expensive handbag reinforces one of the most recognizable traits of the gold digger stereotype—like the "naïve," "trendy" starlets collectively imagined in the context of the Cosby accusations, the gold digger is incompetent, petty, and values material possessions above society's well-being. In the 1700s, Lord Hale exhorted that women "must have choice diet *provided for* them. . . . They spend their parent's or husband's money or estate on costly clothes, new fashions, and changeable entertainments." In the 2000s, Kanye West similarly remarked, "She was supposed to buy your shorty Tyco with your money / She went to the doctor, got lipo with your money."[35] Underlying these characterizations is the idea that women are both uniquely suited to use their bodies to achieve socioeconomic resources and, at the same time, uniquely unsuited to managing those resources.

> The gold digger trades sex for a harder currency. . . . Gold Diggers are not traditionally viewed as being successful in educational, employment, or other economic spheres. Instead, the . . . plan is to "toss them titties around, shake that ass, make that money." . . . Sex may be used to barter for basic needs such as a bag of groceries, getting rent paid, or making sure their lights do not get turned off. However, manicures and pedicures, new clothing, vacations, or having a car note paid are also possible wants.[36]

A tweet proclaims, "[T]his female victim of Jameis Weston is out for some NFL cheese because she can't make money on her own." Others accuse the student of "cash[ing] in" on a "money grab." Embedded in these comments is the idea that leveraging claims of sexual assault is a way for women to overcome "status inequality" and economic insecurity.

The gold digger is an exceptionally powerful trope because, historically, women's frivolity and economic irresponsibility has not been attributed to social factors or even individual personality traits but identified as an inherent biological shortcoming, a lack of capacity for logical reasoning belonging to women as a group. The law traditionally has accepted long-standing assumptions about women as "ultra-connected" to nature or being somehow extra-biological.[37] In his famous brief in *Muller v. Oregon*, a case upholding maximum hour requirements for women workers, for example, Louis Brandeis appealed to (white, elite, male) judges' commonsense that white women's biology and status as "mothers of the race" precluded them from working as many hours as men.[38]

Decisions like *Muller v. Oregon* or *Bradwell v. Illinois*, which relied on similar arguments to uphold the exclusion of women from the practice of law, draw connections between women's biology and their capacity to engage in public life. Legal and social history are replete with similar judicial and legislative pronouncements premised on the Cartesian paradigm that men are logical and deliberate actors while women are superbiological: impetuous, emotional, naturally vengeful. When online commenters use #golddigger, they are exploiting long-standing, biologically based assumptions about sexed and gendered bodies.

The gold digger label is particularly intriguing, however, because it draws on dual—and contradictory—characterizations. On one hand, the image suggests that women are lazy, greedy consumers looking to be taken care of by a "sugar daddy" who will fulfill their consumption-driven desires. On the other hand, however, the gold digger taps into societal apprehensions about manipulative, aggressive women plotting and planning to take down weaker male counterparts, suggesting not only that groups of women are out to manipulate the law but that—as the *Playboy* article suggested back in 1953—the law is subject to manipulation.

Rather than viewing women as a group as passive and illogical, in other incarnations the term suggests anything but incompetence. Amy D. Ronner describes, for example, a gold digger who, in a "perverted entrepreneurial spirit[,] . . . aims to extort the defendant into settlement . . . [M]oney lust . . . propel[s] her to try to dupe a trier of fact into infusing her bank account with ready cash."[39] She is "not . . . a victim, but instead is . . . the villainous perpetrator of a fraud."[40] This conception of the gold digger as a manipulative agent of extortion also infuses online comments about sexual assault complainants.

EXPERT MANIPULATORS

For many online commenters, taking civil, legal action against Jameis Winston transformed Erica Kinsman from a potentially deserving victim into a decisive legal strategist. A tweet provides a handbook as to how accusations against Jameis Winston will proceed, the drama unfolding like a sordid, legal novella:

1. Sloot got fucked

2. She loved it
3. Jameis becomes famous
4. Bitch realizes he's a star and wants money
5. Bitch claims rape
6. Winston wins.

More than twenty years ago, during Mike Tyson's sexual assault trial, witnesses testified that the alleged victim, prior to the assault, had "talked about Tyson's money."[41] In their opening arguments, the defense pointed out that she could become very rich via a civil suit.[42] During his 2005 trial, Michael Jackson's attorney, similarly, portrayed Jackson's accuser and his mother as motivated by money and criticized key witnesses for selling their stories to tabloids versus reporting to the police.[43]

These same comments resonate throughout today's celebrity suits. Former Pittsburgh Steelers player Ben Roethlisberger's lawyer characterized the plaintiff suing him for sexual assault as "disturbed and calculating."[44] A central issue in Cosby's trials was determining who was the "bigger con artist," Cosby or Constand.[45] When Erica Kinsman filed her lawsuit, Winston's attorney responded that "this *stunt* was expected."[46] The first page of Winston's counterclaim for defamation describes Kinsman as engaging the law in a game in which she is "0 for 6" in her claims against the player.

> However, [the alleged victim] has been successful in one major area. She has mounted a false and vicious media campaign to vilify Mr. Winston with the objective of getting him to pay her to go away. [The alleged victim] is motivated by the most insidious [of] objectives—greed.[47]

On an NFL fan site, a poster notes, that "[t]his is not an open rape case. It's a civil suit cash grab timed perfectly to get the most media exposure. If Winston was an actor, and not an athlete, this suit would have been filed a week before the Oscars."

Many of the Cosby accusers also have filed civil suits, inspiring similar reactions from the online public. On a daily news site, one person observes of the spate of civil suits filed against Cosby that "the real business side of this is starting now, the lawsuit for damages. It's all about the money guys and gals. [W]elcome to the real world."[48] Responding to news of the comedian's mistrial, a post on a major news site characterizes that

> [t]he rapidly growing False Rape Accusation Industry suffered a setback today. After a billion dollar campaign to destroy one of the greatest civil rights workers and educators in American History and "America's Dad," they failed to convict.

As described in the previous chapter, a powerful undercurrent on social media identifies "crying rape" as a path to achieve not only wealth but status as a public figure. Tweets express the widespread belief that one's status as a rape survivor readily may be parlayed into a career in broadcasting or reality television. Erica Kinsman is compared to "the new Monica Lewinsky, [since] she got famous off of sexual activity." Other comments about the student suggest an impending "book deal"—"HAHA stupid ass chick trying to get famous."

While some who invoke the term "gold digger" offer stereotypical views of women as "stupid," lacking logic, capability, or personal agency, comments suggesting that Kinsman or other accusers are claiming to have engineered a sexual assault in order to "get famous" evoke a different concern—that of the devious "bitch" who is strategizing to "pull a case" on an unsuspecting wealthy man. This idea that accusers are engaging in "lawfare," deliberately engaging law in order to blackmail or entrap innocent men, stands in contrast to assumptions that women, as a group, lack agency or that they tend to engage in "expressive" behaviors—a sudden letting go of pent-up anger—versus "instrumental" ones, such as plotting or planning.[49]

Myriad online comments reflect a pervasive belief that greedy, vengeful, or regretful women are trying to engage the law to transform a consensual or perhaps "gray area" sexual encounter into a lucrative accusation of sexual assault. As a tweet notes of the Cosby case, the "women are not Cosby's victims. They're the women who sold sex to Cosby. Sell your body for sex, lie to make money, eaassyyyyy."

After being inundated with stories of accusations against Cosby and, before him, Mike Tyson, Kobe Bryant, Ben Roethlisberger, and a host of other celebrities, for some the suit against Jameis Winston seems to take on a tired predictability: "[P]robably just another gold digger trying to get money out of a sports star" or "another slut whore tryna get rich quick." As one person remarks, "of course a bird is gonna try and get money off him." After all, we "[r]eally have to be careful of these types of girls."

On the surface, the observation that an alleged victim has filed a civil suit may seem innocuous, one of several dry facts in a boring procedural history. But in fact these discussions are a roundabout way to malign accusers' character, another means to suggest that an accuser does not fit into the ideal victim stereotype. A commenter on a widely read news site notes, "I am always suspicious of civil complaints for money damages where there is no criminal charge," while another suggests that "[i]f they really wanted to pursue prosecution, then turn down the cash." A reader of a daily paper in a major city gets to the heart of the matter, "What bothers me most about the Cosby rape story is that the victims pursued civil money more than criminal justice." A conservative news reader opines more bluntly, "Any whore will cry rape for a shot at the ghetto lottery."

These characterizations of complainants as "gold diggers" who weaponize their bodies by making false accusations against unwitting male celebrities effect a narrative role reversal in which the accuser becomes the perpetrator and the alleged perpetrator is transformed into the unwitting victim.

A REVERSAL OF FORTUNE

Reflecting on allegations against Winston, a reader of sports news advises, "Forget her. Just a cleat chaser. She's a liar. He is the victim of slander." Tweets exclaim that "Jameis Winston is the victim of attempted EXTORTION" and offer that Kinsman is just "asking for money to shut up. #BLACKMAIL." A response to the story breaking about the Winston accusations on a gossip site inquires, "Who is the victim now?" In reply to a report that Winston might be suing Kinsman for defamation of character, a tweet notes, heartily, "Good to see a victim taking action!" The victim, of course, is not Kinsman but Winston.

Comments like these are replicated across celebrity sexual assault cases. When allegations were waged against hockey player Patrick Kane, fans chimed in, "I feel bad for [him]. . . . Signs huge deal then some gold digger makes shit up." A popular meme emphasizes the player's innocence by superimposing Kane's face on a painting of Jesus Christ. One person tweets of Kane's accuser, "*She* raped him."[50]

After video was released of Ray Rice's attack on his fiancée, some noted that Rice was "the true victim, if it was bad enough she woulda left." A commenter on the Cosby accusations similarly opines, "No longer should a man have to endure this sort of abusive treatment at the hands of vindictive, gold-digging women! So many lives ruined by women's pursuit of 15 minutes of fame and a pile of cash!"

A commenter about the Cosby cases on a conservative site notes that "[w]aiting for 50 years to then be allowed to claim 'Rape' is *insanely predatorial*." Other readers of conservative media refer to allegations against the comedian as a "witch hunt" and "moral panic" akin to the "Salem witch trials." A major news commenter graphically describes how, "[t]his . . . gold-digger . . . *weaponized* her womanhood and cried rape. [It's] a very old hustle." A tweet asks, "Crazy thought. What if Jameis Winston is innocent of rape? . . . Who is the victim now?"

In the view of these commenters, the legal arena is a Hobbesian one in which law can be deployed to blackmail and extort unsuspecting civilians. The irony, of course, is that in these narrative imaginings, it is those people with the least access to resources—in Marc Galanter's view, the legal "have nots"—who are constructed as having law in their corner.[51] As Engel describes, it is those people most likely to need the law to resolve disputes who are also most likely to be dismissed as undeserving "outsiders."[52] In a tightly knit community, neighbors who know one another tend to prefer resolving issues via negotiation and compromise. Resorting to a lawsuit over a dispute is considered unneighborly. It is outsiders who are most likely to need the law to resolve concerns. It is also, however, "socially marginalized or disempowered persons" who, due to factors such as fear of the legal system or lack of access to resources, are most who are likely to "lump it," to avoid making legal claims even when they understand they have experienced something unjust.[53]

Despite what the data show, a barrage of false narratives about tort cases has trained the public to be suspicious of devious attorneys and legal "windfalls." More than thirty years later, for example, people may recall the case of Stella Liebeck, the plaintiff who was awarded $2.7 million by a jury after spilling hot coffee purchased at a McDonald's drive-through. Promoted by conservative tort "reformers" as an example of a frivolous lawsuit, or "jackpot justice," few members of the public are aware that Liebeck sued only after being denied compensation for basic medical costs, that $1.5 million was for punitive damages amounting to about two days of coffee sales for the retailer, or that her third-degree burns were so serious they required skin grafts.[54]

In their description of the varied relationships everyday people have to law and legal institutions, Ewick and Silbey characterize some persons as "with the law"—able to engage the power of the institution to their benefit and, sometimes, even delight in doing so, and others as "before the law"—fearful and in awe of legal processes and therefore unlikely to engage the institution unless absolutely necessary.[55] Ewick's and Silbey's research reinforces that those who are "with the law" are most often the "repeat players"—corporations or persons with the most access to resources. In tweets and online comments, however, it is often the wealthiest party who is recast as the victim and the person with least access to resources as the legal abuser.

Thanks to the propagandist campaigns of tort reform and the vagaries of human nature, we have a collective tendency to scrutinize the behavior and status of civil plaintiffs—*Why did the elderly woman open hot coffee in the car? Why were the parents not looking out for the child who was attacked?* The "inverted" nature of sexual assault trials only compounds this tendency. We pour over every action by the accuser, looking for "evidence" of dispositional tendencies or a less-than-wholesome character. Our conclusions about the character of the alleged victim are informed by biological "knowledge" about women as a class or group. We ignore that, in the civil system, it is those "with the law" who are most likely to win. In the criminal context, it is exceedingly unlikely for professional athletes to be charged with sexual assault, and even less likely for them to be convicted.[56]

The volume of tweets referencing "bitches" who "cry rape" for personal gain suggests a widespread perception that not only are accusers prone to lie but that the legal system itself is up for grabs.

When we situate accusers as interchangeable members of a category—gold diggers, THOTs—these characterizations obscure the complexities—and the costs—inherent in becoming a legal claimant. The U.S. legal system is Byzantine in its requirements but by some miracle, like the "welfare queen" of the 1980s, the gold digger is exceptionally capable not just at navigating a complex legal system but at rigging it in her favor. As discussed in chapter 1, victims like Annie Clark and Emily Doe attest to the multiple, and often unanticipated, hurdles accusers face in reporting crimes and, then, in becoming legally sanctioned victims. Notably Clark, featured in *The Hunting Ground*, refers to the winding road of bringing sexual assault charges as a "game," but not one she is likely to win.

The tort reform movement has contributed to the view that personal injury attorneys are ambulance chasers, "sharks," or worse.[57] On top of a general distaste for attorneys, critiques of alleged victims also often focus on female or "feminist" lawyers like Gloria Allred, suggesting not only fears about resource redistribution but of a gendered redistribution. On a major conservative news site, Allred is described as a ringleader, leading "[s]acrificial lambs to the feminazi alter." A commenter on a more mainstream news site wonders whether Allred is advocating "Feminist justice" or "just a power grab."

Chimamanda Adichie identifies within Nigerian society the idea of "bottom power," the assumption that young women with few resources can mobilize their sexuality to coerce material wealth and social status from wealthy men.[58] Bottom power, Adichie argues, raises a concern that young women are engaged in a campaign of wealth redistribution, threatening the middle class, patriarchal status quo. She explains, however, that "bottom power is actually not powerful; [the woman] just has a good route to tap [into] another person's power."[59] In the end, there is no reallocation of resources. As D'Angelo Barksdale might say, "the king stay the king."

In U.S. society, operating similarly to "bottom power" is the concept of the gold digger, a shorthand means of implying that women have a unique route or access to legal resources based on biology—the assumption that women can use their bodies to manipulate men—and complicity—the idea that biological females as a category are working together toward domination. But, calling a claimant a "gold digger," a "slut," or a "ho" is lashing out against a presumption of women's cultural power, not identifying the group that truly holds the legal cards.

As Kate Manne observes, comments that characterize powerful men accused of sexual assault as "victims" or "targets" do not merely exhibit a lack of empathy for survivors but, importantly, they exhibit a profound lack of understanding of the social, economic, and legal protections available to some alleged perpetrators, particularly celebrity perpetrators. When President Trump describes Justice Brett Kavanaugh, allegations against whom are discussed in the next chapter, as a "great gentleman" for whom he "feel[s] so badly," the president is not just exhibiting a lack of empathy toward the alleged victim but an outpouring of moral solidarity in favor of the accused.[60] Manne characterizes this fellow feeling as "himpathy"—the inappropriate and disproportionate sympathy powerful men often enjoy in cases of sexual assault, intimate partner violence, homicide, and other misogynistic behavior."[61] She writes,

> What makes himpathy so difficult to counter is that the mechanisms underlying it are partly moral in nature: Sympathy and empathy are pro-social moral emotions, which makes it especially hard to convince people that when they skew toward the powerful and against the vulnerable, they become a source of systemic injustice.[62]

A key advancement of the #MeToo movement has been the revelation of just how many allegations of sexual assault and harassment have been suppressed by out-of-court settlements, confidentiality clauses, and nondisclosure agreements, the negotiation of which are overshadowed by a significant imbalance in power.[63] It is not the accusers but the celebrity accused who dictate the terms of these agreements.[64] Even up-and-coming star athletes like Jameis Winston tend to be supported, sheltered, and protected by the institutions that benefit from their skill and status.[65] While, as discussed in chapter 4, factors such as race importantly do shift the power in this calculus, wealth and status most often dictate which party, in this situation, is "with the law," especially in cases where the accused is supported by the resources of a self-protective institution.

The widespread acceptance across the internet of the perpetrator-as-victim narrative suggests that it is the dominant groups within society that continue to shape our cultural images, and that, as Silbey identifies, it is elites that continue to shape law in society.[66] In the twitterverse, it is the alleged victim—the person with comparatively the fewest economic resources—who most often is perceived as holding all the cards. It is easy for commenters to situate sexual assault claimants as having the upper hand; "greedy" women have have existed for centuries.[67]

The idea that there are groups of young women waiting and able to engage the legal system to effect a redistribution of wealth and power impacts not only impressions of women but perceptions of law. In light of recent failures of law as an institution to afford justice, this perception is significant.

THE "GHETTO LOTTERY"

The oft-repeated narrative goes something like this:

> Making these claims . . . certainly gets [the accuser's] name in the news, and the sympathy of thousands. Plus Gloria Allred the famous lawyer calling them to represent. And maybe a book and movie deal if all goes well. And the big prize . . . a potential settlement prize.

A comment on the Cosby accusations on a conservative news site bemoans that "washed up women" are now branding "dating behavior" as "rape" and "misogyny," while another ponders, "Wonder when the rockstar groupie lawsuits will start?" Other comments refer to "a class action gold digger lawsuit" and label criminal allegations as a "retirement plan." A mainstream news reader opines, "There's no way I believe any of these gold-digging ambulance chasing pinheads."

Like the *Playboy* article warning readers about gold diggers in 1953, for many online commenters today, gender is by far the biggest predictor of success in legal claims-making.[68] Online comments display little sympathy for "groupies" who "cry rape from a star" because "[a]ll it takes is one thirsty bitch to cry rape before a perfectly innocent man gets 'rapist' attached to their name. #Kobe #BigBen #Winston." As another tweet puts it, "Every bitch wanna cry rape when it involves a sports star." After all, an age-old avenue for achieving financial or social success is when "woman have sex with a guy and then say its rape when he becomes famous trick. Not this time bitch #FamousJameis #Heisman."

In recent years, civil lawsuits seeking damages for injuries resulting from sexual assaults have more than doubled.[69] The vast majority of these are not only against individuals but, as in Kinsman's case, are also against institutions with so-called deep pockets.[70] In the past twenty years, opportunities to engage the civil legal system in connection with what previously would have been solely criminal cases have radically expanded, due to increased availability of Title VII and Title IX, and the passage of the Violence Against Women Act.[71] The United States Department of Justice itself advocates that victims of sexual assault, where possible, file civil suits.[72] Such suits are an attractive option for those who have experienced injury, not only because individual plaintiffs may recover compensatory and punitive damages but because lower standards of proof and non-unanimous jury requirements make it easier to hold defendants accountable.

For a person who perceives that he or she has suffered a harm, the motive in filing a criminal complaint versus a civil suit may be the same—achieving justice by whatever means necessary.[73] Lininger describes, however, that in the courtroom, evidence that an alleged victim has filed a civil suit is interpreted as indicative of negative traits in the victim's character.[74] He writes that "[e]vidence of parallel civil litigation inflames jurors' instinctive prejudice in much the same way that evidence of prior sexual history inflames prejudice against accusers."[75]

The question of whether victims have filed civil suits or accepted settlements from alleged perpetrators has been brought up in nearly every recent case of sexual assault or harassment allegations against celebrities, from Cosby to Roethlisberger to Nassar.[76] As in a physical courtroom, in the online "courtroom," there is an expectation that genuine sexual assault victims will place their trust in criminal law, which serves the societal objective of getting the "perp" off the streets. In contrast, civil litigation is presumed to reward victims personally—as a commenter on the Cosby case argues, "No one should be able to sue for money when a crime has been committed. If a crime has been committed the criminal needs to go to jail." A slew of similar observations that "victims pursued civil money more than criminal justice" suggest that, in regard to sexual assault accusations, a munificent single-mindedness is expected.

As increasing numbers of alleged victims have been drawn to—or encouraged to turn to—the civil system as a preferred avenue for seeking justice, the public questions their motivations. On top of active smear campaigns against personal injury attorneys, in recent years the public has been privy to the details of numerous large settlements via which sexual assault victims have sought—and sometimes received—billions in compensation from deep-pocketed third parties including universities, religious organizations, and the U.S. government. In the face of these massive awards, the public may begin to think that all plaintiffs alleging sexual assault stand to win the litigation "lottery."

Comments referring to victims who file civil suits as "gold diggers" or presenting "evidence" that victims have accepted "hush money" reflect that legal claims today arise in the shadows of a political movement that has worked hard to reframe public perceptions of personal injury law, lawyers, and claimants.[77] The descriptors that sexual assault claimants are entering the "ghetto lottery" or seeking "jackpot justice" reflect this conservative lens. In identifying claimants as from the "ghetto," online commenters instantly create a particular image of the accuser influenced by both race and class. The alleged victim is situated as an outsider, not an elite member of the status quo like the commenter themselves.

Significantly, in characterizing law as a "lottery" or "jackpot," the institution is recast as fickle, making decisions not based on principle or precedent but on arbitrary, case-by-case factors dependent on the claimant's attractiveness or the shark-like qualities of her attorney. In the past twenty years, in the public discourse, the legal system has been discursively transformed from a distant, difficult-to-access, and unbiased institution to one that is readily manipulated by "ambulance chasing" attorneys and likely to provide unjustified income to civil plaintiffs. Adrian Howe observes,

> The success of the tort "reform" movement . . . has hinged upon this idea that there are greedy or drama-seeking parties who feel injuries

> more acutely than others. Punitive damages, then, are characterized as serving the special interests of a few, demanding plaintiffs rather than penalizing bad actors on behalf of the collective good.[78]

The perception that undeserving, whiny outsiders are making illegitimate claims to resources or are trying to use illicit means to achieve wealth redistribution are not unique to discussions of sexual assault. As Engel writes, individuals' engagement with law not infrequently is perceived as "intru[ding] upon existing relationships, as pretexts for forced exchanges, as inappropriate attempts to redistribute wealth, and as limitations upon individual freedom."[79] His research demonstrates that "social status and power can affect fundamental assumptions about causation and responsibility."[80] "Haves" with greater access to institutional resources—from healthcare, to employment, to the judicial system—may exhibit stoicism in the face of injury, while "have nots" may challenge views of "self-sufficiency in the face of injuries" and emphasize responsibility and accountability.[81] Perceptions of the validity of legal claims are influenced not only by the actual, personal characteristics of the claimant but also by the greater social, legal, and political climate in which such claims are made.

As Engel articulates, "[i]njuries are not objective facts; rather, they are events that humans perceive and interpret within ideational frameworks that reflect a deep interaction between self and culture. . . . [A]lthough nearly all humans are susceptible to pain, they experience and interpret it differently in different social and cultural contexts.[82] He critiques a widespread belief that civil plaintiffs are rational, profit-maximizing actors, noting that "injury victims are not like consumers who coolly and dispassionately choose among different brands of toothpaste. Rather, they are . . . frail and fallible beings . . . [who] may not yet have recovered from a physiologically, emotionally, and psychologically devastating experience."[83] Opinions about those who engage the law reflect social boundaries and in-group and out-group status.[84] That the tort system allocates power away from the state and onto individuals for the reallocation of resources arouses suspicion of dishonest motives not only in sexual assault cases but across all personal injury claims.[85]

Although distrust of the law is present in other personal injury cases, in cases of sexual assault suspicions that plaintiffs are overstating injuries are magnified. Demands that victims show "legitimate" injuries are supported by the continuing and overwhelming influence of rape mythologies and are fueled by a lack of agreement about the precise nature of the injury that has been inflicted in cases of sexual assault. As Lucinda Finley writes, law shapes our collective, societal judgments as to "whether a problem exists or whether a harm has occurred."[86]

Sexual assault law in the United States is no longer explicitly linked to theories of property; however, there is not a consensus on the type of harm wrought by sexual violence. Some advocate continuing a property-based theory of harm, arguing that rape violates possession of oneself.[87] Others argue for criminalizing the violation of sexual agency and autonomy or, more compellingly, for assessing the penalties for rape based on a more complex engagement with potential harms based on multiple factors.[88]

The critique that a Cosby accuser is like a "prostitute" or that Erica Kinsman was hoping for a "book deal" demonstrate an awareness among the public that women's bodies have been and continue to be commodified and, at the same time, a discomfort with the idea that women are asserting sexual autonomy. This fear of the assertion of sexual, bodily autonomy is perhaps most apparent in online comments characterizing groups of women—via their attorneys—as advancing a political agenda by using sexual assault law to abuse men.

CONCLUSION

Social media comments reflect an astute understanding that we are in a moment of cultural crisis concerning not only how we reckon with crimes of gender-based violence but also how best to afford justice in the context of such violence.

While, on one hand commenters respect the criminal justice system, favoring victims who pursue formalities like police reports and rape kits, on the other they exhibit a profound distrust in the law, doubting the capacity of the civil legal system to fairly and equitably allocate resources between plaintiff and defendant. This distrust has developed after years of conservative promotion of "tort reform" accompanied by a profound closing of the courthouse doors to civil claimants. It also has been fostered by the relentless framing by defense attorneys of celebrities as victims and of accusers as looking for a payoff.

One of the greatest accomplishments of the women's movement has been to incorporate more of women's lived experiences into criminal law and procedure. However, as access to legal recourse has increased, so have suspicions that the law is incapable of affording justice in an unbiased manner. In her most recognizable form, justice is blind, but she is also a woman. With legal reforms has risen the public perception of justice as subject to manipulation. At the same time that sexual assault law has been broadened to cover a wider range of real-world circumstances and to incorporate more categories of victims, suspicion has grown that there is a gendered threat encroaching on the status quo.

When sexual assault victims turn to the civil system to seek justice, fears of redistribution of power are amplified. The filing of a civil suit, which for many years has been discursively constructed by tort reformers as an easy way to make a buck, is now characterized on social media as a way for a gold digger or THOT to effect a "come up" in status. In the views of online commenters, lawyers allegedly effecting this unbalanced and unfair wealth redistribution are singled out for their particular anti-male or anti-patriarchy "agenda" and the law is characterized as uniquely susceptible to women's charms or—more accurately—their threats.

There is a popular meme today that states, "It's not pie: Equal rights for others does not mean less rights for you." In the view of many commenters, however, justice is indeed like a pie—a surfeit for some most certainly means a deficit for others. The implication (or accusation) that an accuser is a "gold digger," like the suggestion that an incident took place on the casting couch, emphasizes the superior status of the commenter while it provides social and emotional distance from the events in question. As the accusers in celebrity sexual assault cases are reduced to "gold diggers," "hoes," and "sluts," any crimes that may have occurred become distant spectacles rather than everyday dangers that are part of the fabric of society. Incidences of rape and sexual assault are characterized as individual mistakes of judgment rather than societal problems that you or I might be likely to experience—or to perpetrate.[89]

The continuing influence of the gold digger stereotype emphasizes, too, that achieving and retaining status as an ideal victim is an all-or-nothing proposition. In discussing the 1992 criminal case against Mike Tyson, editorials debated whether alleged survivor Desiree Washington was "a real champion" or "a phoney, a gold digger."[90] Today, filing a lawsuit—in commenters' terms, attempting a "money grab"—casts similar ethical aspersions on a victim's character. As a critic of the Cosby accusers asks, "[W]hat kind of person would take money . . . if someone raped them? Why won't you have them put in jail? Being 'raped' and paid for it . . . doesn't seem right."

NOTES

1. Jessica Luther, "The Jameis Winston Rape Lawsuit Has Some Damaging New Information," *Vice Sports*, April 17, 2015, https://sports.vice.com/en_us/article/wn33gm/the-jameis-winston-rape-lawsuit-has-some-damaging-new-information.
2. Marc Tracy, "Jameis Winston and Woman Who Accused Him of Rape Settle Lawsuits," *New York Times*, December 15, 2016, https://www.nytimes.com/2016/12/15/sports/football/jameis-winston-erica-kinsman-lawsuit.html.
3. Tracy, "Jameis Winston."
4. Luther, "Jameis Winston Rape Lawsuit."
5. Luther, "Jameis Winston Rape Lawsuit."
6. Notably, the settlement did not include any admission of responsibility on the part of the institution. Laura Wagner, "FSU Pays $950,000 to Woman Who Accused Jameis Winston of Sexual Assault," National Public Radio, January 25, 2016, https://www.npr.org/sections/thetwo-way/2016/01/25/464332250/fsu-pays-950-000-to-woman-who-accused-jameis-winston-of-sexual-assault.
7. Tracy, "Jameis Winston."

8. TMZ, "Jameis Winston Alleged Rape Victim Files New Lawsuit," April 16, 2015, http://www.tmz.com/2015/04/16/jameis-winston-civil-lawsuit-alleged-rape-erica-kinsman-florida-state-university/?adid=TMZ_Search_Results.

9. TMZ, "Jameis Winston Victim."

10. During the lawsuit, Winston's attorney alleged that Kinsman had deleted social media posts evidencing her association with a Facebook group of young women that used #FSUCleatChasers to refer to their status as ardent fans of Seminole players. Bud Elliott, "This Is the Letter from Jameis Winston's Attorney to Florida State," *Tomahawk Nation, A Florida State Seminoles Community*, September 24, 2014, https://www.tomahawknation.com/2014/9/24/6840459/letter-jameis-winston-attorney-florida-state-fsu-accuser.

11. Janzen, "Amending," 1090.

12. Peggy Reeves Sanday, *A Woman Scorned: Acquaintance Rape on Trial* (New York: Doubleday, 1996), 149.

13. Sanday, *A Woman Scorned*, 150.

14. Geis, "Lord Hale, Witches," 27.

15. Geis, "Lord Hale, Witches," 27.

16. Geis, "Lord Hale, Witches," 27.

17. Jasmine N. Ross and Nicole M. Coleman, "Gold Digger or Video Girl: The Salience of an Emerging Hip-Hop Sexual Script," *Culture, Health & Sexuality: An International Journal for Research, Prevention, and Care* 13, no. 2 (2011): 158; Hill Collins, *Black Feminist Thought*, 69.

18. Hill Collins, *Black Feminist Thought*, 69.

19. Hill Collins, *Black Feminist Thought*, 69; Dionne P. Stephens and Layli D. Phillips, "Freaks, Gold Diggers, Divas, and Dykes: The Sociohistorical Development of Adolescent African American Women's Sexual Scripts," *Sexuality and Culture* 7, no. 1 (2003): 11, 12. Stephens and Phillips describe how, for African American women, the "ghosts" of past stereotypes are manifested in behavioral norms, such as "the Diva, Gold Digger, Freak, Dyke, Gangster Bitch, Sister Savior, Earth Mother, and Baby Mama."

20. Ann Cammett, "Deadbeat Dads and Welfare Queens: How Metaphor Shapes Poverty Law," *Boston College Journal of Law and Social Justice* 34 (2014): 233, 237.

21. Jennifer A. Sandlin, Jennie Stearns, Julie Garlin Maudlin, and Jake Burdick, "'Now I Ain't Sayin' She a Gold Digger': Wal-Mart Shoppers, Welfare Queens, and Other Gendered Stereotypes of Poor Women in the Big Curriculum of Consumption," *Cultural Studies* 11, no. 5 (2011): 466; Regina Austin, "Nest Eggs and Stormy Weather: Law, Culture, and Black Women's Lack of Wealth," Faculty Scholarship Paper 813, Penn Law: Legal Scholarship Repository (1997), 776.

22. Sandlin et al., "'Now I Ain't Sayin,'" 477.

23. Sandlin et al., "'Now I Ain't Sayin,'" 477.

24. "Gold Digger," lyrics by Kanye West (MetroLyrics, 2003), http://www.metrolyrics.com /gold-digger-lyrics-kanye-west.html.

25. Joanna Bourke, *Rape: Sex, Violence, History* (New York: Counterpoint, 2009), 38.

26. Bourke, *Rape*, 31, fn. 30.

27. hnoss, "Thot" (also "THOT," acronym for "That Ho Over There"), *Urban Dictionary*, March 7, 2017, https://www.urbandictionary.com/define.php?term=Thot.

28. Hill Collins, *Black Feminist Thought*, 69.

29. Lipstick Alley, "'Thot' Things Thread," started by jeansaprincess, August 15, 2015, https://www.lipstickalley.com/threads/thot-things-thread.911948/. Descriptions of THOT activities are often delimited by race, socioeconomic status, and gender. "THOT jobs," for example, include "seasonal worker" positions at a variety of mid- to low-priced retail operations.

30. Armstrong et al., "'Good Girls,'" 107; Jessica Valenti, "In Rape Tragedies, the Shame Is Ours," *The Nation*, April 17, 2013, https://www.thenation.com/article/173911/rape-tragedies-shame-ours#. Jessica Valenti refers to the negative terms we use to describe sexual assault claimants as not "slur[s]" but "designation[s]," describing that

"[w]omen and girls are the ones expected to carry the shame of the sexual crimes perpetrated against them . . . a tremendous load to bear."

31. Roy F. Baumeister and Jean M. Twenge, "Cultural Suppression of Female Sexuality," *Review of General Psychology* 6, no. 2 (2002): 166–203.

32. Sarah McMahon and Lawrence G. Farmer, "An Updated Measure for Assessing Subtle Rape Myths," *Social Work Research* 35 (2012): 72.

33. Elliott McLaughlin, "Janay Rice: Ray Rice was 'Terrified' after Hitting Me," CNN.com, December 1, 2014, https://www.cnn.com/2014/12/01/us/ray-rice-wife-janay-today-show/index.html.

34. Janay Rice's decision to marry Ray Rice also generated an important countermovement, #WhyIStayed, offering many reasons why those who experience intimate partner violence make the decision to remain in violent relationships. "Hashtag Activism in 2014: Tweeting 'Why I Stayed,'" *All Things Considered*, National Public Radio (NPR), December 23, 2014, http://www.npr.org/2014/12/23/372729058/hashtag-activism-in-2014- tweeting-why-i-stayed [http://perma.cc/B8NU-NZWJ].

35. West, "Gold Digger."

36. Dionne P. Stephens and Layli D. Phillips, "Freaks, Gold Diggers, Divas, and Dykes: The Sociohistorical Development of Adolescent African American Women's Sexual Scripts," *Sexuality and Culture* 7, no. 1 (2003): 17–18.

37. Elizabeth Grosz, *Volatile Bodies: Toward a Corporeal Feminism* (Bloomington: University of Indiana Press, 1994); Laura Sjoberg and Caron E. Gentry, eds., *Mothers, Monsters, Whores: Women's Violence in Global Politics* (London: Zed Books, 2007); Patricia Pearson, *When She Was Bad: Violent Women and the Myth of Innocence* (New York: Penguin, 1998).

38. Brief for Defendant in Error, *Muller v. Oregon*, 208 U.S. 412 (1908) (No. 107). Interestingly, it was not Brandeis himself but two women who were responsible for drafting the brief, Josephine Goldmark, a senior staff member at the National Consumers League (NCL) and Brandeis's sister-in-law. The brief was also requested by a woman, NCL leader Florence Kelley. Noga Morag-Levine, "Facts, Formalism, and the Brandeis Brief: The Origins of a Myth," *University of Illinois Law Review* (2013): 60.

39. Amy D. Ronner, "The Cassandra Curse: The Stereotype of the Female Liar Resurfaces in *Jones v. Clinton*," *University of California, Davis Law Review* 31 (1997–1998): 137.

40. Ronner, "The Cassandra Curse," 137.

41. Sanday, *A Woman Scorned*, 235.

42. Sanday, *A Woman Scorned*, 235.

43. Paul Harris, "Courting Disaster," *Observer*, April 16, 2005, https://www.theguardian.com/music/2005/apr/17/michaeljackson.michaeljacksontrial.

44. ESPN.com, "Steelers QB Wants Written Apology," September 16, 2009, http://sports.espn.go.com/nfl/news/story?id=4414936.

45. Jen Kirby, "Cosby Defense Lawyers: Andrea Constand Is a 'Con Artist,'" *Vox*, April 10, 2018, https://www.vox.com/2018/4/10/17219730/bill-cosby-constand-defense-opening-statement-trial.

46. Rachel Axon, "Jameis Winston Files Counterclaim against Accuser Erica Kinsman," *USA Today*, May 9, 2015, http://www.usatoday.com/story/sports/nfl/2015/05/09/jameis-winston-counter-lawsuit-accuser-erica-kinsman-florida-state/27030973/.

47. Axon, "Jameis Winston Files Counterclaim."

48. Filipa Ioannou, Ben Mathis-Lilley, Elliot Hannon, and Lena Wilson, "A Complete List of the Women Who Have Accused Bill Cosby of Sexual Assault," *Slate*, April 26, 2018, http://www.slate.com/blogs/browbeat/2014/11/21/bill_cosby_accusers_list_sexual_assault_rape_drugs_feature_in_women_s_stories.html.

49. Salter, "Justice and Revenge," 238; Sjoberg and Gentry, *Mothers, Monsters*, 37.

50. The affidavit declining prosecution filed by the accuser in Patrick Kane's case cites personal and familial stress as the accuser's reason for no longer cooperating in the case. Sarah Connors, Katie Esmonde, Achariya Rezak, Emily Wang, and Ari Yanover, "The Patrick Kane Case Shows How Much Power Fans Wield in the Way Athlete

Investigations Are Handled," SBNation.com, November 4, 2015, http://www.sbnation.com/2015/11/4/9669752/patrick-kane-accuser-nhl-and-rape-culture.

51. Marc Galanter, "Why the 'Haves' Come Out Ahead: Speculations on the Limits of Legal Change," *Law and Society Review* 9, no. 1 (1974): 95; Engel, "The Oven Bird's Song."

52. Engel, "The Oven Bird's Song."

53. Engel, "The Oven Bird's Song," 323. The vast majority of injuries do not become legal disputes; in order for an injury to become a civil legal dispute, as Felstiner et al. identify, the plaintiff must undergo a process of "naming, blaming, and claiming." Felstiner et al., "Naming, Blaming," 635–36; Morgan, "Risking Relationships," 67.

54. Mark M. Bello, "Twenty-Six Years Later McDonald's Still a "Hot" Topic," *Legal Examiner*, January 16, 2009, https://farmingtonhills.legalexaminer.com/legal/miscellaneous/twenty-six-years-later-mcdonalds-still-a-hot-topic/.

55. Ewick and Silbey, *The Common Place of Law*, 28.

56. Withers describes that, of sixty-four total reported allegations of domestic violence and sexual assault by professional athletes from 2010 through 2014, only one domestic violence allegation—and zero sexual assault allegations—resulted in conviction. Bethany P. Withers, "Without Consequence: When Professional Athletes Are Violent Off the Field," *Harvard Journal of Sports & Entertainment Law* 6, no. 2 (2015): 378–80.

57. Haltom and McCann, *Distorting*.

58. Chimamanda Ngozi Adichie, *We Should All Be Feminists* (New York: Anchor, 2012).

59. Adichie, *We Should All*.

60. Kate Manne, "Brett Kavanaugh and America's 'Himpathy' Reckoning," *New York Times*, Opinion, September 26, 2018, https://www.nytimes.com/2018/09/26/opinion/brett-kavanaugh-hearing-himpathy.html.

61. Manne, "Himpathy."

62. Manne, "Himpathy."

63. Catharine A. MacKinnon, "#MeToo Has Done What the Law Could Not," Opinion, *New York Times*, February 4, 2018, https://www.nytimes.com/2018/02/04/opinion/metoo-law-legal-system.html; Hiba Hafiz, "How Legal Agreements Can Silence Victims of Workplace Sexual Assault," *Atlantic*, October 18, 2017, https://www.theatlantic.com/business/archive/2017/10/legal-agreements-sexual-assault-ndas/543252/.

64. Hafiz, "How Legal Agreements Can Silence."

65. Lisa Wade, "Rape on Campus: Athletes, Status and the Sexual Assault Crisis," *Salon*, March 12, 2017, https://www.salon.com/2017/03/12/rape-on-campus-athletes-status-and-the-sexual-assault-crisis_partner/.

66. Ridgeway, *Framed*, 67.

67. Ridgeway, *Framed*, 4.

68. Sanday, *A Woman Scorned*, 150.

69. Tom Lininger, "Is It Wrong to Sue for Rape?," *Duke Law Journal* 57 (2008): 1557–640.

70. Lininger, "Is It Wrong to Sue?"

71. Morgan, "Risking Relationships," 67, 68.

72. Lininger, "Is It Wrong to Sue?," 1563–64.

73. Lininger, "Is It Wrong to Sue?," 1563–64.

74. Lininger, "Is It Wrong to Sue?," 1560. Lininger observes that courts generally allow "scathing impeachment of accusers" who bring coterminous civil and criminal actions, suggesting that those in authority are uncomfortable with civil suits for rape.

75. Lininger, "Is It Wrong to Sue?," 1564.

76. Kirby, "Cosby Defense Lawyers"; Luther, "The Jameis Winston Rape Lawsuit"; Associated Press, "Judge Denies Motion to Move Case," ESPN.com, September 16, 2009, http://www.espn.com/nfl/news/story?id=4478769.

77. McClellan et al. identify a widespread and mistaken perception among medical professionals that litigants in malpractice cases are more likely to come from low-income families, impressions that lead to differential treatment of poor clients. Frank M. McClellan, Augustus A. White III, Ramon L. Jiminez, and Sherin Fahmy, "Do Poor People Sue Doctors More Frequently? Confronting Unconscious Bias and the Role of Cultural Competency," *Clinical Orthopaedics and Related Research* 470 (2012): 1393–97.

78. Adrian Howe, "The Problem of Privatized Injuries: Feminist Strategies for Litigation," in *At The Boundaries of the Law: Feminism and Legal Theory*, eds. Martha Albertson Fineman and Nancy Sweet Thomadsen (New York: Routledge, 1991), 148. Mendlow argues that tort suits today may be perceived as a form of "institutionalized revenge," driven by the assumption that plaintiffs bring such suits to seek revenge or achieve personal gain rather than to be made whole. Gabriel Seltzer Mendlow, "Is Tort Law a Form of Institutionalized Revenge?," *Florida State Law Review* 39 (2011): 129, 132, 134.

79. Engel, "The Oven Bird's Song," 577.

80. David M. Engel, "Perception and Decision at the Threshold of Tort Law: Explaining the Infrequency of Claims," *DePaul Law Review* 62 (2013): 293, 323.

81. Engel, "Perception and Decision," 292, 323; Galanter, "Why the 'Haves' Come Out Ahead."

82. Engel, "Perception and Decision," 323–24.

83. Engel, "Perception and Decision," 293, 301.

84. Engel, "The Oven Bird's Song," 581.

85. Mendlow, "Is Tort Law . . . Revenge?," 129.

86. Lucinda M. Finley, "Female Trouble: The Implications of Tort Reform for Women," *Tennessee Law Review* 64 (1996–1997): 887.

87. Jed Rubenfeld, "The Riddle of Rape-by-Deception and the Myth of Sexual Autonomy," *Yale Law Journal* 122 (2013): 1372, 1392.

88. Yung, "Rape Law Fundamentals"; Deborah Tuerkheimer, "Sex without Consent," *Yale Law Journal Online* 123 (2013): 352.

89. Moore, "Tracing the Life," 453; Brenner, "Resisting Simple Dichotomies," 507.

90. Ira Berkow, "Sports of the Times; A Champ Named Desiree," *New York Times*, February 25, 1992, http://www.nytimes.com/1992/02/25/sports/sports-of-the-times-a-champ-named-desiree.html.

THREE

Liars

Phi Kappa Psi v. Rolling Stone, LLC

In 2014 *Rolling Stone* magazine published a firsthand account of a sexual assault that allegedly occurred at a fraternity house at the University of Virginia.[1] The article, provocatively titled, "A Rape on Campus," featured a female college student, under the pseudonym "Jackie," who described having been sexually assaulted by seven men at a college party.[2] Published in the midst of copious media coverage of sexual assaults in the military, Title IX lawsuits against several universities, and billion-dollar recoveries for victims across other institutional contexts, the article provided a compelling account of the harms of rape culture and the consequences of an institution's willful ignorance of survivors' complaints. Jackie's narrative brought to life the particular vulnerabilities of a young, female freshman on a large, impersonal campus and gave voice to the frustration—what might be described as a double victimization—that many survivors experience when their accusations are dismissed by those in power.[3] A fellow student observed of the article, "There was a sort of familiar sadness to it."[4] It resonated.

The story, however, wasn't true. Days after the article appeared, comments emerged questioning the veracity of Jackie's account.[5] Readers pointed to hyperbole in the description of the incident, critiqued questionable reporting techniques, and highlighted a lack of corroboration from friends of the complainant.[6] Ultimately, the magazine retracted the article and, in part due to the overwhelming negative attention it received after the retraction, was sold by former owner Jann Wenner.[7]

As with *Kinsman v. Winston*, Jackie's accusations took on a juridical life of their own, spawning multiple, wide-ranging lawsuits.[8] In 2017, a jury awarded UVA dean Sabrina Eramo $3 million for damage to her character resulting from the article.[9] A similar suit by Phi Kappa Psi, alleging the magazine's "wanton destruction" of the fraternity's reputation, was settled for just over $1.5 million.[10] Although not personally named by Jackie, three members of the fraternity also brought individual suits against the magazine, which ultimately settled for undisclosed amounts.[11]

The *Rolling Stone* piece and its aftermath predictably ignited a firestorm across social media. Commenters raced to share opinions about Jackie, questioning her motivation in bringing a false claim—*Was it mental instability? A collapse after a bad grade? Vengeance after a break up?* Like comments about Andrea Constand and Erica Kinsman, a notable feature of online discussions about Jackie is the extent to which they situate the young woman as part of a biologically predetermined group—women who lie about rape.

The previous two chapters explored some of the factors that contribute to online assessments about accusers' status and character and, consequently, opinions about their veracity. "Evidence" that an accuser visited a perpetrator's home alone, that she delayed in filing a police report, or that she filed a civil suit suggests a moral ambiguity and, therefore, a tendency toward an overall lack of truthfulness. In the court of public opinion, feminist campaigns against "slut-shaming" and "victim-blaming" come up against centuries of rape law that are scaffolded on social and biological fallacies about how women, as a group, can, and do, behave.

This chapter delves more deeply into the ways in which long-standing assumptions about women's biology, their "dispositions," tie into modern-day conceptions about accusers' veracity by exploring Jackie, the subject of the *Rolling Stone* debacle, as the embodiment of perhaps the most powerful rape myth today: the myth of the lying accuser.

This chapter intentionally focuses on alleged sexual assault victims who identify as cis women. This is not to ignore that men are also victims. In fact, were prison rapes included in statistics on reported sexual assaults, men would comprise the majority of U.S. sexual assault victims.[12] Similarly, although sexual assault in the military has largely been framed as a women's issue, statistics about the armed forces bear out that, in terms of sheer numbers, men comprise the majority of sexual assault victims by far.[13] Other studies find that male college students report "unwanted and coerced sexual activity" at a level comparable to similarly situated women.[14] Trans men and women experience staggering rates of sexual victimization.[15] Further, recent data from the Centers for Disease Control and Prevention (CDC) highlight not only that women and men can both be perpetrators of sexual assault but that in certain contexts women may be *more likely* to be perpetrators.[16]

Although rape happens to and is committed by people identifying across the sexuality and gender spectrum, the rape of a man is not identical to the rape of a woman. The bodies of female sexual assault accusers, culturally speaking, are read differently than those of male accusers. Men may occasionally be called gold diggers, for example, but the label is generally used to signify a particular (and "biological") type of feminine laziness, consumerism, and greed.[17] When men are accused of visiting the casting couch, it is usually as the person in the position of power. Whether or not accusers are cisgender females, the validity of their claims is determined by sexual assault laws that have been constructed based on assumptions about women.[18]

The intentional focus on cis female survivors is also a product of the gendered discussions taking place in the #MeToo era, something the book discusses in depth in chapter 6. Despite the efforts of researchers like Bennett Capers and Laura Sjoberg to highlight the diversity of sexual assault perpetrators and victims, sexual assault is largely rhetorically constructed in the media and across social network systems as a crime that is *done by* men and *happens to* women.[19] Discourse from social networks to print media to official research reports most often centers on women—usually cisgender, heterosexual women—as the primary victims of sexual assaults. The report from the *First White House Tax Force to Protect Students from Sexual Assault*, disseminated during the Obama administration and taken down in the Trump era, goes so far as to categorize sexual assault as not gender-based violence but "violence against women," emphasizing the need for us to protect "our daughters, our sisters, our wives, our mothers, [and] our grandmothers."[20] The website for the Time's Up campaign follows this dialectic construction, featuring a prominently displayed letter that begins, "Dear Sisters."[21] As the book discusses in part 3, in conversations about #MeToo, men are most often constructed as "bystanders" or "allies" and less frequently included in the victim category.

Although the book acknowledges this gendered dichotomy, it does not intend to build on it but rather to begin to deconstruct it. As described in earlier chapters, one of the problems with the criminal justice system is that it has rarely taken notice of crime victims. In the context of the criminal legal system, unless a story is particularly mysterious or uniquely horrific, victims tend to fade to the periphery, their voices a footnote if ever heard at all.

In contrast, in the context of sexual assault, victimhood often takes on a particular, sometimes notorious, status—a status that is enabled by the construction of sexual assault accusers as female. We celebrate survivors like the athletes who bravely testified against Larry Nassar, and we categorize other victims by hashtag—#dukelacrosse, #tawanabrawley, and #UVAHoax—thereby warning potential, future claimants to be truthful or face potentially severe and lifelong consequences. What this chapter describes as the "Jackie problem" is not that a sexual assault accuser may have lied but rather the continuing resonance of that lie, a statement that remains a cautionary tale years after an alleged incident. The resonance of this lie is rooted in commonsense—and political—assumptions about biology.

Within social movements, there is often a pressure from "respectability politics"—the idea that, in the context of structural oppressions, the behavior of individuals will be seen as negatively reflecting on the group to which they belong.[22] In the Black Lives Matter or the marriage equality movements, the existence of respectability politics may foster pressure to be a "model minority." There is a fear that a misstep by one person could be identified as a reason to withdraw or deny rights and privileges to the whole. The *Philadelphia Inquirer* recently ran an op-ed regarding allegations by actor Jussie Smollett, who self-identifies as an African American and gay man, after the actor was indicted on charges he manufactured hate crime allegations. The essay—entitled, "Jussie Smollett Case a Reminder That One False Accuser Can Hurt All Future Victims"—highlights the fear that minority groups may feel when one of their members is perceived to have engaged in behavior that the majority, however misguidedly, may attribute to the whole.[23] The heart of respectability politics can be summarized in one sentence: "Liars chill the atmosphere for real victims."[24]

Reporting rape carries with it the weight of a similar politics of respectability. Every time an alleged victim reports a sexual assault, she not only places into question her own reputation and character, she risks casting aspersions on the veracity of all other victims coming forward—in the eyes of the police, the judiciary, and, of course, the public. In reporting the alleged harms they suffered, Erica Kinsman, Andrea Constand, and Jackie in an instant became accountable not only to those around them in the present but to countless others who might dare to make claims in the future.

The concern that large groups of women are coming out of the woodwork to lie about rape reflects distrust in the ability of the legal system to provide justice, as discussed in chapters 1 and 2. It is also tied to realizations about the deployment of rape charges as a means to railroad Black men and the role that white women have played in perpetuating injustice. As the book discusses in depth in the following chapters, lying about rape should be taken seriously; the impact of such lies may be significant. False rape accusations have tragically impacted Black men, habitually terrorizing them both within the judicial system and via extralegal lynching. And the public, rightfully, has lost faith in the legal system to be an objective and unbiased arbiter of justice.

Before turning to focus on the ways in which these concerns and anxieties are embodied in alleged perpetrators, however, it is important to spend one more chapter focusing on how sexual assault laws were and continue to be written on the bodies of accusers.

TRUTH OR DARE

This chapter does not take a position on the percentage of false rape claims. Rather, the book accepts, first, that people lie about crime and, second, that we have absolutely no way to know just how often this occurs.

Evidence for the idea that people lie—perhaps a lot—is embedded in the criminal justice system. One example is the ancient practice of swearing in witnesses, purposefully exacting a promise to "tell the truth, the whole truth, and nothing but the truth." Like the threat of prosecution for perjury, this long-standing courtroom ritual is founded on the proposition that, short of divine—or judicial—intervention, most of us might at times be inclined to take a few liberties. During the second Cosby trial, Janice Dickinson was cross-examined by the defense as to why her formal testimony contradicted the story she told about the comedian in her tell-all book. "It's all a fabrication there," Dickinson distinguished. "I wanted the paycheck from the book. . . . [But] [t]oday I am on a sworn Bible."[25]

The tendency of human beings to lie, or at least to sugarcoat the truth, comes up regularly in Fourth Amendment cases. When ascertaining the validity of anonymous tips, for example, courts carefully weigh when public policy justifications for government intrusion outweigh suspicions about an informant's veracity and reliability.[26] The concern that rushed investigations or flawed perceptions might render less-than-truthful testimony from police officers underlies the requirement that probable cause determinations be evaluated by a "neutral and detached magistrate," contrasting calm and unbiased court officials with "zealous" police officers wont to abuse their discretion.[27] In the Fifth Amendment context, high-profile cases, such as those of the Central Park Five and Norfolk Four, not to mention hundreds of DNA exonerations, have brought the topic of false confessions into the limelight.[28] Although some of these confessions turn out to have been coerced, a befuddling number of defendants voluntarily admit to crimes in which they played no role whatsoever.[29]

When a witness lies on the stand, that person is said to have committed an act of perjury and is punished accordingly; but the actions of that person are not attributed to all witnesses going forward. In contrast, however, when a sexual assault accuser like Jackie has lied, her actions reflect not only on her personal, human failings but on all future female claimants. The saying goes: to err is human, to forgive divine. In most cases, the tendency to lie is attributed to *human* nature. In the case of rape, however, lying is regarded as a matter of problematic, gendered biology. Catherine MacKinnon identifies that "women's rights" historically have been segregated as a category separate from "human rights."[30] Similarly, women's frailties long have been culled from the category of human frailties.

Although online discussions about sexual assault engage black-and-white terms like truth and falsity, legally speaking, there is no such thing as a "false" claim. During what is usually a lengthy and complex process, a criminal complaint may be determined to be unfounded, unsupported, unsubstantiated, or baseless, but it is not—at least not technically—designated "false" or "fake." This distinction is not just a semantic one.

Constitutional criminal procedure goes to great pains to distinguish between legal and factual guilt—something may have happened, but without evidence establishing a "fair probability" that it occurred, there is no arrest.[31] If the state cannot prove the defendant's involvement "beyond a reasonable doubt," there can be no conviction. The heart of criminal law is not guilt and innocence but guilt and nonguilt, gradations of truth established painstakingly through the adversarial process.

In this context, an unfounded or unsubstantiated allegation is by no means necessarily a false one. We can see this in cases such as O. J. Simpson's where there may be insufficient evidence to find a defendant guilty beyond a reasonable doubt, but there is nonetheless sufficient evidence for a jury to find him responsible in a civil case. Lisak et al. cite a memorandum from the International Association of Chiefs of Police distinguishing unsubstantiated from false reports:

> The determination that a report of sexual assault is false can be made only if the evidence establishes that no crime was committed or attempted. . . . This should not be confused with an investigation that fails to prove a sexual assault occurred. In that case the investigation would be labeled unsubstantiated. *The determination that a report is false must be supported by evidence that the assault did not happen.*[32]

In other words, an absence of physical evidence, inconsistent statements by the accuser, lack of cooperation, or delayed reporting should not in and of themselves mean that a claim is not truthful.[33]

Do accusers in sexual assault trials really lie more than other alleged victims in the criminal justice system? Maybe. It is impossible to answer based on the data we have available. A recent article by De Zutter and colleagues unhelpfully describes estimates of the percentage of false rape claims in the United States as between 3 percent and 90 percent.[34] Unsurprisingly, the lowest rates of false reports are offered by feminist scholars, sometimes citing an unsupported statistic thrown out by Susan Brownmiller during the 1980s that only 2 percent of rape claims are false.[35] The highest estimates of false claims predictably tend to appear in conservative publications or from data taken directly from interviews with, or observations by, the police.[36]

Based on data from several government offices, including the U.S. Department of Justice, the British Home Office, and the FBI, one recent article places the percentage of unfounded or baseless rape claims at about 8 percent.[37] However, even governmental data can be manipulated or may be incomplete. The Philadelphia Police Department, for example, admits to mislabeling complaints to reduce workload and improve case clearance rates.[38] The thousands of untested rape kits still sitting in crime labs across the United States suggest that other police departments similarly may not have been fully and fairly investigating every report of sexual assault over the past several years.

Lisak and colleagues observe that, the more closely law enforcement procedures are interrogated, the lower the rate of false claims.[39] The researchers identify the ways in which the ideal victim paradigm continues to operate in contemporary law enforcement: "Cases in which the victim is unable or unwilling to cooperate, in which evidence is lacking, in which the victim makes inconsistent statements, or in which the victim was heavily intoxicated frequently get classified as 'unfounded' or 'no-crimed.'"[40]

Further, even allegations that turn out to be wholly unfounded may be based more in mistake than malice.[41] In recent years it has come to light that the single biggest factor in wrongful convictions is mistaken eyewitness testimony. While some eyewitnesses may act out of spite, psychologist Elizabeth Loftus demonstrates that many false identifications happen because our senses fail us in times of trauma.[42] Law enforcement and courtroom procedures, such as lineups, compound these human frailties.[43]

As the social media comments discussed in previous chapters suggest, as a society we do not fully comprehend what, legally speaking, constitutes a criminal sexual assault. Our collective uncertainty about "gray areas" of the law influences not only observers but those directly impacted by crime.[44] Just as the Cosby jurors struggled to situate Bill Cosby's conduct in regard to Andrea Constand in the realm of "recklessness" or "lack of knowledge," many persons who meet the legal criteria for having experienced (or perpetrated) criminal sexual assaults similarly may not see their situation reflected in the "bloodless" language of law.[45]

Tellingly, when the term "sexual harassment" was first coined by MacKinnon in the early 1990s, legal services organizations reported that the initial reaction of many victims was not relief but bewilderment—"You mean I could do something about this?"[46] Michael McCann talks about this difficulty in developing rights consciousness among even the most deserving of victims and claimants.[47] A similar lack of awareness is evident in comments by Dr. Christine Blasey Ford, whose allegations of sexual assault against nominee—now Supreme Court justice—Brett Kavanaugh made headlines in 2018. At the time of the alleged incident, she recounts thinking: "I'm not ever telling anyone this. This is nothing, it didn't happen, and he didn't rape me."[48] She describes that it was years later, after seeking therapy, that she began to recognize the incident as traumatizing.[49]

To add insult to injury, years of categorizing persons—married women, sex workers, men—as outside the parameters of justice means that even those who comprehend that they have experienced what is, or should be, a crime may not feel comfortable in reporting that crime to law enforcement. In fact, data regarding prosecutions of "false" claims show that the law has a record of penalizing some claimants for reporting crimes that later turned out to be true, doubly victimizing those who braved reporting sexual assaults. In this undefined and retributive context, it is understandable that—more than with other crimes—victims both under- and misreport sexual assaults.

Data regarding the crime of robbery show a comparable rate of false or baseless allegations.[50] Taszlitz identifies similarities between robbery and sexual assault:

> In the usual robbery case . . . the victim's identification of the defendant alone results in conviction. This is so even if the lighting conditions were poor and the time for observation brief. . . . Rarely is the robbery victim portrayed as deranged or a liar. But rape is different. With rape, the victim's truthfulness is almost always challenged: she is covering a pregnancy, hiding an affair, seeking revenge for advances spurned. Or the problem is her character: a slut, drug addict, "nut" case, or congenital liar.[51]

We don't often tweet about false complaints of muggings,[52] nor do we usually attribute to robbery victims a particular politics of respectability.

THE #UVAHOAX

As reports emerged identifying the *Rolling Stone* article as a fiction, commenters flocked to social media to defend the brothers of Phi Kappa Psi and to criticize flawed fact-checking by the magazine and its reporter. A torrent of comments, however, zeroed in on Jackie, interrogating the young woman's motivation for coming forward with what looked like yet another false rape claim. Many categorized the undergrad as mentally unstable, engaging pejorative terms like "psycho-liar," "batshit crazy," "nutter," "messed up," and a "fruit cake." On a conservative blog, a commenter classifies Jackie as one of a category—"*another* insane girl." A tweet observes, simply, "Bitches be crazy."

Neither this flurry of psychobiological explanations for female behavior nor the negative terms used to describe mental illness are particularly surprising. We have become, paradoxically, a society in which individuals increasingly seek psychological explanations for nearly every issue or concern. Puzzled by Donald Trump's victory in the 2016 election, liberal voters looked to pop-psychological phenomena—"gaslighting" and "confirmation bias." Yet, as a society we continue to treat those who are mentally ill with fear and disdain.[53]

As discussed previously, explanations of women's actions as predictably irrational or illogical are deeply rooted in "commonsense" ideas about the female sex as physically and emotionally fragile. Criminological researchers identify a tendency to attribute to women "expressive" or illogical aggression—a sudden letting go of pent-up anger—versus "instrumental" focus on plotting and planning crimes.[54] Men's commission of crimes is accepted as a "normal" aspect of society, but when women commit crimes it is deemed unusual or aberrant. Women's engagement in crime is primarily explained in terms of biological weakness or frailty ("bitches be crazy"); co-optation or seduction—women are pawns in a larger scheme; or categorizations of abnormality—women are "whores" or "bad mothers."[55] The idea that women would engage in so-called street crimes for reasons similar to men's—need, desire, conformity to social norms—is rarely part of the conversation.[56] We are surrounded by legal info-tainment that reinforces these "commonsense" myths. Shows like *Snapped*, for example, suggest that criminal behavior by women emerges more commonly out of a sudden, unpredictable rage than from logical, rational deliberation.

As biologically based assumptions inform discussions about female perpetrators, they also influence discussions about sexual assault complainants whom, for years, we have identified as having an almost organic drive to lie.[57] A conservative news reader attributes Cosby's accusers' claims to vengeance, invoking a well-known phrase, "[H]ell has no fury like a woman scorned." The same comment appears in the brief filed by Larry Nassar during his sentencing,[58] while a tweet observes of the alleged events at UVA, "Commonest reason for false rape accusations: revenge, same as for this false accusation . . . #UVAHoax." Conservative commentator Tomi Lahren offers some "final thoughts" on UVA after the lawsuits: "Cry rape. Get sued."

There is a *Simpsons* episode in which Homer is wrongfully accused of sexual harassment.[59] When his accuser, a feminist graduate student, appears on the news to discuss her claim, she apologizes for crying. Her interviewer's reaction is that her "tears say more than real evidence ever could."[60] There is often an assumption that women are "playing the victim," relying on biology to trigger a sympathetic response. A popular argument levied against allowing women in combat goes, when confronted with a wounded woman—even a wounded woman warrior—men cannot resist attempting to save her.[61] Recent research shows that judges and jurors' preconceived notions about gender may even impact their consideration of "hard" neuroscientific evidence, potentially causing them to treat some women with mental illness as more rather than less culpable for their crimes.[62]

Our distrust of the female biology is compounded by our recent romance with unreliable female narrators. We seem to be surrounded by mentally unstable, alcoholic, and less-than-truthful "girls"—*Sharp Ob-*

jects, Gone Girl, Girl on the Train, The Girl Before, An Anonymous Girl. Today's most popular shows and novels feature women who "swoon, hyperventilate and/or pathologically lie their way through . . . adventures."[63] Far from a riot grrrl persona, these contemporary, fragile butterflies, weakened by trauma, often find themselves easily manipulated by determined male perpetrators. Marketed as mysteries, the puzzle for readers of these books is less likely to be *Whodunit?* than *How truthful was she?* Whatever the answer, these fictional works tend to support the idea that women, as a category, rarely end up on the logical side of the Cartesian coin.

Like discussions of the Cosby accusers, comments about Jackie are divided between those dismissing her as silly or crazy and those that categorize her accusations as a shrewd attempt to game the legal system by "crying rape."

A commenter on a popular pop culture magazine site accuses Jackie of being out for the "$$$," while another calls her a "brat" who was "angry her parents couldn't afford for her to attend the more 'prestigious' Brown University." Another participant in a popular online community asks, "Why would a woman make up a rape accusation? Because of the attention she gets." That Jackie might be a mastermind of fake rape claims resonates on Twitter, where commenters label her a "fake rape con artist," "disgusting liar," a "fat lying bitch," and a "serial liar." On a mainstream news site, a comparison is drawn between Jackie and Rachel Dolezal, who gained notoriety as a white woman who for years assumed a Black identity: "It seems to me that this lady is *huckster* along the lines of that faux black woman who was really white. I feel sorry for the young man." *Rolling Stone,* which obviously had a vested interest in placing responsibility for the article fully on the student, took advantage of categorizations of Jackie as an attention-seeking "narcissist," categorizing the student in pleadings as "a really expert fabulist storyteller" who "managed to manipulate" the entire editorial process.[64] On a popular gossip site, a commenter assesses that

> [a] pretty high percentage of the rape cases covered by national media have liars. The reason is because the media is a fly light for narcissist attention seeking people. . . . whereas for most *real rape victims* the idea wouldn't cross their minds.

The unique power of the hashtag has meant that Jackie's accusations continue to resonate with the public more than four years after they have been revealed to be untrue. As suspicions began to surface regarding the accusations, #UVAHoax emerged as a way for interested commenters to follow rapidly unfolding legal developments. Engaging the hashtag in 2014 were comments like, "Is the femenazi . . . at UVA going to issue the fraternities an apology? Of course not, because they are men, and she hates them" and "#UVAHoax #RollingStone This is why we need #mens-rights to be talked about more. Women dont want equal rights, they want GOD rights."

Years later, #UVAHoax still appears as a way to suggest or signify the presence of false sexual assault allegations. A tweet referring to allegations of intimate partner violence against former White House staff secretary Rob Porter observes, "There's FemiNazis on record stating get every guy fired, even if you have to lie. By any means necessary. #dukelacrosse #tawanabrawley #UVARollingStones." Of allegations of child molestation against Alabama senatorial candidate Roy Moore, another tweet notes, "#LockHerUp another attention seeking pathological liar. I'm not sure why there are so many crazy women like that in the US #TawanaBrawley #DukeLacrosse #MattressGirl." In the eyes of many commenters, Jackie's story can be placed in a litany of similar situations:

> [T]he Jameis Winston fake rape where the woman had semen from three different men on her. Then the Ben Roethlisberger rape case where the victim emailed 13 of her friends bragging about the sex. I agree with the person below. Women lie.

Comments situating allegations at UVA in the midst of other, potentially similar instances of false allegations—the infamous Duke lacrosse team events, for example, or Tawana Brawley's claims that she experienced a racially motivated gang rape in the mid-1980s—bring to mind Felman's description of criminal complaints as evoking "legal memory" of events that, for the public, signify something greater than individual facts and circumstances.[65] In the public imagination, false rape accusations gradually become categorized as part of a long and familiar story rather than reflecting particular historical times or specific circumstances.

Today, #UVAHoax is an effective, shorthand way to mobilize a litany of fears, not only about false rape claims but about a widespread institutional failure to provide due process. When in 2016 a Yale basketball captain was expelled from the university after having been accused of sexual assault,[66] a commenter noted, "#UVAHoax #Yale He said, She said. Smells." When reporter Michelle Fields alleged that she had been assaulted by Donald Trump's campaign manager, Corey Lewandowski, tweets reacted that "#MichelleFields was assaulted in exactly the same way the #UVAHoax giel was raped: In her Imagination." On Twitter, in addition to dismissing claims against Roy Moore and Rob Porter, #UVAHoax is invoked in critiquing allegations by pop singer Kesha, game designer Anita Sarkeesian, and the woman who accused hockey player Patrick Kane.

In 2019, the state of Virginia was rocked by revelations that Governor Ralph Northam had included a racist photo on his medical school yearbook page.[67] Soon after the story broke, two women came forward to accuse the next person in line for governor, Justin Fairfax, of having committed sexual assault. In discussing one of the women on Twitter, there are references to UVA—and to Jackie:

> She is risking nothing. She gains notoriety, and is in a field where allegations will be believed, whether true or not, whether substantiated or not. She becomes a martyr if not believed and will secure professional accolades for her bravery! #JustinFairfax #UVAHoax.

Via one hashtag, sets of interconnected comments collaborate to transform an individual accuser from a full-fledged person into a stereotype. The accuser is no longer one person who lied but one of many liars conflating a series of events with distinct facts and circumstances. When, in the midst of mounting accusations against Bill Cosby, Jackie's story was revealed as false, Zara Kessler, a journalist following the case wrote that Cosby's future would no doubt be impacted by Jackie's retraction. Kessler described, "Every . . . accuser is a potential 'Jackie'—although we don't yet know precisely what it means to be a 'Jackie.'"[68]

PRETTY LITTLE LIARS

Jackie is not the first sexual assault accuser in recent memory to have been discovered to have lied about all or part of an alleged incident. In 1989, the name Tawana Brawley entered the vernacular when the fifteen-year-old alleged she had been kidnapped and raped by a group of white men, who then left her naked, in a garbage bag, her body covered in feces-scrawled racial slurs.[69] Championed by civil rights activist Al Sharpton, Brawley's accusations later were ascertained to have been exaggerated if not wholly made up. On social media, Brawley's name is synonymous with the specter of false rape allegations. A recent post on the Cosby allegations asks, for example,

> What is to prevent a woman from totally ruining a man's life and career by making false allegations against him? No evidence? No witnesses. . . . YES, there are MANY women who LIE about abuse. . . . Tawana Brawley, anyone???

A more recent example of a claim some on social media regard as dubious is that of Columbia University student Emma Sulkowicz. Sulkowicz became a subject of debate when, after allegedly having been sexually assaulted by a fellow student, they carried their mattress to class and campus events for an entire year as part of a senior thesis entitled "Carry That Weight."[70] Although Sulkowicz's name may be unfamiliar, you may recognize their continued relevance on social media via #mattressgirl, a hashtag that, like #UVAHoax, is invoked in connection with incidents of questionable rape claims. Around the time of the 2013 incident, posters were hung up in the neighborhood around the campus featuring Sulkowicz's photo with the tag line "Pretty Little Liar."[71]

While Bill Cosby's behavior with Andrea Constand represents an area in which a clear criminal assault—the penetration of an unconscious victim who was unable to consent—is vernacularized as a "gray area," the assault allegedly experienced by Emma Sulkowicz arguably demonstrates something different—a "gray area" encounter that, across the internet, is dismissed as not criminal. In Sulkowicz's description, the assault was a challenging one to prosecute—a consensual encounter that midway turned nonconsensual, with the alleged perpetrator ignoring pleas to stop, then holding Sulkowicz down and anally penetrating them.[72] A recent project by Sulkowicz, *Ceci N'est Pas Un Viol* (*This is not a rape*) encourages visitors to watch several videos of the encounter and then to weigh in on a reenactment of their alleged assault in a comments section, answering tough questions including, "Do you think I am the perfect victim?"[73]

What does it mean to be a Jackie or a Tawana or a #mattressgirl? First and foremost it means that an accuser has been severed from their individual experiences. In the case of Jackie, as well as with Sulkowicz and Brawley, over time, a person who told a lie is discursively transformed into a liar and whatever misrepresentations they may have made are transformed into part of a deliberate hoax. Of all persons to gain this infamous status, one of the most recognizable is Crystal Mangum, whose accusations have a continuing life online via #dukelacrosse. A journalist writes,

> The outcome, for Mangum, is not just that she is seen as a liar, but something worse: She is "The Liar." You don't need to know her story because you know *of* her, of what she represents. Today, someone need only say the word "Duke" in a discussion about sexual violence and for all listening it invokes the specter of a false accuser who cries rape and ruins the lives of innocent men.[74]

And what of the accusers? Mangum, who continues to maintain she was assaulted in 2006, refers to herself as "broken" and her family "torn apart."[75] The extent to which Brawley's name is maligned across the internet has led Brawley herself to change her name.[76]

In the aftermath of sexual assault allegations, there is a contest to frame events—and the winner is almost invariably the party with the most resources. After the Duke Lacrosse allegations, the university engaged in an extensive public relations effort designed to present both the players and the institution itself as "victims of a rogue prosecutor." This stance, which positioned the accused and the institution as "innocent," ignored that the alleged assault had occurred in the context of what was undeniably a less-than-savory situation, a university team—mostly underage students—had hired strippers to perform at a party where drinking was involved.[77] The protestations by the institution importantly overlooked the role that this type of sexual objectification plays in the larger construct of violence.[78]

Lucinda Finley describes the harms that occur when we discursively remove accusers from their personal experiences,

> The grand jury's conclusion . . . that Tawana Brawley was not the victim of a criminal sexual assault by four white men has shaped people's understanding that "nothing happened." The legal pronouncement is deemed definitive of what happened. Few stop to think that when a young black woman in a racist society is found in a garbage bag after having been reported as missing for several days, dazed, her naked body smeared with racial slurs written in feces, "nothing" is not what happened.[79]

Finley's caution against making a leap to judgment in regard to Tawana Brawley remains salient today. As described in the previous chapters, our legal system is built on dichotomies—*martyr* or *gold digger, altruism* or *compensation*, and *victim* or *liar*. Sometimes, however, the liar also is a victim.

Jackie herself still does not admit to manufacturing claims but rather describes that she was suffering from PTSD at the time she was "pressured" by Sabrina Erdely to share her story.[80] As to the details of an assault, she says she can't remember. [81] In labeling Jackie an expert fabulist, this very different story about a troubled young woman pressured to report a gang rape is pushed into the background.

As activists did in the case of Tawana Brawley, women's rights advocates sought to engage Jackie's allegations as a vehicle to identify and address harmful rape culture on college campuses. Ultimately, however, in the court of public opinion there is a focus on incidents as having "happened" or "not happened"—on claims as true or false. As Finley observes, in this race to judgment, not only is personal trauma obscured but the stories of those who "saw in the event the need to express outrage, either will never be heard, or can now [also] be dismissed as 'not true.'"[82]

Just as the idea of the gold digger resonates, fueled by centuries of "commonsense" recognition that women tend to be either manipulative bitches or flighty, irresponsible consumers, the ease with which we brand women "liars" is rooted in biological assumptions that are easily activated in online conversations. Today, #UVAHoax has become but one in a parade of horribles, and Jackie herself a living cautionary tale not only for survivors contemplating coming forward but for all women espousing points of view that potentially challenge the status quo.

"CROOKED" HILLARY

Donald Trump's presidential campaign was notable for its visible slogan "Make America Great Again." In the background, however, the campaign was engaged in an equally—and arguably more successful—initiative that sought to define itself by denigrating its opponent. The most expedient way to accomplish this objective was to brand Hillary Clinton an iconic liar. At rallies throughout the United States, Trump supporters chanted "lock her up," waving posters featuring Hillary Clinton behind bars or in a black-and-white jumpsuit.[83] The hashtag, #crookedhillary, trended on Twitter.[84]

Clinton's personal and career trajectories were not free from legitimate critiques about integrity. Her husband's presidency was clouded by scandals including Whitewater,[85] and his terms in office were plagued by the discovery of his extramarital affair with intern Monica Lewinsky—an affair that, due to the significant power imbalance, is a stretch to call consensual. During and after her tenure as secretary of state, Hillary Clinton, too, was critiqued for using her private email for classified correspondence and for her response to an attack on a U.S. mission in Benghazi, Libya.[86]

Whether or not the conservative framing of Clinton as "crooked Hillary" was based in the candidate's actions, it was facilitated by the "commonsense" familiarity of many of the criticisms launched against the candidate. Susan Bordo describes how a role reversal was accomplished during the 2016 election, as would-be Democratic candidate Bernie Sanders was discursively formed as a champion of social justice and Clinton—who in her career had strongly advocated for universal healthcare, paid childcare, and paid sick leave—was constructed as the "establishment" candidate, benefiting from elite connections to organizations like Goldman Sachs.[87] Bordo describes a "bitter irony" that the male candidate, Sanders, was so easily constructed as "the heart" and Clinton "the head."[88]

Via numerous insulting tweets by President Trump and other conservatives, 2020 presidential candidate Elizabeth Warren, who exaggerated her Native American ancestry, similarly is being politically reenvisioned from a well-intended person who, based on romanticized family lore, misstated her minority heritage into an endemically untruthful plotter who deliberately misrepresented her minority status to gain an unfair economic and political advantage.[89] The president's repeated, dismissive labeling of Warren as "Pocahontas" is significant, in one fell swoop denigrating the bravery of one of very few indigenous female heroes and emphasizing the ways in which Warren herself does not embody these heroic traits.

Chapter 2 engaged how, in the aftermath of sexual assault allegations, powerful men defend themselves by claiming that they are the true "victims," blameless martyrs targeted by women who are intrinsically driven to extort and manipulate. Similarly, when men—cisgender, heterosexual men—lie, their missteps are tied to *human* frailties—pride, perhaps, or ambition. The suggestion that a woman has been less than truthful, however, is readily transformed to signify a chronic and biological lack of honesty. The suggestion that Clinton or Warren is an opportunistic liar resonates because, as we have been told for centuries, women lie. These discourses attributing to Clinton a unique power to manipulate, and resituating her not as an outsider but as possessing the upper hand in the Cartesian divide, are familiar because they have been engaged successfully for centuries to undercut the arguments of women attempting to gain access to, or benefit from, institutional processes formerly reserved for men. Deeply entrenched assumptions tying women's behavior to their character make it easier in the context of female candidates to transform one bad judgment into a "hoax" and a single, untruthful instance into a pattern of predictable behavior of yet another lying woman.

As discussed in chapters 1 and 2, a prevalent feature of social media discussions about sexual assault allegations is that, often, comments purporting to offer "facts" about claimants—that an accuser waited to report an assault, for example, or that they filed a civil lawsuit—are in reality thinly cloaked efforts to cast aspersions on victims' character. The failure to report an alleged crime to the police or the proactive step of filing a civil suit is deemed determinative of fabricated accusations or of greed or a thirst for fame. A lack of bruising or trauma is interpreted as proof that an event must have been a "bad date" or "hook up" on the "casting couch" rather than a real and "brutal" rape. It's a song we may not like but we are drawn to dance to it anyway because we've heard it so many times before.

Unsurprisingly, a comment on a popular, conservative blog implies a connection between the UVA allegations and the Clinton campaign, "The same people defending the fabulist Jackie . . . must have a crossover with those defending/supporting the fabulist Hillary Clinton. . . . They both tell lies upon lies and expect you to believe fantastical stories that any normal person can see right through."[90] Tweets abound engaging #UVA-Hoax in the context of Election 2016, with commenters noting, "Hillary Clinton is the most corrupt woman in US history. #Hillarhoid #UVAHoax and "Vote for Hillary! Four more years of . . . #UVAHoax rape hoaxes." Another Daily Caller commenter observes of Hillary:

> But she's a woman and must be believed. Just ask Monica Lewinsky's Boyfriend's Wife. Unless, of course, it's William Jefferson Blythe Clinton doing the raping in which case all women are nothing but worthless c*nts to her. Oh, the next six months are going to be SO much fun.[91]

The situating of Hillary Clinton—the first female presidential candidate, one of just three female secretaries of state, and one of a significant minority of female senators—as uniquely politically empowered echoes fifteenth-century characterizations by Sir Matthew Hale of wives—deprived of owning property in their own names by law—as singularly able to craftily extort their husbands' fortunes. As Leigh Gilmore characterizes, mainstream media portrayed Clinton as "sinister,"

> [t]he words "email," "lying" and "woman" fell like a series of dominoes. Adding "nothing to investigate" to the string of words never mattered. The deep emotion was tapped: You cannot trust women with power.[92]

In other words, Hillary Clinton had a Jackie problem. Once the candidate was situated as one of a gendered group of liars, the task of the Trump campaign was easy. By association, not only was Clinton herself greedy and unreliable, she was supported by a groundswell of women who, *en masse*, were engaging their unique, biological characteristics to effect dangerous social change. Led by representatives like Gloria Allred, a hallmark of these groups of women is that they are looked upon as having a unique ability to manipulate the law in their favor.

In fall 2018, sexual assault claims yet again were at the forefront of public discussion as the country was riveted by allegations that Supreme Court nominee Brett Kavanaugh had attempted to sexually assault Professor Christine Blasey Ford during a party they both attended while in high school.[93] Ford's accusation first surfaced in September of 2018, immediately prior to the Senate vote on Kavanaugh's confirmation.[94] In late September, Kavanaugh and Ford both testified before the Senate Judiciary Committee in what was described by the *New York Times* as a "duel" in which "two very different versions of the truth, unfolding in the heated atmosphere of gender divides, #MeToo and the Trump presidency, could not be reconciled."[95] Although in the end Kavanaugh narrowly was confirmed by a 50–48 vote, largely split along party lines, a statement by senator Jeff Flake summed up the reaction of moderates on both sides: "There is doubt . . . We'll never move beyond that."

Part 2 of this book focuses on the accused, exploring the ways in which today's socially mediated world brings increasing threats to due process and sometimes noncompensable injury to the reputation of parties who have not been found guilty in a court of law. These next chapters address the potential impact of Ford's allegations on Kavanaugh himself, as he undertakes a position predicated on fairness and neutrality, and on public perceptions of the court as an institution. For the moment, however, I would like to explore this characterization of a Senate confirmation hearing as a "duel" not just between rivals across the political aisle, but across the gender divide.

Although his comments were relatively measured prior to Justice Kavanaugh's confirmation, afterward the president was quick to categorize Kavanaugh as "a man that was caught up in a hoax that was set up by the Democrats" and Ford as telling a story that was "all made up—it was fabricated, and it's a disgrace."[96] Exhibiting both a lack of empathy and confusion about the interrelationship between trauma and memory, the president mocked Ford's testimony,

> How did you get home? I don't remember. How'd you get there? I don't remember. Where is the place? I don't remember. How many years ago was it? I don't know. I don't know. I don't know. I don't know. What neighborhood was it in? I don't know. Where's the house? I don't know. Upstairs, downstairs, where was it? I don't know. . . . But I had one beer. That's the only thing I remember.[97]

He categorized Ford's accusations as part of a "con game."[98]

On Twitter, Ford's accusations likewise are situated as part of an orchestrated plot with varying objectives: to bring down the president, to promote a liberal agenda, to create a crisis of gender. Perhaps eager to deflect from his own questionable status in the spotlight, as Oscar season approached, Donald Trump Jr. tweeted a meme showing Blasey Ford, Nathan Phillips, a Native American activist who had been involved in a recent confrontation with Catholic youth during a right-to-life protest, and Jussie Smollett as nominees in a new category: "Best Performance in a Politically Motivated Hate Crime Hoax."[99] Other tweets compare Dr. Ford to other, paradigmatic liars, describing the professor as "less credible than Crystal Gail Mangum in the Duke Rape Hoax" and her actions as "the biggest hoax since Al Sharpton and Tawana Brawley," actions for which the "Democrats . . . recruited her and groomed her."

As occurred with Jackie and with Crystal Mangum and Tawana Brawley before, a notable characteristic of social media comments critical of Christine Blasey Ford is the extent to which they discount the accuser's own story in order to situate accusations within a larger, often polarized, structure. In Donald Trump Jr.'s characterization, a well-regarded professor making truthful, if potentially unfounded or mistaken, allegations about what she experienced as a young woman is rhetorically transformed into not only a crime but a "hate crime."

That Christine Blasey Ford came forward with allegations under the explicit condition that they remain confidential suggests that she was aware not only of the firestorm the accusations would ignite but the personal price she would pay as an accuser of a prominent political figure. The duel metaphor engaged by the *Times* has turned out to be appropriate; not only Ford's allegations but her person continue to be polarizing. Ford's family fled their home for months due to the number and severity of death threats she received after her testimony.[100]

In late October of 2018 shortly after Justice Kavanaugh's confirmation, a number of Democratic leaders were targeted with bomb threats and suspicious packages.[101] The wave of threats was condemned by conservative conspiracy theorists as a "false flag" attempt by Democrats to grab attention in the wake of unsuccessful hearings.[102] Not surprisingly, some commenters view both the bomb threats and Ford's accusations as part of a larger plot—as the president described, a "con game"—to unseat Republican lawmakers. Others, however, take the rhetoric a step farther, disturbingly comparing Ford not to the targets of suspicious packages but to the bomb itself. "Ford was just a human hoax device," one person tweets, while another remarks, "Last time liberals planted a bomb was Dr. Christine Ford." A third commenter observes, "Dr. Christine Blasey Ford went from being a very fine woman to being an evil hoax."

Perhaps the transformation of the person of Ford herself into a bomb should not be shocking; after all, women's biology has long been deemed to render their actions unpredictable, volatile, and threatening to the status quo. Allegations that women are "crying rape" as part of a con game not only devalue the claims of individuals, they situate an interpersonal issue into the framework of a larger plan or conspiracy. Notably, although some view her as a mastermind or an "expert fabulist," others on social media characterize Jackie as a "girl," overwhelmed by college life and a natural foil for those with an agenda. These constructions of Jackie evoke our legal memory of other, lying girls.[103] Rather than focusing on deterring rape, we have become a society obsessed with deterring liars.

LOCK THEM UP

A video posted on YouTube by men's rights activist TJ Kirk entitled "Feminism & Rape: Belief without Evidence" has over three hundred fifty thousand views and five thousand comments.[104] The bulk of these recommend harsh penalties for accusers who make untruthful allegations of rape. A commenter notes, "As men we need to advocate harsher punishment for people who falsely accuse. That's a way to stop them from happening," while another person writes that "[J]ackie should be put in prison." A third chimes in, "I love the ideas in the comments about false accusers being given jail time and or suit/fines and being put on a list of 'false accusers' . . . There needs to be some real consequences to falsely accusing someone of such a horrendous crime." Someone else suggests that the criminal trial process should be adjusted to reflect more of a search for truth than the current, constitutional reasonable doubt standard: "New System . . . [W]e Get Both Parties Stories if they correlate the Accused goes to Jail if they don't the Accuser Goes to Jail."

A notable undercurrent is the extent to which social network participants would like to see those who make false accusations face severe and sometimes creative sanctions. Some suggest relatively moderate censure for Jackie, demanding the student issue a formal apology or dismissing her from the university. Others suggest that civil law should be engaged to discipline the accuser. Tweets, for example, make observations such as "I hope Phi Kappa Psi sues . . . 'Jackie' for libel"; "I hope Jackie gets the most severe libel lawsuit possible"; and "[C]an every man in every frat sue UVA for slander?" Another asks, "How did the frat make out. They should get at least $80 million. And a new house."

Many, however, craft inventive punishments for false accusers. A YouTube comment suggests that "[f]alse rape accusers must work to pay the damages to those they have falsely accused. Twenty years in a rock quarry ought to do it. Feminists always beg for a man's job anyways." A commenter on a popular general news site suggests, "This young woman made false allegations that seriously damaged innocent people. That's a crime. She should be prosecuted and everything about that should be public record." Another agrees, suggesting that "the women who knowingly bring false rape claims [should be] given the exact same punishment that would've been handed down to their alleged rapist. This same treatment should apply to anyone who knowingly brings a false claim against another person." Another comment similarly notes that "'Jackie' needs to be placed in a nice treatment program for at least 18 months. That's the duration for sex-offender treatment programs in prison." On a feminist site, a comment emphasizes the significance of proportionality,

> My point is that the punishment or penalty for a given offense should scale proportionally to the harm done by the offense. Thus, not all false rape accusations are equal, and so should not be subject to the same penalties. Within the spectrum of harm caused by false rape accusations, the harm caused by "Jackie's" probably false accusation is not deserving of the same reprisal as a false accusation that affirmatively ruins someone's reputation and derails their life in meaningful and significant ways, such as to the degree of harm, humiliation, and derailment to which the Duke lacrosse players were subject.

Identifying the value of social media organizing, a participant in a popular online community suggests a "letter-writing campaign to the district attorney" to "ask for charges to be pressed."

Although some suggest that law as an institution mete out justice for false claims, it is not uncommon for comments to suggest extralegal and often violent punishments. A particularly incensed tweet recommends, "[I]ts time to hunt '#Jackie' down and bring the lying bitch to justice." Others suggest that the penalty for lying about rape should be rape: "I am a male and I want that bitch [Jackie] hammered. The males are scarred. Nail that cunt HARD!!!!!!!!!!!!!!!!" Another writes, "I hope one of the feminazis from NOW get raped and no one believe her thanks to all the rape hoaxes."

Similar comments reverberate across sites discussing sexual assault allegations from Cosby to Weinstein. A tweet notes of Jameis Winston's accuser, for example, "[B]itches that cry rape when they didn't get raped shudd get charged n same sentencing as a rapist imo." Another writes, "If it is found that she purposely made a false allegation of rape, she needs to go to prison for TWICE as long as [Winston would have]." Another person recommends a more intimate solution, "[Winston] should find that bitch who tried to put fake rape charges on him and spit on her." Tweets are particularly menacing in the context of hockey player Patrick Kane's accuser, one decrying, "Hope you get hung bitch" and another observing that the accuser "needs be gangbanged." There is a strong belief among commenters that deterrence is best effected via harsh punishments, for example, of Erica Kinsman a tweet notes, "The girl needs to be charged with falsifying a report" so that others will know that "[r]ape isn't a joke or a meal ticket."

A significant concern raised by commenters is that, if claimants like Jackie are not punished, other accusers will be incentivized to bring false rape allegations. A popular meme featuring a photo of Jackie reads, "Why not Lie About Rape? There's No Penalty If You Do." A tweet asks, "Where's deterrence for the next Jackie?" And a blogger pleads, "Sane peoples of the western world, it is time to set a precedent on false rape allegations!"[105] Similar to the commenter alleging that, in accusing Bill Cosby, Andrea Constand is committing "feminist rape," a commenter on a video-sharing site proclaims of reporter Sabrina Erdely, who broke the Jackie story, "You've just committed 'Fact Rape.' A new form of hate crime." A tweet about Christine Blasey Ford critiques the admonition that we should #believeallwomen, observing, "It's been estimated that as many as 40% of rape allegations are false. That's a very awful statistic. Maybe we should punish the liars? If, Ford lied, what will happen to her? Nothing. But, #Kavanaugh's life can never be fixed."

The vehemence with which online commenters weigh in on the consequences due to Jackie and other false accusers supports that, once a rape accusation becomes public, an accuser's body no longer just belongs to her. What should happen to the accuser—and her body—become matters appropriate for public debate. As described in the introduction, via media discussions, celebrity bodies become public bodies—blank slates onto which societal debates and anxieties are projected.[106] Historically, women's bodies also have been political bodies, legal claimants like Norma McCorvey (better known as "Jane Roe" in the *Roe v. Wade* case) or "Baby M" (the child at the center of a custody battle between a surrogate mother and a biological father), for example, becoming a focus for discussions about reproductive rights and freedoms. As they are constructed and reconstructed in the public imagination, the individual bodies of sexual assault complainants become public battlegrounds. The anger against false claimants is palpable because the political stakes are very high.

Evidenced by #dukelacrosse, #tawanabrawley, and #UVAHoax, not only do sexual assault accusers become the focus of social and political concerns, their claims—more accurately, the presumed falsity of their claims—contribute to a body of "evidence" that women, as a category, are unreliable.

THE POLITICS OF REPRESENTATION

In 2015, *Law & Order: SVU* aired an episode entitled "Devastating Story."[107] The hour-long narrative—nestled in a season that also "ripped from the headlines" scenarios based on Gamergate and the Cosby accusations—bore many similarities to Jackie's case, focusing on the allegations of a young, female student at fictitious Hudson University who alleges she has been raped by four fraternity brothers.

In fact, not one but multiple devastating stories are revealed during the episode. At first, the viewer is drawn in by a red herring. Caught up in the victim-empathetic plot line that is a hallmark of the series, the viewer first assumes that the devastation befalls the victim herself. As the narrative arc unfolds, however, we come to appreciate that the accuser's story has harsh consequences for many others at Hudson. The episode concludes with the discovery that the student's allegations were made up, a fairytale masterminded by an eager, feminist professor who sought to further a feminist agenda—and her scholarly career—by exposing Hudson University as a "rape factory." The "reveal" is that devastation is reserved for the accused, young men now branded "rapists" for life.

The greatest devastation, however, belongs to those victims yet to come—the yet-to-be, "legitimate" rape claimants for whom, seasoned detective Olivia Benson mournfully observes, this case has "set the clock back thirty years."[108] This, perhaps, is the most tragic consequence of all—that the accuser's lies have not only wreaked interpersonal havoc but, in one swoop, have also unraveled a third of a century of hard-fought feminist criminal justice reforms.

Like Detective Benson, online comments about Jackie bemoan the impact the revelation of her false claims will have on future claimants. A tweet remarks, "I want to cry. First #DukeLacrosse Team #fuckup & now #RollingStone's #Jackie story fuck up. #Rape victims are doomed." An undercurrent across websites, both liberal and conservative, is that, in reporting a "fake rape," Jackie has made it worse for other, "real" victims. A commenter on a conservative blog writes, "Faking a rape is disgusting when you consider the effect it has on real rape cases when the deception is discovered." Another observes, "So now false accusations are the norm." A *New York Times* opinion piece regarding the #MeToo movement waxes poetic,

> Maybe it will happen tomorrow or maybe next week or maybe next month. But the Duke lacrosse moment, the Rolling Stone moment, will come. A woman's accusation will turn out to be grossly exaggerated or flatly untrue. And if the governing principle of this movement is still an article of faith, many people will lose their religion. They will tear down all accusers as false prophets. And we will go back to a status quo in which the word of the Angelos is more sacred than the word of the Isabellas. There are limits to relying on "believe all women" as an organizing political principle. We are already starting to see them.[109]

In 2014, the *Atlantic* magazine featured a piece arguing that "the episode [at UVA] [was] terrible news for survivors of rape," explaining that "The next time another Jackie comes forward—even if she is completely honest and has no preconditions—there might not be another national magazine reporter willing to listen."[110]

There is a widespread concern spanning liberal and conservative quarters that, in supporting a false claimant like Jackie, feminist advocates create a situation in which subsequent, real rape victims will not be believed. A major news reader observes, "What i find most disgusting is there are women out there that have been REALLY raped and because of idiots like this it forces people to question the victims because of so many girls who have cried wolf." On a video broadcasting site, there is a complaint that feminists do not care as much about "#Yazdi sex slavery" as about "fake 'Jackie.'" On another forum, a poster observes, "Stupid attention seeking hoes ruining it for the real rape victim." Some, echoing Olivia Benson, request that the accuser "apologize to every single rape victim ever for raising the height of the mountain she'll have to climb to convince people to take her accusations seriously." As one poster in an online community responds, "I like that you mentioned that it makes it harder for real victims. There ARE real victims of rape out there, but they don't show boat after."

Mark Krikorian tweeted about Jackie for the *National Review*, "Every 'outrage' story must now be assumed a hoax until proven otherwise."[111] While another Twitter user created a "poem,"

> Sabrina & Jackie sitting in a tree
> F A N T A S I Z I N G
> First comes lies
> Then comes libel
> Next comes fraternities with litigation

Integral to many posts is the idea of role reversal discussed in the previous chapter—that, in making false accusations, the accuser has become the assailant, and the alleged perpetrator, the target. As one person notes in a popular online community, "We are in the midst of a 'moral panic' about rape, much like the moral panic about child abuse and devil worship in the 1980s." Another notes, "[T]he actual victims in this case were the guys who had their fraternity shut down, their reputations trashed, their lives disrupted and were basically subjected to mob justice." As, the tweet above describes of Supreme Court justice Brett Kavanaugh, now appointed to one of the most impressive posts in the U.S. government—and one of only nine accompanied by lifetime tenure—"[his] life can never be fixed."

CONCLUSION

When they make allegations, sexual assault accusers face a Jackie problem. Their story adds to three centuries of discourse, social and legal, that have situated women as legal outsiders and described them as emotionally driven and biologically determined liars that are easily co-opted for nefarious purposes. On social media, sexist stereotypes operate as evidence, the court of public opinion taking judicial notice of commonsense ideas like "bitches lie."

In addition to the revelation that the protagonist herself has lied, a key revelation in the "Devastating Story" *SVU* episode is that she was persuaded to do so by a fame-seeking feminist professor. Many on social media similarly see Jackie's actions as motivated by a larger, feminist agenda. An aggrieved commenter on a popular celebrity gossip site notes that "[t]he radical feminist viewpoint is the norm in America and in law enforcement." Others invoke phrases such as "feminazi" or "fauxminism" to describe claims of sexual assault, furthering the idea that *real* harms are being ignored or obscured as focus turns toward what is perceived to be another false narrative.

The engagement of the term "hoax" to describe Jackie's accusations and subsequent publication of the *Rolling Stone* article supports this idea that false claimants are often pawns in larger gender wars. Unlike the relatively neutral legal descriptor of an "unsubstantiated claim," a hoax implies a *deliberately* crafted deception. To effect a hoax is to exercise agency in plotting and planning toward a particular end objective, usually fooling the targeted party. Critiques by *Rolling Stone* itself add fuel to the fire, deflecting criticism of the magazine and its employees by labeling Jackie "a really expert fabulist storyteller" who "managed to manipulate" the entire editorial process. A *National Review* article critiquing Jackie's allegations describes them as part of a "feminist catechism that 'all women must be believed.'"[112]

In response to a popular news article urging that we "generally believe" rape claims, commenters write that "feminists really want females to hold all the power in society" and that "[r]ape allegations are the witch hunts of our day." A poster on a major news site writes that "[a]ll these left wing organizations conspire with government agencies and private industries to push a radical agenda," with another noting, "NOW should be dissolved and the leaders fined hefty fines." On a conservative blog, a commenter observes,

> In asserting that women who claim assault should always be taken at their word they leave no other standing for the accused man but to be disbelieved. This inverts the process of justice, innocent untill proven guilty.

As discussed in the previous chapters, sexual assault trials have indeed been an "inverted" process; however, the most problematic part of the system has been that the perpetrator's guilt is determined via focus on the victim. Comments like the one above resemble Friedman's idea of the funhouse mirror; they turn the feminist critique of the law on its head.

As a society, we increasingly have become entranced by girl heroes. In 2012, after being wounded in an attempt to attend school in Afghanistan, Malala Yousafzai became an international symbol of women's oppression and resilience.[113] Since the incident, Malala has become a globally sought-after proponent of women's rights, and her fund has raised billions to support young women's education on a worldwide basis. In 2017, on Wall Street, artist Kristen Visbal's *Fearless Girl* bronze statue quickly became iconic, staring down Arturo Di Modica's *Charging Bull*, presenting not only a literal challenge but a figurative one to the old boys' network and patriarchy.[114] Nike's popular "girl effect" and "play like a girl" campaigns laud powerful strong young women.[115]

On social networks, however, the term "girl" often signifies something short of empowerment. Rather than self-possessed, in social media comments, Jackie more closely resembles the unreliable "girl" narrator imagined by writers of fiction than the powerful "fearless girl." Like the "Devastating Story" *SVU* episode, in the view of many online commenters, Jackie has been co-opted, recruited in favor of a larger feminist agenda that threatens the status quo.

Jackie is not alone in this dubious "girl narrator" category. She is recognizable among legions of unreliable young rape claimants, including Tawana Brawley, Crystal Mangum and, more recently, Lena Dunham and Emma Sulkowicz (the "mattress girl"). Each of these people has a different story about an alleged sexual assault to share, their claims shaped by both similar and distinct societal factors and circumstances. On social media, however, they all suffer from the Jackie problem—their unique circumstances overshadowed by fear of a feminist agenda to co-opt the law—and the presumption that women have a gendered, biologically based predisposition to lie about sexual assault.

Like the "funhouse mirror," online comments using #UVAHoax effect a narrative shift, reframing one person who lied about crime into one of an army of women "crying rape." So defined, the accuser faces a politics of representation, now accountable to any other alleged victim who may come forward in the future. A single lie is seen to cast aspersions on the truthfulness of not one woman but all women.

In repeatedly using labels like "hoax" to describe instances of false rape allegations, the claims of feminist advocates are juxtaposed with the traditional liberal ideal of due process and fairness for defendants. The outcome is that the legal system itself is viewed as untrustworthy and subject to manipulation. As a commenter on a conservative blog writes, describing male targets of rape cases, "There is justice and the system, those of us out of the system will never get justice, just abuse."

Like the conversations attributing a particular type of "bottom power" to gold diggers, the narrative repetition of hordes of women seeking to come after unwitting young men is a deliberate reframing of power that transforms those least disadvantaged into the victims in a given situation. On a major news site, for example, a reader observes that

> [f]alse rape accusations . . . serve a very real purpose. It helps young men know that whenever it's their word against a woman's word, they will be demonized and treated like a damned liar. This comes in handy if the young men eventually get divorced and get slapped with restraining orders and accusations of child abuse as a custody strategy. They'll already be aware that defending themselves is futile.

As Matthew Hale's opinions attest, the idea that law is malleable in the hands of devious female accusers is nothing new. However, social media did not exist when public debates took place about the rulings of Lord Hale or even about the veracity of rape allegations against Mike Tyson or Kobe Bryant. When accusations were made against Tyson and Bryant, the public debated whether accusers were lying on coffee breaks or around the dinner table. After Jackie's accusations were revealed to be false, Twitter trolls threatened to "dox" the student, revealing her full name and address to the millions across the online world.[116] The viciousness with which even suspected liars are treated may not only create personal dangers but is likely to further chill reporting of sexual assault except in the most egregious cases.

The myth of false claimants is one of the most powerful rape myths operating today, not because false claims do not occur but because lying is so often the default presumption. As Adichie observes of stereotypes, "the problem . . . is not that they are untrue, but that they are incomplete. They make one story become the only story."[117] When it comes to high-profile sexual assault accusations, more often than not, the fear of false claims is the primary story, the dominant narrative. When it is discovered that a claimant like Jackie has not been truthful in her accusations, the public response is not surprise but recognition.

Over time, criminal cases become recognized less for their facts than for the ideas they represent. As social media commenters consider the alleged incidents at UVA and their aftermath, the accusations are placed in the context of other alleged incidents, such as #dukelacrosse. The accuser is transformed into one of a series of dishonest and deauthorized female complainants. Today, there is an assumption that women are not only lying about rape for personal gain—a "meal ticket"—but also as part of a larger conspiracy to effect the "end of men." To blame a decline in (white, middle-class) male political power on women as a group ignores the larger global and structural factors at work in such an exchange.

The significance of the myth of false claims is not that such claims do not exist but that their existence is so readily politicized, casting aspersions on accusers not only as individuals but as members of a category of dishonest women. Our eagerness to categorize sexual assault claims as absolutely true or absolutely false signals that, for the majority of us, it is more comfortable to approach the world in terms of dichotomies: innocence and guilt, truth and lies. Our insistence on finding the truth of sexual assault allegations has a significant impact on accusers. In addition, as I discuss in the next few chapters, it also significantly impacts the discursive construction of—and real effects on—perpetrators.

NOTES

1. Adapted and reprinted in part with permission from Honest Victim Scripting in the Twitterverse. 22 William and Mary Journal of Women and the Law 495 (2016). © 2016 William and Mary Journal of Women and the Law.

2. Sabrina R. Erdely, "A Rape on Campus: A Brutal Assault and Struggle for Justice at UVA," *Rolling Stone*, November 19, 2014, http://web.archive.org/web/20141119200349/http://www.rollingstone.com/culture/features/a-rape-on-campus-20141119 (retracted April 5, 2015); "Eramo vs. Rolling Stone Complaint" in *Washington Post*, May 12, 2015, https://www.washingtonpost.com/apps/g/page/local/eramo-vs-rolling-stone-complaint/1692/.

3. Less often recalled than the Jackie story is that, just a few months before the publication of the *Rolling Stone* article, a young woman, Hannah Graham, had been murdered while beginning her sophomore year at UVA. Sarah Ellison, "After A Rape Story, A Murder, and Lawsuits: What's Next for the University of Virginia?," *Vanity Fair*, September 9, 2015, http://www.vanityfair.com/news/2015/09/university-of-virginia-most-horrible-year.

4. Julia Horowitz, "Why We Believed Jackie's Rape Story," *Politico*, December 6, 2014, http://www.politico.com/magazine/story/2014/12/why-we-believed-jackies-story-113365#ixzz4Eri8kjhC.

5. Erik Wemple, "The Full Demise of Rolling Stone's Rape Story," *Washington Post*, December 11, 2014, https://www.washingtonpost.com/blogs/erik-wemple/wp/2014/12/11/the-full-demise-of-rolling-stones-rape-story/?utm_term=.1618c5f9f331.

6. Anna Merlan, "*Rolling Stone* Partially Retracts UVA Story over 'Discrepancies,'" *Jezebel*, December 5, 2014, http://jezebel.com/rolling-stone-partially-retracts-uva-story-over-discrep-1667329573; Ellison, "After A Rape Story."

7. Faced with multiple libel suits, ultimately, the company was sold. Dante A. Ciampaglia, "How Much Did Rolling Stone Magazine Sell For? Penske Media Group Buys Iconic Publication," *Newsweek*, December 21, 2017, http://www.newsweek.com/how-much-did-rolling-stone-magazine-sell-penske-media-group-buys-iconic-754795.

8. Kate Dries, "*Rolling Stone* Reaches a Settlement with Former UVA Administrator Nicole Eramo," *Jezebel*, April 12, 2017, https://jezebel.com/rolling-stone-reaches-a-settlement-with-former-uva-admi-1794250576; Ben Sisario, "*Rolling Stone* Faces Revived Lawsuit over Campus Rape Article," *New York Times*, September 19, 2017, https://www.nytimes.com/2017/09/19/business/media/rolling-stone-virginia-lawsuit.html.

9. Dries, "*Rolling Stone* Reaches"; Sisario, "*Rolling Stone* Faces."

10. Dries, "*Rolling Stone* Reaches"; Sisario, "*Rolling Stone* Faces."

11. Dries, "*Rolling Stone* Reaches"; Sisario, "*Rolling Stone* Faces."

12. Bennett Capers, "Real Rape Too," *California Law Review* 99, no. 5 (2011): 1273.

13. Francine Banner, "Institutional Sexual Assault and the Rights/Trust Dilemma," *Cardozo Public Law, Policy & Ethics Journal* 13 (2015): 165–66.

14. Lara Stemple and Ilan H. Meyer, "Sexual Victimization by Women Is More Common than Previously Known," *Scientific American*, October 10, 2017, https://www.scientificamerican.com/article/sexual-victimization-by-women-is-more-common-than-previously-known/. Recent data from the CDC reveals that over one year, men and women are equally likely to experience nonconsensual sex, and most male victims report female perpetrators. "Over their lifetime, 79 percent of men who were 'made to penetrate' someone else (a form of rape, in the view of most researchers) reported female perpetrators."

15. Human Rights Campaign, "Sexual Assault and the LGBTQ Community," https://www.hrc.org/resources/sexual-assault-and-the-lgbt-community.

16. Stemple and Meyer, "Sexual Victimization by Women."

17. A recent case in which men have been in the spotlight as victims of sexual assault is in the context of allegations against performer Michael Jackson. Notably, a key issue in these cases has not only been the credibility of the accusers themselves but of their mothers. In fact, after Jackson's acquittal in 2005, jurors specifically commented on the veracity of the accuser's mother, noting, for example, that she made jurors "uncomfortable" and had "snapped her fingers" at them. Dan Glaister and David Teather, "Jackson Found Not Guilty," *Guardian*, June 13, 2005, https://www.theguardian.com/world/2005/jun/14/michaeljacksontrial.music.

18. As Russell observes, citing philosopher Louise du Toit, "the abjection of the body caused by the act of rape cannot be generalised to all bodies similarly. The abjection of women during rape occurs against a backdrop of a body already coded as abject: as waste, excess, and mere matter. While the male victim is abjected by his feminisation during rape, this is not directly comparable to the female victim." The act and potential impact of rape also cannot be presumed to be uniform across Black and white female bodies, disabled and nondisabled bodies, and heterosexual versus LGBTQ+ bodies. Yvette Russell. "Woman's Voice/Law's Logos: The Rape Trial and the Limits of Liberal Reform," *Australian Feminist Law Journal* 42, no. 2 (2016): 275–76.

19. Capers, "Real Rape Too"; Laura Sjoberg, *Women as Wartime Rapists: Beyond Sensation and Stereotyping* (New York: New York University Press, 2016).

20. *Not Alone: The First White House Task Force to Protect Students from Sexual Assault* (April 2004) at ii, citing speech by vice president Joe Biden, January 22, 2014, formerly available at https://www.notalone.gov/assets/report.pdf.

21. TIME'S UP website, https://www.timesupnow.com.

22. Osagie K. Obasogie and Zachary Newman, "Black Lives Matter and Respectability Politics in Local News Accounts of Officer-Involved Civilian Deaths: An Early Empirical Assessment," *Wisconsin Law Review* 2016, no. 3 (2016): 543; Mark Simpson, "Respectability Is the New Closet," *Guardian*, June 2, 2009, https://www.theguardian.com/commentisfree/2009/jun/02/gay-stonewall-respectability-closet.

23. Christine Flowers, "Jussie Smollett Case a Reminder That One False Accuser Can Hurt All Future Victims," *Philadelphia Inquirer*, February 18, 2019, https://www.philly.com/opinion/commentary/jussie-smollett-hate-crime-false-accusations-20190218.html.

24. Flowers, "Jussie Smollett Case."

25. Jen Kirby, "Cosby Defense Attorneys Used Personal Attacks to Try to Discredit Witnesses," *Vox*, April 13, 2018, https://www.vox.com/2018/4/13/17234172/bill-cosby-trial-accusers-janice-dickinson-testimony.

26. Kathryn Seligman and Jordan Jaffe, "When Does an Anonymous Tip Provide Reasonable Suspicion for a Stop and Frisk?," First District Appellate Project, http://www.fdap.org/downloads/articles_and_outlines/anonymous_tips.pdf.

27. David E. Steinberg, "Zealous Officers and Neutral Magistrates: The Rhetoric of the Fourth Amendment," *Creighton Law Review* 43 (2010): 1023–24.

28. S. M. Kassin, "The Social Psychology of False Confessions," *Social Issues and Policy Review* 9, no. 1 (2015): 25–51.

29. Kassin, "Social Psychology of False Confessions."

30. MacKinnon, "Women's Human Rights."

31. Rumney, for example, describes how the police in Great Britain would sometimes classify complaints of marital rape as false (otherwise known as "no-criming") despite the fact that the complainant may have been reporting a genuine incident of nonconsensual sex. Philip N. S. Rumney, "False Allegations of Rape," *Cambridge Law Journal* 65 (2006): 130.

32. David Lisak, Lori Gardinier, Sarah C. Nicksa, and Ashley M. Cote, "False Allegations of Sexual Assault: An Analysis of Ten Years of Reported Cases," *Violence Against Women* 16, no. 1 (2010): 1319.

33. Lisak et al., "False Allegations," 1319–20.

34. Andre De Zutter, Robert Horselenberg, and Peter J. van Koppen, "The Prevalence of False Allegations of Rape in the United States from 2006–2010," *Journal of Forensic Psychology* 2, no. 2 (2017): 1–5; Emily Bazelon and Rachael Larimore, "How Often Do Women Falsely Cry Rape?," Slate.com, October 1, 2009, http://www.slate.com/articles/news_and_politics/jurisprudence/2009/10/how_often_do_women_falsely_cry_rape.html (observing that the high 90 percent false rate offered by conservative commentators is usually based in a very limited study of only thirty-four rape complaints made to one police surgeon in Scotland between 1969 and 1974).

35. Lisak et al. observe that the 2 percent statistic sometimes cited by feminist advocates likely reflects statistics offered by Judge Lawrence H. Cook in a talk before the New York City Bar Association allegedly supported by information from the New York City rape analysis squad at the time. No data are available to support these statistics. Lisak et al., "False Allegations," 1319–20.

36. Michelle Malkin, "Beware the Rape Allegation Bandwagon," *National Review*, October 18, 2017, https://www.nationalreview.com/2017/10/metoo-may-exaggerate-prevalence-sex-crimes/ (41 percent false claim rate); Lisak et al., "False Allegations," 1323 (critiquing the data on which such high rates of reporting are based).

37. Citing 1997 Department of Justice data, for example, Rumney calculates that about 8 percent of reported forcible rapes were determined to be unfounded. Rumney, "False Allegations of Rape," 138. Lisak et al. cite a 2005 study by the British Home Office also finding that approximately 8 percent of 2,643 rape claims analyzed over a fifteen-year period were false. Lisak et al., "False Allegations," 1325. A recent report by De Zutter et al. based on "raw crime statistics of the U.S. from the UCR [Uniform Crime Reporting] of the FBI . . . from 1960 until 2010" found that false and baseless allegations comprised about 5 percent of total rape allegations. De Zutter et al., "Prevalence of False Allegations," 4.

38. Rumney, "False Allegations of Rape," 138.

39. Lisak et al., "False Allegations," 1331.

40. Lisak et al., "False Allegations," 1321, 1326.

41. Rumney describes, for example, finding "no-crimed" categorizations by law enforcement in cases which complainants "thought they might have been sexually assaulted while asleep or intoxicated, but subsequent forensic examination indicated that no sexual contact had taken place." Rumney, "False Allegations of Rape," 130. De Zutter et al. similarly describe how the law enforcement category of "unfounded" cases often includes "baseless" cases, meaning that, while allegations may not have

met the legal criteria for a crime, they also were not false or malicious. De Zutter et al., "Prevalence of False Allegations," 2.

42. Elizabeth F. Loftus, *Eyewitness Testimony* (Cambridge: Harvard University Press, 1996).

43. Loftus, *Eyewitness Testimony*.

44. In the 1980s, Mary P. Koss conducted a study in which she asked college students whether they had experienced any events meeting the criteria for rape under the existing Ohio rape statute. Although when asked if they had been raped, most students said no, in fact, one in five undergraduate women met the criteria. However, the students had difficulty defining the actual harm they had experienced as criminal. This possibility that even victims will misidentify acts as not assault significantly impacts not only reporting data but likelihood to seek treatment or counseling. Mary P. Koss, Christine A. Gidycz, and Nadine Wisniewski, "The Scope of Rape: Incidence and Prevalence of Sexual Aggression and Victimization in a National Sample of Higher Education Students," *Journal of Consulting and Clinical Psychology* 55, no. 2 (1987): 162–70; L. M. Orchowski, A. S. Untied, and Christine A. Gidycz, "Factors Associated with College Women's Labeling of Sexual Victimization," *Violence and Victims* 28, no. 6 (2013): 940–58.

45. Bowley and Wodzak, "What Divided the Cosby Jurors?"; Koss et al., "Scope of Rape."

46. Jessica Bennett, "The 'Click' Moment: How the Weinstein Scandal Unleashed a Tsunami," *New York Times*, November 5, 2017, https://www.nytimes.com/2017/11/05/us/sexual-harrasment-weinstein-trump.html.

47. Michael McCann, "The Unbearable Lightness of Rights: On Sociolegal Inquiry in the Global Era," *Law and Society Review* 18, no. 2 (2014).

48. Manne, "Himpathy."

49. Manne, "Himpathy."

50. De Zutter et al., "Prevalence of False Allegations," 4.

51. Taslitz, *Rape and the Culture*, 20.

52. Rumney, "False Allegations of Rape," 146.

53. Alison Kodjak, "Experts Say There's Little Connection between Mental Health and Mass Shootings," *All Things Considered*, NPR, February 23, 2018, https://www.npr.org/2018/02/23/588374658/experts-say-theres-little-connection-between-mental-health-and-mass-shootings.

54. Pearson, *When She Was Bad*; Sjoberg and Gentry, *Mothers, Monsters*.

55. Pearson, *When She Was Bad*.

56. Pearson, *When She Was Bad*.

57. Taslitz, *Rape and the Culture*, 8; Hillary Di Menna, "Sexual Assault Cases Are Our Modern-Day Witch Trials," *Establishment*, July 15, 2016, https://theestablishment.co/sexual-assault-cases-are-our-modern-day-witch-trials-7c955ae5acc (describing how courts often treat women accusers as "carnal liars").

58. "Larry Nassar's Letter Elicits Gasps in a Packed Courtroom," CBS News, January 25, 2018, https://www.cbsnews.com/news/larry-nassar-letter-elicits-gasps-in-packed-courtroom/.

59. "Homer Badman," *The Simpsons*, season 6, episode 9, directed by Jeffrey Lynch, original air date November 27, 1994, on FOX.

60. "Homer Badman," *The Simpsons*.

61. Jane Blair, "Five Myths about Women in Combat," *Washington Post*, May 27, 2011, https://www.washingtonpost.com/opinions/five-myths-about-women-in-combat/2011/05/25/AGAsavCH_story.html?utm_term=.208d65922a9d.

62. Valerie Gray Hardcastle, M. K. Kitzmiller, and Shelby Lahey, "The Impact of Neuroscience Data in Criminal Cases: Female Defendants and the Double-Edged Sword," *New Criminal Law Review* 21, no. 2 (2018): 292.

63. Maureen Corrigan, "What 'Gone Girl' and 'The Girl on the Train' Have Wrought," *Washington Post*, November 1, 2017, https://www.washingtonpost.com/

entertainment/books/what-gone-girl-and-the-girl-on-the-train-have-wrought/2017/01/11/33dcf838-d114-11e6-9cb0-54ab630851e8_story.html?utm_term=.40f649ea340c.

64. Ravi Somaiya, "Rolling Stone Article on Rape at the University of Virginia Failed All the Basics, Report Says," *New York Times*, April 5, 2015, https://www.nytimes.com/2015/04/06/business/media/rolling-stone-retracts-article-on-rape-at-university-of-virginia.html.

65. Felman, *Juridical Unconscious.*

66. Pat Eaton-Robb, "Yale Alumni Contribute to Former Star Athlete's Sex-Expulsion Case," Boston.com, December 2, 2017, https://www.boston.com/sports/college-sports/2017/12/02/yale-alumni-contribute-to-former-star-athletes-sex-expulsion-case.

67. Rachel Axon, "Woman Who Alleged Rape by Fairfax, Maggette Spotlights Issue of Revictimization," *USA Today*, February 13, 2019, https://www.usatoday.com/story/news/nation/2019/02/13/justin-fairfax-corey-maggette-and-issue-rape-revictimization/2857516002/.

68. Zara Kessler, "Rolling Stone Problems Change Cosby Context," *Sydney Morning Herald*, December 9, 2014, https://www.smh.com.au/world/rolling-stone-problems-change-cosby-context-20141209-1232h7.html.

69. Lucinda M. Finley, "Breaking Women's Silence in Law: The Dilemma of the Gendered Nature of Legal Reasoning," *Notre Dame Law Review* 64 (1989): 889.

70. E. Karin Cadoux, "Animating Injury: Trauma Rite as Personal Exhibition and Public Exposition" (Master's Thesis submitted to the Department of Women's Studies, University of Michigan–Ann Arbor, April 3, 2017), 74.

71. Anonymous, "I Am Not a 'Pretty Little Liar,'" *Jezebel*, May 21, 2015, https://jezebel.com/i-am-not-a-pretty-little-liar-1705996719.

72. Richard Pérez-Peña and Kate Taylor, "Fight against Sexual Assaults Holds Colleges to Account," *New York Times*, May 3, 2014, https://www.nytimes.com/2014/05/04/us/fight-against-sex-crimes-holds-colleges-to-account.html.

73. Cadoux, "Animating Injury," 76.

74. Jessica Luther, "'I'm Broken': The Duke Lacrosse Rape Accuser, 10 Years Later: A Decade after Crystal Magnum Accused Duke Lacrosse Players of Raping Her, She Tells Her Story from Inside Prison," Vocativ.com, March 10, 2016, http://www.vocativ.com/295731/im-broken-the-duke-lacrosse-rape-accuser-10-years-later/.

75. Luther, "Crystal Mangum."

76. "Tawana Brawley Rape Hoax Leads To Defamation Damage Payout 26 Years Late," Black Voices, *Huffington Post*, August 5, 2013, https://www.huffingtonpost.com/2013/08/05/tawana-brawley-hoax_n_3709058.html.

77. Barbara Barnett, "Framing Rape: An Examination of Public Relations Strategies in the Duke University Lacrosse Case," *Communication, Culture, & Critique* 1, no. 2 (2008): 192–93.

78. Barnett, "Framing Rape,"192–93.

79. Finley, "Breaking Women's Silence," 889.

80. U.S. Press and Publishing, "'Jackie' Testifies: Rolling Stone Story was 'What I Believed to be True at the Time,'" *Guardian*, October 24, 2016, https://www.theguardian.com/media/2016/oct/24/rolling-stone-defamation-trial-uva-jackie-testifies.

81. U.S. Press, "'Jackie' Testifies."

82. Finley, "Breaking Women's Silence," 889.

83. Avery Anapol, "Trump Supporters Chant 'Lock Her Up' at Campaign Rally," *The Hill*, December 8, 2017, http://thehill.com/homenews/administration/364062-trump-supporters-chant-lock-her-up-at-campaign-rally. An "email controversy," in which Clinton was found to have used personal email for official correspondence while employed as secretary of state, was a prominent topic throughout the presidential debates.

84. Daniel Lavelle, "From 'Slimeball Comey' to 'Crooked Hillary,' Why Trump Loves to Brand his Enemies," *Guardian*, April 17, 2018, https://www.theguardian.com/

us-news/shortcuts/2018/apr/17/presidents-nicknames-slimeball-comey-former-fbi-director.

85. Whitewater Special Report, *Washington Post*, 1998, https://www.washingtonpost.com/wp-srv/politics/special/whitewater/timeline.htm.

86. "Benghazi Mission Attack Fast Facts," CNN Library, June 29, 2018, https://www.cnn.com/2013/09/10/world/benghazi-consulate-attack-fast-facts/index.html.

87. Susan Bordo, "The Destruction of Hillary Clinton: Sexism, Sanders and the Millennial Feminists," *Guardian*, April 2, 2017, https://www.theguardian.com/us-news/commentisfree/2017/apr/03/the-destruction-of-hillary-clinton-sexism-sanders-and-the-millennial-feminists.

88. Bordo, "The Destruction."

89. Annie Linskey, "Ethnicity Not a Factor in Elizabeth Warren's Rise in Law," *Boston Globe*, September 1, 2018, https://www.bostonglobe.com/news/nation/2018/09/01/did-claiming-native-american-heritage-actually-help-elizabeth-warren-get-ahead-but-complicated/wUZZcrKKEOUv5Spnb7IO0K/story.html.

90. Chuck Ross, "UVA Dean Defamed in *Rolling Stone* Article Takes On Major Feminist Organization," *Daily Caller*, June 11, 2016, http://dailycaller.com/2016/06/11/uva-dean-defamed-in-rolling-stone-article-takes-on-major-feminist-organization/.

91. Blake Neff, "UVA Jackie May Have Just Been Caught in Another Big Lie," *Daily Caller*, May 19, 2016, http://dailycaller.com/2016/05/19/uva-jackie-email-liar-new-evidence-lawsuit/.

92. Leigh Gilmore, "It Wasn't Just 'Fake News' Presenting a Fake Hillary Clinton: She Was Held to Impossible Standards," *Salon*, November 26, 2016, https://www.salon.com/2016/11/26/it-wasnt-just-fake-news-presenting-a-fake-hillary-clinton-she-was-held-to-impossible-standards_partner/.

93. Erin Kelly and Jessica Estepa, "Brett Kavanaugh: A Timeline of Allegations against the Supreme Court Nominee," *USA Today*, September 28, 2018, https://www.usatoday.com/story/news/politics/onpolitics/2018/09/24/brett-kavanaugh-allegations-timeline-supreme-court/1408073002/.

94. Blasey Ford sent a letter detailing the allegations to Senator Dianne Feinstein in July of that year; however, at that time, Blasey Ford requested that the allegations not be made public. Kelly and Estepa, "Brett Kavanaugh."

95. Sheryl Gay Stolberg and Nicholas Fandos, "Brett Kavanaugh and Christine Blasey Ford Duel with Tears and Fury," *New York Times*, September 27, 2018, https://www.nytimes.com/2018/09/27/us/politics/brett-kavanaugh-confirmation-hearings.html.

96. David Jackson, "Donald Trump Calls Assault Allegations against Kavanaugh a Democratic 'Hoax,'" *USA Today*, October 8, 2018, https://www.usatoday.com/story/news/politics/2018/10/08/donald-trump-calls-assault-allegations-against-brett-kavanaugh-hoax/1564801002/.

97. Maggie Haberman and Peter Baker, "Trump Taunts Christine Blasey Ford at Rally," *New York Times* , October 2, 2018, https://www.nytimes.com/2018/10/02/us/politics/trump-me-too.html?module=inline.

98. John Fritze, "Trump Unloads on Brett Kavanaugh Accuser: 'She Admits She Was Drunk,'" *USA Today*, September 25, 2018, https://www.usatoday.com/story/news/politics/2018/09/25/donald-trump-deborah-ramirez-admits-she-drunk/1420729002/.

99. Tamar Lapin, "Trump Jr. Compares Christine Blasey Ford to Jussie Smollett in Oscar 'Hoax' Category," *New York Post*, February 24, 2019, https://nypost.com/2019/02/24/trump-jr-compares-christine-blasey-ford-to-jussie-smollett-in-oscar-hoax-category/.

100. Nick Visser, "Christine Blasey Ford Can't Return Home Due to 'Unending' Threats, Lawyers Say," *Huffington Post*, October 8, 2018, https://www.huffingtonpost.com/entry/christine-blasey-ford-home-unending-threats_us_5bbaa112e4b0876eda9f3317.

101. Mairead McArdle, "Wave of Bomb Threats Targets Prominent Democrats," *National Review*, October 24, 2018, https://www.nationalreview.com/news/bomb-threats-target-prominent-democrats-nationwide/.

102. Will Sommer and Kelly Weill, "Trump Allies Insist Bomb Threats against Clinton, Obama, CNN Are 'Pure BS,' a 'False Flag,'" *Daily Beast*, October 24, 2018, https://www.thedailybeast.com/pro-trump-media-insists-bomb-threats-against-clinton-obama-cnn-are-pure-bs-a-false-flag; Kevin Roose, "Debunking 5 (More) Viral Rumors about Kavanaugh's Accusers," *New York Times*, September 26, 2018, https://www.nytimes.com/2018/09/26/us/politics/kavanaugh-fact-check.html.

103. Bourke, *Rape*, 31, fn. 30.

104. Thomas James "TJ" Kirk III, "Feminism & Rape: Belief without Evidence," YouTube, December 13, 2014, https://www.youtube.com/watch?v=YhxYw9t_XMc.

105. Manuel Pfister, "The Great University of Virginia (UVA) Rape Hoax, Jackie Coakley, *Rolling Stone* and Sabrina Rubin Erdely," *The Single Dude's Guide to Life & Travel*, April 7, 2015, http://www.singledudetravel.com/2015/04/the-great-university-of-virginia-uva-rape-hoax-jackie-coakley-rolling-stone-and-sabrina-rubin-erdely/.

106. Cramer, *Pregnant with the Stars*.

107. "Devastating Story," *Law & Order: SVU*, season 16, episode 18, directed by Michael Slovis, original air date April 1, 2015, on NBC.

108. "Devastating Story," *Law & Order: SVU*.

109. Bari Weiss, "The Limits of 'Believe All Women,'" *New York Times*, November 28, 2017, https://www.nytimes.com/2017/11/28/opinion/metoo-sexual-harassment-believe-women.html?_r=0.

110. Olga Khazan, "The *Rolling Stone* Fiasco Is Terrible News for Rape Survivors," *Atlantic*, December 5, 2014, https://www.theatlantic.com/health/archive/2014/12/the-rolling-stone-fiasco-is-terrible-news-for-rape-survivors/383483/.

111. Kessler, "*Rolling Stone* Problems."

112. Mona Charen, "It's High Time Columbia's Mattress Girl Was Discredited," *National Review*, August 4, 2017, https://www.nationalreview.com/2017/08/columbia-university-mattress-girl-emmas-sulkowicz-paul-nungesser-lawsuit-rape-accusation-exonerated/.

113. Malala Fund, https://www.malala.org/malalas-story?g=1&utm_expid=.rFt8T4goQvu3waedVYhuNA.1&utm_referrer=https%3A%2F%2Fwww.google.com%2F.

114. Sarah Cascone, "A Bunch of Bull? Wall Street Firm Behind 'Fearless Girl' Settles Gender Discrimination Suit," *ArtNet*, October 10, 2017, https://news.artnet.com/art-world/fearless-girl-settles-gender-discrimination-suit-1110587. Ironically, the statue turned out not to be an independent artistic effort but a corporate stunt. The statue originally bore a plaque reading, "Know the Power of Women in Leadership/SHE Makes a Difference." It turned out, however, that the "she" in the tag line referred not only to the girl facing the bull, but the ticker symbol for the corporate fund that had sponsored the statue.

115. Maria Hengeveld, "How Nike's Neoliberal Feminism Came to Rule the Global South," *FeministWire*, September 14, 2015, http://www.thefeministwire.com/2015/09/nike-neoliberal-feminism/.

116. Notorious troll Charles C. Johnson was banned from Twitter for such threats. Hanna Rosin, "Trolls Are Outing UVA's 'Jackie.' That's *Rolling Stone*'s Fault Too," *Slate*, December 8, 2014, http://www.slate.com/blogs/xx_factor/2014/12/08/doxxing_jackie_the_vile_and_dangerous_threats_of_charles_johnson_and_other.html.

117. Chimamanda Adichie, "The Danger of a Single Story," TEDGlobal 2009, https://www.ted.com/talks/chimamanda_adichie_the_danger_of_a_single_story/transcript.

II

The Perpetrators

FOUR

Railroaded

State of Mississippi v. Milam and Bryant

In 1955, two white men, J. W. Milam and Roy Bryant, were tried in Mississippi for the murder of a fourteen-year-old African American teenager, Emmett Till.[1,2] The pair were acquitted in just under an hour by an all-white, male jury.[3] Although jurors did not hear her testimony, on the record were statements from Roy's wife, Carolyn Bryant, a white woman who described that Till "grabbed" and "threatened" her in front of her husband's store, then whistled at her before driving away.[4] The pair were acquitted. Just a few months later, Milam and Bryant proudly confessed to having murdered Till, describing to *Look* magazine how they forced the young man from his bedroom, then drove for miles until they reached a river, where they forced Till to remove all his clothes and find a heavy object. The pair then bound Till's feet to the object he had found—an electric fan—and shot and drowned him.[5]

In 2017, more than sixty years after Emmett Till's death, Carolyn Bryant recanted, admitting that her allegations of threats and physical contact were untrue.[6]

Perhaps no other story so profoundly emphasizes what is at stake when sexual assault allegations are made more than that of Emmett Till. Yet, Till's narrative is one that, throughout U.S. history, has been terrifyingly common. The past three chapters have focused on the impacts of the "inverted" process of the rape trial on victims, highlighting how, in centering on the character of accusers, perpetrators' responsibility for sexual assault has been displaced and discounted.

When alleged sexual assault perpetrators are Black, however, the trial process has functioned very differently. While the issue of white women's chastity is front and center when alleged perpetrators are also white, complainants' chastity has rarely been a focus when the accused is not white. Special evidentiary rules permitted juries to draw factual conclusions regarding intent based on the races of alleged victims and perpetrators based on the assumption that white women would never consent to sex with Black men.[7] Capers uses the term "white letter law" to describe this "reallocat[ion] of burdens of proof persuasion" in the context of U.S. rape laws.[8]

Just as distrust of female complainants did not magically evaporate with the abolition of the Hale instruction, the flawed assumptions that contributed to creating additional hurdles for African American and other nonwhite defendants have not magically been eradicated in the contemporary era of "color blindness." Reactions to the Jussie Smollett allegations discussed in chapter 3, for example, demonstrate that nonwhite persons caught up in the criminal justice process continue to be subject to a politics of respectability, whereby there is a fear that the behavior of one person automatically will be imputed to the group to which they belong.

THE PAST IS PRESENT

Social media comments regarding sexual assault cases, particularly those involving white female accusers and Black defendants, reveal an astute public consciousness of and anger about the disproportionate impact criminal justice practices have had on African American men.

Although racism is prevalent across the internet, many comments relating to sexual assault allegations against African American men invoke rape law's horrific past. A major news reader describes Cosby as "yet another black man accused of something by a white person" in what the reader deems a "modern day lynching." A tweet proclaims, "Cosby is Black. If he raped white women in the 60's and 70's, they would have hung him," while another observes, "U mean to tell me Bill Cosby was raping white women in the early 60s and 70s with impunity? They would have hoisted bill up from the finest oak tree." A tweet connects the present to the past via a series of hashtags: "You can't condemn a man 30 years later for something he could've done. #cosby #haditbeenablackwoman #emmettill." Another commenter tweets, "[T]hey killed Emmett Till for whistling at a white woman you think they would let Cosby rape 20 white women."

A tweet regarding Jameis Winston inquires, similarly, "Does To Kill a Mockingbird ring a bell? You should know better." While another Twitter user observes, "The only black men in America who got treated like rich white people by the police this year were Jameis Winston & Bill Cosby."

Although the work of this project so far has been to identify how social media comments perpetuate myths about the criminal justice system, comments like these are premised not in myth but in fact. Fully *three-fourths* of victims of the over four thousand seven hundred documented lynchings that occurred in the United States from 1882–1968 involved Black victims.[9] Of the 4,715 legally sanctioned executions for rape between 1822 and 1946, three-fourths of those executed also were Black men.[10]

These statistics demonstrate that Black defendants not only have faced mob justice for allegations of violation of social codes and norms, they have fared little better in the legal arena. From the Reconstruction era through the time of Jim Crow laws, false rape charges against Black men were common across the South, often arising out of minor violations of the social code, such as Emmett Till's alleged whistling at Caroline Bryant.[11] As Berger writes, "[R]ape for a long time marked the fatal crossroads where racial discrimination and capital punishment encountered each other most dramatically."[12]

Approximately twenty years before the extralegal execution of Emmett Till, an Alabama court weighed the case of the Scottsboro boys, nine young African Americans aged thirteen to nineteen accused of raping two white women, Ruby Bates and Victoria Price, while all were hitching a ride on a freight train to Memphis.[13] During their first trial, the nine were denied contact with their families and were all provided with only one attorney, a real estate lawyer, who met the defendants for the first time on the day their trial began.[14]

Powell v. Alabama, the 1932 case in which the U.S. Supreme Court reversed the Scottsboro convictions, often is presented as a paean to the power of due process, the court heroized in its identification of the nearly wholesale deprivation of representation in a capital case.[15] While *Powell* is a high point for due process, however, the case also is brutal evidence of the law's limits. After the Supreme Court ruling, and now represented by competent counsel, many of the Scottsboro defendants were tried again, only once again to be convicted by all-white, male juries.[16] Those who did not have to endure a retrial were plagued by emotional, mental, and physical illness resulting from their time in prison, and most continued to have brushes with the law. In 2013, the Alabama Board of Pardons and Paroles at last voted to pardon three of the Scottsboro defendants, fourteen years after the last of them had passed away.[17]

Fifty years after Scottsboro, five teenagers, Antron McCray, Kevin Richardson, Yusef Salaam, Raymond Santana, and Korey Wise, were accused and convicted of raping a white female jogger in New York's Central Park.[18] The terms used by the press and politicians to describe the suspects were animalistic, including "wilding," "monsters," a "wolf pack."[19] The vigor with which the public pursued the defendants bore a disturbing resemblance to the celebration of Milam and Bryant for the murder of Emmett Till. Donald Trump famously spent nearly $100,000 on full-page advertisements in four daily papers calling for the return of capital punishment.[20] Years later, after many of the defendants had served their prison terms, a confession revealed that the young men were innocent. A wholly unrelated person, Matias Reyes, was in fact the perpetrator of the Central Park attack. The tragedy of the Central Park Five provides yet another example of how, in the context of a deeply troubled history, allegations of rape have been used to inflict racial terror on African American men.[21]

The racism embedded in the U.S. criminal justice system has not been eradicated. Hand in hand with the "war on drugs" maintained from the Nixon through both Bush administrations came rising support for a crime control system favoring swift justice and long sentences, and dismissing due process as a constitutional "technicality."[22] The privileging of such a crime control system—hallmarks of which are mandatory minimum sentences, three strikes laws, and truth in sentencing policies—has led to a troubling increase in mass incarceration, with a growth rate of more than 400 percent from the 1980s to today.[23] Disproportionately, the impact of such policies has fallen on nonwhite persons.[24] In addition, activism by organizations such as Black Lives Matter and Cop Watch reveals not only ongoing instances of racially motivated police brutality but a trend of municipalities policing the poor, criminalizing poverty via engaging a strategy of levying fines against those least able to pay.[25]

The public's engagement of #emmettill and references to the classic novel, *To Kill A Mockingbird*, in the context of allegations against Bill Cosby and Jameis Winston suggest that society is aware of the failures of due process inhering in the criminal justice system. In comparing contemporary accusations to lynchings, commenters, significantly, are making visible long-standing discriminatory processes and practices. As Felman writes, public criminal allegations reflect "legal memory" that is "constituted . . . by a forgotten chain of cultural wounds."[26] Social media provide commenters with an important forum for not only exposing longstanding trauma and terror inflicted by the criminal justice system but making inroads to social change.

That social media highlight the continued impact of racism on the U.S. criminal justice system is heartening. Online comments suggest that not only is the American public aware of the racist treatment of Emmett Till and the Scottsboro defendants, people are now making critical and thoughtful connections between biases in contemporary law enforcement and historically discriminatory practices of the past. Hashtags linking the prosecution of Bill Cosby to discriminatory prosecutions of other Black defendants signal the public's awareness that the past is present. As a commenter on the site of a popular newspaper explains, "[T]his [criminal justice] system has a very dark history, including extrajudicial killings and racism."

Not all critiques on social media, however, exhibit racial or cultural sensitivity.

FALSE FLAGS, REAL FEARS

The men's rights movement (MRM) is a contemporary offshoot of the men's liberation movement of the 1970s that focuses on issues such as parenting and child custody, reproductive rights, and intimate partner violence as they impact men across society.[27] The movement also is frequently criticized for its anti-feminist rhetoric, promoting men's interests by denigrating women.

A common refrain of the MRM is that men, as a group, are vulnerable to false accusations of rape. Over the past several years, a major focus of MRM activists has been what they identify as an epidemic of unsubstantiated sexual assault claims. One MRM post on YouTube by activist TJ Kirk entitled "Feminism & Rape: Belief Without Evidence," gathered more than five thousand comments. The men's rights subreddit, entitled The Red Pill, has over two hundred eighty thousand subscribers.[28]

Among the comments on MRM-related videos and sites is this one, by a poster identifying as a concerned mother. The commenter writes,

> [M]y biggest worry right now is that some girl or woman, for whatever reason, will point a finger at my son and say "He raped me. I don't have any proof but I will cry the tears and be 'brave' about it." . . . [If] woman is caught lying, rather than get a jail sentence . . . her punishment is usually a slap on the wrist rather than an actual penalty. I find that absolutely fucking terrifying. The last time that mentality was enacted was during the Salem Witch Trials.

Another commenter describes of contemporary rape claims,

> THIS IS HOW LYNCHINGS HAPPEN! . . . I just hate this. I hate how people think destroying someone because they may have done something is fine. If I get fired from my job, lose friends and am kicked out of my apartment, then what? I have no shelter, I lack money, and am now alone in the world. How do I defend myself in court when I cannot feed myself. How can I go though information to prove my innocence when I sleep on the streets? Who will tell me not to commit suicide when it becomes too much?

The previous chapter identified comments like these as infused with gendered assumptions. The idea that women are likely to—and easily can—manufacture wholly false accusations of rape out of greed, spite, or revenge is one of the most damaging rape myths in existence today.

Although they have sexist undertones, however, the comments above also reflect something tangible and important—the concern that current institutional systems of dealing with sexual assault are ineffective in affording due process to alleged perpetrators. These worries that those accused of rape will not receive due process—and that they may face lifelong consequences as a result of a mere accusation—are not myths created by MRA (men's rights activists) trolls. They reflect the legal reality in which we live today.

As described earlier, contemporary penalties on the books for sexual assault have been significantly reduced from those formerly available for rape at common law. In the organization's amicus brief in *Coker v. Georgia*, the ACLU Women's Rights Project—spearheaded by feminist advocate Ruth Bader Ginsburg—advocated for removing what the brief deemed rape law's "crippling 'chivalric protection.'"[29] The brief argued that the severe punishment for perpetrators of rape was a disincentive to reporting the crime. Further, the stiff penalties being imposed for rape did not reflect respect for women victims' autonomy but rather the value placed by men on women's chastity.[30]

As sentences for sexual assault have been gradated, however, other legal and social sanctions for perpetrators have increased. For example, in 2019, a person convicted of a sex-related offense may be required to sign on to a registry that, sometimes for life, will dictate where they are permitted to live and travel, not to mention carrying with it the possibility that every person in their neighborhood will be notified that they are living near a dangerous felon.[31] Researchers argue that sex offender registries, a knee-jerk response to fears of child predation, are rooted in strikingly inaccurate data and are overly broad, requiring registration for offenses ranging from public urination to first-degree rape.[32] If the conviction is for the rape of a child, confinement may also be required—until a felon can prove they are no longer a danger to society.[33]

The significant stigma associated with sex-related offenses makes allegations of sexual assault and harassment appealing fodder for "lawfare," the deployment of law as a weapon in interpersonal or political conflict.[34] In 2017, a sexual harassment complaint against New York senator Chuck Schumer was leaked online.[35] Although it lacked some key information, to the untrained eye the lengthy document appeared to be a complaint filed in a U.S. District Court.[36] Not only did the complaint prove to have been unfounded, it was wholly manufactured.

After Broward County sheriff Scott Israel made public statements regarding the 2018 mass shooting at Marjory Stoneman Douglas High School in Parkland, Florida, six-year-old videos resurfaced online suggesting that the sheriff formerly had an affair with a seventeen-year-old girl.[37] Again, it turned out not only that the target of the smear campaign had not committed statutory rape but that he had never even met his accuser. The videos, in which a young girl tearfully spoke of Israel forcing her to get an abortion, were comprised of lies, solicited from the young woman by an anonymous source via a freelance services site.[38]

Similarly, during Roy Moore's 2017 senate race, an alleged victim approached the *Washington Post* claiming to have been impregnated by the senator when she was just fifteen years old.[39] She claimed, further, that she was driven across state lines by the politician to obtain an abortion.[40]

The accusations, it turned out, had been manufactured by Project Veritas, a right-wing organization that claims to engage in undercover operations in order to uncover media bias.[41] Similar, very questionable allegations have been brought against special counsel Robert Mueller and Democratic hopeful Mayor Pete Buttigieg.[42] Not to mention "Pizzagate," the alleged child-trafficking ring run by Hillary Clinton from a Washington, D.C., pizza parlor.[43]

Originally describing a warfare technique in which navies would hoist the flag of a different nation on vessels to confuse an enemy, today the term "false flag" describes the creation of false online data in order to influence public opinion or to disrupt an enemy's political processes—in other words, political catfishing.[44] The growth of social media has provided increasing opportunities to disseminate conspiracy theories, and to reach an audience susceptible to believing such theories.[45] As accusations of Russian hacking of the 2016 U.S. election attest, false flags are dangerous, not only because they sway individual opinions, but because they erode our trust in institutions.

As the narratives of Caroline Bryant and Ruby Bates attest, the ability to make unfounded rape claims is not new but social media now provide an instantaneous, public forum in which to make such claims, as well as the ability to craft them in a very convincing manner. The Pizzagate child sex ring conspiracy assertions were so convincing they inspired Edgar Welch, a twenty-eight-year-old North Carolina resident, to travel to D.C. and storm Comet Ping Pong with several rounds from his AR-15.[46]

Social media facilitates rapid dissemination, not only of false flag narratives, but of stories about alleged perpetrators that may not be false, but, then again, may not be wholly truthful. In the past year allegations of sexual assault and harassment have unseated hundreds of bankers, chefs, entrepreneurs, and academics.[47] Criminal charges have been few and far between but social consequences abound. Among the famous to resign from high profile positions so far are politician Al Franken, newsperson Matt Lauer, chef Mario Batali, and entrepreneur Steve Wynn.

As stories broke regarding numerous allegations against producer Harvey Weinstein, whose criminal case this book discusses in chapter 6, an ancillary drama unfolded around the "shitty men list," a downloadable, open-access spreadsheet circulated in the entertainment industry listing men who allegedly had engaged in bad behaviors ranging from "weird lunch dates" to rape and physical violence.[48] The ease and anonymity with which viewers could interact with the list was significant because it did away with concerns about stigma and repercussion that could deter individuals from disclosing experiences of harassment and assault. Of course, these same characteristics made the list a dubious one, subject to manipulation. The list's creator, journalist Moira Donegan, currently subject to a defamation suit from a person named on said list, reflects that it

> offered an impartial, rather than adversarial, tool to those who used it. It was intended specifically not to inflict consequences, not to be a weapon—and yet, once it became public, many people immediately saw it as exactly that.[49]

For many, the "shitty men list" also raised the question asked by Amy Schumer at the start of this book—were these men losers or rapists? And should it matter?

Major newspaper *USA Today* offers an interactive calendar where one can visit to see the latest alleged celebrity perpetrator, the number of accusers, and the status of allegations against him.[50] Among 150 current perpetrator statuses is a litany of extralegal consequences: "fired," "resigned," "step[ped] down," "took leave of absence," "suspended," "banned," "company sold," "magazine cancelled," and, disturbingly, "took own life," and "committed suicide."[51] Only one of the people listed on the site, Larry Nassar, so far has been convicted of any crime.

A characteristic of our modern criminal justice system is that the direct impact of punishment in the United States is often eclipsed by its collateral consequences. One might face three to five years in prison for a sex crime but a lifetime of checking the "felon" box on job applications or registering as a sex offender. For many, the harshest result of a criminal conviction in the United States is often not the short-term loss of liberty but the diminishment of personal economic opportunities and exclusion from participation in civic life.[52] Although prison sentences for rape are not formally death sentences, convicted rapists and child molesters face an exponential—and societally and state-sanctioned—risk of violence and lifelong stigma.

The consequences listed for alleged perpetrators on the *USA Today* site—fired, banned, suspended, and, tragically, committed suicide—demonstrate that, in today's socially mediated world, there is a very real danger of being convicted in the court of public opinion based not only on evidence that is admissible in a court of law but on evidence that is incomplete, insufficient, or—even assuming a relatively modest 8 percent rate of false criminal claims—made up.

In addition to Erica Kinsman's accusations against Jameis Winston, *The Hunting Ground* film features another story detailing allegations against a young man named Winston. Harvard law student Kamilah Willingham alleges that a fellow law student, Brandon Winston, assaulted her while she was unconscious.[53] Winston was charged in criminal court, in addition to facing a disciplinary hearing at the university.[54] Ultimately, he was cleared of all charges by the court, acquitted by the panel, and permitted to finish his degree.

Since the 1990s, Title IX, passed to prohibit gender discrimination in schools receiving federal funds, has become the primary mechanism for addressing complaints of sexual assault at colleges and universities.[55] In most proceedings, the standard of proof is less than the "beyond a reasonable doubt" standard of a criminal trial because the consequence for perpetrators identified via these processes is not prison but suspension or expulsion.[56]

Title IX is blunt instrument for handling sexual assault claims. From an alleged victim's perspective, collegiate administrative processes may be biased or ineffective, sometimes resulting in a decision that leaves a victim living in the same dorm or attending the same classes as their perpetrator.[57] From the perspective of the accused, harsh consequences—a career-ending expulsion, for example, or a refusal to provide support for a professional exam—can be handed down based solely on a preponderance of the evidence rather than the higher standard of beyond a reasonable doubt.

Although Brandon Winston was officially cleared of wrongdoing, the aftermath for both parties was far from over. After the release of *The Hunting Ground*, a group of Harvard law professors objected to the film's representations about Brandon in the film.[58] In response, Willingham published a letter addressed to the professors, whom she labeled the "Harvard Law 19," observing that the academics were allowing "a loathsome rape culture to thrive on our campuses and across our country."[59] Willingham urged that Winston's defenders "should be deeply ashamed of yourselves for using such an important issue in such a manipulative way."[60]

In response, Winston's attorneys launched "The Brandon Project" (https://brandonproject.org), a professionally constructed, interactive site that offers letters of support from Winston's family members, video clips from *The Hunting Ground* with "corrective" voice-overs, links to nonprofit advocacy organizations supporting those accused of sexual assault, and pop-ups of texts sent by Willingham to Winston throughout the evening of the alleged incident.[61] When one googles Brandon Winston's name, links to the site promoting Brandon's innocence and critiques of due process pop up amid others promoting victims' rights and heavily critiquing the professors who came to his defense.

The ongoing and very public dispute between Kamilah Willingham and Brandon Winston shows the extent to which legal battles today are not—or not only—fought in the physical courtroom but, sometimes exclusively, in the virtual one. For alleged perpetrators in the recent past, a trial would have been a finite event, a "not guilty" verdict bookmarking the end of an arduous process. While community members might recollect accusations against an everyday person like Brandon Winston, he also might be able to move to a different town or state and conduct his life in relative obscurity, free of allegations of crime.

Today allegations of sexual assault are renewed with any search for a suspect's name on social media, whether by a prospective employer, a friend, or a possible date. A commenter on a men's rights-related YouTube video opines,

> Do you know how difficult it is to get a job or an apartment when a local newspaper states you are a rapist or a criminal in general . . . And newspaper don't usually just delete a false stories . . . The cost of disbelieving a true victim is that the accuser is not convicted. That's really horrible. But I would state that the cost of false accusation is much higher. Because that's at best a rumor about you having raped a girl (with doubts if it maybe true even if proven wrong) and at worst a destroyed life.

On a popular daily news site, a commenter to an article regarding unfounded rape allegations writes of the trauma he experienced after having been accused.

> My girlfriend was raped several years ago. I was falsely accused of rape less than a year ago. I contacted her (I had known her before her incident) because I was desperate for someone to talk to who would understand what I was going through. To my great relief, it turned out that we understood each other very well. From the initial stages of suicidal thoughts and not being able to function to the long-term fear, mistrust, and guilt that are facts of our lives, it turns out that her experience of being raped and mine of being falsely accused of rape were very similar. . . . One important difference, though, is that when she was violated, she received a great deal of help (medical, legal, psychological). Apart from family and friends, I was on my own.

Former *Washington Post* editor Alan Barth wrote of McCarthy-era blacklists that the press is too often an "instrument" that can "inflict punishment by publicity."[62] With even a suggestion on social media that someone is a rapist can come very real social and economic consequences. Bill Cosby, Harvey Weinstein, and Steve Wynn all have encountered the revocation of their honorary degrees from various institutions, based not on criminal convictions but on extralegal bodies determination that allegations against them were "credible."[63]

Chapter 3 addressed the ways in which, via the hashtag, the names of accusers who have made unfounded sexual assault allegations come to represent something beyond the accusers themselves, serving both as a reminder of past harms that have been inflicted and a warning to claimants in the future. The online environment bears similar risks for the accused. Unlike a physical trial, geographically confined and temporally limited, the virtual trial in which Brandon Winston is embroiled potentially will continue for the rest of his life.

However, although the stigma carried by those who have been falsely accused of rape is real, it is not clear that the *threat* of being falsely accused is actually as great as social media comments suggest.

THE LYNCH MOB

Like discussions about victims' "virtue," explicit considerations of the role of race in relationships between alleged victims and perpetrators is no longer formally integrated into the criminal trial process. However, this does not mean that racial biases have ceased to overshadow the criminal justice system. African American male defendants continue to be framed by the media as threatening or menacing, particularly when the victim is white.[64] And data continue to emerge regarding the disparate impact of criminal justice procedures and policies on Black men in other contexts—"stop-and-frisk" or "hot spot" policing policies, the role of cross-racial identification in wrongful convictions, and disparate sentencing in multiple contexts.[65] Recent police-involved shootings of Michael Brown, Eric Garner, Philando Castile, and others reveal continuing systemic injustices profoundly impacting Black men.

While social media comments reveal a public awareness of the unequal treatment Black men have faced at the hands of the U.S. criminal justice system, at the same time, other important aspects of history are being obscured. A significant example is in the discursive, political reframing of the term "lynch mob." As described above, the term lynching carries with it a particular meaning for African American defendants, who have been subjected to legal and extralegal terror. Today, in a virtual sleight of hand, what are very real fears confronted by Black male alleged perpetrators have been transformed into a fear faced by all men, rich or poor, Black or white, young or old. Like the image of the welfare queen described by Cammett—an image deployed to further a political objective—in the online environment today, the term "lynch mob" is being transformed into a description of not racial but gendered oppression.

Like the term "gold digger," the term "lynch mob" appears prominently in conversations discussing contemporary sexual assault accusations. In response to an article about the Cosby mistrial on a popular conservative news site, the term "lynching" appears nine different times. Commenters describe the accusations against the celebrity as a "Gloria Allred lynching" and a "lynching, liberal style." Comments on a major newspaper's site regarding an article detailing social media advocacy to extend statutes of limitations describe

> "public opinion" [as] no more reliable than a lynch mob led by media coverage. #MeToo has generated something of a feeding frenzy lately. I don't doubt that many of the accusations are genuine, but PROVING them in a court of law requires more than sincere testimony from alleged victims.

Others critique recent trials reliant on DNA evidence as "little better than a lynch mob."

Across comment sites, the terms "lynch mob" and "lynching" are used to describe sexual assault allegations involving not only Black but often white suspects. Several comments compare accusations against Bill Cosby to those against another prominent figure, Donald Trump, noting, for example, that "lynching" is "exactly what the Democrats are trying to do to President Trump." Another agrees, "The media is doing the SAME thing to Bill as they are doing with TRUMP." On a major liberal news site, a reader suggests that attorney Gloria Allred "go find some of those women Donald Trump bragged about assaulting" rather than spending time on the Cosby case. A tweet complains of what seems to be a growing list of allegations against public figures, "I was on board w/ #metoo early on. . . . [b]ut the 'movement' is now a chaotic lynch mob. It's been hijacked to destroy & divide progressives." Regarding white NHL player Patrick Kane, a tweet notes, " The press and the social media lynch mob have been telling everyone what to think and what to say about this . . . story," while another calls for the "lynch mob women media who called for Kane's suspension" to apologize. In support of white producer Harvey Weinstein, a tweet notes, "Some tweets out there sound like they want to form a lynch mob, people still have the right to due process even Weinstein."

The specter of the "lynch mob" pops up frequently in response to the legal probe into the Trump administration's Russia dealings. A typical tweet appraises that "[Special Prosecutor Robert] Mueller and his 90% dem lynch mob. Spent millions on a phony witch hunt and President Trump." Another tweet notes that the

> Scarlet Letter is the tip of the iceberg as the Social Media Lynchings of Moore and Weinstein are also reminiscent of To Kill a Mockingbird, prejudging and on the cliff hanger of lynch mob justice in its' ugliest form.

Recently, the spokesperson for Alabama Republican senatorial candidate Roy Moore, who lost the 2017 election by a narrow margin after sexual misconduct allegations plagued him, described how the "lynch mob media" was attacking Republican candidates, characterizing that, "When you have false allegations that are generated by The Washington Post there tends to be a pile-on. . . . That's how a lynch mob works." Tweets chime in that Moore "was not allowed due process. Jury of his peers. He was tried and convicted by #media #dems #rinos #Hollywood—if that's not a #lynchmob" and note that "Roy Moore is being killed without a trial . . . #lynchmob." Another tweet situates the #MeToo movement in historical context:

> The feminists are the ones who have discredited the #metoo movement. It is lynch-mob justice today, just as it was when they used it against Emmit Till. The right believes in Individual justice, which involves actual proof beyond anonymous accusations.

More recent accusations against then-Supreme Court nominee Brett Kavanaugh are characterized similarly, a tweet noting, "Kavanaugh is the one being judged—by a lynch mob," and another describing an unnamed group "conspire[ing] to hang . . . Kavanaugh in the court of public opinion without due process."

Comments that situate rape accusations against African American men in a long and troubled history of legal and extralegal lynching serve an important function, highlighting the injustices that continue to be perpetuated by the U.S. criminal justice system. However, the application of the term "lynch mob" to describe accusations against a figure like Roy Moore, a white, West Point–educated judge,[66] is not just ironic. It suggests that, in this moment of crisis, legal discourse is being reshaped in a manner that risks obscuring centuries of oppression.

One of the most extreme examples of the reinvention of the term "lynch mob" appears in a comment from a reader responding to an article about the UVA allegations on a conservative blog site. The reader complains that, under the Obama administration, attorney general "Loretta Lynchmob" was likely to initiate "disbarment proceedings against lawyers with the temerity to challenge a rape accuser." Lynch was, of course, the first African American woman to be appointed to the attorney general position.

Although many virtual commenters engage the idea of the lynch mob to discuss the specific challenges faced by African American men in the criminal legal system, a surprising number engage the term "lynch mob" to convey something entirely different. These commenters purport that false rape allegations are being made as a means of threatening not just nonwhite men but *all* men.

Today, many question whether racist, xenophobic, and sexist comments by President Trump are simply faux pas or whether they are "dog whistles," coded language that is being constructed to marshal a white neonationalist faction, not only within the United States, but globally.[67] As they are retweeted, comments that might have seemed like insults—such as a statement that Mexicans are rapists or that Muslim Americans are inciting hate—are transformed into partisan calls to arms, stereotypical images colonizing and obscuring the realities of individual, lived experiences. The deployment of coded language is common in the virtual world, forming what Hughey and Daniels call a "social stenography" that is purposefully designed "to hide the intended meanings behind posts and status updates from parents and moderators."[68]

In the eyes of legal scholars, the incorporation of law into popular culture has largely been categorized mistake or caricature—everyday impressions forming a *My Cousin Vinny*-esque parody that is rooted in benign misapprehension.[69] However, genial and distant characterizations of understanding of law in popular culture ignore the ways in which, across social media, acts of oppression against racial minorities are deliberately being reframed into acts of aggression against an enfranchised majority. By engaging terms like "lynch mob" to describe sexual assault allegations, commenters are promoting what David Altheide calls a "politics of fear"; as violent crime rates decline, the fear mongering among the public contributes to the achievement of political and economic goals.[70]

Conversations about sexual assault do not occur in isolation, but are political debates that relate to other conversations regarding immigration, reproductive rights, and the First Amendment. A conservative dog whistle in recent years has been the reframing of the "Black Lives Matter" declaration with the assertion that "All Lives Matter." Premised in a history of systemic racism, the core of the Black Lives Matter movement has been to proclaim that African Americans should at last have a seat at the table, that minorities are entitled to the unbiased treatment by the criminal justice system that white counterparts historically have received. To counter the assertion that Black lives matter with the idea that all lives matter implies that, rather than seeking equal treatment, African Americans are asking for better treatment, a categorization that ignores how systemic racism continues to negatively impact members of minority communities.

Tweets and comments comparing current accusations against powerful, white political figures to allegations against Tom Robinson, the poor, African American man falsely accused of rape in *To Kill A Mockingbird*, similarly overlook the intersections of race, class, and gender in an attempt to reframe false accusations solely in terms of a gendered dichotomy. Engaging a term like "lynch mob" to describe complaints against a rich, white man obscures the fact that three-fourths of the individuals who have been lynched in the United States were persons of color. Like "gold digger," the term also effects a role reversal by implying that—in Adichie's terms—some sort of a "bottom power" agenda motivates accusers.

Comments comparing the allegations against Roy Moore or Donald Trump to the lynching of Emmett Till distort the fact that lynching was not an expression of power against *male* bodies but "a means of exercising white power over black male bodies."[71] The racial harms inflicted as part of sexual assault law—and its intersectional problems—are obscured when lynching is reframed as gendered practice and when the most powerful are represented as targets and victims.

WITCH HUNTS

Used somewhat interchangeably with the term "lynch mob" is the related charge that rape allegations are being manufactured as part of a feminist "witch hunt." In response to a video discussing false rape claims on a popular video site, a viewer writes that it is "McCarthyism all over again." Numerous others recall the "Salem Witch Trials," when

> [A] bratty bunch of bratty girls accused people of being witches, and said people had to (somehow) prove they were not witches or else be burned at the stake. . . . This "Listen and Believe" notion is a bit like that in the sense that people accused of rape are now, essentially, guilty until proven innocent.

Although the featured video is discussing claims of a white female accuser against white male victims, a commenter notes that

> [t]he Jury in "To Kill a Mockingbird" had it right, she said the black man raped her and they believed her despite multitudes of evidence that she was clearly lying. I guess Feminists got something different out of that book than I did.

In another forum, journalist Sabrina Erdely, who reported Jackie's claims at UVA, is described as a member of a "coven" of liars. A commenter notes that the "rape liars . . . are here to ensure the witch hunt for men continues unabated."

In 2017, President Trump famously used the term "witch hunt" to describe his status as the object of an investigation by special prosecutor Robert Muller, which he described as the "single greatest witch hunt of a politician in American history."[72] The president is not the only one to engage the metaphor. Woody Allen, Liam Neeson, Matt Damon, and George Clooney all use the term "witch hunt" to describe the contemporary atmosphere surrounding sexual assault.[73] Bill Cosby's attorney, Monique Pressley also employed it to describe charges against the comedian.[74]

Historically, "lynch mob" describes not generalized violence against men but a specific form of terrorism inflicted on Black men; likewise, the term "witch hunt" has a particular, and gendered, meaning. As described in the previous chapter, witch hunts were a particular form of state violence exacted by governments primarily against women and others who stepped outside societal norms or challenged power structures. The label "witch" was a controlling image engaged to define outsiders and to uphold and maintain the discriminatory status quo.

Compiled by Inquisitors Jakob Sprenger and Heinrich Kramer, the fifteenth century treatise *Malleus Maleficarum* explained why witches were more likely to be found among women than men:

> [Women] are more credulous . . . more impressionable . . . they have slippery tongues . . . she is more carnal than a man . . . they are more prone to abjure the faith . . . women also have weak memories. . . . As she is a liar by nature, so in her speech she stings while she delights us. . . . [S]he is an imperfect animal, she always deceives.[75]

Allegations of witchcraft were not only made against women; however, their impact on women arguably was more significant. When witch trials came to prominence in Europe in the 1400s, women had no voice at all in the formal mechanisms of disputing. Legal status for women was afforded only as dependents, slaves, or property. Notably, the *first time* women were accorded "independent legal status" of any kind in a courtroom was when they offered evidence as suspected witches.[76]

There is a unique connection between rape law and witchcraft. Until the 1990s, a sexual assault victim pressing charges in a U.S. court might have come up against the Hale instruction, the caution to jurors that rape was a charge easily made and difficult to disprove.[77] The author of the instruction and first to offer it was Sir Matthew Hale, the jurist, known for his disdain of idle wives discussed in chapter 2, who reached his prime in the early fifteenth century.[78] Hale presided over trials for both rape and witchcraft, and his opinions were outliers in both contexts.[79] During the latter, Hale became notorious for having sentenced two young women to death based on sketchy "evidence" that the girls had vomited pins, "cursed horses," and somehow engineered "lice of extraordinary bigness" and a "popping toad," accusations that were treated with skepticism even in the mid 1500s.[80] In a time marked by misogyny, Hale drew attention for his dismissive opinions about marital rape, holding—in contrast to fellow justices—that a husband could never be guilty of rape committed upon a "lawful wife," since "by their mutual matrimonial consent and contract the wife hath given up herself in this kind unto her husband, which she cannot retract."[81]

Hale's famous and long-standing instruction about the accusation of rape being "easily" made and hard to disprove originated in a treatise on magic with which the lord was enamored. The book was not about rape but the supernatural, noting that "[t]he accusation [of witchcraft] was easy to make and hard to disprove."[82] Hale transposed the phrase so that an invocation that was once offered to protect women against charges of witchcraft was now applied to insulate men against charges made *by* women in the context of rape.

The Hale instruction, offered by judges in some U.S. jurisdictions until the 1990s, is not the only vestige of biological assumptions that continue to cling to sexual assault law. Professor John Wigmore's 1940 treatise on evidence, produced hundreds of years after Hale's pronouncements, emphasizes the importance of admitting evidence of female chastity in rape cases: "There is, however, at least one situation in which chastity may have a direct connection with veracity, viz, when a woman or young girl testifies as complainant against a man charged with a sexual crime—rape, rape under age, seduction, assault." Wigmore explains that,

> Modern psychiatrists have amply studied the behavior of errant young girls and women coming before the courts in all sorts of cases. Their

> psychic complexes are multifarious, distorted partly by inherent defects, partly by diseased derangements or abnormal instincts, partly by bad social environment, partly by temporary physiological or emotional conditions. One form taken by these complexes is that of contriving false charges of sexual offenses by men. The unchaste (let us call it) mentality finds incidental but direct expression in the narration of imaginary sex-incidents of which the narrator is the heroine or the victim.[83]

Taking a page from Hale, Wigmore strongly advocated that no jury should be allowed to deliberate regarding an alleged sexual offense unless the "social history and mental makeup" of the complainant were first thoroughly examined by a physician.[84]

Like the designation of the gold digger, characterizations of women as "more prone [than men] to abjure the faith" or of "greedy appetite" are not random insults but controlling images, politicized distinctions that have served, and continue to serve, the important, strategic purpose of excluding women as a group or category from the elite, male-dominated status quo. As Bourke argued about turn-of-the-century descriptions of young immigrant girls as "lying as easily as morphine fiends," the persistent framing of women as, biologically, liars is a political one, implying that men as a category are more logical, and more likely to be truthful.[85]

In chapter 2, the book discusses how the frequent appearance of the term "gold digger" across social media is effecting a politicized role reversal in which sexual assault accusers are transformed into extortionists and the celebrities accused into innocent targets. Similarly, today, not only is it most commonly men in power who claim to be the objects of witch hunts but, in a blatant, discursive rejection of power dynamics, it is the "witches" who are identified as doing the targeting. After Bill Cosby's sentencing, his defense team made a public statement. The attorneys attributed the jury's verdict to systemic racism, given "what this country has done to black men for centuries."[86] But they did not stop there. The lawyers went on to describe Cosby's conviction as a product of a "sex war," comparing allegations against the comedian to those against Brett Kavanaugh.[87]

As Silbey describes, there is a "gap" between law on the books and law in society, and it is usually the most powerful or elite who control how definitions are negotiated within this space.[88] Looking closely at the discursive (de)volution of the terms "lynch mob" and "witch hunt" on social media provides a lens into how definitions are being debated in a moment of crisis and into who is controlling the discourse. In April 2018, the Equal Justice Initiative opened the National Memorial for Peace and Justice, a physical monument "to the legacy of enslaved black people, people terrorized by lynching . . . humiliated by racial segregation and Jim Crow."[89] Around the same time, hundreds of tweets proclaimed that white, rich, elderly men such as Donald Trump, Roman Polanski, Harvey

Weinstein, and Roy Moore must be protected from the pressures of the #metoo "lynch mob."

This is not a harmless sleight of hand but a political framing. Not every historical moment is up for grabs but, legally speaking, this one is. Out of the debates that occur on social media, the trajectory of legal history is being altered.[90] Perhaps the most significant danger in redefining the idea of the witch hunt is that, while such processes historically were conducted by governments against citizens, now allegations of witch hunts arise in disputes pitting citizen against citizen or, in the cases of Roy Moore and Donald Trump, citizens against the state. The term "witch hunt"—coined to describe a situation in which, based on insufficient evidence, the government targeted nonconforming parties—now, disturbingly, is being transmogrified to describe unlawful attempts by "outsiders" to usurp governmental power. The least powerful are the ones being categorized as holding the cards.

Notably, the discursive transformation of powerful women into witches is a bipartisan effort. When counselor to the president Kellyanne Conway seemed exceptionally quiet for a few weeks in early 2017, a popular meme featured a photo of the stockinged feet of the Wicked Witch of the East sticking out from under Dorothy's house, with the tag line, "Where is Kellyanne?"[91] Both Conway and presidential confidante Omorosa Manigault Newman have been portrayed in comedy sketches as "stalking" the president.[92] Across the political fence, women who are engaging in public, political speech are recast as aberrant—witches and bitches.

INTERSECTIONALITY

As discussed in earlier chapters, contemporary rape law is deeply embedded in and affected by race and by gender. Although contemporary laws on their face are race and gender neutral, such laws are not blank slates. The history of using rape law as a weapon of terror against the Black community should not be swept up in the wake of contemporary "color-blind" jurisprudence. While this chapter critiques the gendered reframing of rape accusations as a witch hunt, it does not intend to erase white women's role in effecting this terror.

As the dust settles after the 2016 election, and as participants in #MeToo consider next steps, it is essential to identify and learn from the socioeconomic and racial schisms that have hampered the sexual assault reform movement since its inception. Feminism is in the midst of a period of reckoning during which women of color are being recognized for longstanding contributions to social change and white women are being called out for the role many have played in furthering racist, classist, and even misogynist oppressions.

Mary Louise Fellows and Sherene Razack identify the "hierarchical relations" that historically have functioned within the women's movement, observing that it is more comfortable to call out the systems that oppress us, and much more challenging to identify and confront the systems of oppression in which we ourselves are dominant.[93] Morgan Jerkins describes that, although white women today are more likely to categorize themselves as oppressed rather than oppressors, in focusing on the ways in which they themselves have been oppressed, white feminists have created an artificial distance between their actions and the potential impact of those actions on nonwhite people. Jerkins observes,

> We need to realize that white feminine fear does not produce innocuous behavior, but a kind of harassment that often leads to racial trauma. If we are ever going to meaningfully address racial injustice in this country, we must unpack the power of this fear and understand how it is inextricably linked to discrimination, police brutality and other forms of racial terrorism. For it is through someone's baseless apprehension that people like myself are only a phone call away from being exterminated.[94]

Carolyn Bryant's recantation of her damning allegations against Emmett Till comes at a time during which the feminist movement is beginning, hopefully, to acknowledge the long-standing role white women have played in promoting harmful social policies.[95] Stephanie Jones-Rogers, for example, powerfully identifies the ways in which white women, not merely trapped in the home, in fact actively participated in Southern slave markets.[96] Stacey Patton and others have begun to call out what have been labeled "#beckys," white women notifying law enforcement about ordinary actions of African Americans that they view as threatening or out of place.

Patton's description of one of these white women might have described Caroline Bryant fifty years ago. Patton writes that, because white women don't *feel* privileged, they are inclined to claim power by asserting it over others. She observes,

> History, as well as the voting patterns of white women, show that white women will endure the antipathy of misogyny for the benevolence of patriarchy. . . . Their position as white women, vulnerable, fragile, and in need of protection places them above and distanced from the violence and death that defines the conditions of Blacks, Muslims, and immigrants in this country. It's an easy choice white women have made over and over again.[97]

The description is a recognition that, while white women historically may have been politically powerless, as a group they were culturally powerful,

> They had "pretty" power—which was lethal. White women weaponized their tears and femininity to assert their power over Black lives.

> From Emmett Till to the Scottsboro boys, white women would cry for attention and make false rape claims and white supremacist men were eager to believe it and exact violent retribution for crimes not committed. Today, they continue testing their power over black bodies and manipulating white male hatred and state authority to see if they'll "defend" them.[98]

Social media discussions about sexual assault allegations and media coverage often support the idea that claimants are being marshaled by attorneys like Gloria Allred as part of a white feminist "power grab." An article in defense of Aziz Ansari in the *Atlantic* complains,

> I thought it would take a little longer for the *hit squad* of privileged young white women to open fire on brown-skinned men. I had assumed that on the basis of intersectionality and all that, they'd stay laser focused on college-educated white men for another few months. But we're at warp speed now, and the revolution—in many ways so good and so important—is starting to sweep up all sorts of people into its conflagration: the monstrous, the cruel, and the simply unlucky. Apparently there is a *whole country full of young women* who don't know how to call a cab, and who have spent a lot of time picking out pretty outfits for dates they hoped would be nights to remember. They're angry and temporarily powerful, and last night they destroyed a man who didn't deserve it.[99]

Although, as discussed above, the potential consequences of being labeled a rapist in today's society are indeed frightening, the *Atlantic* author's categorizing the claims of one person regarding an incident she deems to have been harmful *to her* into the deliberately focused actions of "witch hunt" or "hit squad" is problematic. Where the piece—like many online comments—veers astray is in the assessment of the allocation of power. In identifying a "whole country full of angry young women," and in ascribing both intent and power to "destroy" men to those women, the author echoes many online commenters. However, while it may be Ruby Bates who set the wheels in motion to convict the Scottsboro defendants, it was a flawed legal system that ultimately destroyed them.

Alison Edwards sought to point out the role of systemic oppressions in her response to the publication of Susan Brownmiller's treatise about white women's rape, *Against Our Will*, in the 1970s. She wrote,

> What is more important [than discussions of sexual assault is that] the unemployment rate for non-whites is double that of whites. . . . [t]here is an increase in the police and prison repression of third world communities. The U.S. economic system, itself built on world-wide violence, is in crisis. As people sit home, frustrated, unable to find work, often without the most elementary necessities, they lash out at each other.[100]

While identifying a "hit squad of privileged white women opening fire" importantly calls out the highly problematic role of white women in making unfounded claims that have upheld and supported discriminatory structures, it does not address the power dynamics that have inspired and encouraged such claims. It is also an open question whether, in this new era of social media, cultural power—in Patton's terms, "pretty" power—is in fact akin to legal or political power or if, as Adichie describes of "bottom power" in Nigeria, cultural power is in fact an impotent attempt to latch on to the power of others. If we fail to identify the role of the state in perpetuating violence and racial and socioeconomic inequalities, a vital moment for the renegotiation of power may be lost.

CONCLUSION

In the forty years between the 1980s and today, incarceration rates in the United States have risen by more than 400 percent.[101] This wave of mass incarceration disproportionately has impacted Black men who, until recently, were being imprisoned at a rate more than five times that of whites.[102] While the media focus has been on the role of drug sentencing in fostering these disparities, the war on drugs does not tell the whole story of mass incarceration. Black males remain likely to be overidentified and overprosecuted for most criminal offenses, including sex-related offenses.[103] According to the Innocence Project, at least fourteen African American men who have been proven innocent via DNA evidence were convicted based on mistaken cross-racial identification as part of a rape or murder of a white female victim.[104] There is a danger that extralegal processes such as university Title IX proceedings, which have no requirement that institutions provide data regarding race and accusations, may be continuing to further the ongoing, symbiotic relationship between rape and racism.[105]

The power and pervasiveness of social media today mean that, in the context of sexual assault, it is not only victims, but the accused, who face potentially harsh and stigmatizing treatment. Comments across social media reflect that the public understands and appreciates the harms that may result from an unjustified accusation of rape, particularly for nonwhite suspects and defendants. Not uncommonly, online comments situate the harms allegedly experienced by victims in the context of a racist U.S. history that has relied on the claims of white, female accusers in order to enact terror against Black men.

The contemporary concept of "lynch mobs" and "witch hunts" being discussed on social media today, however, often bear little relation to their historical predecessors. The categorization of rape allegations as "mob justice" or akin to lynching are like the image of the 1650s "witch" and the 1980s "welfare queen"—deliberate efforts to effect political transformations by misidentifying or obscuring structures of power, operating in service of an elite and patriarchal status quo.

Commenters who assert that a media "lynch mob" is set on taking down Donald Trump or Roy Moore create an offensive and false equivalence between the allegations against a white billionaire and those against a disenfranchised Black youth like Emmett Till. In doing so, the unique hardships identified by the Supreme Court in *Powell v. Alabama* are ignored. Similarly, rampant characterizations of rape accusations as "witch hunts" conducted *by* rather than *against* witches obscure a deeply problematic history in which law most often has been engaged by white male elites to maintain power by delimiting women as a category.

With the assertion that "mobs" of feminists—the implication often being white feminists—are using sexual assault law as a weapon in greater gender wars has come a significant shift in ideas about due process. During the Warren era, rights expansion was identified as a liberal objective, the Democratic insistence on due process juxtaposed against the conservative, Republican crime control system of justice. Today's social media comments frame liberals—often feminist liberals—as seeking to forgo due process in order to effect swift, efficient justice against perpetrators of sexual assault.

Comments like those identifying Gloria Allred as a ringleader of the "feminazis" often are categorized as "backlash" against advancements to law effected by the women's movement. However, in reality, feminist attempts to change rape law, such as abolishing the death penalty or gradating penalties for degrees of sexual assault, have been accompanied by laws and policies that have expanded rather than shrunk the carceral state.[106] This trajectory may be exacerbated under the current, crime control–friendly administration which, for example, argues for reinstating capital punishment for some non-homicide crimes.[107] Online discourse privileges the dichotomous "us versus them" rhetoric of "sex wars," pitting arguments that the liberal, feminist needle has not swung far enough against those that the needle has swung too far. It is possible, however, that true feminist change to sexual assault law, change that both provides justice to victims and protects the due process of perpetrators, remains elusive.

NOTES

1. This chapter was adapted and reprinted in part with permission from *Honest Victim Scripting in the Twitterverse*. 22 William and Mary Journal of Women and the Law 495 (2016). © 2016 William and Mary Journal of Women and the Law.

2. Sheila Weller, "How Author Timothy Tyson Found the Woman at the Center of the Emmett Till Case," *Vanity Fair*, January 26, 2017, https://www.vanityfair.com/news/2017/01/how-author-timothy-tyson-found-the-woman-at-the-center-of-the-emmett-till-case?mbid=social_twitter.

3. Weller, "How Tyson Found."

4. Weller, "How Tyson Found." The case at the time was publicly labeled "the wolf-whistle murder."

5. The story as told to *Look* by the perpetrators may not be entirely accurate. For example, some researchers believe that Milam and Bryant may have omitted involvement of accomplices. Devery Anderson, "Widow of Emmett Till Killer Dies Quietly, Notoriously," *USA Today*, February 27, 2014, https://www.usatoday.com/story/news/nation/2014/02/27/emmett-till-juanita-milam/5873235/.

6. Weller, "How Tyson Found." There is some debate regarding whether Bryant indeed recanted, as her words were not recorded. Jerry Mitchell, "Bombshell Quote Missing from Emmett Till Tape. So, Did Caroline Bryant Donham Really Recant?, *Mississippi Clarion Ledger*, August 21, 2018, https://www.clarionledger.com/story/news/2018/08/21/emmett-till-carolyn-bryant-donham-recant-quote-missing/1017876002/.

7. Wiggins, "Rape, Racism," 111.

8. Capers, "Real Rape Too," 1349; Harris, "Race and Essentialism," 233–34. Angela Harris describes how, like gender, race is often presumed to be a "biological categor[y], Black becoming 'the name for a category of people who are by nature morally and intellectually inferior'; just as 'women (read white) are morally superior—naturally caring, self-sacrificing, all-suffering—but intellectually deficient and inherently irrational.'"

9. "History of Lynchings," NAACP, http://www.naacp.org/history-of-lynchings/.

10. Wiggins, "Rape, Racism," 107.

11. "Lynching in America," Equal Justice Initiative.

12. Vivian Berger, "Man's Trial, Woman's Tribulation: Rape Cases in the Courtroom," *Columbia Law Review* 77, no. 1 (1977): 4.

13. *Powell v. Alabama*, 287 U.S. 45 (1932).

14. *Powell v. Alabama*.

15. *Powell v. Alabama*.

16. Kelly Kazek, "The Sad Ends of the Scottsboro Boys: Their Lives in Brief Biographies," AL.com, April 15, 2013, http://blog.al.com/breaking/2013/04/the_sad_ends_of_the_scottsboro.html.

17. Alan Blinder, "Alabama Pardons 3 'Scottsboro Boys' After 80 Years," *New York Times*, November 21, 2013, https://www.nytimes.com/2013/11/22/us/with-last-3-pardons-alabama-hopes-to-put-infamous-scottsboro-boys-case-to-rest.html.

18. "About *The Central Park Five*," PBS, http://www.pbs.org/kenburns/centralparkfive/about-central-park-five/.

19. Brentin Mock, "How Our Fear of 'Wilding' Colored the Central Park Five Case," *Grist*, July 8, 2014, https://grist.org/cities/how-our-fear-of-wilding-colored-the-central-park-five-case/.

20. Sarah Burns, "Why Trump Doubled Down on the Central Park Five," Opinion, *New York Times*, October 17, 2016, https://www.nytimes.com/2016/10/18/opinion/why-trump-doubled-down-on-the-central-park-five.html.

21. Another similar story is that of the Groveland Four, pardoned in January 2019, seventy years after false allegations were made against them. https://www.miamiherald.com/news/politics-government/state-politics/article224282780.html.

22. Francine Banner, "Narrowing the Construction of 'Innocence': Societal and Constitutional Consequences," in *Controversies in Innocence Cases in America*, ed. Sarah Lucy Cooper (London: Ashgate, 2014), 159–74.

23. "Fact Sheet: Trends in U.S. Corrections," The Sentencing Project, June 2018, https://sentencingproject.org/wp-content/uploads/2016/01/Trends-in-US-Corrections.pdf.

24. "Trends," The Sentencing Project.

25. Peter Edelman, "In 2017, It's Still a Crime to Be Poor," *Nation*, November 3, 2017, https://www.thenation.com/article/the-price-of-justice/.

26. Felman, *Juridical Unconscious*.

27. Michael A. Messner, *Politics of Masculinities: Men in Movements* (Lanham, MD: Rowman & Littlefield, 2000): Peter Finocchiaro, "Is the Men's Rights Movement Growing?," *Salon*, March 29, 2011, https://www.salon.com/2011/03/29/scott_adams_mens_rights_movement/.
28. Reddit, The Red Pill, https://www.reddit.com/r/TheRedPill/.
29. Murray, "Inequality's Frontiers," citing Brief Amici Curiae for the ACLU et al. at 11, *Coker*, 433 U.S. 584 (No. 75-5444), 1976 WL 181482, at *11.
30. Murray, "Inequality's Frontiers."
31. Yung, "Rape Law Fundamentals," 16.
32. Yung, "One of These Laws," 372–73; Mears, *American Criminal Justice Policy*, 81.
33. Yung, "One of these Laws," 372–73; Anderson, "Campus Sexual Assault," 1955 (noting that from 2001 to 2010 eighteen states increased terms of incarceration applicable to rape, while others "lifted punishment ceilings and even built higher floors. For example, the share of federal sexual offenders subject to mandatory minimum sentences rose from five percent in 2001 to fifty-one percent in 2010."); Mears, *American Criminal Justice Policy*, 81–82.
34. "About Lawfare: A Brief History of the Term and the Site," Lawfare Blog, https://www.lawfareblog.com/about-lawfare-brief-history-term-and-site.
35. Michael Edison Hayden, "Fake News Story about Chuck Schumer Implodes after Pro-Trump Conspiracy Theorists Claim Source Went Dark," *Newsweek*, December 13, 2017, http://www.newsweek.com/fake-news-story-chuck-schumer-implodes-747384.
36. Jordain Carney, "Schumer Pursuing Legal Action after Fake Sexual Harassment Accusations," *The Hill*, December 13, 2017, http://thehill.com/homenews/senate/364706-schumer-pursuing-legal-action-after-fake-sexual-harassment-accusations.
37. Veronica Stracqualursi, "Woman Admits Accusations against Broward County Sheriff are 'Fake,'" CNN, March 23, 2018, https://www.cnn.com/2018/03/23/politics/florida-sheriff-hoax-videos/index.html.
38. Stracqualursi, "Woman Admits."
39. Aric Jenkins, "The *Washington Post* Says a Woman Tried to Give Them a Fake Roy Moore Story," *Time*, November 28, 2017, http://time.com/5038629/jaime-phillips-roy-moore-washington-post-project-vertias-james-okeefe/; Weiss, "The Limits of Believe."
40. Jenkins, "Fake Roy Moore Story."
41. Bari Weiss, "The Limits of Believe."
42. Tim Fitzsimons and Brandy Zadrozny, "Man Says Buttigieg Never Assaulted Him, Blames Conservative Activists for Claim," *NBC News*, April 30, 2019, https://www.nbcnews.com/feature/nbc-out/man-says-buttigieg-never-assaulted-him-blames-conservative-activists-claim-n1000241; Jon Swaine, "FBI Asked to Investigate Suspected Double Hoax against Mueller," *Guardian*, October 30, 2018, https://www.theguardian.com/us-news/2018/oct/30/robert-mueller-fbi-hoax.
43. Andrew Breiner, "Pizzagate, Explained: Everything You Want to Know about the Comet Ping Pong Pizzeria Conspiracy Theory but Are Too Afraid to Search for on Reddit," *Salon*, December 10, 2016, https://www.salon.com/2016/12/10/pizzagate-explained-everything-you-want-to-know-about-the-comet-ping-pong-pizzeria-conspiracy-theory-but-are-too-afraid-to-search-for-on-reddit.
44. Jason Wilson, "Crisis Actors, Deep State, False Flag: The Rise of Conspiracy Theory Code Words," *Guardian*, February 21, 2018, https://www.theguardian.com/us-news/2018/feb/21/crisis-actors-deep-state-false-flag-the-rise-of-conspiracy-theory-code-words; Levi Maxi, "False Flags in Cyberspace: Targeting Public Opinion and Political Will," *Cipher Brief*, March 6, 2018, https://www.thecipherbrief.com/false-flags-cyberspace-targeting-public-opinion-political-will.
45. Wilson, "Crisis Actors.
46. Breiner, "Pizzagate."
47. "The Harvey Weinstein Effect," *USA Today*, https://www.usatoday.com/pages/interactives/life/the-harvey-weinstein-effect/.

48. Doree Shafrir, "What to Do with 'Shitty Media Men'?," BuzzFeedNews.com, October 12, 2017, https://www.buzzfeednews.com/article/doree/what-to-do-with-shitty-media-men#.raZYroJL6; Katie McDonough, "This Was Always Going to Hurt," *Splinter*, October 13, 2017, https://splinternews.com/this-was-always-going-to-hurt-1819434482 (noting that the Shitty Media Men list was "derailed before it could develop meaning").

49. Constance Grady, "Shitty Men List Creator Moira Donegan on the Year in #MeToo," Vox.com, October 16, 2018, https://www.vox.com/culture/2018/10/16/17955392/moira-donegan-interview-me-too-shitty-media-men-list.

50. "Weinstein Effect," *USA Today*.

51. "Weinstein Effect," *USA Today*.

52. Sarah B. Berson, "Beyond the Sentence—Understanding Collateral Consequences," *National Institute of Justice Journal* 272, https://www.nij.gov/journals/272/Pages/collateral-consequences.aspx.

53. Jeannie Suk Gersen, "Shutting Down Conversations about Rape at Harvard Law," *New Yorker*, December 11, 2015, https://www.newyorker.com/news/news-desk/argument-sexual-assault-race-harvard-law-school.

54. Gersen, "Shutting Down Conversations."

55. Banner, "Institutional Sexual Assault."

56. In 2011, approximately 80 percent of colleges and universities were using a preponderance standard to assess responsibility of perpetrators for sexual assault. During the Obama administration, a "Dear Colleague" letter formally announced an administrative preference for the preponderance standard, rather than the higher standard of clear and convincing evidence used in some civil trials. The Trump administration has rescinded this formal preference for the lower standard of proof, although most colleges and universities continue to use the criterion of preponderance of the evidence. Kathryn Joyce, "The Takedown of Title IX," *New York Times Magazine*, December 5, 2017, https://www.nytimes.com/2017/12/05/magazine/the-takedown-of-title-ix.html.

57. Hannah Brenner, "Opinion: DeVos' New Guidelines on Handling Campus Sexual Assault Raise Risk of Another MSU," Op-Ed, *Detroit Free Press*, January 26, 2018, https://www.freep.com/story/opinion/contributors/2018/01/26/msu-title-9/1065913001/

58. Gersen, "Shutting Down Conversations."

59. Kamilah Willingham, "To the Harvard 19: Do Better," Medium.com, March 24, 2016, https://medium.com/@kamily/to-the-harvard-law-19-do-better-1353794288f2.

60. Willingham, "Do Better."

61. The Brandon Project: Facts Matter, http://brandonproject.org.

62. Glenn Frankel, *High Noon: The Hollywood Blacklist and the Making of an American Classic* (London: Bloomsbury, 2017), 12.

63. Bianca Quilantan, "U. of Pennsylvania Revokes Honorary Degrees to Steve Wynn and Bill Cosby," *Chronicle of Higher Education*, February 1, 2018, https://www.chronicle.com/article/U-of-Pennsylvania-Revokes/242415.

64. Today, biases in the media may be more implicit than overt. For example, Dixon and Linz found that prejudicial information about the background of defendants was twice as likely to be mentioned by local newscasters in cases where there was a nonwhite defendant and a white victim. Travis L. Dixon and Daniel Linz, "Race and the Misrepresentation of Victimization on Local Television News," *Communication Research* 27, no. 5 (2000): 547–73.

65. "Race and Wrongful Convictions," The Innocence Project, June 24, 2010, https://www.innocenceproject.org/race-and-wrongful-convictions/.

66. Jess Bidgood, Richard Fausset, and Campbell Robertson, "For Roy Moore, a Long History of Combat and Controversy," *New York Times*, November 18, 2017, https://www.nytimes.com/2017/11/18/us/roy-moore-alabama.html.

67. Karen Grigsby Bates, "'Rapists,' 'Huts': Trump's Racist Dog Whistles Aren't New," NPR, January 13, 2018, https://www.npr.org/sections/codeswitch/2018/01/13/577674607/rapists-huts-shitholes-trumps-racist-dog-whistles-arent-new.

68. Hughey and Daniels, "Racist Comments," 337.
69. Sherwin, *Popular Culture and Law*, xiii; Friedman, "Popular Legal Culture," 7.
70. Altheide, *Terrorism*.
71. Brenner, "Resisting Simple Dichotomies," 523; Bennett Capers, "The Unintentional Rapist," *Washington University Law Review* 87 (2010): 1345, 1390.
72. Sahil Chenoy, Jessia Ma, and Stuart A. Thompson, "Trump's Growing Obsession with the 'Witch Hunt,'" Opinion, *New York Times*, August 22, 2018, https://www.nytimes.com/interactive/2018/08/22/opinion/trump-cohen-mueller-investigation.html (observing that, in just one year, President Trump tweeted about "witch hunts" more than 110 times.)
73. Anna Livsey, "Liam Neeson Says Harassment Allegations Are Now 'A Witch-Hunt,'" *Guardian*, January 13, 2018, https://www.theguardian.com/film/2018/jan/13/liam-neeson-says-harassment-allegations-have-become-a-witch-hunt; Paul Chi, "Clooney and Damon: Weinstein Scandal Will Lead to a 'Massive, Systemic Change,'" *Vanity Fair*, October 23, 2017, https://www.vanityfair.com/hollywood/2017/10/george-clooney-matt-damon-harvey-weinstein-suburbicon-witch-hunt.
74. Whitney Gaspard, "Bill Cosby's Lawyer Monique Pressley Calls It Quits," *Essence*, August 16, 2018, https://www.essence.com/news/bill-cosbys-lawyer-monique-pressley-calls-it-quits/.
75. Geis, "Lord Hale, Witches," 37.
76. Anne L. Barstow, *Witchcraze: A New History of the European Witch Hunts* (New York: HarperCollins, 1995), 41
77. Geis, "Lord Hale, Witches," 26.
78. Geis, "Lord Hale, Witches," 26.
79. Geis, "Lord Hale, Witches," 26.
80. Geis, "Lord Hale, Witches," 32, 41. Geis describes that, rather than merely reflecting contemporary, "commonsense" views of women, Hale's viewpoint was disputed by other jurists of the time, with some fellow justices specifically disputing Hale's outlier position with regard to a husband's conjugal rights.
81. Geis, "Lord Hale, Witches," 40.
82. Geis, "Lord Hale, Witches," 26.
83. Anderson, "Campus Sexual Assault," 1948, citing John Henry Wigmore, *A Treatise on the Anglo-American System of Evidence in Trials at Common Law* §924a, at 459 (3d ed. 1940).
84. Denise R. Johnson, "Prior False Allegations of Rape: Falsus in Uno, Falsus in Omnibus?," *Yale Journal of Law and Feminism* 7, no. 2 (1995): 252, 253, fn. 51.
85. Bourke, *Rape*, 31, fn. 30; Hill Collins, *Black Feminist Thought*, 68, 225–26.
86. Julia Jacobs, "Cosby's Team Alleges Racism and Sexism, Calling Him a Victim of a 'Sex War,'" *The New York Times*, September 25, 2018, https://www.nytimes.com/2018/09/25/us/cosby-jail-racist-sex-war.html.
87. Jacobs, "Cosby's Team."
88. Silbey, "After Legal Consciousness."
89. "Lynching," Equal Justice Initiative.
90. Abeysekara, *Colors*, 4, fn. 10.
91. Susan Chira, "Sexist Political Criticism Finds a New Target: Kellyanne Conway," *New York Times*, March 5, 2017, https://www.nytimes.com/2017/03/05/us/kellyanne-conway-sexist-political-criticism.html.
92. Chira, "Sexist Political Criticism."
93. Mary Louise Fellows and Sherene Razack, "The Race to Innocence: Confronting Hierarchical Relations among Women," *Journal of Gender, Race and Justice* 1 (1998): 335–52.
94. Morgan Jerkins, "Why White Women Keep Calling the Cops on Black People," *Rolling Stone*, July 17, 2018, https://www.rollingstone.com/politics/politics-features/why-white-women-keep-calling-the-cops-on-black-people-699512/.
95. For example, when the [nine] Scottsboro defendants were convicted in *Powell v. Alabama*, the court overlooked evidence that the accusers had been traveling across

state lines for the purposes of prostitution. Wiggins, "Rape, Racism," 127. However, while there were social pressures for the women to lie, it is also true that Victoria Price seems to have done so with particular relish, embellishing the story of the alleged assault with details about the assailants wielding weapons and promising to make her pregnant, leading one observer of the trial to note that it would be a "wonder" if the Scottsboro defendants' attorney got "out alive." "The Scottsboro Accusers," PBS, http://www.pbs.org/wgbh/americanexperience/features/scottsboro-ruby-bates-and-victoria-price/.

96. Stephanie Jones-Rogers, *They Were Her Property: White Women as Slave Owners in the American South* (New Haven: Yale University Press, 2019).

97. Stacey Patton, "Why #MeToo Needs to Talk about Predatory White Women," *Dame,* October 23, 2018, https://www.damemagazine.com/2018/10/23/why-metoo-needs-to-talk-about-predatory-white-women/.

98. Patton, "White Women." The treatment of sexual assault accusers across social media supports this idea that privilege is least visible to those who have it. Fiona Smith, "Privilege Is Invisible to Those Who Have It: Engaging Men in Workplace Equality," *Guardian,* June 7, 2016, https://www.theguardian.com/sustainable-business/2016/jun/08/workplace-gender-equality-invisible-privilege. Jerkins identifies white women as "weaponiz[ing] fear." Jerkins, "Why White Women Keep Calling."

99. Caitlin Flanagan, "The Humiliation of Aziz Ansari," *Atlantic,* January 14, 2018, https://www.theatlantic.com/entertainment/archive/2018/01/the-humiliation-of-aziz-ansari/550541/.

100. Alison Edwards, "Rape, Racism, and the White Women's Movement: An Answer to Susan Brownmiller," Sojourner Truth Organization (STO), http://www.sojournertruth.net/rrwwm.html.

101. "Trends," The Sentencing Project.

102. "Trends," The Sentencing Project.

103. Capers, "Real Rape Too"; Janet Halley, "Trading the Megaphone for the Gavel in Title IX Enforcement," *Harvard Law Review Forum* 128 (2015): 103–17.

104. "African American Wrongful Convictions Today," The Innocence Project, March 29, 2013, https://www.innocenceproject.org/african-american-wrongful-convictions-today/.

105. Halley, "Trading the Megaphone," 108.

106. Yung, "Rape Law Fundamentals"; Halley, "Trading the Megaphone"; Kristin Bumiller, *In an Abusive State: How Neoliberalism Appropriated the Feminist Movement Against Sexual Violence* (Durham, NC: Duke University Press, 2008).

107. Philip Bump, "Trump's Death-Penalty Advocacy Hopes to Make America 1990 Again," *Washington Post,* March 16, 2018, https://www.washingtonpost.com.

FIVE

Monsters

People of the State of California v. Brock Allen Turner

In June 2015, Stanford University student Brock Turner was arrested after two witnesses saw Turner digitally penetrating a young woman who appeared to be unconscious. Turner faced a jury trial, and was convicted on three felony counts of sexual assault.[1] Although the conviction carried a potential sentence of ten or more years, the consequences Turner faced were lighter: six months in county jail, followed by three years of formal probation, registration as a sex offender, and participation in a sex offender rehabilitation program.[2] The case gained widespread attention after the online publication of an impact statement by the victim, Emily Doe, which described her frustration that, even though the case included the "classic" requirements of both physical evidence and corroborating witnesses, Doe faced an exhausting and uphill battle to secure Turner's conviction and, in her view, markedly insufficient sentence.[3]

While victim impact statements have been in practice for a while, the viral dissemination of Doe's statement was something new. Not only did social media enable the widespread sharing—for the first time—of a very personal narrative describing in detail not only the immediate aftermath but the ongoing impact of sexual assault, but social network sites opened invigorating opportunities for people to engage with one another in dialogue about the consequences faced by Turner and, importantly, to debate about what those consequences should have been.

Across feminist websites like Jezebel and Babe.net, and everyday news outlets like *USA Today* and People.com, commenters offer similar sentiments not only about Turner's sentence but about character of the man himself. Posters on one feminist site observe that Turner should "be in jail for the rest of his miserable fucking life" and describe "how vile he is," "how deserving he is of a long, torturous, detestable life." A post recommends that "we put the definition [of rape] with [Turner's] face up on some billboards for all those who still don't know what rape is or what it looks like."

Most complain that Turner's sentence was a "slap on the wrist." One person describes it as an "absolute fucking outrage [about] how our judicial system deals with rape." Another suggests, "I know we like to complain about mandatory minimums for nonviolent drug offenses but it sounds like that is something that would help in the case of rape, i.e. you get 3 years minimum regardless of mitigating factors and it goes up from there depending on severity."

On another feminist site, a story that refers to Turner as "human garbage" in its title draws comments exclaiming, "He gets 3 months . . . like what in the ACTUAL FUCK?" One person observes, angrily, that "[t]he whole system is fucked [when] [p]eople get more prison time for shoplifting than sexual molestation of a child." Another implores, "Jesus christ dude. Someone just take him out."

Like the social media comments identifying discriminatory impacts of the law discussed in the previous chapter, these comments about Brock Turner's sentence suggest something positive—that the general public recognizes that injustices to victims, as well as racial and socioeconomic injustices for perpetrators, are deeply embedded in the U.S. criminal justice system. Posts about the Turner case accurately observe that "most rapists aren't convicted." Others raise concerns about how privilege might have operated in the context of Turner's trial, for which the presiding judge was a fellow Stanford alumnus. A reader on a feminist site wonders, what if

> [Turner] were a drop out who was not white . . . would [he] have had so many advocates[?] . . . So many people rushing to save his life and not ensure that he was stigmatized to the nth degree. So many people listening to his friends or family or willing to side with them because they fear what it means to have that privilege stripped away. That benefit of the doubt.

A similar comment argues that Turner should have been expected to behave better due to his status.

> Our society routinely shows us that young, wealthy, white men are viewed as having made mistakes when they end up being called "defendant." The attitude is always "This person fucked up, but they aren't a *bad person.*" I disagree, this guy *is* a bad person, as are others of his ilk. They have *everything*, the world works in their favor but it's still not enough. . . . They still can't keep their noses clean? They still can't help but abuse others? Fuck em.

Memes circulated comparing the sentence received by Turner to a much longer sentence handed down to Black Vanderbilt University athlete Corey Batey for what commenters argued was a similar offense.[4] A post simply notes, "Let's be real, black and brown rapists would never receive minimum sentences out of fear that jail would be 'detrimental' to their well-being. Fuck everything about this."

As another commenter on a site geared toward feminist readers notes of Turner's penalties, "If anything this will just embolden him, and all other rapists like him. All they have to do is take a sip of beer and they won't go to 'real' prison." Another person raises important issues of race and sexual assault when they sarcastically remark about the judge's sentencing, "I am sure he would have sent a young black defendant with no budding athletic career on his way with the same slap on the wrist." A commenter on the blog of an iconic feminist magazine observes,

> We need to look at what's fair. . . . It's not right that a black man can get twenty-five years or so for rape and a white man can get six months. We need to have equal justice and protection for all victims of rape.

A mainstream news article announces, "Martha Stewart Spent More Time in Jail than Brock Turner!"

Through the identification of privilege and, as the chapter discusses below, the resulting activism in which virtual advocates have engaged—lobbying successfully for expanded statutes of limitations and penalties for sexual assault as well as for the recall of *People v. Turner* judge Aaron Persky—we may, finally, be making important inroads toward eradicating the systemic gender, racial, and socioeconomic biases that stubbornly persist throughout all stages of the criminal justice process.

However, while the virtual court has been swift in its response to the sentencing of Brock Turner, fewer people are interrogating whether the process of virtual sentencing, in fact, has been fair.

For many members of the online public, accusations against Bill Cosby and Jameis Winston raise concerns about systemic failures. For many reasons, including the race of the accused and presumptions about the moral character of accusers, in those cases due process concerns loom large in the public imagination. Although racist, sexist, and classist comments are common in the context of Winston and Cosby, on social media the public also demonstrates an awareness about the racially biased history of the criminal justice system and, specifically, the operation of sexual assault laws within that system.

The Brock Turner case—largely conceptualized as featuring an elite, white male perpetrator and an extremely sympathetic victim—signifies something very different for the virtual jury than the Winston and Cosby allegations. Rather than a triumph of due process, over and over again, Turner's relatively light sentence is held out as an example of the failure of the system in delivering swift and decisive justice. In the actual courtroom, Turner's trial may have exemplified a surfeit of due process, potentially riddled with favoritism premised in gender, race, and socioeconomic inequalities. In the court of public opinion, in contrast, Turner's trial and conviction has been brutal, conclusive, and effective, suggesting that social media not only provide a powerful forum in which social justice may be promoted but in which a cold shoulder is turned to constitutional protections.

A DEGRADATION OF STATUS

Of Brock Turner, a commenter on a major mainstream news site writes, "People who would rape a defenseless woman behind a dumpster aren't normal." Another notes that "[p]redators exist. Sharks exist. We must take the steps to protect ourselves. We cannot educate sociopaths to not rape in the same way we cannot tell serial killers not to murder." A third echoes, "[R]ape of an unconscious victim is . . . indicative of pathology that many forensic psychologists believe is hard-wired. . . . This young man will reoffend, and perhaps next time kill his victim. We can only hope he takes his own life first in the meantime."

An interesting facet of Turner's case was that he was not a celebrity but an everyday individual who became a public figure by virtue of media coverage and social media discussion of his crime. Friedman identifies that, based on a combination of the type of a criminal event and its timing, trials of everyday people can become "celebrity trials."[5] He writes that

> [p]robably not one person out of a million had heard of Lizzie Borden or Sam Sheppard or Claus von Bülow or Scott Peterson or the Menendez brothers before they became enmeshed in the web of criminal justice. Once they did so, however, they became household names.[6]

Today, Brock Turner's image appears next to the definition of sexual assault in a criminal justice textbook, leading one commenter on a feminist site to remark that, despite his brief jail sentence, "[a]t least we'll always have this horrible mugshot of him next to the literal textbook definition of rape."

Harold Garfinkel refers to criminal trials as "status degradation ceremonies," ritualistic processes through which individuals who have transgressed social norms are moved from the category of acceptable members of society to outsiders and "others." As one can see in the conversations about whether Bill Cosby's actions were "real rape" discussed in chapter 1, or in the collective participation in defining gold digger and THOT in chapter 2, it is by identifying and describing deviance that we, collectively, establish what is normal.[7] As conversations about Brock Turner take place on social media, the public is navigating a process through which a formerly at least somewhat socially acceptable bad actor is transformed into a horrific monster.

Over the same period of time as the public debated the Turner case, a status degradation also was being effected in the case of former Team USA Gymnastics doctor Larry Nassar, who in late 2017, Larry Nassar was sentenced to 175 years in prison after pleading guilty to seven counts of first-degree criminal sexual conduct.[8] Allegations against Nassar first gained public attention in 2016 when, after years of complaints of sexual misconduct, female athletes started to go public with descriptions of having been sexually assaulted by the doctor. Over two years, more than two hundred accusers described instances in which the doctor had digitally penetrated them under the guise of treatment, sometimes with their parents present.

If discourse condemning sexual assault perpetrators as aberrant is evident in the Turner case, it is expanded tenfold in discussions about Nassar. A comment on a major news site notes of Nassar's case that "[t]hese poor girls won't be able to lead normal lives because of this monster." A post on a gossip site asks, "What's the point of putting someone in prison for life who has no possibility of getting out? Because our moronic system does not allow us to execute them."

It is easy to understand the swiftness and uniformity with which the court of public opinion rushed to render its verdict in the case of Nassar, who pled guilty to abusing and molesting hundreds of victims, including children, as well as possessing child pornography. As Garfinkel identified, it is in expressing our collective, moral outrage against outsiders that we reinforce insider group solidarity.[9] Via the status degradation process of a criminal trial, a person who was very recently one of *us* is transformed into a totally different person, a "distinct social object" from the individual we knew before.[10] The news media document this transition via interviews with neighbors or coworkers who either attest that they had "no idea" about the perpetrators criminality or identify signs that the person was "evil" all along.[11]

Not all status degradation ceremonies are successful. It takes a particular act or actor to muster the necessary collective, unified opinion of disdain. The Nassar degradation ceremony worked exceptionally well because it brought together even oppositional portions of society in agreement on one issue—it is wrong to abuse a position of power to molest hundreds of children.

While the universal outcry against Nassar is immediately understandable, the rapid and largely unified condemnation of Brock Turner, an "average" young man who committed a first offense, is perhaps more surprising. Strikingly similar words are used to describe Turner and Nassar across social media sites, conservative and liberal—including "predator," "monster," "evil"—although Larry Nassar, by his own admission, committed hundreds of assaults and Turner only confessed to one. For the perpetrators, the effect of their collective, ceremonial casting out from society has been the same—to render them one-dimensional in the public eye. One can see the conclusion of the status degradation process clearly in social media conversations about Nassar, widely described as a "monster," and about Brock Turner, now featured as an exemplary "rapist" in the introduction to a criminal justice textbook. Once a bad actor is determined by *us* to be a "monster," his status is degraded to well outside the norm of ordinary human behavior, and restorative and rehabilitative models of justice no longer apply.

The Turner case, in particular, is notable for the speed and finality with which this rhetorical transition from ordinary criminal actor to monster took place, suggesting that, although the tendency to demonize or dehumanize perpetrators predates social media, online forums enable status degradation to occur more efficiently than ever before. The reductive tendencies of the online environment connect posters to one another via the least common denominator, and encourage them to develop in-groups by defining and demeaning outsiders.

In dehumanizing perpetrators, however, we risk perpetuating the same problems that inhere in the dehumanization of victims. As we focus on the inherent "evil" or "monstrousness" of the bad actor, the focus becomes "less on the crime itself and more on the character of the assailant."[12] As described throughout this book, sexual assault trials demand a "relational and fixed" "victim/perpetrator framework."[13] We not only demand that survivors meet the "ideal victim" stereotype, but we also apply "real rape" stereotypes to alleged perpetrators. "[I]f a party is not recognizable as a perpetrator because he or she fails to conform to the behavior and motivations expected of that role, then there is no recognizable rape."[14]

MONSTER CREATION AND THE REAL RAPE MYTH

One of the primary aims of this book is to identify the insidious, overarching power of real rape myths across social media. As the first few chapters have pointed out, social media conversations suggest that, despite reforms in legislation, we have a long way to go in eradicating rape myths as they impact victims. We may have moved away from quite literally "slut-shaming" accusers for what they wore, but we continue to believe and support most fully those victims who come closest to meeting ideal (and unrealistic) expectations.

As discussed in connection with false claims in chapter 3, the more stereotypically "true" rape myths appear—the more they seem to comport with our commonsense knowledge—the harder they are to identify and confront. Social media comments about Brock Turner suggest that, in addition to striving to minimize the impact of rape myths on victims, we need to examine and address how these myths impact perpetrators and alleged perpetrators.

On culture blog Medium.com, Zachary Elwood outlines some important ways in which news coverage and social media discussions advanced a mistaken public misunderstanding of the Turner case, beginning with the classification of the case as "rape." Technically under California law at the time, Elwood describes, Turner was not convicted of rape, which required sexual intercourse, but of sexual assault based on digital penetration of an unconscious victim.[15] Despite the legal definitions of his crimes, headlines repeatedly referred to Turner as a "convicted rapist," with former website xoJane.com describing the event as an "incredibly horrific rape case" and the *LA Times* reporting a "brutal attack."[16]

Discussions about the location of the incident also elided the truth. Although the victim described the attack as occurring near a dumpster, the police report describes the incident as occurring in a "high visibility area with high foot traffic."[17] Nonetheless, media reports seized on the dumpster element to categorize the crime as "degrading" and Turner's actions as "secretive."[18] Elwood highlights a CNN article embellishing, in opposition to the police report, that "Turner took the victim to a dimly lit, isolated area and sexually assaulted her *behind* a dumpster."

One might be tempted to ask why these seemingly semantic or arcane distinctions matter. Turner's actions clearly were abhorrent. But when it comes to legal decision-making, it is important to keep in mind that small details are neither irrelevant nor semantic. Just this term, for example, the Supreme Court rendered a decision regarding the guilt of a defendant based on its holding that the term "dwelling" in a burglary statute could apply to a mobile home or tent.[19] Perhaps more importantly, labeling Turner's actions correctly matters because those actions *were* terrible as they occurred.

Whether or not it was legally defined as rape, Brock Turner's digital penetration of an unconscious woman was a bad act on its own. By discursively amplifying Turner's actions—and in shifting the formal legal language of "unconscious digital penetration" to the more sensational descriptor of "rape"—media outlets are engaging in more than just simplification. This is a vernacularization of law that once again upholds real rape myths, exaggerating what occurred on the Stanford campus to sway public opinion out of any "gray area" and closer to the identification of the act as a "real and true rape" and, consequently, Turner as a "real rapist."

Across social media, Brock Turner's attorney is vilified for arguing that, rather than intending to commit rape—a legal category that at the time required intercourse—his client intended to perform "outercourse" with Emily Doe, seeking sexual gratification without direct penis to vagina contact.[20] Although the descriptor of "outercourse" is unfortunate, critiques of these arguments about Turner's intent as "splitting hairs" ignore the extent to which there is an overwhelming pressure to situate criminal sexual assault in black-and-white terms, and for the state to situate acts within a "real rape" paradigm.[21] The Brock Turner case could have opened up opportunities, now foreclosed, for public discussion about what acts in fact should constitute crimes, what harms result from such acts, and how perpetrators should be punished. In actuality, however, these potential debates were, as frequently happens in the context of sexual assault, obscured in favor of dichotomous approaches to defining crime, victims, and perpetrators.

Echoing ideas of vernacularization, retired Santa Clara County Superior Court judge LaDoris Cordell argues that the transformation of Brock Turner's actions in public discourse from sexual assault to rape is not accidental but political. She identifies that the media purposefully advanced a "false narrative" engaging the word rape rather than the more precise, legally applicable definition of Turner's alleged conduct.[22] This chapter discusses below some of the impacts of public outcry about Turner's sentence, including the passage of California administrative bills 2888 and 701, which expand the definition of rape in the state and eliminate probation in cases where victims were intoxicated or unconscious.[23] After the bills' passage, the *LA Times* editorial staff joined together in an op-ed critiquing AB 2888, arguing that the bill was "headline-driven," "tailored to the circumstances of [the Turner] case and the unpopular sentence that followed."[24] The staff decried, "Headlines trump thinking in criminal justice."[25]

It is not only in the discursive constructions of his actions but in descriptions of him as a person that the status degradation of Brock Turner is accomplished. In the first three chapters, this book discusses how our collective attention to the character of alleged sexual assault victims serves to obscure potentially important conversations about the societal or systemic factors that enable sexual assaults to occur. We eschew discussions of systemic rape culture in favor of focusing on the character flaws or blameworthiness of the individual accuser.

Our thirst for dispositional explanations impacts not only our impressions of victims but of perpetrators. As described earlier, Scully and Marolla identify a tendency to identify perpetrators of sexual assault as abnormal or pathological.[26] One can see this tendency on social media, as Brock Turner is labeled "garbage," a "sick," "serial predator" who must be put away. As previously mentioned, one comment observes, "People who would rape a defenseless woman behind a dumpster aren't *normal*." A similar comment notes that "A *normal* person's reaction to an unconscious person behind a dumpster would be to call 911 and render aid. A psychopath's response would be to attack that person."

Defining Brock Turner as a "psychopath" or "predator" falls into the pattern, identified by Scully and Marolla and discussed in chapter 1, of treating sexual assault as different from other crimes, and of labeling rapists as further outside societal boundaries than other criminal perpetrators. Mary Koss, the researcher whose landmark studies during the 1980s remain the foundation for the statistic that one in five college-aged women is likely to be sexually assaulted, argues that the association of commission of rape with a tendency toward serial predation is supported by flawed academic research.[27] While criminal justice policy makers, urged by the public, rushed to accept the idea that campus rapes were being committed by serial predators, the likelihood of serial predation was much lower than proclaimed.

This tendency to single out rape as exceptional rather than part of the fabric of society like "ordinary" crimes obscures the extent to which those most likely to commit sexual assaults are usually not strangers but, in fact, are the very people whom we know and love. Portrayals of Turner, before the crime, describe him as an "ordinary" boy with an extraordinary talent. Receiving far less publicity than Doe's impact statement were the forty-four letters written by Turner's family members, friends, and teachers from the city in which he grew up, midsized working class Dayton, Ohio.[28] His swim coach wrote that Brock was "quiet and unassuming" and did not exhibit "an assumption of privilege" the coach saw in "other star athletes."[29] His current boss, the owner of a small company that times running, bicycle, and triathlon races, discusses the consequences for Turner of losing a Stanford education, describing how, as a lifetime sex offender registrant, he is relegated to pursuing minimum wage employment.[30] His best friends describe him as "modest" and "kindhearted."[31] Overall, the letters submitted to the court, many from fellow eighteen-year-olds, depict Turner as a person far from the "Fisher Price–level lesson for recognizing white privilege" that the *Guardian* newspaper argues he represents, or about whom a commenter on a feminist site observes:[32]

> The wealthy white cishet male athlete often displays an extraordinary level of violence and indifference towards other members of its group, particularly females. Scientists have been monitoring this individual, who they've named "Brock Turner, Rapist" . . . [Turner] will not face any *further* penalty for this extraordinary display of sociopathic privilege.

In contexts other than sexual assault, the criminal justice system is making at least some strides toward reform, incorporating holistic strategies like restorative justice or exploring alternatives to sentencing via specialty or treatment courts. We strive to understand drinking to excess or addiction to opioids as not only a disease but a symptom; the abuse of drugs and alcohol increasingly is being recognized as a way of dealing with a lack of social support in the context of an increasingly demanding society. In the Turner case there was no dispute that both parties were significantly intoxicated.[33] The memo Turner provided to the court described a connection between his drinking to excess and the difficulties he faced as a middle-class midwesterner in adjusting to the elite, Silicon Valley lifestyle at Stanford. Turner wrote that

> [c]oming from a small town in Ohio, I had never really experienced celebrating or partying that involved alcohol.

Turner's statement, signaling both confusion and displacement is far from the old boys' network, "white privilege cake with a frosting on top" case that was trumpeted so widely across social media networks.[34] Whether or not one believes Turner's statement should have mitigated his sentence, developing a better understanding about Brock Turner's experience could be helpful in gaining understanding about the motivations of perpetrators and, perhaps, in preventing sexual assault.

On the surface, widespread online characterizations of Turner as a "monster" and a "predator" appear to advance feminist ideals. However, it is less than clear that increasing punishment for the crime of sexual assault is the best way to achieve the long-illusive objective of justice for victims. Further, defining a first-time offender like Brock Turner as a "classic" or "serial" rapist seems to cut against feminist identifications of rape culture, which encourage us to recognize that the crime committed by Brock Turner was not *extrinsic to* or *outside of* societal norms but rather a product of larger cultural interactions.

Katie Roiphe critiques that accepting common characterizations of perpetrators as "leering monsters you have to steer around, as if in a video game" cause us to risk missing a more nuanced, and important, analysis that could improve the criminal justice system.[35] Rather than asking what it was about Turner that made him into a rapist, it may be more useful to focus on what it was about Stanford—or Dayton, Ohio—or U.S. culture, more generally—that created an environment in which he felt enabled or, more problematically, encouraged to digitally penetrate an unconscious woman. The assumption that Brock Turner was a "monster" all along, widely shared across social networks, obfuscates the ways we, as a society, may have participated in creating the monster.

JAILHOUSE JUSTICE

Like comments about "false" sexual assault accusers, online comments about convicted perpetrators are particularly vicious. A comment to a popular magazine announcing Turner's appeal remarks, "[I]t would be great if a motorcycle gang rounded him up and the boys showed him a really good time," while others call to "castrate him" and advocate "tak[ing] the perpetrator out." Suggestions for extralegal justice abound, such as, "Please someone just do us all a favor and take this punk for a ride to the desert." One person implores, "[F]ind his address and let's go have a little chat with this garbage."

Comments on Larry Nassar's sentencing predictably exhibit an even more retributive quality, not infrequently suggesting that the most appropriate penalty for rape is rape. A commenter on a popular gossip site jokes about the doctor, "[m]y psychic sees broomsticks and mop handles in his future." Others observe, "He's gonna get that foot long special for the rest of his life" and "[h]e is going to get to suck a lot of studs in prison. That is no longer considered a punishment."

On a feminist news site, commenters allude more cryptically that Nassar will get "jailhouse justice," offering that the doctor "is a child molester, I heard they don't do so well in prison."

Whenever sexual assault allegations are made against public figures, similar comments emerge. In regard to Bill Cosby, a commenter on a popular newspaper observes, "I guess he'll be using his Fat Albert with his cellmate," while another jests, "Dear Bill, if your cellmate (cellie) offer you Quaaludes, think twice!" A commenter on a different widely read newspaper describes,

> One can only hope that a very large and powerful inmate takes a liking to Mr. Cosby. Then he will have an inkling of what these women have endured at his hands.

Comments advocating that perpetrators face "jailhouse justice" raise important philosophical questions about the purpose of criminal punishment. There is a movement today toward restorative, community-based justice and embracing rehabilitation rather than retribution, particularly in connection with nonviolent offenses. Many of us understand that communities are decimated as a result of what, in many cases, has proven to be a "cradle to prison pipeline" and the harms resulting from warehousing individuals for longer and longer periods of time.[36]

Around the same time as Brock Turner was sentenced, a Brooklyn judge was praised for his holistic approach in in the case of Chevelle Nesbeth, a mother and college student, who had been convicted of drug dealing.[37] Although the justice department advocated that she should spend two to three years in prison, the judge cited the impact of the collateral consequences she would face even without having prison time—a bar on grants to pay for college, the inability to apply for a passport, being evicted from public housing, and a suspension of her driver's license.[38] When the public weighed in on social media, by and large they felt these infringements were more than enough to penalize the young and well-intentioned mom.[39]

When it comes to sexual assault, however, commenters tend to argue that sentences should be longer, harsher, and more retributive. Jill Lepore cites former prosecutor Scott Sundby's categorization of current views on sexual assault as advocating almost biblical punishments: "Hey, we all get to pick up a rock and throw it at this person!" Brock Turner may have been punished too lightly in the view of many commenters, but it is important to recognize that he was punished, serving time in jail, registering as a sex offender for life, dismissed from Stanford University, barred from the university's swim team, and now a "poster child" for rape across social and print media.[40]

As described above, after Turner's sentencing, social media activists successfully lobbied the California legislature and governor to bolster penalties for sexual assault, expanding the definition of rape to include the digital penetration of an unconscious person, eliminating probation as an option in cases where the victim was unconscious, and adding new mandatory minimum sentence provisions.[41]

This call for a multidimensional expansion of the reach of the criminal justice system in connection with sexual assault brings up some troubling questions. First, if serving three months in the county jail and the attendant collateral consequences faced by Brock Turner was too little punishment, what is the right amount? We are in a period of time in which overall violent crime rates, including rates of sexual assault, are down. In addition, in regard to many other offenses—drug crimes, gambling, even intimate partner violence—there is a movement toward de-incarceration and "diverting" suspects out of the criminal justice pipeline via therapeutic approaches, such as treatment, rehabilitation, and restorative justice. The movement toward a crime control system in dealing with rape stands in contrast to this overall trend, making one wonder whether we have thought sufficiently about what goals are going to be met by this expansion of the legal net.

Further, and importantly, we must ask who is likely to be most impacted by these lengthened statutes of limitations, expanded definitions, and mandatory minimum sentences. As identified by social media commenters themselves, it is the privileged who continue to be most able to evade the worst of punishments, due perhaps to judicial "old boys' networks" but also because of access to a pipeline of good lawyers. Historically, Black and other nonwhite persons have been likely to receive more stringent sentences for all crimes but particularly for sexual assault crimes. Brock Turner may be a catalyst for advocating harsher penalties, but elite white men are highly unlikely to be the persons who are most significantly impacted by such penalties.

As highlighted throughout the book, there is a strong societal tendency to pathologize perpetrators of sexual assault and to distinguish the harms of sexual assault from those caused by other "street" crimes. This tendency to prefer an "eye for an eye" approach to punishment fits into a long history of distinguishing sexual assault from other crimes and, consequently contributes to distinct expectations reserved for sexual assault perpetrators and victims. However, the definition of sexual assault as outside the boundaries of normal behavior and condemnation of perpetrators as outside the fabric of society contributes to the continued prevalence of "real rape" myths.

As she sentenced perpetrator Larry Nassar, judge Rosemarie Aquilina made several noteworthy statements. At one point during the proceeding she observed that she was signing the doctor's "death warrant." At another, she mentioned that, if it were up to her, she "would allow some or many people to do to him what he did to others."[42] The judge's comments reflect sentiments advocating prison rape that are common across social media, particularly when it comes to discussions of "monsters" like Nassar and Turner. Although cloaked in the rhetoric of justice, these calls of "rape for rape" do no favors for advancing the feminist cause. Rather, statements like these serve to normalize rape culture by presenting sexual assault as a normal and natural by-product of incarceration.

In a nation comprised of many vulnerable populations, prisoners are arguably the most vulnerable to sexual assault. According to the Bureau of Justice Statistics (BJS), about two hundred thousand people are sexually violated in prison on an annual basis.[43] Rates of sexual assault against inmates are about *thirty times* the rates in the civilian population.[44] Prisoners are likely to underreport crimes, and statutes like the Prison Litigation Reform Act mean they have significantly less access to legal recourse than nonincarcerated counterparts.[45] Our contemporary system of mass incarceration disproportionately impacts the poor and disproportionately incarcerates nonwhite defendants. To suggest that rape not only is likely to but *should* occur in the prison system encourages sexual violence to be committed by and against those with the least power to object. For a judge to even tacitly advocate the perpetuation of rape in the context of such overwhelming oppression is highly problematic. And words have effects. Just hours after being placed in the general population in Tuscon, Arizona, Larry Nassar reported having been assaulted by fellow inmates.[46]

In considering what punishments are appropriate for sexual assault cases, it is important, too, to reckon with the impact of collateral consequences. As described in chapter 4, in U.S. society today, punishment is often less about a term in jail or prison and more about the related and after-effects of incarceration. A person who commits a felony might serve less than a year in prison but, in some states, might lose the right to vote or to hold particular employment. The commission of one crime can mean a lifetime of lost economic opportunities from checking the "felon" box on job applications. Ex-offenders may face a term on a registry or additional months or years of confinement. The offender-funded model of justice means that many people who are released from jail or prison—or their families—must pay thousands of dollars to compensate the state for the costs of their confinement. For many, consequences that once were "collateral" to punishment now form the heart of criminal sanctions.

Only a miniscule number of those revealed to have been perpetrators via #MeToo have faced formal legal sanctions. Yet, many have faced censure within the communities of which they formerly were a part. Throughout fall 2017, as accuser after accuser came forward, the consequences Harvey Weinstein faced were swift and sharp. He was fired from his production company, which subsequently filed for bankruptcy and was sold to investors at a deep discount.[47] Weinstein was suspended from the British Academy of Film and Television Arts, banned for life from the Producers Guild of America, and became the second person ever expelled from the Academy of Motion Picture Arts and Sciences.[48] In addition, the businessman was stripped of the W. E. B. Du Bois Medal he received from Harvard University for his contribution to African and African American culture,[49] and forced to return the honorary bachelor's degree he received on the basis of "experiential credits" from his undergraduate institution, the State University of New York at Buffalo.[50] Queen Elizabeth II is considering revoking Weinstein's title as a Commander of the Order of the British Empire, a disgraced status shared by dictators Benito Mussolini and Robert Mugabe, and France allegedly plans to take away Weinstein's Legion of Honor award.[51] Other well-known alleged perpetrators have faced a similar loss of social and economic opportunities.

The swift and sure revocation of social status confronted by many accused as part of the #MeToo movement raises important questions about the role of law in these cases. When it comes to sexual assault, the custom of dealing with perpetrators extralegally is well-founded. The record of courts in affording justice to victims, providing due process for perpetrators, and protecting members of the community is, to put it bluntly, abysmal. Do we need the imprimatur of a legal process if the heart of punishment—its collateral sanctions—has been accomplished?

The celebration at the arrest and impending trial of Harvey Weinstein suggest that the role of law as an institution remains significant. In May 2018, the disgraced producer painstakingly staged a "perp walk" designed to evoke particular responses in the public. In what Doreen St. Félix describes as a "rush," those waiting to see justice served witnessed Weinstein not only cuffed but escorted by a female detective through the same neighborhood where he allegedly committed many attacks.[52] The accused clearly attempted to garner public support from those on his side of the "gender war," wearing a nonthreatening baby blue sweater and toting biographies of Broadway producers who were falsely maligned during the "witch hunts" of the McCarthy era.[53]

A *New York Times* article offers that the sight of "Weinstein in handcuffs was a 'start' to justice for his accusers."[54] Accusers affirm a need to send a "message" that they argue can only be accomplished via visible, formal legal proceedings. One observer of the case describes the textbook role of law in effecting general deterrence, noting, "If someone of his stature can be taken down by our legal system . . . then someone in a much lower position who thinks they can wield power over women might think twice."[55] Others describe witnessing the arrest and trial process as cathartic.[56] Similar comments were made after Cosby's sentencing, a tweet noting that "We, the women, now have real hope for justice" and another hailing a "new day in rape culture, a new day in the women's movement, a new day for feminism."[57]

This celebration of Weinstein and Cosby in handcuffs might be viewed as demonstrating a renewed faith in the legal system, a recognition that formal legal systems have the capacity to afford justice to victims in a way that socially imposed sanctions cannot. Despite some accusers' claims that justice *begins* with the institution of a formal criminal process, however, it is hard to believe that an image of Weinstein in handcuffs has much more than a symbolic value. In preparation for trial, Weinstein allegedly has employed multiple public relations companies to dig up dirt on accusers, whom his attorneys have already accused of stirring up the #MeToo movement to impose "mob rule."[58] Dichotomous battles rage across Twitter as to whether the mogul is a "monster" or "sociopath," and whether his accusers are honest victims or greedy "gold diggers" out for cash. In this era of confirmation bias, it is hard to believe that the formal pronouncement of guilt or lack of guilt will sway many arguments. Just as if Brock Turner had succeeded in his 2018 appeal, it is likely the response of a large portion of the public would have been outrage rather than acceptance.

Echoing de Tocqueville, the crown jewel of the American justice system is its ability to mete out unbiased justice that is insulated from the frenzied roar of the crowd. As the Cosby trial suggests, however, isn't it pretense to suggest that law can be applied in a vacuum in this era of social media? It remains to be seen whether it is possible to exclude the frenzied crowd that is banging on the courthouse door.

Legal cases today are complicated by the fact that discussions on social media are not just centered on the defendants and victims, online commenters also focus their attention on the other participants in criminal trials—the lawyers who advocate for clients and the state, and the judges who hand down legal decisions. As discussed in earlier chapters, the past several years have seen rough seas for attorneys, more frequently represented in the media as "sharks" and "ambulance chasers" than as rights-vindicating heroes. The advent of social media means that it is not only defendants like Brock Turner or Larry Nassar who may become reluctant celebrities. Online commenters also debate and dissect the words and deeds of attorneys and judges. And, as described below, the verdict regarding these individuals also may be harsh and swift.

FIRST THING WE DO, LET'S KILL ALL THE LAWYERS

Immediately after news of Brock Turner's sentence caught the public eye, commenters began to ask why the judge in the case, Aaron Persky, had handed down such a seemingly light sentence. When it was discovered that Persky also had attended Stanford University and had been a student athlete, assumptions about the existence of an "old boys' club" grew rampant. A commenter on a major newspaper writes that this

> rich, white, spoiled brat. . . . got the white glove treatment from this "judge." If this perpetrator had been any other color, race, and socioeconomic level, etc., he would be in state prison. This "judge" also assaulted this young woman. If my daughter had been the victim . . . I would have taken steps to mete out my own justice on both of these men.

A similar comment on the same site observes that "[t]he victim was raped twice. Once by assailant, and again by judge." " Excusing Judge Persky for this ridiculous sentence," another person writes, "makes no more sense than his excusing the rapist for the sexual assault." Another notes, ominously, "[The judge] keeps focusing on the rights of the criminal. . . . He should be looking at both sides, but he seems to keep overlooking the victim, the evidence, and the witnesses. . . . Actions have consequences, and judges shall be judged too." Others malign the process of judging more generally,

> Most judges (NOT ALL) are basically lawyers who can't hack it in the dog eat dog business of law . . . What is the old saying "Those who can't do, teach. And those who can't teach, teach gym." Well those who can't lawyer, teach law school, and those who can't teach law school . . ."

Another commenter cuts to the chase, just calling Persky a "misogynistic hypocritical pig." One commenter on a feminist site writes, "I'm hoping (and pledge to support) ANY qualified candidate who steps forward to crush this monster and put an end to his career." While a comment on the blog of an iconic women's magazine observes,

> Judge Persky has a responsibility to the people to say that rape is wrong. It's not three months, it's not six months, it's not two years, twelve years—it's a lifetime of pain that you will go through. And I really sincerely hope that we can hold him accountable . . . for what he made a poor student go through.

Many comments about Judge Persky are not attacks on his reasoning but ad hominem attacks, calling into question his character by labeling him, by association, a rapist and "monster."

Second-guessing outcomes and sentencing decisions in criminal cases has become a pastime in the United States, with verdicts in cases against

Jodi Arias, Casey Anthony, and Bill Cosby debated and disputed in public forums. However, in this era of social media, the Brock Turner case offered a novel opportunity; through virtual networks, the public not only was able to exchange opinions about Judge Persky's decision but to convert those opinions into social and legislative change.

As described above, empowered by social media outlets, online commenters unsatisfied with the version of justice handed down in Turner's case successfully lobbied to change statutes of limitations and lengthen sentences for some sexual assault crimes.[59] In addition, in June 2018, a majority of California voters voted to recall Judge Persky from his position.[60] It was the first recall of a judge in the state in eighty-six years.[61] The recall campaign, chaired by a professor at Stanford Law School, became a political cause célèbre, and was financed by over $1 million raised via crowdsourcing on social media.[62] More than one million people signed on to the petition to recall the judge on change.org.[63]

Persky began to face consequences from his decision well before the recall. In response to widespread public critiques of the judge, jurors began to refuse to serve on cases over which he presided, and the judge was reassigned from criminal court to the civil division.[64]

While the negative reaction to Judge Persky was widespread, his colleagues debated the merits of recalling the judge. During the highly contentious recall campaign, some colleagues praised Persky's attention to due process and his concern about the collateral consequences of contemporary convictions. Many saw a threat to judicial discretion and independence inherent in the recall campaign. One Persky supporter observes of recall advocates: "They'd rather have judges that respond to the mob."[65] A retired California judge similarly voices concern that the recall represents "a dangerous threat to the independence of the judiciary" and may be

> terrible for racial justice. . . . If it succeeds, it sends a message to every judge on every court in California and really beyond. . . . A lot of the defendants are young people, and mostly males, of color—Latino and African-American. They are the ones who are going to receive the sentencings of these judges who are going to be hesitant, if not fearful, to impose a leniency in a sentence.[66]

Another judge observes, "When judges believe that they will lose their careers for making unpopular but lawful decisions, they may lack the courage to stand up for the rights of minorities or others needing protection from powerful majorities."[67]

Cleared of wrongdoing by a California judicial oversight panel, Persky himself has offered only one statement in defense of his actions, noting,

> California law requires every judge to consider rehabilitation and probation for first-time offenders. It's not always popular, but it's the law,

> and I took an oath to follow it without regard to public opinion or my opinions as a former prosecutor.[68]

The campaign against Persky is now held out as a threat to other judges, some of whom are expressing concerns that they too might be "Persky'd."[69]

Persky's decision in the case was not wholly unsupported. Rather than the ten-to-fourteen-year possible maximum for the crimes of which Turner was accused, the defendant's probation officer—a representative of the interests of the state—recommended that the defendant receive a four-to-six-month sentence, based on the belief that the defendant's level of intoxication affected his ability to form the required intent in regard to a serious crime of "attempt."[70] As noted earlier, the court received numerous letters from Turner's friends and family attesting to his work ethic and character.

Media descriptions of Persky's decision, however, paint a picture of unfettered judicial discretion being meted out to protect an elite old boys' club. Damon Young writes in the *Guardian* that "Judge Persky took the souffle out of the oven, tasted it, and said: 'You know what this souffle is missing? A dollop of white privilege. Actually forget a dollop. This needs a quart of that shit.'"[71] Similar descriptions of Turner's sentencing are pervasive across print and social media.

Perhaps as far from Judge Persky as one can get on the ideological fence is the judge who presided over Larry Nassar's sentencing, Rosemarie Aquilina, clearly an advocate for swift and retributive justice. In addition to suggesting that she supported Larry Nassar being raped while incarcerated, the judge appeared to relish sentencing Nassar to two lifetimes in prison, offering comments such as "[p]rison is no place for a human being to live."[72]

On social media some critique the Judge Aquilina's statements, their criticisms at times invoking the stereotypical, biologically rooted assumptions about female behavior examined in earlier chapters. A poster on an article about the sentencing on a major news site writes, for example, "I hope she [the judge] practiced being less emotional. Oh well. Women are emotional." Others express concern that personal opinion is being injected into what should be an unbiased process:

> The public would rather see "Judge Judy" ostracize and browbeat a supposedly guilty person than actually see the duty carried out and executed with professionalism and righteous intent.

The vast majority of online comments regarding Aquilina, however, are overwhelmingly positive. A poster on a major news site objects to fellow commenters' criticisms of the judge, "I bet if the judge had been a man, no one would have said a thing." Others call her "a goddamn hero" and note, "I wish Judge Aquilina had the opportunity to handle sentence for Brock Turner." A comment notes poetically of the judge,

> All the power to her.
> Women are taking the power now!
> We're cleaning house!!!
> Hope he suffers in jail.

Exploring public discussion of judges and attorneys can provide an important lens into how we feel about law itself.[73] In 1770, John Adams famously defended six British soldiers who fired into a crowd during what became known as the Boston Massacre. Adams, who earned sentence reductions or acquittals for all six, later referred to his role in the trial as "one of the best Pieces of Service I ever rendered my Country," noting that condemning the soldiers to death would have been "as foul a Stain upon this Country as the Executions of the Quakers or witches."[74] Adams was so celebrated for this public service in defending the much-maligned soldiers that historians credit the trial as a reason for his election to the presidency.

One has to wonder how Adams, the consummate defense attorney, would be treated today in a world in which, far from accolades, the attorneys for Larry Nassar received rape and death threats as a result of their vigorous representation of their client.[75] Contemporary examples suggest not well. In Spring 2019, the position of Harvard dean for Ronald S. Sullivan Jr. was not renewed after the attorney accepted a position on Weinstein's defense team, a position from which he has since withdrawn.[76] Students protested that Sullivan's role as dean was not consonant with his defense of the producer, identifying Sullivan's decision as "trauma inducing."[77] Students' critiques of Sullivan flourished, despite that he previously had represented the family of Michael Brown in a wrongful death suit against the city of Ferguson, Missouri. Randall Kennedy, a friend and colleague of Sullivan's whose work has been instrumental in exposing racial injustice in the criminal justice system, refers to the dean's dismissal as a "thorough embarrass[ment]" fueled by

> anger at anyone daring to breach the wall of ostracism surrounding Mr. Weinstein, even for the limited purpose of extending him legal representation. [The students] want to make him, a person still clothed with the presumption of innocence, more of an untouchable before trial than those who have been convicted of a crime.[78]

In 2016, candidate Donald Trump invited three of Bill Clinton's accusers to the second presidential debate. Accompanying these alleged victims was Kathy Shelton. A victim of child sexual abuse, Shelton had encountered Hillary Clinton when Clinton defended Shelton's abuser in 1975.[79] In including Shelton among the accusers Trump's message was clear—those who vigorously represent alleged sexual predators are no better than predators themselves.

As has been emphasized throughout this book, when it comes to sexual assault, the court of public opinion gravitates toward one-dimensional explanations of legal cases and parties—a particular case is "about race" or "about gender," a victim is truthful or a liar, and a perpetrator is either innocent or a monstrous predator. The online comments about judges Aquilina and Persky highlight that the public responds best when fact finders' behaviors comport with this idealized, black-and-white vision of law.

Whether based in elitism, concerns of due process, or both, Judge Persky's sentencing of Brock Turner was complex, implicating issues of socioeconomic and racial privilege, but also raising questions about due process and mass incarceration. It is impossible to articulate in just 280 characters the numerous factors, positive and negative, that contributed to the judge's decision. On the other hand, Judge Aquilina's strongly worded warnings to the "monster," Larry Nassar, fit readily into mythologies that Jill Lepore refers to as "as old as stoning."[80] The message during Nassar's sentencing was familiar and clear: rapists are sick, pathological predators who are beyond redemption.

As social media offer the public a new way to exclude "unworthy" victims and to enact new and creative punishments on would-be perpetrators, the virtual world also offers the public new means to assert control over those who are responsible for representing these parties. As evidenced by comments regarding Gloria Allred as a "serial victim maker," in the socially mediated universe, there is little love for lawyers. In connection with the UVA allegations, commenters on a conservative blog call for disbarment of the attorneys who agreed to represent *Rolling Stone*,[81] causing one attorney who represented the magazine to remark that "we [the lawyers] are the ones . . . being tried."[82] Another commenter on the UVA allegations advocates "[S]hutting down ALL law schools for 30 years" and passing a law that "[l]awyers cannot run for public office." The commenter writes, "I know it's a dream but WOW what a dream. TRUMP = Businessman Hillary = Lawyer, liar."[83]

Over time, what was once a simmering public disapproval of lawyers has grown into a full-fledged disdain of a field seen as replete with "ambulance chasers" and extortionists. Attorneys involved in high-profile cases commonly receive death threats. In May 2019, Christopher Darden, known for having served on the prosecution team against OJ Simpson, resigned from his defense of Eric Holder, accused of killing rapper Nipsey Hussle. He blamed online threats to his and his family's safety for the resignation, explaining that "these days . . . cowards don't send letters instead they sit anonymously behind keyboards threatening a man's mother and children."[84] Darden expressed dismay at the threat constitutional protections posed by virtual commenters,

> After centuries of a history of black men hung from trees without trial, or after the thousands of cases of black men tried, convicted and executed without counsel. . . . I cannot understand why in 2019 some

people would deny a black man his 6th Amendment right to counsel of his choice.

When it comes to female attorneys, threats frequently focus not just on death but rape. Larry Nassar's attorney describes an anonymous comment on a web intake form threatening, to "rape your children. And then rape you in front of your children. And then murder your children in front of you but let you live."[85] Michele Dauber, who engineered the campaign to recall Judge Persky, received a "glitter bomb" from a company called ShipYourEnemiesGlitter.com accompanied by a note reading, "Since you are going to disrobe [Judge Aaron] Persky, I am going to treat you like 'Emily Doe.' Let's see what kind of sentencing I get for being a rich white male."[86]

A CARCERAL FEMINISM

While women receive the worst of violent threats online, it is important to note that women are not only targets of but also advocates for violence, particularly state violence. Just a cursory glance at the comments in Turner's case and appeal on sites like Jezebel, Babe.net, and in *Ms. Magazine* that offer feminist-centered content reveal numerous calls to "castrate all rapists" or regrets that Turner was not "sentenced to some kind of hard labor." Although it was Turner's constitutional right to appeal his conviction and sentence, one commenter observes that he "should get a double sentence for pressing his luck." Others praise Persky's removal, one noting that "Persky was a bad judge and the fact that he was removed by California voters is a good reminder of what the voices of a younger generation are capable of." A responder to the comment agrees that "[p]ublic defenders loved him. If the voices of a younger generation are for less leniency for rapists, I'm ok with it. Vote more indeed!"

The identification of a millennial trend toward expanding the carceral state may not be inaccurate. As the women's movement successfully has advocated for reforms, such as expanding the definitions of sexual assault and broadening the range opportunities for early intervention, feminist advocates arguably have paid too little attention to the potential impact this expanded net of laws may have on defendants, particularly nonwhite defendants. The 1951 case of *McQuirter v. State*,[87] often taught in criminal law classrooms, illustrates the potential dangers for African American male alleged perpetrators when victims' rights are expanded. The complainant in the case is a married woman, Mrs. Allen, who alleged that McQuirter "followed" her and her children from a diner to the home of a neighbor at around 8:00 p.m. on a summer evening. McQuirter argued he was merely waiting for a friend.[88] The question in the McQuirter case is whether this evidence was sufficient for a jury to convict the defendant of an attempt to commit an assault with the intent to rape.

In the law school classroom, the case, in which the court ultimately upholds the conviction, tends to be divisive. While some students identify racism at the heart of a false accusation on Mrs. Allen's part, others argue that the case supports early intervention, citing the underappreciated dangers of stalking and hypothesizing that a rape was stopped from taking place.[89]

Over the past thirty years, criminal laws have been revised to encompass numerous behaviors that formerly might have been deemed immoral but not illegal. Sexual assault laws have been revised to include marital rape and to encompass both male and female perpetrators. Statutes have been drafted that criminalize not only penetration but nonconsensual touching and coercion.[90] As sexual assault has grown as a crime category, the net of the state has grown exponentially. Collateral consequences such as registration requirements have been attached to convictions for many sex crimes.[91] In an acknowledgment of rape culture and gateway behaviors, statutes have been passed in all fifty states penalizing "surveillance behaviors," such as waiting outside a victim's home or "spying" on a victim.[92] Thirty-eight states penalize nonconsensual distribution of pornography, otherwise known as "revenge porn."[93]

Today, there are many strong voices arguing for expansion of the criminal law to provide for stricter sentences for rapists and to extend statutes of limitations to further extend this net of criminal law. Many of these belong to feminist legal scholars who argue for criminalizing a greater and greater range of offenses contributing to rape culture. Erin Sheley, for example, advocates a "broken windows" theory of rape law enforcement that would provide greater arrest powers to law enforcement in the context of street harassment.[94] Franks argues for more extensive legislation regarding revenge porn.[95] Others advocate that more arrests should be made for upskirt photography, known as "creepshots."[96]

Like "locker-room talk," catcalling is part and parcel of rape culture, and tolerance of the behavior a signal that a greater society may be tolerant of sexual assault. However, there is a significant question as to whether making such conduct illegal is the best way to accomplish the greater objectives of the feminist movement, particularly in light of cases like *McQuirter*, which demonstrate the impact broken windows interventions may have on non-white defendants. Bumiller identifies that, while early sexual assault reforms—for example, shelter systems—were constructed outside the state, today many feminist sexual assault reforms are being embraced by the state, bearing a danger of appropriation.[97] Similarly, Emily L. Thuma argues that efforts at feminist reform "won the mainstream but lost the movement," as the motion toward accountability for individual perpetrators was used as a "critical lever of legitimacy for expanding the carceral state."[98] She identifies a "rape-racism nexus," whereby

> when white feminists treat rape solely as an issue of male supremacy and demand a "get tough response from the police and courts, they will not only fail to stem rape but strengthen a criminal justice system pervaded by racism and class bias—the same system that harms and ensnares women.[99]

There is a great deal of research exposing the ways in which crime control policies such as mandatory minimum sentencing and parole "reform" have negatively and disproportionately impacted racial minorities and socioeconomically disadvantaged individuals. However, race and poverty are much less often part of conversations when it comes to discussing feminist advancements in criminal law. There is a lot of conversation surrounding how policies advocating earlier intervention in potential sexual assaults or advocating ongoing offender registries arguably benefit victims and potential victims; however, there is less public discourse regarding the potential infringement of such interventions on the due process of alleged perpetrators, particularly nonwhite alleged perpetrators.

Like *McQuirter*, *State v. Rusk*, is instructive. *Rusk* is a landmark case ultimately stands for the idea that a victim's subjective belief should be part of the analysis of whether he or she has acted reasonably in the context of rape.[100] The appellate court's ultimate decision that a victim's subjective, yet reasonable, belief should be considered was a victory for the women's movement that served as the basis for changing many rape statutes to no longer reflect the harmful and unrealistic expectation that victims should have "fought back to the utmost."[101] Janet Halley argues, however, that feminists have failed to answer the vital question of what happens when subjective beliefs—as Mrs. Allen's likely were—are founded on racist fears and myths.[102]

Phyllis Crocker observes a tendency of feminists to "isolate our anger at the violence against a woman by thinking it impossible to represent, or understand, a man on death row who killed that woman"; however, "[t]he tragedy of the woman's death and the tragedy of the defendant's life" are in fact "interrelated"—"[w]hat occurs to a woman on a personal level is not merely individual but informed by and part of political, social, and cultural beliefs and forces."[103] Janet Halley relatedly cautions that the "badness of rape" should not be used as a motivating factor for other atrocities, for example, to start a war, or to encourage other rapes.[104]

Comments on social media sites suggest that, despite these cautions, when it comes to sexual assault, feminists generally favor and have put their faith in the expansion of the carceral state. Bauman describes that the violence we suffer in society is not only interpersonal violence, the form on which we tend to focus, but structural violence. In the process of condemning the interpersonal violence committed by Brock Turner, online commenters fall into this trap, advocating that violence committed by individuals will be reduced by bolstering the power of the state.

In this desire for expansion of the arm of social control, many feminists have entered into what Lepore refers to as a "bad marriage" with conservative politicians.[105] For example, today's prohibitions against stalking, revenge pornography, or sexting draw feminist support based on the idea that criminalization will work toward ending rape culture while simultaneously garnering the support of conservatives seeking to penalize sexuality based on more Puritan ideals.[106] Katie Roiphe proposes,

> In some ways, if we take the imaginative leap, the world Twitter feminists are envisioning—scrubbed clean of anyone hitting on anyone, asking for phone numbers, leaning over to kiss someone without seeking verbal permission—seems not that substantively far away from the world of Mike Pence saying he will never eat alone with a woman who is not his wife. This odd convergence reveals something critical about the moment: the complicated ways in which we may be snatching defeat from the jaws of victory.[107]

Laura Kipnis observes that this is not a new phenomenon. "There have always been puritanical versions of feminism competing with more emancipatory versions. The so-called radical feminists of the second wave—the designation was always a misnomer—were shortsighted Puritans, even aligning themselves with Christian conservatives to fight the demon pornography (just as some first-wave feminists joined with Prohibitionists to fight the demon rum)."[108] A proposal to extend statutes of limitations or enhance sentencing for rape might be advanced based on a feminist desire to, finally, secure some modicum of justice for victims and the conservative, retributive ideal of swift and efficient justice. Both risk having the same end, intended or unintended, of creating discriminatory criminal justice policies.

REDEMPTION

The political trials of Turner and Nassar emphasize that it is not only accusers who face judgment by the court of public opinion. The character of the perpetrator, too, is interrogated and evaluated through social media commentary. While Turner and Nassar have been sentenced and are firmly entrenched in the "monster" category, what of the other accused perpetrators—Jameis Winston, Bill Cosby, or Harvey Weinstein—who for many remain in that liminal category between "normal" person and social "outcast"?

An important distinction among perpetrators and alleged perpetrators is the way they have chosen to engage the law. In the eyes of the armchair quarterbacks who closely follow the litigation game, like alleged victims, alleged perpetrators are not free to behave in any way they please. A refrain in Kanye West's *Gold Digger* is: "If you ain't no punk holla, 'We want prenup!'"[109] The phrase implies that those who do not engage the legal mechanisms available to them to ward off potential "gold diggers" are "punks." Like gold digger, bitch, and ho, "punk" is a gendered term, originating in prisons and referencing to the "bottom" in a coercive sexual relationship.[110] In other words, those who "let" themselves be "targeted" by ambitious women and do not use law as a shield are themselves undeserving victims. The roles are transposed and a new relationship is forged where the former victim is now, at least legally speaking, in the dominant position and the alleged perpetrator is a feminized "punk."

On Twitter, comments abound reflecting the sentiment that, if they are actually innocent, accused perpetrators of sexual assault will deploy any and all legal mechanisms available to defend their honor and exact punishment against their accusers. Brandon Winston's flashy Brandon Project site serves as a counterpoint to Emma Sulkowicz's *Ceci N'est Pas Un Viol*, both examples of the ways in which "innocence" today is best achieved through savvy and expensive virtual interventions. Via Winston's pop-up text messages and Sulkowicz's video, both invite us to be bystanders of the alleged assaults, and lead us to their own, particular conclusions.

Just like the expectation that it is easy for a money-minded gold digger to "throw a case" at a celebrity, the assumption that law is easy to use as a sword or as a shield harms the accused by ignoring that lawsuits are costly and time-consuming. The conception that a defendant is a "punk" if he does not countersue is contrasted by the Winston cases, which wound their way through the courts for years before settlements were reached in 2017, and the number of civil suits making their way through the courts relating to Cosby and Weinstein. Although celebrities benefit not only from wealth but from the support of institutions and networks that are both invested in their success and, often, contractually obligated to support them, as Ewick and Silbey point out, the status of being "with the law"—able to deploy law in one's favor—even for the wealthy, depends on context.[111] A real estate developer may, for example, feel exceedingly confident of winning property disputes but out of her depth when it comes to a DUI charge. Ronald Sullivan, the Harvard dean defending Harvey Weinstein, remarks that, although they might have the upper hand in a civil court, even the power of powerful men pales in comparison to the resources of the U.S. government.[112]

On the interactive *USA Today* site that is mentioned in chapter 4, one can scroll, daily, to see not only the latest alleged perpetrator, the number of accusers who have spoken out against them, and the status of allegations, but also—importantly—the perpetrator's response to the allegations.[113] In addition to the statuses like "fired" and "took own life" described earlier, the site notes that Ethan Kath, frontman of band the Crystal Castles, is "suing for defamation" and that rapper Nelly "will countersue" after having been accused.[114]

In addition to the latest revelation of sexual assault, in 2018 the U.S. public was captivated by the story of President Trump's alleged affair with a pornographic actress, Stormy Daniels. A major part of the story was whether Trump had paid "hush money" to Daniels in order to ensure her silence about the indiscretion, conveying the idea that settling a lawsuit might be evidence of guilt.[115]

As discussed in chapter 2, online comments show that accepting "hush money"—that is, settling a civil lawsuit—is damning for accusers, signifying that they have stepped out of the ideal victim category by pursuing "civil money and not criminal justice." Casting aside collective well-being for personal considerations cuts against the idea that crime victims, and especially female crime victims, will act out of a single-minded generosity. Alleged perpetrators also face similar expectations that they will defend their honor to the fullest. As a commenter on a popular sports-related site describes about the settlement of *Kinsman v. Winston*,

> Not in a million years would I ever settle. This is a green light to every other bottom feeder that he is free game. He should have fought it if for nothing else to send a message to the people looking for a paycheck that they were not getting one. As an aside why settle if you're innocent?

A similar post on the same site remarks, "Clearly he did it. The innocent would have wanted to go to trial and win." A commenter recommends that "Famous Jameis should sue that bitch, her family, and the police," while another remarks "Jameis's next move is to sue the fuck out of that bitch for defamation and slander." A tweet advises that "Winston lawyers need to go for slander and defamation of character." Conflating criminal and civil law, a tweet notes,

> Why doesn't the girl get charged with slander in Winston's case. Tarnished his name because he's a stud and you're a dum bitch #checkplease.

Just as gender stereotypes are at work behind comments regarding women accusers, however, they also operate in the background of comments like these voicing expectations for male alleged perpetrators. Peggy Reeves Sanday describes the significance of male heroes in society, observing that "we are a nation that thirsts for male heroes and thrives on warrior dreams."[116] "American identity [is] . . . linked with masculine heroism": "[t]he rugged, solitary man, who is larger than life questing for glory."[117] In this context, celebrities' successes most often are attributed to individual action—grit—rather than luck, suggesting that social mobility is gained via talent and hard work.[118] A trained athlete is often portrayed as putting in blood, sweat, and tears, while a plaintiff who secures economic benefit via the civil system is seen as attempting to achieve success without effort.

The focus on success as attributable to "grit"—a combination of hard work and resilience—is a neoliberal invention that reinforces the idea that any of us might someday be a celebrity. As described earlier, research suggests that college athletes are significantly underprosecuted for a large range of crimes compared to their similarly situated nonathlete counterparts.[119] This underenforcement likely is due to a variety of factors, including prompt attention by attorneys, confusion as to how to proceed when university authorities are involved, and intimidation of witnesses.[120] Whatever opinion one may have about Jameis Winston's actions in regard to Erica Kinsman, the case and the numerous resulting civil suits provide a textbook example of the bungled investigation that can result when institutional and civilian authorities intersect regarding sexual assault allegations. Nonetheless, there is a pervasive idea among commenters that, since even athletes and celebrities can be "targeted" for prosecution, it does not bode well for the average Joe. As a comment warns, "ANY bitch u fucked can get out the bed rite after and fry u for rape. Please dont act like Jameis is diff than anybody else." As Manne suggests, when it comes to celebrities being accused, the public's capacity for "himpathy" is unparalleled.

Cases against celebrities are larger than life, representative of something bigger than themselves. Underlying many comments is a collective fear that, when the masculinity of celebrities is threatened by the feminine (or feminist) charge of rape, the masculinity of every other man is also threatened. Dowd and colleagues observe that, while men and boys may have a collective privilege, like their female counterparts, they "operate in a gendered context and collectively experience . . . harm as a result of the social construction of what it means to be a boy or man."[121] In this context, one female victim's achievement of a "come up" is perceived as indicative of a larger, systemic shift or bias. Similar to the way the rape of a victim is often seen as impacting society as a whole, the failure of alleged perpetrators to respond appropriately to the threat of a false claim is also viewed as a collective failure. When accusations emerged against Patrick Kane, a hashtag campaign, "#IStandwith88," emerged to defend the player. Tweets bearing the hashtag remark, "Raise your hand if you've ever felt personally victimized by #PatrickKane accuser" and "the city of Chicago stands with Patrick Kane."

As discussed in chapter 1, to attain ideal victim status female survivors of sexual assault are expected to act solely, or at least primarily, in the public interest, reporting promptly to the police, exhibiting visible trauma, and perhaps engaging in a public education campaign about assault. Men who are accused also face societal expectations. Social media commenters expect "innocent" men to wield law as a sword and shield, fighting any accusation to the utmost, exhibiting a legal masculinity. The failure to meet this masculine legal paradigm may be deemed as falling outside the bounds of "normal" behavior. For African American men alleged to be perpetrators, the anticipation that they will fight to clear their reputations is likely to be even stronger, consonant with the historical stereotype that they are the most likely perpetrators.

In the new world of #MeToo, like the "casting couch," the label "hush money" discussed in chapter 2 may be taking on a new meaning. Formerly reserved for maligning those who accepted money in exchange for silence after an assault, the term now presents a new challenge for the accused. A preoccupation in 2018 has been whether President Trump knew of secret payments by his lawyer, Michael Cohen, to adult film star Stormy Daniels after her alleged affair with the mogul.[122] The focus on those offering, rather than those accepting, payments in settlement of sexual assault claims is potentially revolutionary. It is an acknowledgment that those who are able to offer to pay for confidentiality and nondisclosure agreements are the persons who, in Ewick and Silbey's terms, are "with the law" and thus positioned to engage the law as a weapon to silence those who might challenge their status or authority.

Defending such "hush money" payments, however, now presents new challenges for alleged perpetrators who may have been encouraged by corporate entities to settle claims rather than face the gauntlet of the court of public opinion.

CONCLUSION

Over more than thirty years Roman Polanski's alleged victim, Samantha Geimer, has given many different answers in response to the question of why she does not support bringing charges against the director. One relates to what she sees as striking similarities in the court of public opinion's treatment of both her and her alleged assailant. Geimer observes that, at first, "I was a drug-doing Lolita who had cornered him. . . . Now . . . everyone is calling him a pedophile, the insults have switched."[123]

Andrew Miltenberg, an attorney who represents both alleged victims and alleged perpetrators in Title IX proceedings, has similar things to say about one of his cases, in which he is defending a university student against charges of sexual assault, to the *New York Times*:

> The whole thing is a [expletive]: terrible for him, terrible for her, terrible for the parents. . . . [I]f the process is broken, it's broken at least as

> much for victims as the accused. That correction can become overcorrection in either direction. The pendulum swings both ways. It shouldn't . . . but I don't know how to stop it.[124]

As suggested in previous chapters and discussed in the final part of this book, there is a cost to the broad identification of women as victims that so far has been part of #MeToo. As Laura Kipnis, Katie Roiphe, and others identify, there is a risk that the degree to which women have exercised agency in recent years may be undermined by defining them, collectively, as naïve and unsuspecting "girls" preyed upon by vicious "monsters."

While it is important to recognize the Cassandra-like status accusers like Rose McGowan have been relegated to endure for years, the categorization of young "girl" victim and "monstrous" predator reflects a problematic situation of #MeToo as part of a larger, gendered war rather than as an inclusive movement aimed toward ending rape culture. During Larry Nassar's sentencing, gymnast and anti-rape advocate Rachael Denhollander, asked what fellow survivor Aly Raisman described as a "simple yet powerful question," "How much is a little girl worth?"[125]

The question indeed is powerful, but it is anything but simple. Like the judge's comments about sexual assault and its victims, the observation draws on centuries of legal history in which victims' worth have been determined by their status—little old ladies, little (white) girls valued more highly than other victims in the harsh context of the criminal justice system. Her words eerily bring to mind the decades during which rape was recognized only as a crime of property and not one damaging to survivors' autonomy. The question also raises the issue of punishment, suggesting that the "price" of violation may be compensated by years of incarceration.

As the groundswell of support for survivors has grown, there is an increasing movement to secure justice for victims by imposing harsh and often extralegal or collateral punishments on perpetrators. Feminist pleas to increase sentences for rape or to expand the reach of criminal law stand in contrast to what one might expect to be the usual liberal position against mass incarceration, but they fit into a trajectory of feminism that has relied on identifying the unique and debilitating harms of rape to emphasize the validity of survivors' claims. Today, many conversations among liberal feminists about sexual assault bear a disturbing resemblance to those of staunch conservatives, both calling for expanded statutes of limitations, increased policing, and longer prison terms and casting restorative justice and rehabilitation outside the narrative.

Social media are a powerful influence on legal processes. Not only has virtual activism surrounding the Turner case impacted Aaron Persky's judicial tenure, public opinion also has influenced California law. As a result of the national outrage inspired by Turner's conviction, the state expanded the definition of rape to encompass sexual assaults accomplished without threat or physical force, eliminated probation as an option for offenders where victims are intoxicated or unconscious, and imposed new mandatory minimum sentences for sexual assaults.[126] After they became aware of the inability of many Cosby accusers, due to passage of time, to get their day in court, seven women from around the United States who allege they were assaulted joined together in a grassroots campaign, EndRapeSOL.[127] As a result of lobbying by the organization, as of 2018, six states have altered statutes of limitations to eliminate or significantly extend those imposed on sexual assault.[128]

In the 1980s, a bipartisan fear of judicial independence led to the passage of the sentencing guidelines that, thanks to statutory definitions and mandatory minimum sentencing, played a major part in the rise in the mass incarceration of men—and women—of color.[129] In calling for reforms to sexual assault law we need to remember that "[p]olice are often purveyors of violence and that prisons are always sites of violence."[130] As Alexander describes, mass incarceration is a form of state violence that harms not only offenders but families and communities, particularly communities of color.[131] As the unified social degradation of Brock Turner attests, feminists, and particularly white feminists, have not stopped to consider the unique and powerful harm that is created when we advocate meeting one form of violence with another.

One thing is clear, the court of public opinion has spoken and it is powerful. In Brock Turner's case a trial was held and a legal decision handed down that included not just formal punishment but a lifetime of collateral consequences. Across social media, commenters weighed in, stating that not only were the consequences for Turner not sufficient but the process itself was corrupt. Via discussions across social media and crowdsourced petitions, the general public added their own collateral consequences, ensuring that the name Brock Turner will forever be accompanied by the label rapist.

On the other hand there is Weinstein. Like many others on *USA Today*'s list of alleged perpetrators, he is seemingly suffering some of the collateral consequences of conviction—civil exclusion, societal disdain, economic costs—before any formal decision about his guilt has been—or perhaps ever will be—made. As a trial looms, the producer and his accusers are spending millions on public relations campaigns, recognizing that, regardless of any verdict handed down in an actual trial, the verdict that matters is going to be delivered on social media.

NOTES

1. The counts on which Brock Turner was convicted include assault with intent to commit rape of an intoxicated or unconscious person, sexual penetration of an intoxicated person, and sexual penetration of an unconscious person. Victor Xu, "Brock

Turner Sentenced to Six Months in County Jail, Three Years Probation," *Stanford Daily*, June 2, 2016, https://www.stanforddaily.com/2016/06/02/brock-turner-sentenced-to-six-months-in-county-jail-three-years-probation/.

2. Xu, "Brock Turner Sentenced."

3. Miller, "Stanford Sex Assault Survivor."

4. Jordan Buie, "Brock Turner, Cory Batey Meme Causing Stir on Social Media," *Tennessean*, June 8, 2016, https://www.tennessean.com/story/news/crime/2016/06/08/brock-turner-corey-batey-meme-causing-stir-social-media/85590654/.

5. Friedman, *The Big Trial*, 161.

6. Friedman, *The Big Trial*, 161.

7. Erickson, *Wayward Puritans*; Black, "Crime as Social Control," Garfinkel, "Conditions of Successful Degradation."

8. Char Adams, "Former USA Gymnastics Doctor Larry Nassar Pleads Guilty to Sexually Abusing Girls in Michigan," *People*, November 22, 2017, http://people.com/sports/larry-nassar-pleads-guilty-sexual-abuse-gymnasts/.

9. Garfinkel, "Conditions of Successful Degradation," 420.

10. Garfinkel, "Conditions of Successful Degradation," 421.

11. Garfinkel, "Conditions of Successful Degradation," 421, 422.

12. Phyllis L. Crocker, "Feminism and Defending Men on Death Row," *St. Mary's Law Journal* 29 (1998): 982.

13. Brenner, "Resisting Simple Dichotomies," 505, 508; Thomas A. Mitchell, "We're Only Fooling Ourselves: A Critical Analysis of the Biases Inherent in the Legal System's Treatment of Rape Victims," *Buffalo Journal of Gender, Law and Social Policy* 18 (2010): 98–100.

14. Brenner, "Resisting Simple Dichotomies," 505.

15. Zachary Elwood, "Examining Public Anger and Certainty in the Brock Turner Case and Sentencing," Medium.com, September 11, 2016, https://medium.com/@apokerplayer/examining-public-anger-and-certainty-in-the-brock-turner-case-and-sentencing-869c66201c11.

16. Elwood, "Examining Public Anger."

17. Elwood, "Examining Public Anger" (emphasis mine).

18. Elwood, "Examining Public Anger." Turner himself attempted to get a new trial on the grounds that descriptions of a trash bin as a dumpster were prejudicial. Lauren Hepler, "Campaign to Recall Judge in Stanford Sexual Assault Case Morphs into a Culture War," *San Jose Inside*, March 21, 2018, https://www.sanjoseinside.com/2018/03/21/campaign-to-recall-judge-in-stanford-sexual-assault-case-morphs-into-a-culture-war/.

19. *United States v. Stitt*, No. 17–765 (2018).

20. Daniel Victor, "Brock Turner Wanted Only 'Outercourse,' Lawyer Argues in Appeal," *New York Times*, July 26, 2018, https://www.nytimes.com/2018/07/26/us/brock-turner-victim-outercourse-appeal.html.

21. Victor, "Brock Turner."

22. Hepler, "Campaign to Recall."

23. Ford, "How Brock Turner Changed."

24. *The Times* Editorial Board, "Rape Bill in Response to Brock Turner Case Shows Headlines Trump Thinking in Criminal Justice," *Los Angeles Times*, July 21, 2016, https://www.latimes.com/opinion/editorials/la-ed-rape-sentence-bill-20160630-snap-story.html.

25. *Times* Editorial Board, "Rape Bill."

26. Scully and Marolla, "Riding the Bull."

27. Kevin M. Swartout, Mary P. Koss, and Jacquelyn W. White et al., "Trajectory Analysis of the Campus Serial Rape Assumption," *JAMA Pediatrics* 169, no. 12 (2015): 1148–54 (noting that, "[a]lthough a small group of men perpetrated rape across multiple college years, they constituted a significant minority of those who committed college rape and did not compose the group at highest risk of perpetrating rape when entering college").

28. "Court Documents: Stanford Rape Case, *People v. Brock Allen Turner* (9/9)," *Los Angeles Times*, June 10, 2016, http://documents.latimes.com/people-v-brock-allen-turner-99/.
29. "Court Documents," *Los Angeles Times*.
30. "Court Documents," *Los Angeles Times*.
31. "Court Documents," *Los Angeles Times*.
32. Damon Young, "The Stanford Sexual Assault Case: A White Privilege Cake with Vanilla Frosting on Top," *Guardian*, June 9, 2016, https://www.theguardian.com/society/2016/jun/09/standford-rape-case-white-privilege-brock-turner (referring to the Turner decision as a "white privilege cake with vanilla frosting on top").
33. Elwood, "Examining Public Anger."
34. Young, "The Stanford Sexual Assault Case."
35. Katie Roiphe, "The Other Whisper Network: How Twitter Feminism Is Bad for Women," *Harper's*, August 22, 2018, https://harpers.org/archive/2018/03/the-other-whisper-network-2/.
36. Alexander, *New Jim Crow*.
37. Matt Kaiser, "Was Brock Turner's Sentence Too Lenient?," *Above the Law*, June 16, 2016, https://abovethelaw.com/2016/06/was-brock-turners-sentence-too-lenient/?rf=1.
38. Kaiser, "Was Brock Turner's Sentence?"
39. Kaiser, "Was Brock Turner's Sentence?"
40. Lepore, "The Rise of the Victims'-Rights Movement."
41. Ford, "How Brock Turner Changed."
42. Lovisa Stannow, "No One Deserves to be Raped—Not Even Larry Nassar," *Los Angeles Times*, January 28, 2018, http://www.latimes.com/opinion/opinion-la/la-ol-stannow-larry-nassar-prison-rape-20180128-story.html.
43. Elizabeth Stoker Bruenig, "Why Americans Don't Care about Prison Rape," *Nation*, March 2, 2015, https://www.thenation.com/article/why-americans-dont-care-about-prison-rape/.
44. Stannow, "No One Deserves"; Bruenig, "Why Americans Don't Care."
45. Bruenig, "Why Americans Don't Care."
46. Scott Neuman, "Lawyers for Larry Nassar Say He Was Assaulted in Federal Prison," NPR, July 26, 2018, https://www.npr.org/2018/07/26/632564447/lawyers-for-larry-nassar-say-he-was-assaulted-in-federal-prison.
47. Chris Isidore, "Remains of the Weinstein Company Sold—To the Only Real Bidder," CNN, May 2, 2018, http://money.cnn.com/2018/05/02/media/weinstein-company-bidder/index.html.
48. "Harvey Weinstein Sacked after Sexual Harassment Claims," BBC News, October 9, 2017, http://www.bbc.com/news/business-41546694.
49. "Harvey Weinstein Sacked," BBC News.
50. "Harvey Weinstein Timeline: How the Scandal Unfolded," BBC News, May 25, 2018, http://www.bbc.com/news/entertainment-arts-41594672; John DellaContrada, "UB Statement Regarding SUNY Honorary Degree Recipient Harvey Weinstein," University at Buffalo News Release, October 11, 2017, http://www.buffalo.edu/news/releases/2017/10/020.html.
51. Mike Miller, "Child Molesters, Human Rights Abusers and Maybe Harvey Weinstein: What It Takes to Have the Queen Revoke Your Honorary Title," *People*, October 26, 2017, http://people.com/movies/child-molesters-human-rights-abusers-and-maybe-harvey-weinstein-what-it-takes-to-have-the-queen-revoke-your-honorary-title/.
52. Doreen St. Félix, "The Rush of Seeing Harvey Weinstein's Perp Walk," *New Yorker*, May 25, 2018, https://www.newyorker.com/culture/annals-of-appearances/the-rush-of-feeling-seeing-harvey-weinsteins-perp-walk-arrest.
53. St. Félix, "The Rush."

54. Melena Ryzik, "Weinstein in Handcuffs Is a 'Start to Justice' for His Accusers," *New York Times,* May 25, 2018, https://www.nytimes.com/2018/05/25/nyregion/metoo-accusers-harvey-weinstein.html.

55. Ryzik, "Weinstein in Handcuffs."

56. Lux Alptraum, "Seeing Harvey Weinstein in Handcuffs Was Cathartic but It Doesn't Solve Society's Sexual Abuse Problem," NBC News, May 26, 2018, https://www.nbcnews.com/think/opinion/seeing-harvey-weinstein-handcuffs-was-cathartic-it-doesn-t-solve-ncna877701.

57. Ron Allen and Daniel Arkin, "Bill Cosby Accusers Cry, Rejoice after He Is Sentenced to Prison Time," NBC, September 26, 2018, https://www.nbcnews.com/storyline/bill-cosby-scandal/bill-cosby-accusers-cry-rejoice-after-he-sentenced-prison-time-n913086.

58. Janet Street-Porter, "Harvey Weinstein's PR Machine Means that the Battle for Justice Is Far from Over," *Independent*, May 25, 2018, https://www.independent.co.uk/voices/harvey-weinstein-arrested-bail-me-too-pr-bill-cosby-a8369341.html.

59. Ryzik, "Weinstein in Handcuffs."

60. Richard Gonzales and Camila Domonoske, "Voters Recall Aaron Persky, Judge Who Sentenced Brock Turner," NPR, June 5, 2018, https://www.npr.org/sections/thetwo-way/2018/06/05/617071359/voters-are-deciding-whether-to-recall-aaron-persky-judge-who-sentenced-brock-tur.

61. Gonzales and Domonoske, "Voters Recall."

62. Hepler, "Campaign to Recall."

63. Hepler, "Campaign to Recall."

64. Hepler, "Campaign to Recall."

65. Hepler, "Campaign to Recall."

66. Gonzales and Domonoske, "Voters Recall."

67. Gonzales and Domonoske, "Voters Recall."

68. Cleeve R. Wootson Jr., "The Judge in the Infamous Brock Turner Case Finally Explains His Decision a Year Later," *Washington Post*, July 2, 2017, https://www.washingtonpost.com/news/grade-point/wp/2017/07/02/the-judge-in-the-infamous-brock-turner-case-finally-explains-his-decision-a-year-later/?utm_term=.c74ddb8e8fbf.

69. Hepler, "Campaign to Recall."

70. Elwood, "Examining Public Anger."

71. Young, "The Stanford Sexual Assault Case."

72. Josh Hafner, "The Judge in the Larry Nassar Trial: Incredible Quotes to Victims and Their Abuser," *USA Today*, January 24, 2018, https://www.usatoday.com/story/news/nation-now/2018/01/24/judge-larry-nassar-trial-incredible-quotes-victims-and-their-abuser/1061691001/.

73. Haltom and McCann, *Distorting*.

74. John Adams, *Diary and Autobiography of John Adams, Volumes 1–4 (1755–1804)*, eds. L. H. Butterfield, Leonard C. Faber, and Wendell D. Garrett (Cambridge, MA: Belknap Press, 1961), 79.

75. Tresa Baldas, "Larry Nassar's Lawyer Gets Death Threats in MSU Sex Abuse Case. 'It's Been Insane,'" *Detroit Free Press*, January 31, 2018, https://www.freep.com/story/news/local/michigan/2018/01/31/nassar-lawyer-death-threats-msu/1083909001/.

76. Isaac Chotiner, "A Harvard Law School Professor Defends His Decision to Represent Harvey Weinstein," *New Yorker*, March 7, 2019, https://www.newyorker.com/news/q-and-a/a-harvard-law-school-professor-defends-his-decision-to-represent-harvey-weinstein.

77. Randall Kennedy, "Harvard Betrays a Law Professor—and Itself," *New York Times*, May 15, 2019, https://www.nytimes.com/2019/05/15/opinion/race-identity/harvard-law-harvey-weinstein.html.

78. Kennedy, "Harvard Betrays."

79. Josh Gerstein, "Meet the Four Clinton Accusers."

80. Lepore, "The Rise of the Victims'-Rights Movement."

81. Ross, "UVA Dean Defamed."
82. Alanna Durkin Richer, "Attorneys Make Final Pitch to Jurors in *Rolling Stone* Trial," *Associated Press*, November 2, 2016, https://apnews.com/38f01c70406b43d68b60b6b7690302ab.
83. Ross, "UVA Dean Defamed."
84. Kimberley Richards, "Attorney Chris Darden to Stop Representing Nipsey Hussle's Accused Killer," *The Huffington Post*, May 10, 2019, https://www.huffpost.com/entry/chris-darden-nipsey-hussle-attorney-withdraw-eric-holder_n_5cd5e87de4b0796a95dc05d6.
85. Baldas, "Larry Nassar's Lawyer Gets Death Threats."
86. "Stanford Professor Speaks Out on Arrest of Suspect in White Powder Threat," *Bay City News*, NBC, March 1, 2018, https://www.nbcbayarea.com/news/local/Stanford-Professor-Speaks-Out-on-Arrest-of-Man-Suspected-in-White-Powder-Threat-475607163.html.
87. Capers, "The Unintentional Rapist."
88. Capers, "The Unintentional Rapist."
89. As Capers points out, had the accused in the *McQuirter* case been white, it is unclear that Mrs. Allen would have been apprehensive in the first place. And, if she did report being followed by a white man, it is not apparent whether law enforcement would have viewed the behavior as threatening or merely an attempt at seduction. Capers, "The Unintentional Rapist."
90. Tracy and Whitman, "Rape and Sexual Assault."
91. Yung, "One of These Laws"; Mears, *American Criminal Justice Policy*, 81–82.
92. "The Model Stalking Code Revisited: Responding to the New Realities of Stalking," National Center for Victims of Crime, http://victimsofcrime.org/docs/default-source/src/model-stalking-code.pdf?sfvrsn=12 at 14.
93. "Revenge Porn Laws by State," FindLaw, https://criminal.findlaw.com/criminal-charges/revenge-porn-laws-by-state.html.
94. Erin Sheley, "A Broken Windows Theory of Sexual Assault Enforcement," *Journal of Law and Criminology* 108, no. 3 (2017): 455–510.
95. Mary Anne Franks, "'Revenge Porn' Reform: A View from the Front Lines," *Florida Law Review* 69 (2017): 1255–337.
96. Marc Tran, "Combatting Gender Privilege and Recognizing a Woman's Right to Privacy in Public Spaces: Arguments to Criminalize Catcalling and Creepshots," *Hastings Women's Law Journal* 26 (2015): 185.
97. Bumiller, *Abusive State*.
98. Emily L. Thuma, *All Our Trials: Prisons, Policing, and the Feminist Fight to End Violence* (Urbana, Chicago, and Springfield: University of Illinois Press, 2019), 7.
99. Thuma, *All Our Trials*, 32.
100. Halley, "Trading the Megaphone," 109.
101. Halley, "Trading the Megaphone," 109.
102. Halley, "Trading the Megaphone," 109.
103. Crocker, "Feminism and Defending Men," 984, 1007.
104. Janet Halley, "Rape in Berlin: Reconsidering the Criminalisation of Rape in the International Law of Armed Conflict," *Melbourne Journal of International Law* 9, no. 1 (2008): 78.
105. Lepore, "The Rise of the Victims'-Rights Movement."
106. "Are Anti-sexting Laws Out of Control?," MSNBC, July 10, 2014, https://www.msnbc.com/all-in/watch/are-anti-sexting-laws-out-of-control-301682243741.
107. Roiphe, "The Other Whisper Network."
108. Laura Kipnis, "What We Lose When Sex Is All about Danger," *The Cut*, https://www.thecut.com/2017/03/laura-kipnis-unwanted-advances-excerpt.html.
109. West, "Gold Digger."
110. Mary Anne Franks, "How to Feel Like a Woman, or, Why Punishment Is a Drag," *UCLA Law Review* 61 (2014): 566.
111. Ewick and Silbey, *The Common Place of Law*.

112. Chotiner, "A Harvard Professor."
113. "The Harvey Weinstein Effect," *USA Today*.
114. "The Harvey Weinstein Effect," *USA Today*.
115. Dylan Matthews, "Michael Cohen's Hush Money Payments to Stormy Daniels and Karen McDougal, Explained," *Vox*, August 21, 2018, https://www.vox.com/2018/8/21/17765348/michael-cohen-guilty-plea-stormy-daniels-hush-money.
116. Sanday, *A Woman Scorned*, 49; Gray Cavender, "Media Construction of Athletics: Normalization and Deviance," Chapter 4 in *Routledge Handbook on Deviance*, eds. Stephen E. Brown and Opher Setina (New York: Routledge, 2017), 34–44.
117. Monica J. Casper and Lisa Jean Moore, *Missing Bodies: The Politics of Visibility* (New York: New York University Press, 2009), 133.
118. Rebecca Tiger, "Celebrity Gossip Blogs and the Interactive Construction of Addiction," *New Media and Society* 17 (2013): 343–44.
119. Paula Lavigne, "Lawyers, Status, Public Backlash Aid College Athletes Accused of Crimes," ESPN, June 15, 2015, http://espn.go.com/espn/otl/story/_/id/13065247/college-athletes-major-programs-benefit-confluence-factors-somes-avoid-criminal-charges.
120. Lavigne, "Lawyers, Status."
121. Nancy E. Dowd, Nancy Levit, and Ann McGinley, "Feminist Legal Theory Meets Masculinities Theory," chapter 1 in *Masculinities and the Law*, ed. Ann McGinley and Frank Rudy Cooper (New York: New York University Press, 2012), 25–50. Others attribute the defense of celebrities accused of sexual violence to morally loftier ideals. Boisseau argues, consonant with the Blackstonian formulation, that "false accusations provide the basis for one of the most poignant narratives of injustice because we have the sense that someone punished for a specific, discrete act that they did not commit is entirely innocent, not only of that discrete act but in some sort of existential sense of the word." Tracy Jean Boisseau, "Response to 'The Duke Rape Case Five Years Later: Lessons for the Academy, the Media, and the Criminal Justice System' by Dan Subotnik," *Akron Law Review* 45 (2012): 927.
122. Toluse Olorunnipa, "How Trump Story on Cohen's Hush-Money Payments Shifted over Time," *Bloomberg*, August 24, 2018, https://www.bloomberg.com/news/articles/2018-08-24/how-trump-story-on-cohen-s-hush-money-payments-shifted-over-time; and Andrew C. McCarthy, "On Hush Money, the President's Best Defense Is Lack of Criminal Intent," *National Review*, August 25, 2018, https://www.nationalreview.com/2018/08/trump-cohen-hush-money-president-had-lack-of-criminal-intent/.
123. Cieply, "Samantha Geimer."
124. Mark Landler, "Trump, Saying 'Mere Allegation' Ruins Lives, Appears to Doubt #MeToo Movement," *New York Times*, February 10, 2018, https://www.nytimes.com/2018/02/10/us/politics/trump-porter-me-too-movement.html?action=click&module=Top%20Stories&pgtype=Homepage.
125. Aly Raisman, "Rachael Denhollander," *Time Magazine 100 Most Influential People of 2018*, http://time.com/collection/most-influential-people-2018/5217581/rachael-denhollander/.
126. Ford, "How Brock Turner Changed."
127. Sydney Ember and Graham Bowley, "After Bill Cosby, States Shift on Statutes of Limitations in Sexual Assault Cases," *New York Times*, November 6, 2016, https://www.nytimes.com/2016/11/07/arts/television/after-bill-cosby-states-shift-sexual-assault-statutes-of-limitations.html.
128. Ember and Bowley, "After Bill Cosby."
129. Provine, *Unequal Under Law*.
130. Victoria Law, "Against Carceral Feminism," *Jacobin*, October 17, 2014, https://www.jacobinmag.com/2014/10/against-carceral-feminism/.
131. Alexander, *The New Jim Crow*.

III

Crowdsourcing the Law

SIX

Reckoning

People v. Weinstein

During the 1990s, the films produced by the Weinstein Company, led by CEO Harvey Weinstein, earned hundreds of Oscar nominations. The producer was praised for his activism on behalf of AIDS awareness and medical research. Weinstein promoted his wife's fashion label into a multimillion-dollar business, demanding that actors in his films appear at public events in Marchesa gowns. Ronan Farrow describes that Weinstein, "ha[d] been thanked more than almost anyone else in movie history, ranking just after Steven Spielberg and right before God."[1]

In 2016, however, Weinstein's empire began to crumble. The company invested in a series of less-than-successful films. Then, in the fall of 2017, the *New York Times* and the *New Yorker* reported that dozens of women had been sexually harassed or sexually assaulted by the mogul.[2] Thus far, more than eighty women, among them prominent actors Uma Thurman, Ashley Judd, and Lupita Nyong'o, have come forward to accuse Weinstein of inappropriate sexual behaviors ranging from exhibitionism to rape.[3] Multiple civil suits have been filed alleging that the producer engaged in battery and quid pro quo sexual harassment.[4] In May 2018, Weinstein was arrested in New York City for the alleged rape and sexual abuse of two different women, and it appears the fallout is far from over.[5]

As disclosures surged suggesting the extent of Weinstein's alleged behavior, actress Alyssa Milano tweeted,

> Suggested by a friend: If all the women who have been sexually harassed or assaulted wrote "Me too" as a status, we might give people a sense of the magnitude of the problem. If you've been sexually harassed or assaulted write "me too" as a reply to this tweet.[6]

Milano was quoting Tarana Burke, an activist who launched the hashtag while coming to terms with her own traumatic past.[7] The #MeToo movement rapidly took on a global significance. In Italy, survivors tweeted about #quellavoltache (that time when), as French victims were encouraged to flag harassers with #BalanceTonPorc (snitch out your pig).

#MeToo built on earlier hashtag campaigns, such as #GrabYourWallet and #NotOkay, which attracted millions of participants.[8] As a result of organizing over social media, in March 2017, millions marched worldwide on behalf of women's rights, many wearing hand-knit, pink, cat-eared hats to call out the president's vulgar comments and the administration's overall lack of support for women's concerns. As the social movement took shape, claims of sexual harassment and institutional nonresponsiveness implicated companies including Uber, Google, and Fox News.[9]

Although the Trump administration's policies are, to put it mildly, less than woman-friendly, the president's practice of using social networks as a platform for engaging in politics in fact may have helped to empower oppositional social movements like #MeToo.[10] Although social media were in the background in earlier administrations, the Trump presidency has shifted the role of such platforms from ancillary to primary tools of political messaging.[11]

The stylistic parameters dictated by social networks combined with factors like anonymity, disinhibition effects, and the president's own personality, have contributed to a phenomenon whereby, as political discourse is engaged online, politics have grown exponentially more combative.[12] Pew Research Center identifies that since the 2016 election "angry" reactions on Facebook are much more common than "love" reactions.[13] News media in the United States have become the most polarized of any democratic nation, with readers increasingly refusing to seek out information across the political divide.[14]

Increasing access to social media and growing anger fuel the #MeToo movement. After more than thirty years of activist, feminist interventions in the law, under many metrics the movement has revolutionized law on the books but has had painfully little success in effecting practically meaningful reforms. Crimes of sexual assault continue to be marked by low clearance rates and failures in reporting. Rape kits sit untested. Mistaken assumptions about false claims and liars thrive. Were it two years ago, this book might have concluded that Carol Smart's prediction in the 1990s of feminist changes to law being a Pyrrhic victory still held true.

The #MeToo movement, however, is a game changer, channeling collective frustration at years of institutional indifference into demands for social and legal reforms. The breadth of the movement, and the changes to sentencing and statutes of limitations that it has inspired may signify a seismic shift, not only in the power among the members of the general public to effect legal change, but in their perception of themselves as change agents. MacKinnon characterizes #MeToo as having a "butterfly" effect, that "the right small human intervention in an unstable political system can sooner or later have large complex reverberations."[15] She writes that, at last her own "'flights of activism' . . . are producing 'storms, sometimes tornados, in gender relations through law.'"[16] As MacKinnon describes, after years of attempts at feminist interventions, the movement seems to be on the precipice of achieving what centuries of IRL social protest have been unable to accomplish.[17]

The impact of #MeToo is visible in comments after the guilty verdict in the Cosby case. A reader on a major news site remarks,

> I hope this really is a new day. I hope that, if someone like Cosby or Weinstein actually faces consequences for abusing and sexually assaulting their fellow human beings, those who commit these crimes who are not famous will also be held accountable. No more smearing the accuser, no more making excuses for male privilege. Real consequences. What a relief.

Another notes, "[N]ow there may be consequences for sexual assault and misconduct. People will think twice before they abuse each other. . . . The old tricks of smearing the accusers didn't work this time."

What is the potential of a virtual social movement like #MeToo in regard to law, and what is its peril? The answer depends in large part on how democratic and inclusive social networks turn out to be.

The successful recall campaign of judge Aaron Persky in the Brock Turner case, as well as the numerous changes to sexual assault and rape statutes across the United States, attest to the strength and the unifying power of social media. However, it is an open question whether these changes, accomplished rapidly through the will of a virtual majority, are investing in traditional legal structures and institutions or refuting them. The answer, probably, is both.

There has yet to be a true test of the #MeToo movement's impact on law. The significance of the movement in the Cosby trial was emphasized only by its glaring and deliberate absence.[18] Yet, as described in chapter 1, #MeToo did likely play a role in arguably the most significant portion of the trial, the decision about admission of evidence. The import of the social movement on the potential trials of Weinstein and others remains to be seen, although one can guess that the overwhelming interest in the producer's prosecution already is making the criminal process much more transparent by significantly reducing the likelihood of a plea offer.

#METOO: ITS PROMISE AND PERIL

For many participants, #MeToo has been not only inspirational but revolutionary. Articles describe the hashtag, posted as a Facebook status twelve million times in the movement's first twenty-four hours, as an "avalanche," a "deluge," and a "reckoning."[19] For many, posting #MeToo marked the first time they had publicly spoken about having been harassed or assaulted, even to family or close friends.[20] One can only imagine the numbers of calls and emails that took place after relatives, accustomed to seeing vacation pictures, were confronted with the initially cryptic statement.

Although, as highlighted in the introduction, the internet has proven to be a toxic space for women, it is also potentially a liberating one. Carrie Rentschler comments that the online environment has empowered feminist bloggers "to respond to rape culture, and hold accountable those responsible for its practices when mainstream news media, police and school authorities do not."[21] She describes how the internet enables young women to be "response-able witness[es]" to catcalls, harassment, and rape jokes, documenting and responding to bad behaviors with network-based strategies such as mobile phone video or Google mapping.[22]

While online activism has been parodied as "slacktivism," the virtual environment in reality has been a location that has enabled change that is significant and, perhaps, more democratically effected than ever before. Notably, women are more than twice as likely to sign online petitions and more likely to be involved in virtual organizing, "bypassing the gatekeepers, simply by sheer mass—forcing attention on the issues they deem important."[23] Active participants in virtual forums are not only influencing legislative change and outcomes in criminal cases, they have accomplished significant inroads with regard to issues like repealing the "tampon tax."[24] Via social media, feminists, and particularly feminists from less visible sectors of society, can fill in information that national media coverage may have glassed over or ignored.[25]

Significantly, although young women may be "attacked" or "policed" by other commenters, women of color point out that, for nonwhite women, tangible physical spaces also may feel unsafe. While the digital world may be perceived as an unusually toxic environment by a white woman, it may be interpreted differently by someone who regularly experiences harassment and exclusion in everyday life. [26] As Kaba and Smith explain, "Twitter may be toxic—but so is the world."[27] For non-white commenters, the digital environment can feel safer than the real-life world because

> despite not being protected spaces . . . [i]n these digital spaces, instances of abuse can be addressed without the physical confrontation required to speak up in offline public spaces. Reactions to violence can be contemplated and crafted without the anxiety that comes with an altercation at close proximity. When a woman is cornered on her Twitter feed, she need not go it alone; rather, there is often a heightened sense of collectivity among fellow hashtaggers. When trolls do appear, their toxic words are likely to be met with a group of women who

> stand up to them, advocate for one another, and stake ownership over the digital dialogue.[28]

As recent identifications of Permit Patties and Barbeque Beckies attest, people of color are surveilled even as they engage in innocuous, everyday activities. Ryan Bowles-Eagle explains that "[u]ltimately, hashtag activism . . . is not only about mobility but about the ability to loiter, to linger without needing a reason—something the architecture of a digital space like Twitter is designed to foster."[29]

Unquestionably, the #MeToo movement has inspired survivors personally to speak out and, as it has gained steam, discussions about rape culture, slut-shaming, and toxic masculinity have been moved further into the mainstream.[30] The collective calling out of friends and coworkers as potential perpetrators and harassers online has made many people more aware of the latent dangers around them in real life. As a professional in the entertainment industry wrote of the so-called shitty men list, "Over the course of the day, I had several conversations with female friends who asked a variation of the same question: *This man is close to me, either professionally or personally; what is my role here?*"[31] Others have been encouraged to consider how their own experiences fit into the larger construct of rape culture. As one participant in the movement reflected,

> I've never really thought about these moments cumulatively before. . . . In part, because they seem so "small" compared to what many have experienced—not worthy of consideration.[32]

This statement highlights how the #MeToo campaign has permitted and encouraged persons who have experienced sexual assault and harassment to view what they may have previously dismissed as "minor" violations and humiliations not as isolated events but as part of a larger rape culture. This realization of a collective, shared experience is unprecedented. In January 2016, about a million people were talking about sexual harassment on Twitter; in January 2018, almost eight million people had something to say about the topic.[33] Even if #MeToo does not have clear next steps, simply identifying the magnitude of sexual harassment and assault is a profound accomplishment.[34]

While #MeToo has inspired some to identify what they have experienced as a part of a greater rape culture, it also has created a perhaps less-comfortable space in which people can envision their roles as participants in fostering social and work environments that have been conducive to abuse and assault.[35] The 2017 Dictionary.com Word of the Year was "complicit."[36] Our societal interest in the term reflects the idea that criminal responsibility is not only reserved for perpetrators but for those who aid and abet them. As sexual assault allegations have been revealed across varied fields, discussions concern not only the alleged perpetrators themselves but often those who have, tacitly or directly, supported their bad behavior. The idea of "whisper networks," for example, has become a popular way to describe groups of persons—usually women—who shared warnings about suspected harassers and perpetrators with select friends and colleagues but not to a wider and potentially more vulnerable audience.[37]

Like underground publications in times of political oppression, these networks of women have been praised for exhibiting agency; however, they are also problematic in their failure to publicly identify alleged perpetrators, leaving the most vulnerable to assault unprotected.[38] Collective self-reflection about our own and others' participation in covering up allegations has also been an important part of the #MeToo movement.[39] Uma Thurman's February 2018 statement to the *New York Times* describing encounters with Harvey Weinstein, for example, reads more like a confession than the narrative of a survivor, conveying her regret that her silence had contributed to a "cloud cover" encouraging "lambs" to walk "into the slaughter."[40]

The public emergence of a "sensational" criminal case can lead to a crisis moment, opening up a space for the public to voice opinions, not just about guilt or innocence, but about larger issues of race, class, and gender, free from the anxieties that overshadow in-person conversations. The disclosure that a serious crime has occurred brings up issues of public safety but also raises complex moral and ethical questions. In a case like that of Susan Smith, who drowned her children, the public debates concern, not only of guilt or innocence, but the deeper question of what it means to be a good or bad mother.[41] When, in 2016, a grand jury in St. Louis County failed to indict Darren Wilson, the officer accused of homicide against Michael Brown, conversations took place that not only rehashed facts in the case but confronted racism, poverty, and the role of discriminatory criminal justice practices in imposing structural violence.

In this moment of #MeToo, space has been opened up for the renegotiation of legal meaning. Discussions about complicity mark yet another instance in which a formal, legal term is being vernacularized and perhaps reenvisioned in the public imagination. Yet, as openings arise for discussion and redefinition, it is important to take stock of not only the promise of #MeToo but the movement's potential pitfalls.

A "GENDERED" BINARY

As discussed in the introduction, former Trump administration chief strategist and former CEO of Breitbart, Steve Bannon, identifies a threat to political conservatives from an "anti-patriarchy movement" that he predicts will be "stronger than the tea party."[42] Similar perspectives are in abundance among social media commenters who identify covens of angry women—witches, gold diggers, lynch mobs—waiting in the wings, eager to supplant men in positions of power.

In the views of many internet posters, sexual assault accusations form an important part of a larger and unsettling, gendered upheaval that is taking place across society. As discussed in earlier chapters, there is a belief that men in power are being targeted by and are falling "victim" to lawfare deployed by "feminazis" like Gloria Allred. The witch hunts and lynch mobs described in chapter 4 evidence a widespread moral panic about impending gender wars. Across online forums, there is extensive support for the idea that sexual assault laws have been and are being constructed by women to punish and penalize men. As a commenter on a popular video site writes,

> The way the laws are written sexual assault is anything the woman thinks it is. Trying to kiss a woman and being rejected can be sexual assault. Flirting with a woman who you find out later is not interested can be sexual assault. Trying to hold hands with [a] woman who is not interested can be sexual assault. Sexual assault according to the way American laws are written is anything that the woman feels is unwanted sexual advances. Which could be anything she doesn't like and takes it be something that she thinks is sexual. When it comes to SEX all men are evil and all women are angels—RIGHT?

On the site of a popular weekly entertainment magazine, a commenter explains,

> When it comes to sex the man is always wrong and the woman is always right—the way the *feminist laws* are written. There are many feminist women's groups who lobby the government and make the government and Law enforcement believe that all men are evil and all women are angels that can do no wrong when it comes to SEX.

On a conservative blog, a comment notes, "Winking is sexual assault. You be careful now."

While the identification that women as a category are out to take down all men is extreme, it is not incorrect to identify that, so far, the #MeToo movement appears to have been constructed along gendered lines. As people began to retweet and repost Alyssa Milano's request that "all the *women* who have been sexually harassed or assaulted" write "me too," some changed the word "women" to "persons." Rapidly, fissures emerged. Was the social movement meant to call out men's violence against women and girls or was its objective to identify gender-based violence against all persons? Some men who posted #MeToo were called out as "colonizers" attempting to piggyback on a campaign meant to protect a more marginalized group.[43] Helena Theixos argues that the centering of women's voices in the movement is purposeful: "The prioritizing of the heretofore silenced voice is a hallmark feature of this new activism. . . . Prioritizing the silenced victim's voices is a conscious choice, in direct reaction to and in defiance of a culture of silencing."[44]

In response to #MeToo, a group of established Hollywood women, including Reese Witherspoon, established the TIME'S UP Legal Defense Fund. The website for campaign features a prominently displayed letter that begins, "Dear Sisters."[45] Via mechanisms like the "shitty men list," men are being defined as the likely perpetrators of sexual assault and women constructed as victims or survivors. In much of the discourse surrounding the movement, there are roles for sympathetic men as allies or bystanders but not as victims of violence themselves.

This construction of sexual assault along a gendered divide is troubling. Across institutional contexts—prisons, the military, the Catholic church—men are not only the majority of sexual assault perpetrators but they also comprise the vast majority of victims. Defining sexual assault crimes in terms of a gender binary serves to exclude some survivors from the justice system's protections. The harm from this exclusion is felt by many men personally. Chris Brown, who accused conductor James Levine of sexual assault, describes that, while he admires the women posting the "me too" status, the movement itself has only furthered his "loneliness as a past victim."[46] Similarly, Andrew Schmutzer, as a non-cis female survivor, characterizes his status as "always an adjunct."[47] Data demonstrate that reporting rates among men are lower than those among women, most likely because social stigma and shame are greater within the male victim population.[48] The vast majority of research on sexual assault focuses on cis female victims, as do representations of rape, sexual assault, and sexual harassment across the media. There is a danger that this collective reluctance to view men as genuine victims serves to perpetuate rape culture; we are more likely to favor an eye for an eye approach to the punishment of Turner or Nassar if rape of men, or rape in prison is not "real rape."

The framing of #MeToo so far not only ignores that men are victims of rape in the direct, literal sense but in the broader sense that men, too, are impacted by structural violence. Men themselves are not bystanders to but are actively being harmed by patriarchy.[49] As contemporary discussions of complicity by those speaking out against Weinstein attest, women are both beneficiaries of and victims in systems of oppression. This is also true of men.

The calls to expand incarceration and retributive justice that have accompanied the #MeToo movement risk intensifying this problem by continuing to focus on individual rather than structural violence. Across the criminal justice system, it has not been conservative but bipartisan reforms that have led to the curbing of judicial discretion and to longer and longer sentences. Advocacy by members of the feminist movement has contributed to mandatory arrest policies for both men and women in the context of allegations of intimate partner violence, to a lessened availability of parole, and to moral panics about sex offenders, stalking, and other sex-based offenses.

Perhaps the most significant contribution of social media is the newfound ability to mobilize affinity groups instantaneously around a particular social issue or problem. Just a small sample of the ways in which social media have been used to effect legal change in the past few years includes not only the landmark recall of Judge Persky but an ongoing and growing movement to significantly extend or abolish statutes of limitation relating to sexual assault.[50] Neither the movement toward extending statutes of limitations in relation to crimes of sexual violence nor the cry to remove biased judges is new; the crime control reforms fit into the neoliberal trend toward expanding the carceral state that has been going on for years. Now, however, social media and social networks are providing an unprecedented tool for efficiently mobilizing large and seemingly disparate groups of people around a single issue in an instant.

There is also concern about who, really, is included in the social movement. Founder Tarana Burke, Ashwini Tambe, and others describe that, so far, the faces out in front—in social media language, the "influencers"—have been largely cisgender white women.[51] As a result, Tambe critiques that the movement so far has largely centered on white women's pain.[52] Edwards' criticism of the framing of the women's movement in the 1970s may hold true today: the "analysis, that women's shared oppression by men outweighs all potential for alliances along other lines" sets up a framework in which "Happy Rockefeller has more in common with a Black woman in an auto plant than has a male Black autoworker."[53]

Phyllis Chesler asks, "Will [#MeToo] be able to change the working conditions of farm and factory workers? More important, how will we be able to monitor and intervene in the daily work lives of female agricultural workers, waitresses, secretaries, housekeepers, bar tenders, miners, students, soldiers and prostituted women?"[54] She ponders whether, in fact, these women's "working lives will become harder, harsher, if powerful men lose their sexual perks in the office and have to *pay* to treat women badly."[55] Transgender women, too, experience sexual violence at rates equal to or greater than nontransgender women. As Levine notes, "the attribution of violence against women to male domination offers little to those women who happen to be male-assigned. This is of particular concern in legal contexts."[56]

The recent deluge of disclosures across the entertainment industry, and perhaps telling silences across other industries, demonstrate that, until very recently, the word of even relatively privileged white women would not have been believed over that of male colleagues and bosses. The allegations against Harvey Weinstein tellingly mark the first time in which the accusers of sexual assault are potentially more famous and richer than the accused. As *Time Magazine* asks, rhetorically, in its "Silence Breakers" article: "When movie stars don't know where to go, what hope is there for the rest of us? What hope is there for the janitor who's being harassed by a co-worker but remains silent out of fear she'll lose the job she needs to support her children? For the administrative assistant who repeatedly fends off a superior who won't take no for an answer? For the hotel housekeeper who never knows, as she goes about replacing towels and cleaning toilets, if a guest is going to corner her in a room she can't escape?"[57]

The #MeToo movement faces a Catch-22. It is the very fact that famous, primarily white, elite, cis female women are speaking out that gives #MeToo its power. Out in front of the social movement are women who are both "famous" and "familiar," a tried and true strategy for success.[58] At the Oscar ceremony in early 2017, actor Frances McDormand addressed the necessity for those in power in the entertainment industry to demand that any project on which they work contain an "inclusion rider," a proviso that any workers associated with the project represent a real commitment toward diversity and equality.[59] After the Oscar speech, the actor partnered with a law firm to create a template that could be inserted into employment contracts, requiring that production teams interview women and members of underrepresented groups.[60] The only persons who can demand such a rider, though, are the people who have established their power. So far, it is mostly white and universally economically privileged women who have achieved status within the Hollywood entertainment machine who, at last, seem to have come close to feeling as though they can speak out without facing massive repercussions. What fuels the movement's power also creates its potential to be exclusionary.

The troubled history of the women's movement, dating back to Florence Kelley, Louis Brandeis, and the National Consumers League (NCL), demonstrates that it is highly problematic when women speak on behalf of others. While the NCL advocated for female elevator operators and laundry workers in the early 1900s, white women activists were able to protest against oppression because women of color were employed as domestic workers at their homes.[61] Although protections for white women workers in factories were enacted in the late 1800s, it was not until the 1970s when African American women domestic workers were afforded workplace protections such as minimum wage or maximum hour restrictions.[62]

Across liberal and conservative social media sites it is common for posters to suggest imposing longer or mandatory minimum sentences for sexual assault crimes, continuing to overlook and obscure the impact those changes may have on communities of color. St. Félix tweets, you "can just feel the intersectional framework, which hadn't even truly been instituted, slipping from the discourse in favor of gender binary."[63] There are many nonwhite women—Anita Hill, Shonda Rhimes, Salma Hayek, Lupita Nyong'o, and others—in visible positions within the #MeToo and #TimesUp movements; however, in the overarching and largely one-dimensional reframing of the movement as one about gender, the distinct and important interests of these women of color risk being swept under the rug yet again. As both bell hooks and, more recently, Roxanne Gay, articulate, the question of "who gets to be angry" is a political one.[64] The answer to that question is being debated and disputed in the context of #MeToo.

The TIME'S UP Legal Defense Fund is attempting to raise awareness around these issues of inclusiveness. On its website, the fund's very first objective is "to help less privileged women—like janitors, nurses and workers at farms, factories, restaurants and hotels—protect themselves from sexual misconduct and the fallout from reporting it."[65] Ancillary to the TIME'S UP legal campaign is a promising, inclusive project begun by director and producer Shonda Rhimes, labeled 50/50 by 2020, an initiative that aims for inclusion across the entertainment industry, not only in terms of gender, but also sexual orientation, race, disability status, and other characteristics.[66] Yet one has to wonder if calls for inclusiveness pale in comparison to the draw of #YesAllWomen. To become an effective movement for social change #MeToo also must contend with the powerful draw of biological explanations that appeal not only to fatalists like Steve Bannon but to participants in the movement themselves, raised on decades of "commonsense," gendered truths.

UNREASONABLE WOMEN?

When Ruth Bader Ginsburg argued for abolition of the death penalty for rape in *Coker v. Georgia*, she was confronting, on behalf of the ACLU Women's Rights Project, more than a century of legal arguments that relied on essentialist, gendered differences to advance legal protections for women.[67] In *Muller v. Oregon*, Louis Brandeis famously—and lengthily—appealed to (white, male) judges' commonsense that white women's status as "mothers of the race" should preclude them from working as many hours as male counterparts.[68] In the criminal context, alienation of affection statutes and statutory rape laws all reflected the idea that women were in more need of protection than men, largely because their economic value decreased when they were "defiled."[69]

These arguments were not crafted only by men. They were engineered and advanced by women activists, conscious that biologically based arguments might increase the likelihood of success of their legal arguments.[70] Over time, feminists scholars and activists have employed arguments that women are naturally more caring and empathetic—or even more impressionable—than men in a pragmatic effort to secure legal policies favorable to women. Lenore Walker's theory of learned helplessness, a foundational element of battered spouse syndrome, for example, is founded on the hypothesis that female victims who have been subjected to repetitive, severe trauma at the hands of men may be rendered incapable of fighting back against an active assailant.[71] Cahn critiques this idea that

> [a] reasonable woman. . . . will certainly not respond aggressively or resort to violence herself. The reasonable woman thus becomes a victim who needs protection; when her actions can be portrayed as those of a victim, she is protected by the courts. Other women do not, unfortunately, fit the reasonable woman stereotype.[72]

While some survivors may be passive or frozen in the face of oppression, others may fight back or behave in ways that do not comport with typically "feminine" reactions. Diagnoses like battered woman syndrome or rape trauma syndrome are helpful as explanations for why *some* victims of sexual assault may not promptly report, but they should not be imposed as expectations for *all* victims.[73]

Critics identify a danger that the #MeToo movement, like the theory of learned helplessness, is being centered around the idea that women, as a category, are in need of protecting. Condoleezza Rice exhorts, "Let's not turn women into snowflakes. Let's not infantilize women."[74] A recent article in the *New Republic* notes that #MeToo so far has given voice to

> a shared experience of what has been *done to us* by others. It turns out that this is an extraordinarily effective way to raise consciousness online. But it has a passive quality. And this allows certain presumptions—about men and women, about feminism and misogyny—to rush in, so that they undergird a once-in-a-generation opportunity to redefine gender politics.[75]

Laura Kipnis queries whether the movement resonates with so many women because of echoes of legal protectionism: "[T]here's something reassuringly familiar—at least timeless—about these tales of female peril, even amidst the supposed sexual free-for-all of hookup culture."[76] It is not unusual for social movements, even those ostensibly advocating for women's rights, to draw on traditional, gendered stereotypes. Pamela Aronson, for example, identifies how anti-war activism engaged "gendered frames" to advance more radical objectives.[77] Daphne Merkin dramatically observes that the #MeToo movement might be creating a "victimology paradigm for young women . . . in which they are perceived to be . . . as frail as Victorian Housewives."[78] Fears that #MeToo replicates rather than challenges images of women as in need of protection bring to mind Judge Aquilina's comments during the sentencing of Larry Nassar, referring to rape as uniquely traumatizing and survivors as not everyday women but as superhumanly strong.[79]

Sexual assault law is haunted by our tendency to construct law in the binary—victims are either brave survivors or gold diggers, perpetrators are innocent targets of extortion or monsters. Across social media, those whom we believe are revered as "ideal victims"; they are traumatized, uber-emotional, and concerned with the impact of their experience on society as a whole. The unlucky persons whom we disbelieve are cast outside the norm by applying labels like "gold digger," "prostitute," "THOT," "liar," or "bitch." When it comes to actual victims, experiences and manifestations of trauma are often devalued or discounted.

Chapter 3 addressed the societal tendency, exacerbated on social media, to transform one woman who lies into an example of the prototypical liar. The cumulative effect of centuries of maligning women accusers means that, as Leslie Jamison articulates, when "we start talking about wounded women, we risk transforming their suffering from an aspect of the female experience into an element of the female constitution."[80] For this reason, some refuse to post #MeToo status, arguing that, like rape law historically has done, the movement places the responsibility for registering and defining the parameters of a sexual assault on victims' shoulders.[81] Tarana Burke comments, "I want to teach people to not lean into their trauma. You can create the kind of joy in your life that allows you to lean into that instead."[82] For some, telling their stories may be cathartic, but this does not mean that they need to tell them to the world or to tell them on demand.

In the background is the question of whether women, really, would be better than men at accomplishing fair and effective legal reforms. In the 1990s, political scientist Francis Fukuyama wrote an article notoriously imagining the benefits that would emerge—fewer wars, more empathy—if women reigned in international politics.[83] Katha Pollitt, Barbara Ehrenreich, and other feminist scholars rapidly responded that, not only were men not biologically predisposed to war but women, when given the opportunity, also tend to embrace a power-hungry militarism.[84] Just think of the Alma Coin character in the novel, *Mockingjay* (the final book in *The Hunger Games* series), played in the film by Julianne Moore. Coin is the "good guy" until, suddenly, she isn't.[85]

As Sjoberg identifies, although they comprise a small number of perpetrators, women have participated in perpetuating wartime rape in greater numbers than one might imagine.[86] Today, women comprise about 14 percent of child sex abusers of male children, and 6 percent of sex abusers of female children.[87] Fourteen percent may not seem like a high number until one considers that a staggering 28 percent of youths age fourteen to seventeen report having been sexually victimized over the course of their lifetimes.[88]

Women in power have proven themselves to be capable of Weinstein-like behaviors. A prominent example is Miki Agrawal, the founder of Thinx period underwear.[89] Employees accuse the former CEO of commenting on

> the size and shape of her employees' breasts, an employee's nipple piercings, her own sexual exploits, her desire to experiment with poly-

> amory, her interest in entering a sexual relationship with one of her employees, and the exact means by which she was brought to female ejaculation

as well as touching "an employee's breasts and ask[ing] her to expose them, routinely chang[ing] clothes in front of employees, and conduct[ing] meetings via videoconference while in bed, apparently unclothed."[90]

After a Title IX proceeding, New York University found philosopher Avital Ronell responsible for sexually harassing a male graduate student.[91] Among the accusations levied against the academic were that she required the student to lie in her bed, repeatedly kissed and touched him, and refused to work with him if he did not reciprocate her advances.[92] In a refrain that sounds strikingly familiar, Ronell argues her behaviors were "campy" while the student describes them as "stalking."[93]

In summer 2018, a newspaper revealed that one of the most outspoken accusers of Harvey Weinstein, Asia Argento, had paid a young, male actor $380,000.[94] In the letter outlining his claims, the actor alleged that he experienced ongoing trauma as a result of sexual battery Argento perpetrated on him when he was seventeen and she was thirty-eight.

The revelation of accusations against these women and disclosures by others of "complicity" in suppressing potentially damning information about suspected perpetrators supports the idea that, as the feminist movement has long argued, sexual assault is an exercise of power. Women have participated in—or at least condoned—sexual violence much more frequently that we tend to acknowledge. Continuing feminist calls for expanded prison sentences suggest that women as a category are not opposed to expanding the carceral complex, even if that expansion happens to perpetuate a long-standing and intractable institutional rape culture.

As one reporter notes, "It's hard to escape a sense that feminists see the moment as one of sisterly revenge against men."[95] However, "the view that men as a group are the primary enemy of women as a group . . . overlooks the connection between the social condition of women and their role in the process of production."[96] It is only "[b]y viewing their status as a product of social relations rather than biology, [that] women can devise a strategy for liberation based on alliances with other groups fighting oppression."[97] As Hannah McCann wrote after allegations surfaced against Avital Ronell, "we are called to rethink our emphasis on gender in the first place: perhaps what needs greater attention is who has the power to speak? Who has the power to mobilise accounts of the 'truth'—whether that be the accused, . . . defenders, or otherwise—and who does not?"[98]

To truly be a "reckoning," Tarana Burke tweeted, the #MeToo movement must shift from talking about "individuals" toward discussing the structural factors contributing to rape culture.[99] We need to reckon with the feminist movement's thirst for carceral solutions."

THE MADDING CROWD

As the torrent of accusations against Weinstein continued throughout 2017 and early 2018, actor Tom Hanks commented to BBC News of the producer, "We're at a watershed moment, this is a sea change. . . . His last name will become a noun and a verb. It will become an identifying moniker for a state of being for which there was a before and an after."[100]

Hank's prediction has proven true. The producer's strikingly rapid and comprehensive fall from grace has been given a nickname, the "Weinstein Effect";[101] #weinsteined has become a way to describe the experiences of both those who have experienced harassment or assault by a serial attacker and those accused of engaging in such behavior. The *National Review* argues that based on the number of his accusers, "it's time for Bill O'Reilly to be Weinsteined."[102] An article in *Architect Magazine* queries when its industry will be Weinsteined, calling out a culture of "deep-seated male bias" that long has impeded women's success in the profession.[103] Advisers in the financial services industry admonish employers to prepare for the "Weinstein effect" by crafting robust complaint and investigation procedures.[104]

For some, the harshest outcome after a criminal conviction in the United States is not the temporary loss of liberty but the lifelong diminishment of opportunity for not only personal economic success but for participation in civic life.[105] Unquestionably, #MeToo already has fostered "collateral damage"—not bloodless statistics but actual human casualties. The *USA Today* site discussed earlier lists among the accused not just individuals like Larry Nassar, convicted of multiple counts of sexual assault against children, but men accused of other "sexual misconduct, ranging from inappropriate texts to groping to rape."[106] Listed alongside Nassar and Weinstein on the site are those who have ardently denied a single harassment allegation.[107] The group of men whom the newspaper records as having been fired or demoted includes, in addition to persons accused of rape or sexual assault, men who have been identified as having had arguably consensual relationships with staff members and even those who are merely alleged to have had "sexually themed conversations."[108]

Just prior to his announcement that he was entering the 2020 presidential race, Joe Biden, former vice president and an outspoken advocate against sexual violence, was accused by several women of inappropriate touching.[109] What we now recognize as a predictable debate emerged. Was Biden's behavior, as representative Lucy Flores characterized it, "demeaning and disrespectful," or was he simply "Uncle Joe," an out of touch "bumbler" who—if the allegations are accurate—sniffed and kissed an unknown young woman's head out of mere cluelessness. As first set forth in the introduction, the movement has yet to deeply interrogate what Roiphe calls a "problem of scale," determining what behavior qualifies as criminal—or at least disqualifying of a public position—and what is merely creepy.[110] Thus far, Biden seems to have escaped the allegations relatively unscathed, the verdict tending toward average Joe versus sexual predator in the court of public opinion. As we are well aware, however, the will of the mob can be fickle and fierce.

What of the falsely accused? Some participants in #MeToo adhere to the idea that the reputational or economic damage that may be done to some wrongfully accused men pales in comparison to centuries of harm done to women in the context of sexual assault. Emily Lindin, a columnist at *Teen Vogue*, sums her position on Twitter:

> I'm actually not at all concerned about innocent men losing their jobs over false sexual assault/harassment allegations. If some innocent men's reputations have to take a hit in the process of undoing the patriarchy, that is a price I am absolutely willing to pay.[111]

Heather Jo Flores explains this line of thinking on *Vox*, asking,

> Does an abusive man lose his home, his family, his career, his community? Because these are the things that women often have to give up in order to get away from abuse. More often than not, the woman/victim loses everything and the man/abuser keeps it all and moves on to his next victim, who is either oblivious or hoodwinked into thinking she'll change him.[112]

Suzanna Danuta Walters asks, provocatively, "Why can't we hate men?"[113] After all, strikingly few men seem to have paid significant consequences for alleged sexual assaults, and they do commit the vast majority of violence.[114] After years of horrific treatment of women by the criminal justice system, a significant mass of supporters of #MeToo suggest that, for perpetrators, a loss of a job or a little bit of reputational damage is no big deal. A common argument is that, for most of the accused, sexual assault allegations will prove to have been a small bump in the road.

Historically, a woman's loss of sexual honor "ruined" her forever, whereas men's loss of honor could be reclaimed by vindicating attacks on women's chastity.[115] Today, there remains the possibility that via counseling, attendance at support groups, and participation in advocacy and community service, and a really good PR team, some of those accused in the tidal wave of #MeToo may be able to regain social and economic status, even—some might say, ironically—to become leaders in the movement themselves.[116]

Regardless of whether some of those accused will be able to recover, however, the truth is that others have faced psychological, emotional, or even fatal, physical consequences as a result, not of a legal decision, but of reputational damage inflicted by an angry mob. The acknowledgment by some women that these are consequences we are "willing to pay" are tone deaf and exclusionary. As Tambe observes,

> [I]t is worth keeping in mind that the primary instrument of redress in #MeToo is public shaming and criminalization of the perpetrator. This is already too familiar a problem for black men. We know the history of how black men have been lynched based on unfounded allegations that they sexually violated white women. We know how many black men are unjustly incarcerated. The dynamics of #MeToo, in which due process has been reversed—with accusers' words taken more seriously than those of the accused—is a familiar problem in black communities. Maybe some black women want no part of this dynamic.[117]

Within just one year, the #MeToo movement so far has accomplished a judicial removal, the strengthening of state sexual assault laws, the extension of statutes of limitation, and the firing or otherwise shaming of numerous alleged perpetrators. It is vital to ask what role, if any, due process has in this new and swift race to justice.

#METOO AND DUE PROCESS

On its face, the TIME'S UP Legal Defense Fund chaired by Anita Hill seems to be signaling a new faith in the institution of law in affording justice to victims. It is emblematic that Hill, who was failed so profoundly by the process during Justice Clarence Thomas's Supreme Court nomination and confirmation hearings, has taken on a visible, leading role in an organization promoting legal services for women experiencing sexual harassment.[118] The efforts and monies committed so far to bolstering the TIME'S UP Legal Defense Fund, as well as the Persky recall campaign and petitions to reform sentencing and statutes of limitations evidence, suggest a strong commitment by feminists to strengthening the capacity of law as an institution to deal with sexual assault. As many accusers have identified, it is only when we finally see alleged perpetrators in handcuffs that we can truly know that justice is being delivered

Janet Halley critiques, however, what she identifies as a "governmental feminism," noting that, as the women's movement shifts from advocacy into legal decision-making, there is a risk of lack of attention to procedural fairness.[119] Halley is part of the "Harvard 19," the group of law professors who critiqued the representations of Kamilah Willingham's case in the film *The Hunting Ground*. In their letter characterizing the law student's allegations and its aftermath, Halley and others remarked that "[p]ropaganda should not be allowed to erase [a] just outcome."[120]

The opinions of some #MeToo activists do seem to turn Blackstone's formulation on its head, deeming it irrelevant if one innocent man is convicted as long as a hundred guilty ones are caught. This attitude risks expanding the crime control system and curtailing the nascent movement toward therapeutic jurisprudence and restorative justice. There is also the old adage—be careful what you wish for. While liberals tend to remember with fondness the era of Earl Warren as chief justice of the U.S. Supreme Court, there is perhaps too little attention paid to the aftershocks of the Warren court's decisions, when pleas to recall the judge and his like-minded colleagues appeared across the South in what Joel Cohen describes as "a strident campaign that would make 'Three Billboards' blush."[121] In 2009, the chief justice and two associate justices who formed the Iowa Supreme Court majority that legalized same-sex marriage were voted out, not due to a grassroots campaign conducted by constituents but as a result of money pouring in from outside, conservative political action committees enabled by the *Citizens United* decision.[122]

The United States has a troubling history of residents attempting to achieve justice outside the courthouse doors. In the Jim Crow era, it was not uncommon for lynch mobs to break into jails and kidnap men awaiting trial, the crowd preferring to exact extralegal punishments on Black suspects rather than to entrust the meting out of justice to the slower and potentially fallible courts. Recent recall campaigns, and the treatment of confirmed perpetrators, highlight that social media empower society to enact more and greater collateral consequences to punishment than ever before. When public shaming can lead to bankruptcies, firings, divorce, and other consequences, is law still necessary to provide justice and to effect social control?

With relatively few civil cases pending and almost no arrests or convictions, so far the task of penalizing alleged bad actors has been mainly left to the corporations and institutions that employ them. Akin to a system of Pigouvian taxes, these entities are largely unaccountable to the state but instead face a risk of economic sanctions in the form of diminishment of profits due to boycotts or public protest.[123] For example, when allegations of sexual harassment brought Uber's policy of dealing with such claims via arbitration into the spotlight, it was a social media campaign urging riders to delete the Uber application that pressed the company to revise the policy.[124] There is a bill being proposed in the New York State legislature proposing to incentivize corporate policies using actual taxation, eliminating city tax breaks for corporations that knew about but did not respond to sexual harassment by employees.[125] A key objective of the TIME'S UP campaign is to promote similar legislation "to penalize companies that tolerate persistent harassment, and to discourage the use of nondisclosure agreements to silence victims."[126]

While advocating corporate attention to—or, more accurately, castigating corporate inattention to—issues of sexual harassment is positive, concerns arise when legal processes, and particularly criminal legal processes, are put into the hands of nonlegal entities. These concerns are clear in the university context, where Title IX is heavily criticized for failing to provide justice to alleged victims and alleged perpetrators, particularly perpetrators who are non-white.[127] It is also true in the context of institutions like prisons, the military, and religious organizations, which continue to face accusations of obscuring significant and widespread issues with sexual assault. The "fearless girl" staring down the Wall Street bull is more than emblematic here, signifying, on one hand, the distinct power of one young woman's voice and, on the other, the capacity of an organization to corrupt that voice and deploy it to unintended ends.[128]

Donald Black theorized that the role of law in effecting social control was at its height when the social control effected by other important institutions—the family, education, religious organizations—were at their weakest.[129] Today, supplanting the family and religious institutions are corporations, which play an instrumental role in helping to establish societal mores and norms. As corporations exercise an increasing responsibility in policing sexual harassment and assault, there is an argument that the role of law in resolving claims—and in promoting justice—may be diminished.

CONCLUSION

Crowdsourcing—mobilizing the masses to effect legal and social change—is the source of the #MeToo movement's power. But, while we can see that many people are participating in a movement, we cannot begin to know *why* those people are participating.[130] Part of the #MeToo movement's collective appeal is that participants bring their own reasons for posting the status—healing, sympathy, solidarity, revenge all may be part of the motivation.

To date, the TIME'S UP Legal Defense Fund has received more than $21 million and counting in crowdsourced donations. Are these persons clamoring to donate truly activists, or have social media turned us all into digital bystanders rather than invested, grassroots participants?[131] Skeptics of #MeToo highlight other hashtag campaigns—#itsnotokay, #listenandbelieve, #WhyIStayed, #YouOkSis, #EverydaySexism—some of which have faded away or been colonized by those with opposing points of view.[132] McGuire argues, "You don't tear down the walls of patriarchy with a tweetstorm."[133]

Today, however, maybe you do. For years the story of Kitty Genovese has been circulated as an example of the "bystander effect"—the theory that the larger the group of observers to a criminal act, the more likely it is that people will stand by and do nothing.[134] Recently, however, research has shown that most theories about Genovese had it wrong. Rather than standing by helplessly as they watched a young woman being murdered, additional information revealed over the years confirms that her neighbors tried to help in what ways they could, sometimes at personal risk.[135]

Jeremy Heimans and Henry Timms describe the change in power being effected by social media as "new power," writing that "old power" was "held by few, jealously guarded," while "new power" operates "like a current"—it is "open, participatory, and peer-driven."[136] Not merely observers, participants on social networks, such as those engaged in contributing to TIME'S UP or posting a #MeToo status, are evaluating, revising, and reinventing sexual assault law. Thus far, discriminatory myths, "commonsense" raced and gendered assumptions, and the polarizing platforms of social networks have proven to be a dangerous combination, driving participants toward embracing binaries and away from due process.

Moments of crisis, however, are moments of possibility. As evidenced by the eight million people discussing sexual harassment on Twitter and the more than twelve million posting #MeToo as a status on Facebook, new opportunities have arisen to have vital conversations about law. Suddenly, the world is not only discussing concepts such as rape culture and victim-blaming, it is debating whether conduct does or does not fit into the "real rape" paradigm, whether Black defendants are being "railroaded," and whether a particular sentence was meted out based on racial or socioeconomic privilege.

The importance of making legal power structures visible cannot be underestimated. The institution of law is structured first and foremost to protect those in power, often via a lack of transparency.[137] One reason why labels of gold digger, witch, or monster are effective is that they mask power structures, purposefully constructing an imagined world in which control belongs to those least likely to have it.

As a result of #MeToo and other social media conversations, the public has shifted from talking about "hush money" and indictment of "gold diggers" and guilty "serial predators" to discussing how corporations and elite defendants have deployed confidentiality and nondisclosure agreements to secure the silence of marginalized victims. From Cosby I to Cosby II, the casting couch similarly began to be transformed from a location in which greedy starlets manipulate "lecherous" but unsuspecting old men to a place where predators deliberately stalk targets. These discussions suggest that social media can enable the public not only to focus on the people involved in sexual assaults but on the societal structures that enable such assaults to occur. A significant step forward for the movement so far has been exposing how forced arbitration, nondisclosure agreements, . . . and confidential settlements have operated for years to silence victims."[138]

There are significant problems with this new social movement that may only be exacerbated should #MeToo adhere to its current trajectory. The ubiquitous and problematic framing of sexual assault as an issue pitting women against men reflects the tendency to view criminal cases in terms of either race or gender rather than acknowledging how intersectional concerns pervade U.S. sexual assault law. There is also the literal exclusion that continues to take place—an exclusion of transgender persons, men, women of color, lesbians and gay men, incarcerated persons, and others—that disturbingly mirrors the exclusions that have long inhered in rape law itself.

Lastly, there is the problem of the crowd, an entity that too often moves toward a swift and unreflective form of justice. Despite calls to "equalize" punishments among perpetrators, there is a disturbing trend to treat due process as a technicality.

When one looks at other significant social movements it is important to realize that #MeToo is a beginning. Sexual assault laws reflect not years but centuries of social patterns of dismissal and dehumanization. As the philosophies and practices of influencers in other social movements attest, for radical social and legal change to occur, moments of profound discomfort are required. The question for those who want to effect positive legal change is how, in this era of "new power," to channel the momentum of #MeToo. If indeed it is an offshoot of the existing feminist movement—a fourth wave—the question is how to guide it toward, at last, embracing its own inclusion rider. This is a vital concern that requires not only mobilization but redirection of the trend from the current, distinctly carceral, version of feminism.

In the end, we are left with the overarching question of the place of law in this new social structure. As Christie describes, the job of lawyers is to take away the truth, to "steal" conflicts in an attempt to smooth things over, to win for one party, to make conflict go away.[139] Today, social media have a unique and unprecedented Robinhood-like power to steal claims back and to place them in the hands of everyday people, in MacKinnon's words, to do "what the law could not."[140] Public opinion does not just influence law, public opinion *is* law. Whether resolved via negotiation, such as settlement or plea bargain, or abandoned based on fear, evidentiary barriers, or inertia, it is a fact that the overwhelming majority of potential criminal and civil cases today do not go to trial. In a system increasingly geared toward expediency and efficiency, social media may provide the ideal platforms for punishments to be served quickly and decisively. Is the court of public opinion just one? The jury is out.

NOTES

1. Ronan Farrow, "From Aggressive Overtures to Sexual Assault: Harvey Weinstein's Accusers Tell Their Stories," *New Yorker*, October 23, 2017, https://www.newyorker.com/news/news-desk/from-aggressive-overtures-to-sexual-assault-harvey-weinsteins-accusers-tell-their-stories.

2. Farrow, "From Aggressive Overtures"; Jodi Kantor and Megan Twohey, "Harvey Weinstein Paid Off Sexual Harassment Accusers for Decades," *New York Times*, October 5, 2017, https://www.nytimes.com/2017/10/05/us/harvey-weinstein-harassment-allegations.html.

3. Emma Dibdin, "A Full List of Harvey Weinstein's Accusers and Their Allegations," *Elle*, December 13, 2017, https://www.elle.com/culture/a12838402/a-full-list-of-harvey-weinsteins-accusers-and-their-allegations/.

4. Matthew Haag and James C. McKinley Jr., "Lawsuit against Weinstein Might Open Door to Criminal Charges," *New York Times*, May 2, 2018, https://www.nytimes.com/2018/05/02/nyregion/harvey-weinstein-sexual-assault.html.

5. Kate Samuelson, "Harvey Weinstein Arrested on Charges of Rape, Sex Abuse and More," *Time*, May 25, 2018, http://time.com/5291392/harvey-weinstein-arrested/.

6. Lisa Respers France, "#MeToo: Social Media Flooded with Personal Stories of Assault," CNN, October 16, 2017, https://www.cnn.com/2017/10/15/entertainment/me-too-twitter-alyssa-milano/index.html.

7. Sandee LaMotte, "How #MeToo Could Move from Social Campaign to Social Change," CNN, November 9, 2017, https://www.cnn.com/2017/10/30/health/metoo-legacy/index.html.

8. #NotOkay was created by Kelly Oxford, an author, in response to the release of the Trump "pussy grab" tape. At its height, the #NotOkay campaign was generating fifty tweets per minute. Another significant, recent hashtag campaign was #GrabYourWallet, a movement to rid retail stores in the United States of Trump brand products. Megan Maas, Heather McCauley, Amy E. Bonomi, and S. Gisela Leija, "'I Was Grabbed by My Pussy and Its #NotOkay': A Twitter Backlash Against Donald Trump's Degrading Commentary," *Violence Against Women* 24, no. 14 (2018): 3; Sarah Halzack, "Grab Your Wallet: The Woman Who Began Boycott of Trump Products in US Retailers," *Independent*, February 14, 2017, https://www.independent.co.uk/news/world/americas/grab-your-wallet-trump-boycott-products-us-retailers-shannon-coulter-nordstrom-donald-jr-ivanka-eric-a7579776.html.

9. Lydia Dishman, "This 'Me Too' Timeline Shows Why 2017 Was a Reckoning for Sexism," *Fast Company*, December 6, 2017, https://www.fastcompany.com/40504569/this-me-too-timeline-shows-why-2017-was-a-reckoning-for-sexism.

10. Baker, "Penn Professors Mull."

11. Baker, "Penn Professors Mull."

12. Baker, "Penn Professors Mull"; the president's approach to Twitter has been referred to by some as "schoolyard bully tactics." Andrew Buncombe, "Donald Trump One Year On: How the Twitter President Changed Social Media and the Country's Top Office," *Independent*, January 17, 2018, https://www.independent.co.uk/news/world/americas/us-politics/the-twitter-president-how-potus-changed-social-media-and-the-presidency-a8164161.html.

13. German Lopez, "The Rise of Rage in Social Media Politics, in One Chart," *Vox*, July 18, 2018, https://www.vox.com/policy-and-politics/2018/7/18/17588120/trump-politics-anger-facebook-pew.

14. Brett Edkins, "Report: U.S. Media among Most Polarized in the World," *Forbes*, June 27, 2017, https://www.forbes.com/sites/brettedkins/2017/06/27/u-s-media-among-most-polarized-in-the-world-study-finds/.

15. MacKinnon, *Butterfly Politics*, 1.

16. MacKinnon, *Butterfly Politics*, 1.

17. MacKinnon, "#MeToo Has Done"; Catharine A. MacKinnon, *Butterfly Politics* (Cambridge: Harvard University Press, 2017).

18. When Cosby jurors were asked about #MeToo, they routinely answered that "Not once were race or the #MeToo movement ever discussed, nor did either factor into our decision . . . Simply put, we were asked to assess the credibility of Ms. Constand's account of what happened to her, and each one of us found her account credible and compelling." Claudia Rosenbaum, "Bill Cosby's Jury Says #MeToo and Race Weren't Factors in His Guilty Verdict," BuzzFeedNews.com, April 30, 2018, https://www.buzzfeed.com/claudiarosenbaum/bill-cosby-jury-speaks-out?utm_term=.ogXQjqaAqR#.vhPJDVnqVX; Kirby, "Bill Cosby's Retrial."

19. Renkl, "The Raw Power."

20. Renkl, "The Raw Power."

21. Carrie A. Rentschler, "Rape Culture and the Feminist Politics of Social Media," *Girlhood Studies* 7, no. 1 (2014): 67.

22. Rentschler, "Rape Culture," 69.

23. Jessica Bennett, "Behold the Power of #Hashtag Feminism," *Time*, September 10, 2014, http://time.com/3319081/whyistayed-hashtag-feminism-activism/.

24. The Conversation, "Not Another Online Petition! But Here's Why You Should Think before Deleting It," *The Conversation*, January 29, 2019, https://theconversation.com/not-another-online-petition-but-heres-why-you-should-think-before-deleting-it-110029.

25. Sherri Williams, "Black Feminists Resist Violence with Hashtag Activism," *Feminist Media Studies* 15, no. 2 (2015): 343.

26. Mariame Kaba and Andrea Smith, "Twitter Is Toxic. And So Is the Rest of the World," *The Nation*, April 17, 2014, https://www.thenation.com/article/where-twitter-and-feminism-meet/.

27. Kaba and Smith, "Twitter Is Toxic."

28. Ryan Bowles Eagle, "Loitering, Lingering, Hashtagging: Women Reclaiming Public Space Via #BoardtheBus, #StopStreetHarassment, and the #EverdaySexism Project," Feminist Media Studies 15, no. 2 (2015): 352.

29. Ryan Bowles Eagle, "Loitering, Lingering, Hashtagging."

30. Bennett, "The 'Click' Moment."

31. McDonough, "This Was Always Going to Hurt."

32. Jonathan Mahler, "For Many Women, Trump's 'Locker Room Talk' Brings Memories of Abuse," *New York Times*, October 10, 2016, https://www.nytimes.com/2016/10/11/us/politics/sexual-assault-survivor-reaction.html.

33. Abby Ohlheiser, "How #MeToo Really Was Different, According to Data," *Washington Post*, January 22, 2018, https://www.washingtonpost.com/news/the-intersect/wp/2018/01/22/how-metoo-really-was-different-according-to-data/?utm_term=.b88662a4a5f1.

34. Sophie Gilbert, "The Movement of #MeToo," *Atlantic*, October 16, 2017, http://www.theatlantic.com/entertainment/archive/2017/10/the-movement-of-metoo/542979/

35. Suzannah Weiss, "#MeToo Has Made Me See Anyone Is Capable of Sexual Abuse—Including Me," *Establishment*, February 1, 2018, https://theestablishment.co/metoo-has-made-me-see-anyone-is-capable-of-sexual-abuse-including-me-6455f93309a9.

36. Bill Chappell, "'Complicit' Is the Word of the Year in 2017, Dictionary.com Says," NPR, November 27, 2017, https://www.npr.org/sections/thetwo-way/2017/11/27/566763885/complicit-is-the-word-of-the-year-in-2017-dictionary-com-says; "Why One Dictionary Made 'Complicit' Its Word of the Year," *All Things Considered*, NPR, November 20, 2017, https://www.npr.org/2017/11/30/567572975/why-one-dictionary-made-complicit-its-word-of-the-year.

37. Roiphe, "The Other Whisper Network"; Alex Press, "It's Time to Weaponize the 'Whisper Network,'" *Vox*, October 17, 2017, https://www.vox.com/first-person/2017/10/16/16482800/harvey-weinstein-sexual-harassment-workplace.

38. Press, "It's Time to Weaponize."

39. Maureen Dowd, "This Is Why Uma Thurman Is Angry," Opinion, *New York Times* , February 3, 2018, https://www.nytimes.com/2018/02/03/opinion/sunday/this-is-why-uma-thurman-is-angry.html.
40. Dowd, "This Is Why."
41. Harris, "Myths of Race and Gender."
42. Oppenheim, "Steve Bannon Warns Trump."
43. M. Yvonne Taylor, "Why #MeToo Can Be for Men, Too," *Houston Chronicle*, October 16, 2017, https://www.houstonchronicle.com/local/gray-matters/article/Why-MeToo-can-be-for-men-too-12281653.php.
44. Helena Theixos, "Feminist Perspectives on the Apology of Louis CK and the #MeToo and #TimesUp Movements," *Media Watch* 9, 2018, 268.
45. TIME'S UP website, https://www.timesupnow.com.
46. Associated Press, "Some Male Sexual Assault Victims Feel Left Behind by #MeToo," NBC News, April 19, 2018, https://www.nbcnews.com/news/us-news/some-male-sexual-assault-victims-feel-left-behind-metoo-n867386.
47. Associated Press, "Some Male Sexual Assault."
48. Associated Press, "Some Male Sexual Assault."
49. MenEngage Alliance, UN Women, "Men, Masculinities."
50. Scott Anderson, "Statute of Limitation on Sexual Assault Extended under New Michigan Laws," WXYZ.com, June 12, 2018, https://www.wxyz.com/news/statute-of-limitation-on-sexual-assault-extended-under-new-michigan-laws.
51. Notably, the movement has included very visible statements by women of color, including lawyer Anita Hill, producer Shonda Rhimes, gymnast Gabby Douglas, and actors Lupita Nyong'o, America Ferrera, Eva Longoria, and Salma Hayek. However, Tambe argues that, with these exceptions, it largely is "white women's pain that is centered in popular media coverage." Ashwini Tambe, "Reckoning with the Silences of #MeToo," *Feminist Studies* 44, no. 1 (2018): 199.
52. Tambe, "Reckoning," 199.
53. Edwards, "Rape, Racism."
54. Phyllis Chesler, "My Questions about the #MeToo Moment," Phyllis-Chesler.com written for *Huffington Post*, January 5, 2018, https://phyllis-chesler.com/articles/my-questions-about-the-metoo-moment.
55. Chesler, "My Questions."
56. Levine, "Sexual Scripts," 329.
57. Zacharek et al., "Silence Breakers."
58. Megan Garber, "Is This the Next Step for the #MeToo Movement?," *Atlantic*, June 2, 2018, https://www.theatlantic.com/entertainment/archive/2018/01/beyond-me-too-can-times-up-effect-real-change/549482/.
59. Garber, "Is This the Next Step?"
60. Jennifer Calfas, "How Frances McDormand's Oscar Speech 'Super-Charged' a Significant Change in Hollywood over the Last Year," *Money*, February 22, 2019, http://money.com/money/5636361/frances-mcdormand-oscars-inclusion-riders/.
61. Nancy Woloch, *A Class by Herself: Protective Laws for Women Workers, 1890s–1990s* (Princeton, NJ: Princeton University Press, 2017).
62. Woloch, *A Class By Herself.*
63. Josephine Livingstone, "The Task Ahead for Feminism," *New Republic*, November 17, 2017, https://newrepublic.com/article/145850/task-ahead-feminism.
64. Roxanne Gay, "Who Gets to Be Angry?," *New York Times*, June 10, 2016, https://www.nytimes.com/2016/06/12/opinion/sunday/who-gets-to-be-angry.html; bell hooks, *Killing Rage: Ending Racism* (New York: Holt Paperbacks, 1996); Rebecca Traister, *Good and Mad: The Revolutionary Power of Women's Anger* (New York: Simon & Schuster, 2018).
65. Cara Buckley, "Powerful Hollywood Women Unveil Anti-harassment Action Plan," *New York Times*, January 1, 2018, https://www.nytimes.com/2018/01/01/movies/times-up-hollywood-women-sexual-harassment.html?action=click&module=Most%20Popular&pgtype=Homepage&_r=0.

66. 50/50 by 2020, https://5050by2020.com.
67. Woloch, *A Class By Herself.*
68. Woloch, *A Class By Herself.*
69. Tenzer, "#MeToo, Statutory Rape Laws," 8.
70. Legal arguments must fulfill the sometimes conflicting dual objectives of advancing long-term political or philosophical goals. For example, in the effort to gain African American representation in unions, attorneys like Charles Hamilton Houston aligned with political conservatives intent on union busting in order to further the objectives of both advancing a conservative political agenda and securing additional representation for Black workers in unions (Woloch, *A Class By Herself*) while, first and foremost, granting clients immediate relief if possible.
71. Susan Stefan, "The Protection Racket: Rape Trauma Syndrome, Psychiatric Labeling, and Law," *Northwestern University Law Review* 88 (1994): 1328; Naomi R. Cahn, "Looseness of Legal Language: The Reasonable Woman Standard in Theory and in Practice," *Cornell Law Review* 77, no. 6 (1992): 1398–446.
72. Cahn, "Looseness," 1416.
73. Stefan, "The Protection Racket," 1328.
74. Jason Silverstein, "#MeToo Movement Could Turn Women into 'Snowflakes' and Make Men Resent Them, Condoleezza Rice Says," *Newsweek*, January 14, 2018, http://www.newsweek.com/metoo-movement-women-snowflakes-condoleezza-rice-780939; Masha Gessen, "Sex, Consent, and the Dangers of 'Misplaced Scale,'" *New Yorker*, November 27, 2017, https://www.newyorker.com/news/our-columnists/sex-consent-dangers-of-misplaced-scale.
75. Livingstone, "The Task Ahead."
76. Laura Kipnis, "What We Lose."
77. Pamela Aronson, "Gender and Feminist Consciousness," *The Oxford Handbook of U.S. Women's Social Movement Activism*, eds. Holly McCammon, Verta Taylor, Jo Reger, and Rachel L. Einwohner (New York: Oxford University Press, 2017), 337.
78. Tenzer, "#MeToo, Statutory Rape Laws," 31–32; Daphne Merkin, "Publicly, We Say #MeToo. Privately, We Have Misgivings," *New York Times*, January 5, 2018, https://www.nytimes.com/2018/01/05/opinion/golden-globes-metoo.html.
79. Laura Kipnis, "What We Lose" (describing that "the big story of the moment" is that "[s]ex is dangerous; it can traumatize you for life. Rape is endemic and predators are everywhere").
80. Leslie Jamison, "Grand Unified Theory of Female Pain," *VQR* (Spring 2014), https://www.vqronline.org/essays-articles/2014/04/grand-unified-theory-female-pain.
81. Flores, "I Refuse to Post 'Me Too.'"
82. Harris, "She Founded #MeToo."
83. Francis Fukuyama, "Women and the Evolution of World Politics," *Foreign Affairs* (September/October 1998), https://www.foreignaffairs.com/articles/1998-09-01/women-and-evolution-world-politics.
84. Barbara Ehrenreich, Katha Pollitt, et al., "Fukuyama's Follies: So What if Women Ruled the World?," *Foreign Affairs* (January/February 1999), https://www.foreignaffairs.com/articles/1999-01-01/fukuyamas-follies-so-what-if-women-ruled-world (noting that "women have proved themselves no less susceptible than men to the passions of militaristic nationalism").
85. Suzanne Collins, *The Hunger Games: Mockingjay* (New York: Scholastic, 2010).
86. Sjoberg, *Women as Wartime Rapists.*
87. "Statistics on Perpetrators of Child Sexual Abuse," National Center for Victims of Crime, http://victimsofcrime.org/media/reporting-on-child-sexual-abuse/statistics-on-perpetrators-of-csa.
88. "Statistics on Perpetrators," National Center for Victims of Crime.
89. Noreen Malone, "Sexual-Harassment Claims against a 'She-E.O.,'" *The Cut*, https://www.thecut.com/2017/03/thinx-employee-accuses-miki-agrawal-of-sexual-harassment.html.
90. Malone, "Sexual-Harassment Claims."

91. Zoe Greenberg, "What Happens to #MeToo When a Feminist Is the Accused?," *New York Times* , August 13, 2018, https://www.nytimes.com/2018/08/13/nyregion/sexual-harassment-nyu-female-professor.html.
92. Greenberg, "What Happens to #MeToo?"
93. Greenberg, "What Happens to #MeToo?"
94. Kim Severson, "Asia Argento, a #MeToo Leader, Made a Deal with Her Own Accuser," *New York Times*, August 19, 2018, https://www.nytimes.com/2018/08/19/us/asia-argento-assault-jimmy-bennett.html.
95. Kyle Smith, "Feminists Seize the Moment for Sisterly Revenge," *National Review*, February 5, 2018, https://www.nationalreview.com/2018/02/katie-roiphe-harpers-essay-common-sense/.
96. Edwards, "Rape, Racism."
97. Edwards, "Rape, Racism."
98. Hannah McCann, "Big Reputations: Who Has the Power to Speak #MeToo," *Australian Humanities Review* 63 (2018): 186.
99. Amanda Arnold, "How #MeToo Leaders Are Responding to the Asia Argento Allegations," *The Cut*, https://www.thecut.com/2018/08/metoo-respond-rose-mcgowan-amber-tamblyn-asia-argento.html.
100. "Tom Hanks Says No Way Back for Harvey Weinstein," BBC News, October 19, 2017, http://www.bbc.com/news/entertainment-arts-41678196.
101. "The Harvey Weinstein Effect," *USA Today*.
102. David French, "It's Time for Bill O'Reilly to Be Weinsteined," *National Review*, October 23, 2017, https://www.nationalreview.com/corner/its-time-conservatives-banish-bill-oreilly-progressives-are-banishing-harvey-weinstein/.
103. Aaron Betsky, "Waiting to Be Weinsteined: When Will Accusations of Sexual Harassment Arise in Architecture?," *Architect Magazine*, November 21, 2017, http://www.architectmagazine.com/practice/waiting-to-be-weinsteined-when-will-accusations-of-sexual-harassment-arise-in-architecture_o.
104. Nathaniel M. Glasser, "The Weinstein Effect: #MeToo Allegations in the Financial Services Industry," *Take 5 Newsletter* (November 2017), https://www.ebglaw.com/news/five-issues-in-focus-for-financial-services/#_para1.
105. Sarah B. Berson, "Beyond the Sentence—Understanding Collateral Consequences," *National Institute of Justice* 272 (2013), https://www.nij.gov/journals/272/Pages/collateral-consequences.aspx.
106. "The Harvey Weinstein Effect," *USA Today*.
107. "The Harvey Weinstein Effect," *USA Today*.
108. Laura Kipnis highlights cases of firings of several men for misconduct such as having consensual affairs with staff or having conversations with sexual themes or making rejected passes. Kipnis, "What We Lose."
109. Stephanie Zacharek, "What Men—and Women—Can Learn from Joe Biden's 'Inappropriate Touching,'" *Time*, April 25, 2019, http://time.com/5578143/biden-inappropriate-touching/.
110. Roiphe, "The Other Whisper Network."
111. Weiss, "The Limits of 'Believe.'"
112. Flores, "I Refuse to Post 'Me Too.'"
113. McCann," Big Reputations," 188.
114. Walters, a professor, is now the subject of a Title IX complaint because of expressing these views. McCann, "Big Reputations," 188.
115. Flores, "I Refuse to Post 'Me Too.'"
116. Lucia Graves, "How Famous Men Toppled by #MeToo Plot Their Comeback," *Guardian*, May 27, 2018, https://www.theguardian.com/world/2018/may/27/metoo-sexual-assault-claims-accused-men-plot-redemption-charlie-rose-mario-batali; "The #MeToo Movement and Les Moonves," NPR, August 5, 2018, https://www.npr.org/2018/08/05/635748549/the-metoo-movement-and-les-moonves.
117. Tambe, "Reckoning," 200.

118. Sarah Boboltz, "Anita Hill Tapped to Cure Hollywood's Epidemic of Sexual Misconduct with New Commission," *Huffington Post*, December 16, 2017, https://www.huffingtonpost.com/entry/anita-hill-hollywood-antisexual-misconduct-commission_us_5a356680e4b040881beb0dcb.

119. Halley, "Trading the Megaphone," 106.

120. Ashe Schow, "19 Harvard Law Professors Pen Letter Denouncing 'The Hunting Ground,'" *Washington Examiner*, November 11, 2015, https://www.washingtonexaminer.com/19-harvard-law-professors-pen-letter-denouncing-the-hunting-ground.

121. Joel Cohen, "Recalling Judges Just Because We Don't Like Their Decisions?," *The Hill*, March 23, 2018, http://thehill.com/opinion/judiciary/379648-recalling-judges-just-because-we-dont-like-their-decisions.

122. Cohen, "Recalling Judges."

123. Jonathan S. Masur and Eric A. Posner, "Toward a Pigouvian State," *University of Pennsylvania Law Review* 164 (2015): 93.

124. Michigan Automotive News, "Uber Will No Longer Force Victims of Sexual Assault into Private Arbitration," MLive.com, May 15, 2018, https://www.mlive.com/auto/index.ssf/2018/05/uber_will_no_longer_force_arbi.html.

125. Natalie Olivo, "NY Bill Would Deny Tax Credits over Sexual Harassment," *Law360*, October 16, 2017, https://www.law360.com/articles/974896/ny-bill-would-deny-tax-credits-over-sexual-harassment.

126. Buckley, "Powerful Hollywood Women."

127. For example, Corey Rayburn Yung's hypothesizes that colleges and universities underreport sexual assault, based on data demonstrating that schools' reports of campus sexual assault on average rise by over 40 percent during periods of investigation by the Department of Education. Corey Rayburn Yung, "Concealing Campus Sexual Assault: An Empirical Examination," *Psychology, Public Policy, and Law* 21, no. 1 (2015): 6.

128. Cascone, "A Bunch of Bull?"; *Entrepreneur Magazine* similarly highlights "branding lessons" to be learned from Nike's defense of Colin Kaepernik, the NFL player who controversially took a knee during the National Anthem, a campaign that at once emphasizes the corporation's "values" and secures the loyalty of a young (and growing) customer base. Manish Dudharejia, "4 Branding Lessons from Nike's Colin Kaepernick Ad," *Entrepreneur*, October 22, 2018, https://www.entrepreneur.com/article/321130.

129. Black, "Crime as Social Control."

130. Sultana Lubna Alam and John Campbell, "Role of Relational Mechanisms in Crowdsourcing Governance: An Interpretive Analysis" (Completed Research Paper, Proceedings of the Nineteenth Americas Conference on Information Systems, Chicago, Illinois, August 15–17, 2013).

131. Clyde Haberman, "What the Kitty Genovese Killing Can Teach Today's Digital Bystanders," *New York Times*, June 4, 2017, https://www.nytimes.com/2017/06/04/us/retro-report-bystander-effect.html?hp&action=click&pgtype=Homepage&clickSource=story-heading&module=second-column-region&region=top-news&WT.nav=top-news.

132. LaMotte, "How #MeToo Could Move."

133. Angelina Chapin, "Don't Count On 'Me Too' to Sway the Bill Cosby Jury," *Huffington Post*, April 19, 2018, https://www.huffingtonpost.com/entry/bill-cosby-me-too_us_5ad74918e4b03c426daa2fca.

134. Haberman, "What the Kitty Genovese Killing Can Teach."

135. Haberman, "What the Kitty Genovese Killing Can Teach."

136. Jeremy Heimans and Henry Timms, *New Power: How Power Works in Our Hyperconnected World—and How to Make It Work for You* (New York: Doubleday, 2018), 16–17.

137. Minna J. Kotkin, "How the Legal World Built a Wall of Silence around Workplace Sexual Harassment," *Washington Post*, October 20, 2017, https://www.washingtonpost.com/outlook/how-the-legal-world-built-a-wall-of-silence-around-

workplace-sexual-harassment/2017/10/20/ac1f41dc-b2b1-11e7-9e58-e6288544af98_story.html?utm_term=.c37867127452.

138. MacKinnon, "#MeToo Has Done."

139. Christie, "Conflicts," 4.

140. MacKinnon, "#MeToo Has Done."

Bibliography

Abeysekara, Ananda. *Colors of the Robe: Religion, Identity, and Difference*. Columbia: University of South Carolina Press, 2002.

"About Lawfare: A Brief History of the Term and the Site." Lawfare Blog. https://www.lawfareblog.com/about-lawfare-brief-history-term-and-site.

"About *The Central Park Five*." PBS. http://www.pbs.org/kenburns/centralparkfive/about-central-park-five/.

Abrams, Jamie. "The #MeToo Movement: An Invitation for Feminist Critique of Rape Crisis Framing." Paper No. 2018–5, University of Louisville Legal Research Paper Series, April 6, 2018.

Adams, Char. "Former USA Gymnastics Doctor Larry Nassar Pleads Guilty to Sexually Abusing Girls in Michigan." *People*, November 22, 2017. http://people.com/sports/larry-nassar-pleads-guilty-sexual-abuse-gymnasts/.

Adams, John. *Diary and Autobiography of John Adams, Volumes 1–4 (1755–1804)*, edited by L. H. Butterfield, Leonard C. Faber, and Wendell D. Garrett. Cambridge, MA: Belknap Press, 1961.

Adichie, Chimamanda Ngozi. "The Danger of a Single Story." TEDGlobal 2009. https://www.ted.com/talks/chimamanda_adichie_the_danger_of_a_single_story/transcript.

———. *We Should All be Feminists* . New York: Anchor, 2012.

Adler, Lindsey. "Aly Raisman Is Ready to Burn It All Down." Deadspin.com, January 19, 2018. https://deadspin.com/aly-raisman-is-ready-to-burn-it-all-down-1822234455.

"African American Wrongful Convictions Today." The Innocence Project, March 29, 2013. https://www.innocenceproject.org/african-american-wrongful-convictions-today/.

Alam, Sultana Lubna, and John Campbell. "Role of Relational Mechanisms in Crowdsourcing Governance: An Interpretive Analysis." Completed Research Paper, Proceedings of the Nineteenth Americas Conference on Information Systems, Chicago, Illinois, August 15–17, 2013.

Alexander, Michelle. *The New Jim Crow: Mass Incarceration in the Age of Colorblindness*. New York: New Press, 2012.

Allen, Ron, and Daniel Arkin. "Bill Cosby Accusers Cry, Rejoice after He Is Sentenced to Prison Time." NBC, September 26, 2018. https://www.nbcnews.com/storyline/bill-cosby-scandal/bill-cosby-accusers-cry-rejoice-after-he-sentenced-prison-time-n913086.

Alptraum, Lux. "Seeing Harvey Weinstein in Handcuffs Was Cathartic but It Doesn't Solve Society's Sexual Abuse Problem." NBC News, May 26, 2018. https://www.nbcnews.com/think/opinion/seeing-harvey-weinstein-handcuffs-was-cathartic-it-doesn-t-solve-ncna877701.

Altheide, David. *Terrorism and the Politics of Fear*. Lanham, MD: AltaMira Press, 2006.

Anapol, Avery. "Trump Supporters Chant 'Lock Her Up' at Campaign Rally." *The Hill*, December 8, 2017. http://thehill.com/homenews/administration/364062-trump-supporters-chant-lock-her-up-at-campaign-rally.

Anderson, Benedict. *Imagined Communities: Reflections on the Origin and Spread of Nationalism*. London: Verso, 1991.

Anderson, Devery. "Widow of Emmett Till Killer Dies Quietly, Notoriously." *USA Today*, February 27, 2014. https://www.usatoday.com/story/news/nation/2014/02/27/emmett-till-juanita-milam/5873235/.

Anderson, Michelle J. "Campus Sexual Assault Adjudication and Resistance to Reform." *Yale Law Journal* 125 (2016): 1947.

———. "Negotiating Sex." *Southern California Law Review* 78 (2005): 1423.

Anderson, Scott. "Statute of Limitation on Sexual Assault Extended under New Michigan Laws." WXYZ.com, June 12, 2018. https://www.wxyz.com/news/statute-of-limitation-on-sexual-assault-extended-under-new-michigan-laws.

Anderson, Tre'vell. "Hannibal Buress: The Comic Who Kindled the Cosby Firestorm." *Los Angeles Times*, December 31, 2015. http://beta.latimes.com/entertainment/tv/showtracker/la-et-st-hannibal-buress-cosby-joke-20151231-story.html.

Anonymous. "I Am Not a 'Pretty Little Liar.'" *Jezebel*, May 21, 2015. https://jezebel.com/i-am-not-a-pretty-little-liar-1705996719.

———. "Stanford Sexual Assault Case Survivor Emily Doe Speaks Out." *Glamour*, November 1, 2016. https://www.glamour.com/story/women-of-the-year-emily-doe.

"Are Anti-sexting Laws Out of Control?" MSNBC, July 10, 2014. https://www.msnbc.com/all-in/watch/are-anti-sexting-laws-out-of-control-301682243741.

Armstrong, Elizabeth A., Laura T. Hamilton, Elizabeth M. Armstrong, and J. Lotus Seeley. "'Good Girls': Gender, Social Class, and Slut Discourse on Campus." *Social Psychology Quarterly* 77, no. 2 (2014): 100, 102.

Arnold, Amanda. "How #MeToo Leaders Are Responding to the Asia Argento Allegations." *The Cut*. https://www.thecut.com/2018/08/metoo-respond-rose-mcgowan-amber-tamblyn-asia-argento.html.

Aronson, Pamela. "Gender and Feminist Consciousness." The Oxford Handbook of U.S. Women's Social Movement Activism (eds. Holly McCammon, Verta Taylor, Jo Reger, and Rachel L. Einwohner). New York: Oxford University Press, 2017: 333–53.

Ash, Erin, Jimmy Sanderson, Chenjerai Kumanyika, and Kelly Gramlich. "'Just Goes to Show How These Hoes Try to Tear Men Down': Investigating Twitter and Cultural Conversations on Athletic Ability, Race, and Sexual Assault." *Journal of Sports Media* 12, no. 1 (2017): 70.

Associated Press. "Bill Cosby Trial: Only 2 Accusers Can Testify, Judge Rules." *Times-Picayune*, February 24, 2017. https://www.nola.com/crime/index.ssf/2017/02/bill_cosby_trial_accuser_testi.html.

———. "Bill Cosby's Defense Gives Closing Argument." DW.com, December 6, 2017, https://www.dw.com/en/bill-cosbys-defense-gives-closing-argument/a-39219996.

———. "Cosby Lawyers Say Prosecutors Using 'Casting Couch' Cliché." VOA News, November 1, 2016. https://www.voanews.com/a/bill-cosby-sexual-assault-trial-lawyers-prosecutors-casting-couch-cliche/3574708.html.

———. "Judge Denies Motion to Move Case." ESPN.com, September 16, 2009. http://www.espn.com/nfl/news/story?id=4478769.

———. "Read Excerpts from Bill Cosby's 2005–2006 Quaalude Deposition." *Los Angeles Times*, May 23, 2016. http://www.latimes.com/local/lanow/la-me-ln-bill-cosby-quaalude-deposition-excerpts-20160523-snap-story.html.

———. "Shouting Matches Break Out at Cosby Hearing." *USA Today*, December 13, 2016. https://www.usatoday.com/story/life/people/2016/12/13/cosby-judge-to-weigh-potential-testimony-of-13-other-women/95366650/.

Austin, Regina. "Nest Eggs and Stormy Weather: Law, Culture, and Black Women's Lack of Wealth." Faculty Scholarship Paper 813. Penn Law: Legal Scholarship Repository (1997), 776.

Axon, Rachel. "Jameis Winston Files Counterclaim Against Accuser Erica Kinsman." *USA Today*, May 9, 2015. http://www.usatoday.com/story/sports/nfl/2015/05/09/jameis-winston-counter-lawsuit-accuser-erica-kinsman-florida-state/27030973/.

———. "Woman Who Alleged Rape by Fairfax, Maggette Spotlights Issue of Revictimization." *USA Today*, February 13, 2019. https://www.usatoday.com/story/

news/nation/2019/02/13/justin-fairfax-corey-maggette-and-issue-rape-revictimization/2857516002/.

Bailey, Alyssa. "Kim Kardashian is Studying to Become a Lawyer and Plans to Take the Bar in 2022," *Elle*, April 10, 2019, https://www.elle.com/culture/celebrities/a27101447/kim-kardashian-studying-to-become-lawyer/.

Bailey, Sarah Pulliam. "How the Mom Internet Became a Spotless, Sponsored Void." Outlook. *Washington Post*, January 26, 2018. https://www.washingtonpost.com/outlook/how-the-mom-internet-became-a-spotless-sponsored-void/2018/01/26/072b46ac-01d6-11e8-bb03-722769454f82_story.html.

Baker, Brandon. "Penn Professors Mull President Trump's Effect on Political Communications." *Penn Today*, August 9, 2018. https://penntoday.upenn.edu/news/penn-professors-mull-president-trumps-effect-political-communications.

Baker, Katie J. M. "Here's the Powerful Letter the Stanford Victim Read to Her Attacker." BuzzFeedNews.com, June 3, 2016. https://www.buzzfeednews.com/article/katiejmbaker/heres-the-powerful-letter-the-stanford-victim-read-to-her-ra.

Baldas, Tresa. "Larry Nassar's Lawyer Gets Death Threats in MSU Sex Abuse Case: 'It's Been Insane.'" *Detroit Free Press*, January 31, 2018. https://www.freep.com/story/news/local/michigan/2018/01/31/nassar-lawyer-death-threats-msu/1083909001/.

Banner, Francine and Nicholas Paron. "'Hell Hath No Fury . . .': Gendered Reactions to the Cosby Mistrial across Liberal and Conservative News Media Sites." In Debbie Ging and Eugenia Siapera (Eds.), *Gender Hate Online: Understanding the New Anti-Feminism*, Chapter 8, Palgrave MacMillan, 2019 (in press).

———. "Institutional Sexual Assault and the Rights/Trust Dilemma." *Cardozo Public Law, Policy & Ethics Journal* 13 (2015): 165–66.

———. "'It's Not All Flowers and Daisies': Masculinity, Heteronormativity and the Obscuring of Lesbian Identity in the Repeal of 'Don't Ask, Don't Tell.'" *Yale Journal of Law and Feminism* 24, no. 1 (2012): 73.

———. "Methodological Approaches to Studying Crime and Popular Culture in New Media." In *The Oxford Encyclopedia of Crime, Media, and Popular Culture*, edited by Nicole Ratter and Michelle Brown. New York: Oxford University Press, 2017. http://criminology.oxfordre.com/view/10.1093/acrefore/9780190264079.001.0001/acrefore-9780190264079-e-171.

———. "Narrowing the Construction of 'Innocence': Societal and Constitutional Consequences." In *Controversies in Innocence Cases in America*, edited by Sarah Lucy Cooper. London: Ashgate, 2014.

Baraniuk, Chris. "How Twitter Bots Help Fuel Political Feuds." *Scientific American*, March 27, 2018. https://www.scientificamerican.com/article/how-twitter-bots-help-fuel-political-feuds/.

Barkan, Steven E. *Law and Society: An Introduction*. New York: Pearson, 2008.

Barnes, Robert. "Rebuking Trump's Criticism of 'Obama Judge,' Chief Justice Roberts Defends Judiciary as 'Independent,'" *The Washington Post*, November 21, 2018, https://www.washingtonpost.com/politics/rebuking-trumps-criticism-of-obama-judge-chief-justice-roberts-defends-judiciary-as-independent/2018/11/21/6383c7b2-edb7-11e8-96d4-0d23f2aaad09_story.html?utm_term=.6724fa63bfd2.

Barnett, Barbara. "Framing Rape: An Examination of Public Relations Strategies in the Duke University Lacrosse Case." *Communication, Culture, & Critique* 1, no. 2 (2008): 179–202.

Barstow, Anne L. *Witchcraze: A New History of the European Witch Hunts*. New York: HarperCollins, 1995.

Bates, Karen Grigsby. "'Rapists,' 'Huts': Trump's Racist Dog Whistles Aren't New." National Public Radio, January 13, 2018. https://www.npr.org/sections/codeswitch/2018/01/13/577674607/rapists-huts-shitholes-trumps-racist-dog-whistles-arent-new.

Baumeister, Roy F., and Jean M. Twenge. "Cultural Suppression of Female Sexuality." *Review of General Psychology* 6, no. 2 (2002): 166–203.

Bazelon, Emily, and Rachael Larimore. "How Often Do Women Falsely Cry Rape?" Slate.com, October 1, 2009. http://www.slate.com/articles/news_and_politics/jurisprudence/2009/10/how_often_do_women_falsely_cry_rape.html.

Beard, Mary. *Women & Power: A Manifesto*. New York: Liveright, 2017.

Beitsch, Rebecca. "#MeToo Movement Has Lawmakers Talking about Consent." *Huffington Post*, January 24, 2018. https://www.huffingtonpost.com/entry/metoo-movement-has-lawmakers-talking-about-consent_us_5a6758dfe4b06bd14be5067f.

Bello, Mark M. "Twenty-Six Years Later McDonald's Still a "Hot" Topic." *Legal Examiner*, January 16, 2009. https://farmingtonhills.legalexaminer.com/legal/miscellaneous/twenty-six-years-later-mcdonalds-still-a-hot-topic/.

"Benghazi Mission Attack Fast Facts." CNN Library, June 29, 2018. https://www.cnn.com/2013/09/10/world/benghazi-consulate-attack-fast-facts/index.html.

Benkler, Yochai, Robert Faris, Hal Roberts, and Ethan Zuckerman. "Study: Breitbart-Led Right-Wing Media Ecosystem Altered Broader Media Agenda."*Columbia Journalism Review*, March 3, 2017. https://www.cjr.org/analysis/breitbart-media-trump-harvard-study.php.

Bennett, Jessica. "Behold the Power of #Hashtag Feminism." *Time*, September 10, 2014. http://time.com/3319081/whyistayed-hashtag-feminism-activism/.

———. "The 'Click' Moment: How the Weinstein Scandal Unleashed a Tsunami." *New York Times*, November 5, 2017. https://www.nytimes.com/2017/11/05/us/sexual-harrasment-weinstein-trump.html.

Benshoff, Laura. "Bill Cosby Sentenced to at Least 3 Years in State Prison for Sexual Assault." NPR, September 25, 2018. https://www.npr.org/2018/09/25/651065803/bill-cosby-sentenced-to-at-least-3-years-in-state-prison.

Bergehed, Katarina. "Sex without Consent Is Rape. Sweden's Move to Recognize That Means Fewer Women Will Have to Say #MeToo." *Time*, May 23, 2018. http://time.com/5288303/sweden-affirmative-consent-rape-law/.

Berko, Anat, and Edna Erez. "Gender, Palestinian Women, and Terrorism: Women's Liberation or Oppression?" *Studies in Conflict and Terrorism* 30, no. 6 (2007): 493–519.

Berkow, Ira. "Sports of the Times; A Champ Named Desiree." *New York Times*, February 25, 1992. http://www.nytimes.com/1992/02/25/sports/sports-of-the-times-a-champ-named-desiree.html.

Berson, Sarah B. "Beyond the Sentence—Understanding Collateral Consequences." *National Institute of Justice Journal* 272 (2013). https://www.nij.gov/journals/272/Pages/collateral-consequences.aspx.

Betsky, Aaron. "Waiting to Be Weinsteined: When Will Accusations of Sexual Harassment Arise in Architecture?" *Architect Magazine*, November 21, 2017. http://www.architectmagazine.com/practice/waiting-to-be-weinsteined-when-will-accusations-of-sexual-harassment-arise-in-architecture_o.

Bidgood, Jess, Richard Fausset, and Campbell Robertson. "For Roy Moore, a Long History of Combat and Controversy." *New York Times*, November 18, 2017. https://www.nytimes.com/2017/11/18/us/roy-moore-alabama.html.

Black, Donald. "Crime as Social Control." *American Sociological Review* 48, no. 1 (1983): 34–45.

Blair, Jane. "Five Myths about Women in Combat." *Washington Post*, May 27, 2011. https://www.washingtonpost.com/opinions/five-myths-about-women-in-combat/2011/05/25/AGAsavCH_story.html?utm_term=.208d65922a9d.

Blinder, Alan. "Alabama Pardons 3 'Scottsboro Boys' After 80 Years." *New York Times*, November 21, 2013. https://www.nytimes.com/2013/11/22/us/with-last-3-pardons-alabama-hopes-to-put-infamous-scottsboro-boys-case-to-rest.html.

Boboltz, Sarah. "Anita Hill Tapped to Cure Hollywood's Epidemic of Sexual Misconduct with New Commission." *Huffington Post*, December 16, 2017. https://www.huffingtonpost.com/entry/anita-hill-hollywood-antisexual-misconduct-commission_us_5a356680e4b040881beb0dcb.

Boisseau, Tracy Jean. "Response to 'The Duke Rape Case Five Years Later: Lessons for the Academy, the Media, and the Criminal Justice System' by Dan Subotnik." *Akron Law Review* 45 (2012): 927.

Bordo, Susan. *The Destruction of Hillary Clinton*. Brooklyn: Melville House, 2017.

———. "The Destruction of Hillary Clinton: Sexism, Sanders and the Millennial Feminists." *Guardian*, April 2, 2017. https://www.theguardian.com/us-news/commentisfree/2017/apr/03/the-destruction-of-hillary-clinton-sexism-sanders-and-the-millennial-feminists.

Bourke, Joanna. *Rape: Sex, Violence, History*. New York: Counterpoint, 2009.

Bowley, Graham. "Potential Cosby Jurors Are Asked About #MeToo Bias." *New York Times*, April 2, 2018. https://www.nytimes.com/2018/04/02/arts/television/bill-cosby-trial-jury-selection.html.

Bowley, Graham, and Matthew Haag. "Cosby Jury Says Accuser's Credibility, Not #MeToo, Led to Guilty Verdict." *New York Times*, April 30, 2018. https://www.nytimes.com/2018/04/30/arts/television/cosby-juror-interview-gma.html.

Bowley, Graham, and Sophie Wodzak. "What Divided the Cosby Jurors? Words, for One Thing." *New York Times*, June 30, 2017. https://www.nytimes.com/2017/06/30/arts/television/bill-cosby-jurors-mistrial-wording-unconscious.html?_r=0.

boyd, danah m., and Nicole B. Ellison. "Social Network Sites: Definition, History, and Scholarship." *Journal of Computer-Mediated Communication* 13, no. 1 (2007): 210–30.

Bradley, Laura. "Alec Baldwin Complains John Oliver Has Turned Talk Shows into 'Grand Juries.'" *Vanity Fair*, December 6, 2017. https://www.vanityfair.com/hollywood/2017/12/alec-baldwin-john-oliver-stephen-colbert-talk-shows-grand-juries.

Brandon Project, The: Facts Matter. http://brandonproject.org.

Braudel, Fernand. *On History* . Chicago: University of Chicago Press, 1980.

Breiner, Andrew. "Pizzagate, Explained: Everything You Want to Know about the Comet Ping Pong Pizzeria Conspiracy Theory but Are Too Afraid to Search for on Reddit." *Salon*, December 10, 2016. https://www.salon.com/2016/12/10/pizzagate-explained-everything-you-want-to-know-about-the-comet-ping-pong-pizzeria-conspiracy-theory-but-are-too-afraid-to-search-for-on-reddit.

Brenner, Alletta. "Resisting Simple Dichotomies: Critiquing Narratives of Victims, Perpetrators, and Harm in Feminist Theories of Rape." *Harvard Journal of Law and Gender* 36 (2013): 505.

Brenner, Hannah. "Opinion: DeVos' New Guidelines on Handling Campus Sexual Assault Raise Risk of Another MSU." *Detroit Free Press*, January 26, 2018. https://www.freep.com/story/opinion/contributors/2018/01/26/msu-title-9/1065913001/.

Brown, Stacy. "Bill Cosby Paid Andrea Constand $3.5M in 2006 Settlement." *Page Six*, March 10, 2018. https://pagesix.com/2018/03/10/bill-cosby-paid-andrea-constand-3-5m-in-2006-settlement/.

Brownmiller, Susan. *Against Our Will: Men, Women, and Rape*. New York: Open Road Media, 2013.

Bruenig, Elizabeth Stoker. "Why Americans Don't Care About Prison Rape." *Nation*, March 2, 2015. https://www.thenation.com/article/why-americans-dont-care-about-prison-rape/.

Buckley, Cara. "Powerful Hollywood Women Unveil Anti-harassment Action Plan." *New York Times*, January 1, 2018. https://www.nytimes.com/2018/01/01/movies/times-up-hollywood-women-sexual-harassment.html?action=click&module=Most%20Popular&pgtype=Homepage&_r=0.

Buie, Jordan. "Brock Turner, Cory Batey Meme Causing Stir on Social Media." *Tennessean*, June 8, 2016. https://www.tennessean.com/story/news/crime/2016/06/08/brock-turner-corey-batey-meme-causing-stir-social-media/85590654/.

Bulinski, Maximilian A., and J. J. Prescott. "Online Case Resolution Systems: Enhancing Access, Fairness, Accuracy, and Efficiency." *Michigan Journal of Race and Law* 21, no. 2 (2016): 205–48.

Bumiller, Kristin. *The Civil Rights Society: The Social Construction of Victims*. Baltimore: Johns Hopkins University Press, 1992.

———. *In an Abusive State: How Neoliberalism Appropriated the Feminist Movement Against Sexual Violence*. Durham, NC: Duke University Press, 2008.

Bump, Philip. "Trump's Death-Penalty Advocacy Hopes to Make America 1990 Again." *Washington Post*, March 16, 2018. https://www.washingtonpost.com.

Buncombe, Andrew. "Donald Trump One Year On: How the Twitter President Changed Social Media and the Country's Top Office." *Independent*, January 17, 2018. https://www.independent.co.uk/news/world/americas/us-politics/the-twitter-president-how-potus-changed-social-media-and-the-presidency-a8164161.html.

Berger, Vivian. "Man's Trial, Woman's Tribulation: Rape Cases in the Courtroom." *Columbia Law Review* 77, no. 1 (1977): 4.

Burgess, Ann Wolbert, and Lynda Lytle Holmstrom. "Rape Trauma Syndrome." *American Journal of Psychiatry*, February 12, 2015. https://ajp.psychiatryonline.org/doi/abs/10.1176/ajp.131.9.981.

Burns, Sarah. "Why Trump Doubled Down on the Central Park Five." Opinion. *New York Times*, October 17, 2016. https://www.nytimes.com/2016/10/18/opinion/why-trump-doubled-down-on-the-central-park-five.html.

Burt, Martha R. "Cultural Myths and Supports for Rape." *Journal of Personality and Social Psychology* 38, no. 2 (1980): 217–30.

Butler, Bethonie. "Focus of Jussie Smollett Assault Investigation Has 'Shifted,' Chicago Police Say." *Washington Post*, February 16, 2019. https://www.washingtonpost.com/arts-entertainment/2019/02/15/chicago-police-say-there-is-no-evidence-jussie-smolletts-assault-claims-are-hoax/?utm_term=.f1521e8e9fe7.

Cacciola, Scott. "Victims in Larry Nassar Abuse Case Find a Fierce Advocate: The Judge." *New York Times*, January 23, 2018. https://www.nytimes.com/2018/01/23/sports/larry-nassar-rosemarie-aquilina-judge.html.

Cadoux, E. Karin. "Animating Injury: Trauma Rite as Personal Exhibition and Public Exposition." Master's Thesis submitted to the Department of Women's Studies, University of Michigan–Ann Arbor, April 3, 2017.

Cahn, Naomi R. "Looseness of Legal Language: The Reasonable Woman Standard in Theory and in Practice." *Cornell Law Review* 77, no. 6 (1992): 1398–446.

Calfas, Jennifer. "How Frances McDormand's Oscar Speech 'Super-Charged' a Significant Change in Hollywood over the Last Year." *Money*, February 22, 2019. http://money.com/money/5636361/frances-mcdormand-oscars-inclusion-riders/.

Cammett, Ann. "Deadbeat Dads and Welfare Queens: How Metaphor Shapes Poverty Law." *Boston College Journal of Law and Social Justice* 34 (2014): 233, 237.

Capers, Bennett. "Real Rape Too." *California Law Review* 99, no. 5 (2011): 1273.

———. "The Unintentional Rapist." *Washington University Law Review* 87 (2010): 1345, 1390.

Card, Claudia. "Rape as a Weapon of War." *Hypatia* 11, no. 4 (1996): 5–18.

Carlson, Tucker. "We Are Offering an Apology—And It Has to Do with Joe Biden and Anti-human Hysteria," Fox News, April 4, 2019, https://www.foxnews.com/opinion/tucker-carlson-we-are-offering-an-apology-and-it-has-to-do-with-joe-biden-and-anti-human-hysteria.

Carney, Jordain. "Schumer Pursuing Legal Action after Fake Sexual Harassment Accusations." *The Hill*, December 13, 2017. http://thehill.com/homenews/senate/364706-schumer-pursuing-legal-action-after-fake-sexual-harassment-accusations.

Carr, Austin, and Harry McCracken. "'Did We Create This Monster?' How Twitter Turned Toxic." Fast Company, April 4, 2018. https://www.fastcompany.com/40547818/did-we-create-this-monster-how-twitter-turned-toxic.

Cascone, Sarah. "A Bunch of Bull? Wall Street Firm behind 'Fearless Girl' Settles Gender Discrimination Suit." *ArtNet*, October 10, 2017. https://news.artnet.com/art-world/fearless-girl-settles-gender-discrimination-suit-1110587.

Casper, Monica J., and Lisa Jean Moore. *Missing Bodies: The Politics of Visibility*. New York: New York University Press, 2009.

Cavender, Gray. "Media Construction of Athletics: Normalization and Deviance," chapter 4 in *Routledge Handbook on Deviance*, edited by Stephen E. Brown and Ophir Setiha. New York: Routledge, 2017.

Chamallas, Martha. *The Measure of Injury: Race, Gender, and Tort Law*. New York: New York University Press, 2010.

Chang, Alvin. "The Facebook and Cambridge Analytica Scandal, Explained with a Simple Diagram." *Vox*, May 2, 2018. https://www.vox.com/policy-and-politics/2018/3/23/17151916/facebook-cambridge-analytica-trump-diagram.

Chapin, Angelina. "Don't Count on 'Me Too' to Sway the Bill Cosby Jury." *Huffington Post*, April 19, 2018. https://www.huffingtonpost.com/entry/bill-cosby-me-too_us_5ad74918e4b03c426daa2fca.

Chappell, Bill. "'Complicit' Is the Word of the Year in 2017, Dictionary.com Says." National Public Radio, November 27, 2017. https://www.npr.org/sections/thetwo-way/2017/11/27/566763885/complicit-is-the-word-of-the-year-in-2017-dictionary-com-says.

Charen, Mona. "It's High Time Columbia's Mattress Girl was Discredited." *National Review*, August 4, 2017. https://www.nationalreview.com/2017/08/columbia-university-mattress-girl-emmas-sulkowicz-paul-nungesser-lawsuit-rape-accusation-exonerated/.

Chenoy, Sahil, Jessia Ma, and Stuart A. Thompson. "Trump's Growing Obsession with the 'Witch Hunt.'" Opinion. *New York Times*, August 22, 2018. https://www.nytimes.com/interactive/2018/08/22/opinion/trump-cohen-mueller-investigation.html.

Chesler, Phyllis. "My Questions about the #MeToo Moment." Phyllis-Chesler.com written for *Huffington Post*, January 5, 2018. https://phyllis-chesler.com/articles/my-questions-about-the-metoo-moment.

Chi, Paul. "Clooney and Damon: Weinstein Scandal Will Lead to a 'Massive, Systemic Change.'" *Vanity Fair*, October 23, 2017. https://www.vanityfair.com/hollywood/2017/10/george-clooney-matt-damon-harvey-weinstein-suburbicon-witch-hunt.

Chira, Susan. "Sexist Political Criticism Finds a New Target: Kellyanne Conway." *New York Times*, March 5, 2017. https://www.nytimes.com/2017/03/05/us/kellyanne-conway-sexist-political-criticism.html?

Chotiner, Isaac. "A Harvard Law School Professor Defends His Decision to Represent Harvey Weinstein." *New Yorker*, March 7, 2019. https://www.newyorker.com/news/q-and-a/a-harvard-law-school-professor-defends-his-decision-to-represent-harvey-weinstein.

Christie, Nils. "Conflicts as Property." *British Journal of Criminology* 1, no. 17 (1977): 4.

———. "The Ideal Victim." In *From Crime Policy to Victim Policy*, edited by E. A. Fattah. London: Palgrave Macmillan, 1986.

Ciampaglia, Dante A. "How Much Did *Rolling Stone* Magazine Sell For? Penske Media Group Buys Iconic Publication." *Newsweek*, December 21, 2017. http://www.newsweek.com/how-much-did-rolling-stone-magazine-sell-penske-media-group-buys-iconic-754795.

Cieply, Michael. "Samantha Geimer, Victim in Roman Polanski Sex Case, Strongly Defends Him Inside and Outside of Court." Deadline.com, June 9, 2017. http://deadline.com/2017/06/samantha-geimer-roman-polanski-victim-defends-director-hearing-1202109259/.

Cipriani, Casey. "Marisa Hargitay's Rape Kit Documentary Came to Life Because of Olivia Benson—Yes, Really." Bustle, April 13, 2018. https://www.bustle.com/p/mariska-hargitays-rape-kit-documentary-came-to-life-because-of-olivia-benson-yes-really-8778963.

Cohen, Joel. "Recalling Judges Just Because We Don't Like Their Decisions?" *The Hill*, March 23, 2018. http://thehill.com/opinion/judiciary/379648-recalling-judges-just-because-we-dont-like-their-decisions.

Cohen, Stanley. *Folk Devils and Moral Panics: The Creation of the Mods and Rockers*. London: Oxford University Press, 1972.

Collins, Ronald K.L. "FAN 200 (First Amendment News) Mary Anne Franks, 'The Free Speech Fraternity.'" *Concurring Opinions*, September 20, 2018. https://concurringopinions.com/archives/2018/09/fan-200-first-amendment-news-mary-anne-franks-the-free-speech-fraternity.html.

———. "FAN 200 (First Amendment News) Ruthann Robson, 'The Cyber Company Town.'" *Concurring Opinions*, September 20, 2018. https://concurringopinions.com/archives/2018/09/fan-200-first-amendment-news-ruthann-robson-the-cyber-company-town.html.

Collins, Suzanne. *The Hunger Games: Mockingjay*. New York: Scholastic, 2010.

Connors, Sarah, Katie Esmonde, Achariya Rezak, Emily Wang, and Ari Yanover. "The Patrick Kane Case Shows How Much Power Fans Wield in the Way Athlete Investigations are Handled." SBNation.com, November 4, 2015. http://www.sbnation.com/2015/11/4/9669752/patrick-kane-accuser-nhl-and-rape-culture.

Conversation, The. "Not Another Online Petition! But Here's Why You Should Think before Deleting It." *The Conversation*, January 29, 2019. https://theconversation.com/not-another-online-petition-but-heres-why-you-should-think-before-deleting-it-110029.

Corrigan, Maureen. "What 'Gone Girl' and 'The Girl on the Train' Have Wrought." *Washington Post*, November 1, 2017. https://www.washingtonpost.com/entertainment/books/what-gone-girl-and-the-girl-on-the-train-have-wrought/2017/01/11/33dcf838-d114-11e6-9cb0-54ab630851e8_story.html?utm_term=.40f649ea340c.

Corrigan, Rose. *Up against a Wall: Rape Reform and the Failure of Success*. New York: New York University Press, 2014.

"Court Documents: Stanford Rape Case, People v. Brock Allen Turner (9/9)." *Los Angeles Times*, June 10, 2016. http://documents.latimes.com/people-v-brock-allen-turner-99/.

Cramer, Renée Ann. *Pregnant with the Stars: Watching and Wanting the Celebrity Baby Bump*. Palo Alto: Stanford University Press, 2015.

Crocker, Phyllis L. "Feminism and Defending Men on Death Row." *St. Mary's Law Journal* 29 (1998): 982.

Cuklanz, Lisa M., and Sujata Moorti. "Television's 'New' Feminism: Prime-Time Representations of Women and Victimization." *Critical Studies in Media Communication* 23, no. 4 (2006): 303.

Dastagir, Alia E. "Some Say One False Report Could Cripple the #MeToo Movement. Is Progress that Fragile?" *USA Today*, December 8, 2017. https://www.usatoday.com/story/news/2017/12/08/analysis-movement-metoo-but-heres-why-were-still-talking-believewomen/923156001/.

Daughtry, Timothy. "Seven Signs of Liberal Privilege." Townhall.com, September 20, 2017. https://townhall.com/columnists/timothydaughtry/2017/09/20/seven-signs-of-liberal-privilege-n2384136.

de Tocqueville, Alexis. "Chapter VI: Judicial Power in the United States." *Democracy in America* (1831). https://www.marxists.org/reference/archive/de-tocqueville/democracy-america/ch06.htm.

De Zutter, Andre, Robert Horselenberg, and Peter J. van Koppen. "The Prevalence of False Allegations of Rape in the United States from 2006–2010." *Journal of Forensic Psychology* 2, no. 2 (2017): 1–5.

Delgado, Richard. "Storytelling for Oppositionists and Others: A Plea for Narrative." *Michigan Law Review* 87, no. 8 (1989): 2416.

DellaContrada, John. "UB Statement Regarding SUNY Honorary Degree Recipient Harvey Weinstein." University at Buffalo News Release, October 11, 2017. http://www.buffalo.edu/news/releases/2017/10/020.html.

Dent, Mark. "Bill Cosby to Face Multiple Accusers in Upcoming Sexual Assault Trial." *Deadline*, March 15, 2018. https://deadline.com/2018/03/bill-cosby-andrea-constand-judge-multiple-accusers-to-testify-in-constand-trial-1202338879/.

Di Menna, Hillary. "Sexual Assault Cases Are Our Modern-Day Witch Trials." *Establishment*, July 15, 2016. https://theestablishment.co/sexual-assault-cases-are-our-modern-day-witch-trials-7c955ae5acc.

Dibdin, Emma. "A Full List of Harvey Weinstein's Accusers and Their Allegations." *Elle*, December 13, 2017. https://www.elle.com/culture/a12838402/a-full-list-of-harvey-weinsteins-accusers-and-their-allegations/.

Dishman, Lydia. "This 'Me Too' Timeline Shows Why 2017 Was a Reckoning for Sexism." *Fast Company*, December 6, 2017. https://www.fastcompany.com/40504569/this-me-too-timeline-shows-why-2017-was-a-reckoning-for-sexism.

Dixon, Travis L., and Daniel Linz. "Race and the Misrepresentation of Victimization on Local Television News." *Communication Research* 27, no. 5 (2000): 547–73.

Dowd, Maureen. "This Is Why Uma Thurman Is Angry." Opinion. *New York Times*, February 3, 2018. https://www.nytimes.com/2018/02/03/opinion/sunday/this-is-why-uma-thurman-is-angry.html.

Dowd, Nancy E., Nancy Levit, and Ann McGinley. "Feminist Legal Theory Meets Masculinities Theory." Chapter 1 in *Masculinities and the Law*, edited by Ann McGinley and Frank Rudy Cooper. New York: New York University Press, 2012.

Dreamer's Club. "Date Rape." *Urban Dictionary*, February 18, 2005. https://www.urbandictionary.com/define.php?term=date%20rape.

Dries, Kate. "*Rolling Stone* Reaches a Settlement with Former UVA Administrator Nicole Eramo." *Jezebel*, April 12, 2017. https://jezebel.com/rolling-stone-reaches-a-settlement-with-former-uva-admi-1794250576.

Dudharejia, Manish. "4 Branding Lessons from Nike's Colin Kaepernick Ad." *Entrepreneur*, October 22, 2018. https://www.entrepreneur.com/article/321130.

Dunlap, Bridgette. "How California's New Rape Law Could Be a Step Backward." *Rolling Stone*, September 1, 2016. https://www.rollingstone.com/culture/culture-news/how-californias-new-rape-law-could-be-a-step-backward-250347/.

Eagle, Ryan Bowles. "Loitering, Lingering, Hashtagging: Women Reclaiming Public Space Via #BoardtheBus, #StopStreetHarassment, and the #EverdaySexism Project." *Feminist Media Studies* 15, no. 2 (2015): 349–53.

Eaton-Robb, Pat. "Yale Alumni Contribute to Former Star Athlete's Sex-Expulsion Case." Boston.com, December 2, 2017. https://www.boston.com/sports/college-sports/2017/12/02/yale-alumni-contribute-to-former-star-athletes-sex-expulsion-case.

Edelman, Lauren B. *Working Law: Courts, Corporations, and Symbolic Civil Rights*. Chicago: University of Chicago Press, 2016.

Edelman, Peter. "In 2017, It's Still a Crime to Be Poor." *Nation*, November 3, 2017. https://www.thenation.com/article/the-price-of-justice/.

Edgers, Geoff. "Bill Cosby's 'Far from Finished' Tour Pushes On. But Will It Be His Last?" *Washington Post*, March 24, 2015. https://www.washingtonpost.com/entertainment/bill-cosbys-far-from-finished-tour-pushes-on-will-it-be-his-last/2015/03/24/d665bee4-cf1f-11e4-8a46-b1dc9be5a8ff_story.html?utm_term=.00b04ea08d2e.

Edkins, Brett. "Report: U.S. Media among Most Polarized in the World." *Forbes*, June 27, 2017. https://www.forbes.com/sites/brettedkins/2017/06/27/u-s-media-among-most-polarized-in-the-world-study-finds/.

Edwards, Alison. "Rape, Racism, and the White Women's Movement: An Answer to Susan Brownmiller." Sojourner Truth Organization (STO). http://www.sojournertruth.net/rrwwm.html.

Egan, Nicole Weisensee. "Bill Cosby Accuser Andrea Constand Threatens to Withdraw from Criminal Investigation." People.com, October 27, 2015. https://people.com/crime/bill-cosby-accuser-andrea-constand-threatens-to-withdraw-from-investigation/.

Ehrenreich, Barbara, Katha Pollitt, et al. "Fukuyama's Follies: So What if Women Ruled the World?" *Foreign Affairs* (January/February 1999). https://www.foreignaffairs.com/articles/1999-01-01/fukuyamas-follies-so-what-if-women-ruled-world.

Elliott, Bud. "This Is the Letter from Jameis Winston's Attorney to Florida State." *Tomahawk Nation, A Florida State Seminoles Community*, September 24, 2014. https://www.tomahawknation.com/2014/9/24/6840459/letter-jameis-winston-attorney-florida-state-fsu-accuser.

Ellison, Louise, and Vanessa E. Munro. "A Stranger in the Bushes, or an Elephant in the Room? Critical Reflections upon Received Rape Myth Wisdom in the Context of a Mock Jury Study." *New Criminal Law Review: An International and Interdisciplinary Journal* 13, no. 4 (2010): 781–801.

Ellison, Sarah. "After A Rape Story, A Murder, and Lawsuits: What's Next for the University of Virginia?" *Vanity Fair*, September 9, 2015. http://www.vanityfair.com/news/2015/09/university-of-virginia-most-horrible-year.

Elwood, Zachary. "Examining Public Anger and Certainty in the Brock Turner Case and Sentencing." Medium.com, September 11, 2016. https://medium.com/@apokerplayer/examining-public-anger-and-certainty-in-the-brock-turner-case-and-sentencing-869c66201c11.

Ember, Sydney, and Graham Bowley. "After Bill Cosby, States Shift on Statutes of Limitations in Sexual Assault Cases." *New York Times*, November 6, 2016. https://www.nytimes.com/2016/11/07/arts/television/after-bill-cosby-states-shift-sexual-assault-statutes-of-limitations.html.

Engel, David M. "The Oven Bird's Song: Insiders, Outsiders, and Personal Injuries in an American Community." *Law and Society Review* 18, no. 4 (1984).

———. "Perception and Decision at the Threshold of Tort Law: Explaining the Infrequency of Claims." *DePaul Law Review* 62 (2013): 293, 323.

———. "Vertical and Horizontal Perspectives on Rights Consciousness." *Indiana Journal of Global Legal Studies* 19, no. 2 (2012): 426.

"*Eramo vs. Rolling Stone* Complaint." *Washington Post*, May12, 2015. https://www.washingtonpost.com/apps/g/page/local/eramo-vs-rolling-stone-complaint/1692/.

Erdely, Sabrina R. "A Rape on Campus: A Brutal Assault and Struggle for Justice at UVA." *Rolling Stone*, November 19, 2014. http://web.archive.org/web/20141119200349/http://www.rollingstone.com/culture/features/a-rape-on-campus-20141119. Retracted April 5, 2015.

Erickson, Kai. *Wayward Puritans: A Study in the Sociology of Deviance*. New Haven, CT: Yale University Press, 2004.

Estrich, Susan. *Real Rape*. Cambridge: Harvard University Press, 1988.

Ewick, Patricia, and Susan S. Silbey. *The Common Place of Law: Stories from Everyday Life*. Chicago: University of Chicago Press, 1998.

"Fact Sheet: Trends in U.S. Corrections." The Sentencing Project, June 2018. https://sentencingproject.org/wp-content/uploads/2016/01/Trends-in-US-Corrections.pdf.

Farrow, Ronan. "From Aggressive Overtures to Sexual Assault: Harvey Weinstein's Accusers Tell Their Stories." *New Yorker*, October 23, 2017. https://www.newyorker.com/news/news-desk/from-aggressive-overtures-to-sexual-assault-harvey-weinsteins-accusers-tell-their-stories.

Fellows, Mary Louise, and Sherene Razack. "The Race to Innocence: Confronting Hierarchical Relations among Women." *Journal of Gender, Race and Justice* 1 (1998): 335–52.

Felman, Shoshana. *The Juridical Unconscious: Trials and Traumas in the Twentieth Century*. Cambridge: Harvard University Press, 2002.

Felstiner, William L. F., Richard L. Abel, and Austin Sarat. "The Emergence and Transformation of Disputes: Naming, Blaming, Claiming." *Law and Society Review* 15, no. 3/4 (1980–1981): 638.

50/50 by 2020. https://5050by2020.com.

Finlayson, Lorna. "Can the Law be Feminist?" *London Review of Books* 30, no. 2 (January 2018): 29–31. https://www.lrb.co.uk/v40/n02/lorna-finlayson/can-the-law-be-feminist.

Finley, Lucinda M. "Breaking Women's Silence in Law: The Dilemma of the Gendered Nature of Legal Reasoning." *Notre Dame Law Review* 64 (1989): 889.

———. "Female Trouble: The Implications of Tort Reform for Women." *Tennessee Law Review* 64 (1996–1997): 887.

Finocchiaro, Peter. "Is the Men's Rights Movement Growing?" *Salon*, March 29, 2011. https://www.salon.com/2011/03/29/scott_adams_mens_rights_movement/.

Fisher, Bonnie S., Leah E. Daigle, and Francis T. Cullen. *Unsafe in the Ivory Tower: The Sexual Victimization of College Women*. Los Angeles: Sage, 2010.

Fitzsimons, Tim and Brandy Zadrozny, "Man Says Buttigieg Never Assaulted Him, Blames Conservative Activists for Claim," *NBC News*, April 30, 2019, https://www.nbcnews.com/feature/nbc-out/man-says-buttigieg-never-assaulted-him-blames-conservative-activists-claim-n1000241.

Flanagan, Caitlin. "The Humiliation of Aziz Ansari." *Atlantic*, January 14, 2018. https://www.theatlantic.com/entertainment/archive/2018/01/the-humiliation-of-aziz-ansari/550541/.

Fletcher, George P. *A Crime of Self-Defense: Bernhard Goetz and the Law on Trial*. Chicago: University of Chicago Press, 1988.

Flores, Heather Jo. "I Refuse to Post 'Me Too' as My Facebook Status. How About Men Post 'I Ignored It and I Won't Anymore' Instead?" *Independent*, October 17, 2017. https://www.independent.co.uk/voices/harvey-weinstein-facebook-me-too-sexual-assault-abuse-men-should-post-too-a8004631.html.

Flowers, Christine M. "Jussie Smollett Case a Reminder that One False Accuser Can Hurt All Future Victims." *Philadelphia Inquirer*, February 18, 2019. https://www.philly.com/opinion/commentary/jussie-smollett-hate-crime-false-accusations-20190218.html.

Ford, Matt. "How Brock Turner Changed California's Rape Laws." *Atlantic*, October 1, 2016. https://www.theatlantic.com/news/archive/2016/10/california-law-brock-turner/502562/.

Fox, Andrea. "5 Gadgets That Alert Drinkers to Date Rape Drugs." EfficientGov.com, May 22, 2017. https://efficientgov.com/blog/2017/05/22/5-date-rape-drug-detectors/.

Fox, Jesse, Carlos Cruz, and Ji Young Lee. "Perpetuating Online Sexism Offline: Anonymity, Interactivity, and the Effects of Sexist Hashtags on Social Media." *Computers in Human Behavior* 52 (2015): 437–38.

France, Lisa Respers. "#MeToo: Social Media Flooded with Personal Stories of Assault." CNN, October 16, 2017. https://www.cnn.com/2017/10/15/entertainment/me-too-twitter-alyssa-milano/index.html.

Franiuk, Renae, Jennifer L. Seefelt, Sandy L. Cepress, and Joseph A. Vandello. "Prevalence and Effects of Rape Myths in Print Journalism." *Violence Against Women* 14, no. 3 (2008): 290.

Frankel, Glenn. *High Noon: The Hollywood Blacklist and the Making of an American Classic*. London: Bloomsbury, 2017.

Franks, Mary Anne. "How to Feel Like a Woman, or, Why Punishment Is a Drag." *UCLA Law Review* 61 (2014): 566.

———. "'Revenge Porn' Reform: A View from the Front Lines." *Florida Law Review* 69 (2017): 1255–337.

French, David. "It's Time for Bill O'Reilly to Be Weinsteined." *National Review*, October 23, 2017. https://www.nationalreview.com/corner/its-time-conservatives-banish-bill-oreilly-progressives-are-banishing-harvey-weinstein/.

Frenkel, Sheera, and Daisuke Wakabayashi. "After Florida School Shooting, Russian 'Bot' Army Pounced." *New York Times*, February 19, 2018. https://www.nytimes.com/2018/02/19/technology/russian-bots-school-shooting.html.

Friedman, Lawrence M. *The Big Trial: Law as Public Spectacle*. Lawrence: University Press of Kansas, 2015.

———. "Popular Legal Culture: Law, Lawyers, and Popular Culture." Chapter 1 in *Popular Culture and Law*, edited by Richard K. Sherwin. Aldershot, England: Ashgate, 2006.

Fritze, John. "Trump Unloads on Brett Kavanaugh Accuser: 'She Admits She Was Drunk.'" *USA Today*, September 25, 2018. https://www.usatoday.com/story/news/politics/2018/09/25/donald-trump-deborah-ramirez-admits-she-drunk/1420729002/.

Fukuyama, Francis. "Women and the Evolution of World Politics." *Foreign Affairs* (September/October 1998). https://www.foreignaffairs.com/articles/1998-09-01/women-and-evolution-world-politics.

Fuller, Lon L. *The Morality of Law*, revised edition. New Haven: Yale University Press, 1969.

Galanter, Marc. "Why the 'Haves' Come Out Ahead: Speculations on the Limits of Legal Change." *Law and Society Review* 9, no. 1 (1974): 95.

Garber, Megan. "Is This the Next Step for the #MeToo Movement?" *Atlantic*, June 2, 2018. https://www.theatlantic.com/entertainment/archive/2018/01/beyond-metoo-can-times-up-effect-real-change/549482/.

Gardner, Eriq. "Janice Dickinson Scores Huge Appellate Wins in Bill Cosby Defamation Case." *Hollywood Reporter*, November 21, 2017. https://www.hollywoodreporter.com/thr-esq/janice-dickinson-scores-huge-appellate-wins-bill-cosby-defamation-case-1060782.

Garfinkel, Harold. "Conditions of Successful Degradation Ceremonies." *American Journal of Sociology* 61, no. 5 (1956): 420–24.

Garland, David. "On the Concept of Moral Panic." *Crime, Media, Culture: An International Journal* 4, no. 1 (2008): 10.

———. "What is a 'History of the Present'? On Foucault's Genealogies and Their Critical Preconditions." *Punishment & Society* 16, no. 4 (2014): 367, 372.

Gaspard, Whitney. "Bill Cosby's Lawyer Monique Pressley Calls It Quits," *Essence*, August 16, 2018, https://www.essence.com/news/bill-cosbys-lawyer-monique-pressley-calls-it-quits/.

Gay, Roxanne. "Who Gets to Be Angry?" *New York Times*, June 10, 2016. https://www.nytimes.com/2016/06/12/opinion/sunday/who-gets-to-be-angry.html.

Geis, Gilbert. "Lord Hale, Witches, and Rape." *British Journal of Law and Society* 5, no. 1 (Summer 1978): 42.

Gersen, Jeannie Suk. "Shutting Down Conversations about Rape at Harvard Law." *New Yorker*, December 11, 2015. https://www.newyorker.com/news/news-desk/argument-sexual-assault-race-harvard-law-school.

Gerstein, Josh. "Meet the Four Clinton Accusers who Joined Trump." Politico.com, October 9, 2016. https://www.politico.com/story/2016/10/clinton-accusers-donald-trump-debate-229444.

Gessen, Masha. "Sex, Consent, and the Dangers of 'Misplaced Scale.'" *New Yorker*, November 27, 2017. https://www.newyorker.com/news/our-columnists/sex-consent-dangers-of-misplaced-scale.

Gilbert, Sophie. "The Movement of #MeToo." *Atlantic*, October 16, 2017. https://www.theatlantic.com/entertainment/archive/2017/10/the-movement-of-metoo/542979/.

Gilmore, Leigh. "It Wasn't Just 'Fake News' Presenting a Fake Hillary Clinton: She Was Held to Impossible Standards." *Salon*, November 26, 2016. https://www.salon.com/2016/11/26/it-wasnt-just-fake-news-presenting-a-fake-hillary-clinton-she-was-held-to-impossible-standards_partner/.

Glaister, Dan, and David Teather. "Jackson Found Not Guilty." *Guardian*, June 13, 2005. https://www.theguardian.com/world/2005/jun/14/michaeljacksontrial.music.

Glaser, Paul Michael, dir. *The Running Man*. Los Angeles: TriStar Pictures, 1987.

Glaspell, Susan. *Trifles*. In *Literature: A World of Writing*, edited by David L. Pike and Ana M. Acosta. New York: Pearson Longman, 2011.

Glasser, Nathaniel M. "The Weinstein Effect: #MeToo Allegations in the Financial Services Industry," *Take 5 Newsletter* (November 2017), https://www.ebglaw.com/news/five-issues-in-focus-for-financial-services/#_para1.

Gonzales, Richard, and Camila Domonoske. "Voters Recall Aaron Persky, Judge Who Sentenced Brock Turner." National Public Radio, June 5, 2018. https://

www.npr.org/sections/thetwo-way/2018/06/05/617071359/voters-are-deciding-whether-to-recall-aaron-persky-judge-who-sentenced-brock-tur.

Gottfried, Jeffrey, and Elisa Shearer. "News Use across Social Media Platforms 2016." Pew Research Center, May 26, 2016. http://www.journalism.org/2016/05/26/news-use-across-social-media-platforms-2016/.

Grady, Constance. "Shitty Men List Creator Moira Donegan on the Year in #MeToo," Vox.com, October 16, 2018, https://www.vox.com/culture/2018/10/16/17955392/moira-donegan-interview-me-too-shitty-media-men-list.

Graves, Lucia. "How Famous Men Toppled by #MeToo Plot Their Comeback." *Guardian*, May 27, 2018. https://www.theguardian.com/world/2018/may/27/metoo-sexual-assault-claims-accused-men-plot-redemption-charlie-rose-mario-batali.

Greenberg, Zoe. "What Happens to #MeToo When a Feminist Is the Accused?" *New York Times*, August 13, 2018. https://www.nytimes.com/2018/08/13/nyregion/sexual-harassment-nyu-female-professor.html.

Gross, Samantha J. "After Nearly 70 Years, Florida Clemency Board Pardons Groveland Four." *Miami Herald*, January 13, 2019. https://www.miamiherald.com/news/politics-government/state-politics/article224282780.html.

Grosz, Elizabeth. *Volatile Bodies: Toward a Corporeal Feminism*. Bloomington: University of Indiana Press, 1994.

Haag, Matthew, and James C. McKinley Jr. "Lawsuit against Weinstein Might Open Door to Criminal Charges." *New York Times*, May 2, 2018. https://www.nytimes.com/2018/05/02/nyregion/harvey-weinstein-sexual-assault.html.

Haberman, Clyde. "What the Kitty Genovese Killing Can Teach Today's Digital Bystanders." *New York Times*, June 4, 2017. https://www.nytimes.com/2017/06/04/us/retro-report-bystander-effect.html.

———. "When Youth Violence Spurred 'Superpredator' Fear." *New York Times*, April 6, 2014. https://www.nytimes.com/2014/04/07/us/politics/killing-on-bus-recalls-superpredator-threat-of-90s.html.

Haberman, Maggie, and Peter Baker. "Trump Taunts Christine Blasey Ford at Rally." *New York Times*, October 2, 2018. https://www.nytimes.com/2018/10/02/us/politics/trump-me-too.html?module=inline.

Hafiz, Hiba. "How Legal Agreements Can Silence Victims of Workplace Sexual Assault." *Atlantic*, October 18, 2017. https://www.theatlantic.com/business/archive/2017/10/legal-agreements-sexual-assault-ndas/543252/.

Hafner, Josh. "The Judge in the Larry Nassar Trial: Incredible Quotes to Victims and Their Abuser." *USA Today*, January 24, 2018. https://www.usatoday.com/story/news/nation-now/2018/01/24/judge-larry-nassar-trial-incredible-quotes-victims-and-their-abuser/1061691001/.

Halley, Janet. "Rape in Berlin: Reconsidering the Criminalisation of Rape in the International Law of Armed Conflict." *Melbourne Journal of International Law* 9, no. 1 (2008): 78.

———. "Trading the Megaphone for the Gavel in Title IX Enforcement." *Harvard Law Review Forum* 128 (2015): 103–17.

Halliday, Simon, and Bronwen Morgan. "I Fought the Law and the Law Won? Legal Consciousness and the Critical Imagination." *Current Legal Problems* 66 (2013): 2.

Haltom, William, and Michael McCann. *Distorting the Law: Politics, Media, and the Litigation Crisis*. Chicago: University of Chicago Press, 2004.

Halzack, Sarah. "Grab Your Wallet: The Woman Who Began Boycott of Trump Products in US Retailers." *Independent*, February 14, 2017. https://www.independent.co.uk/news/world/americas/grab-your-wallet-trump-boycott-products-us-retailers-shannon-coulter-nordstrom-donald-jr-ivanka-eric-a7579776.html.

Haque, Umair. "Why Twitter's Dying (and What You Can Learn From It)." HuffPost (blog), October 28, 2015. http://www.huffingtonpost.com/umair-haque/why-twitters-dying-learn-from-it_b_8401542.html.

Hardaker, Claire, and Mark McGlashan. "'Real Men Don't Hate Women': Twitter Rape Threats and Group Identity." *Journal of Pragmatics* 91 (2016): 82.

Hardcastle, Valerie Gray, M. K. Kitzmiller, and Shelby Lahey. "The Impact of Neuroscience Data in Criminal Cases: Female Defendants and the Double-Edged Sword." *New Criminal Law Review: An International and Interdisciplinary Journal* 21, no. 2 (2018): 292.

Harding, Kate. "Gray Matters: How Rape in Pop Culture Became a Matter of Opinion." *Bitch*, August 2, 2018. https://www.bitchmedia.org/article/rape-in-pop-culture-became-matter-of-opinion.

Harris, Aisha. "She Founded #MeToo. Now She Wants to Move Past the Trauma," *The New York Times*, October 15, 2018, https://www.nytimes.com/2018/10/15/arts/tarana-burke-metoo-anniversary.html.

Harris, Angela P. "Race and Essentialism in Feminist Legal Theory." *Stanford Law Review* 42 (1989–1990).

Harris, Cheryl I. "Myths of Race and Gender in the Trials of O. J. Simpson and Susan Smith —Spectacles of Our Times." *Washburn Law Journal* 35 (1996): 226.

Harris, Paul. "Courting Disaster." *Observer*, April 16, 2005. https://www.theguardian.com/music/2005/apr/17/michaeljackson.michaeljacksontrial.

"The Harvey Weinstein Effect." *USA Today*. https://www.usatoday.com/pages/interactives/life/the-harvey-weinstein-effect/.

"Harvey Weinstein Sacked after Sexual Harassment Claims." BBC News, October 9, 2017. http://www.bbc.com/news/business-41546694.

"Harvey Weinstein Timeline: How the Scandal Unfolded." BBC News, May 25, 2018. http://www.bbc.com/news/entertainment-arts-41594672.

Harvey-Jenner, Catriona. "The Number of Women Who Troll Online Will SHOCK You." *Cosmopolitan*, May 26, 2016. https://www.cosmopolitan.com/uk/reports/news/a43626/women-half-online-trolls/.

"Hashtag Activism in 2014: Tweeting 'Why I Stayed.'" *All Things Considered*. National Public Radio, December 23, 2014. http://www.npr.org/2014/12/23/372729058/hashtag-activism-in-2014-tweeting-why-i-stayed.

Hayden, Michael Edison. "Fake News Story about Chuck Schumer Implodes after Pro-Trump Conspiracy Theorists Claim Source Went Dark." *Newsweek*, December 13, 2017. http://www.newsweek.com/fake-news-story-chuck-schumer-implodes-747384.

Heimans, Jeremy, and Henry Timms. *New Power: How Power Works in Our Hyperconnected World—and How to Make It Work for You*. New York: Doubleday, 2018.

Held, Amy. "More Than 140 'Sister Survivors' of Larry Nassar Abuse Are Honored at ESPYS." National Public Radio, July 19, 2018. https://www.npr.org/2018/07/19/630440282/more-than-140-sister-survivors-of-larry-nassar-abuse-are-honored-at-espys.

Hendricks, Jaclyn. "The Side of McKayla Maroney You Haven't Seen Before." *New York Post*, May 15, 2017. https://nypost.com/2017/05/15/the-side-of-mckayla-maroney-you-havent-seen-before/.

Hengeveld, Maria. "How Nike's Neoliberal Feminism Came to Rule the Global South." *FeministWire*, September 14, 2015. http://www.thefeministwire.com/2015/09/nike-neoliberal-feminism/.

Henneberger, Melinda. "Bill Cosby Mistrial Shows Sexual Assault Laws Must Change." Opinion. *USA Today*, June 17, 2017. https://www.usatoday.com/story/

opinion/2017/06/17/bill-cosby-mistrial-sexual-assault-laws-must-change-melinda-henneberger-column/102824708/.

Hennessey-Fiske, Molly, Matt Pearce, and Jenny Jarvie. "Texas School Shooter Killed Girl Who Turned Down His Advances and Embarrassed Him in Class, Her Mother Says." *Los Angeles Times*, May 20, 2018. http://www.latimes.com/nation/la-na-texas-shooter-20180519-story.html#.

Henry, Nicola, and Anastasia Powell. "Embodied Harms: Gender, Shame, and Technology-Facilitated Sexual Violence." *Violence Against Women* 21, no. 6 (2015): 769–70.

Hepler, Lauren. "Campaign to Recall Judge in Stanford Sexual Assault Case Morphs into a Culture War." *San Jose Inside*, March 21, 2018. https://www.sanjoseinside.com/2018/03/21/campaign-to-recall-judge-in-stanford-sexual-assault-case-morphs-into-a-culture-war/.

Hill Collins, Patricia. *Black Feminist Thought: Knowledge, Consciousness, and the Politics of Empowerment*. New York: Routledge, 2000.

Hill, Kashmir. "Facebook Manipulated 689,003 Users' Emotions for Science." Forbes.com, June 28, 2014. http://www.forbes.com/sites/kashmirhill/2014/06/28/facebook-manipulated-689003-users-emotions-for-science/#2bfad356704d.

"History of Lynchings." NAACP. http://www.naacp.org/history-of-lynchings/.

hnoss. "Thot" (also "THOT," acronym for "That Ho Over There"). *Urban Dictionary*, March 7, 2017. https://www.urbandictionary.com/define.php?term=Thot.

Holbrook, Evans. "Change in the Meaning of Consortium." *Michigan Law Review* 22 (1923): 2, 6.

hooks, bell. *Killing Rage: Ending Racism*. New York: Holt Paperbacks, 1996.

Hornaday, Ann. "Enough with Naming and Shaming: It's Time for Restorative Justice in Hollywood." *Washington Post*, February 1, 2018. https://www.washingtonpost.com/lifestyle/style/enough-with-naming-and-shaming-its-time-for-restorative-justice-in-hollywood/2018/02/01/416ccf80-0518-11e8-b48c-b07fea957bd5_story.html?utm_term=.a1cbf977c01e.

Horowitz, Julia. "Why We Believed Jackie's Rape Story." *Politico*, December 6, 2014. http://www.politico.com/magazine/story/2014/12/why-we-believed-jackies-story-113365#ixzz4Eri8kjhC.

Houlihan, Michael, and Bonnie Harvey. "How Crowdsourcing Is Shaping the Future of Everything." Entrepreneur.com, January 13, 2018. https://www.entrepreneur.com/article/307438.

Howe, Adrian. "The Problem of Privatized Injuries: Feminist Strategies for Litigation." In *At The Boundaries of the Law: Feminism and Legal Theory*, edited by Martha Albertson Fineman and Nancy Sweet Thomadsen. New York: Routledge, 1991.

Hsu, Tiffany. "For Many Facebook Users, a 'Last Straw' That Led Them to Quit." *New York Times*, March 21, 2018. https://www.nytimes.com/2018/03/21/technology/users-abandon-facebook.html.

Hughey, Matthew W., and Jessie Daniels. "Racist Comments at Online News Sites: A Methodological Dilemma for Discourse Analysis." *Media, Culture & Society* 35, no. 3 (2013): 334.

Human Rights Campaign. "Sexual Assault and the LGBTQ Community." https://www.hrc.org/resources/sexual-assault-and-the-lgbt-community.

Hutton, Julia. "Compensating for Mass Murder." *Atlantic*, April 2, 2015. https://www.theatlantic.com/business/archive/2015/04/compensating-for-mass-murder/389174/.

The-Injury-Lawyer-Directory.com. "Contributory Negligence vs. Comparative Negligence." https://the-injury-lawyer-directory.com/contributory-negligence-vs-comparative-negligence/.

Ioannou, Filipa, Ben Mathis-Lilley, Elliot Hannon, and Lena Wilson. "A Complete List of the Women Who Have Accused Bill Cosby of Sexual Assault." *Slate*, April 26, 2018. http://www.slate.com/blogs/browbeat/2014/11/21/bill_cosby_accusers_list_sexual_assault_rape_drugs_feature_in_women_s_stories.html.

Isidore, Chris. "Remains of the Weinstein Company Sold—To the Only Real Bidder." CNN, May 2, 2018. http://money.cnn.com/2018/05/02/media/weinstein-company-bidder/index.html.

Jackson, David. "Donald Trump Calls Assault Allegations against Kavanaugh a Democratic 'Hoax.'" *USA Today*, October 8, 2018. https://www.usatoday.com/story/news/politics/2018/10/08/donald-trump-calls-assault-allegations-against-brett-kavanaugh-hoax/1564801002/.

Jacobs, Julia. "Cosby's Team Alleges Racism and Sexism, Calling Him a Victim of a 'Sex War,'" *The New York Times*, September 25, 2018, https://www.nytimes.com/2018/09/25/us/cosby-jail-racist-sex-war.html.

"Jameis Winston Alleged Rape Victim Files New Lawsuit." TMZ, April 16, 2015. http://www.tmz.com/2015/04/16/jameis-winston-civil-lawsuit-alleged-rape-erica-kinsman-florida-state-university/?adid=TMZ_Search_Results.

James, Mike. "George Pell, Once Australia's Most Senior Catholic, Sentenced to 6 Years for Child Sex Abuse." *USA Today*, March 12, 2019. https://www.usatoday.com/story/news/world/2019/03/12/catholic-church-george-pell-six-years-child-sex-case/3146864002/.

Jamison, Leslie. "Grand Unified Theory of Female Pain." *VQR* (Spring 2014). https://www.vqronline.org/essays-articles/2014/04/grand-unified-theory-female-pain.

Janzen, Sydney. "Amending Rape Shield Laws: Outdated Statutes Fail to Protect Victims on Social Media." *John Marshall Law Review* 48, no. 4 (2015): 1087–118.

Jenkins, Aric. "The *Washington Post* Says a Woman Tried to Give Them a Fake Roy Moore Story." *Time*, November 28, 2017. http://time.com/5038629/jaime-phillips-roy-moore-washington-post-project-vertias-james-okeefe/.

Jerkins, Morgan. "Why White Women Keep Calling the Cops on Black People." *Rolling Stone*, July 17, 2018. https://www.rollingstone.com/politics/politics-features/why-white-women-keep-calling-the-cops-on-black-people-699512/.

Johnson, Denise R. "Prior False Allegations of Rape: Falsus in Uno, Falsus in Omnibus?" *Yale Journal of Law and Feminism* 7, no. 2 (1995): 252, 253, fn. 51.

Jones-Rogers, Stephanie. *They Were Her Property: White Women as Slave Owners in the American South*. New Haven: Yale University Press, 2019.

Joyce, Kathryn. "The Takedown of Title IX." *New York Times Magazine*, December 5, 2017. https://www.nytimes.com/2017/12/05/magazine/the-takedown-of-title-ix.html.

Kaba, Mariame, and Andrea Smith. "Twitter Is Toxic. And So Is the Rest of the World." *The Nation*, April 17, 2014. https://www.thenation.com/article/where-twitter-and-feminism-meet/.

Kaiser. "Amy Schumer on Her 'Friend' Aziz Ansari: It's Not a Crime, But It's Not Cool." *Celebitchy*, February 1, 2018. http://www.celebitchy.com/565075/amy_schumer_on_her_friend_aziz_ansari_its_not_a_crime_but_its_not_cool/.

Kaiser, Matt. "Was Brock Turner's Sentence Too Lenient?" *Above the Law*, June 16, 2016. https://abovethelaw.com/2016/06/was-brock-turners-sentence-too-lenient/?rf=1.

Kantor, Jodi, and Megan Twohey. "Harvey Weinstein Paid Off Sexual Harassment Accusers for Decades." *New York Times*, October 5, 2017. https://www.nytimes.com/2017/10/05/us/harvey-weinstein-harassment-allegations.html.

Kaplan, Tracey. "Recall Aftermath: Will the Removal of Judge Aaron Persky Prompt a New Legal Battle?" *Mercury News*, June 6, 2018. https://www.mercurynews.com/2018/06/06/judge-persky/.

Kassin, S. M. "The Social Psychology of False Confessions." *Social Issues and Policy Review* 9, no. 1 (2015): 25–51.

Kazek, Kelly. "The Sad Ends of the Scottsboro Boys: Their Lives in Brief Biographies." AL.com, April 15, 2013. http://blog.al.com/breaking/2013/04/the_sad_ends_of_the_scottsboro.html.

Kelly, Erin, and Jessica Estepa. "Brett Kavanaugh: A Timeline of Allegations against the Supreme Court Nominee." *USA Today*, September 28, 2018. https://

www.usatoday.com/story/news/politics/onpolitics/2018/09/24/brett-kavanaugh-allegations-timeline-supreme-court/1408073002/.

Kennedy, Randall. "Harvard Betrays a Law Professor—and Itself," *New York Times*, May 15. 2019, https://www.nytimes.com/2019/05/15/opinion/race-identity/harvard-law-harvey-weinstein.html.

Kerr, Emma. "The Latest Assault Victim since *The Keepers* Comes Forward with New Sexual Abuse Story." Oxygen.com, February 8, 2018. https://www.oxygen.com/crime-time/the-latest-assault-victim-since-the-keepers-comes-forward-with-new-sexual-abuse-story.

Kessler, Zara. "*Rolling Stone* Problems Change Cosby Context." *Sydney Morning Herald*, December 9, 2014. https://www.smh.com.au/world/rolling-stone-problems-change-cosby-context-20141209-1232h7.html.

Khazan, Olga. "The *Rolling Stone* Fiasco Is Terrible News for Rape Survivors." *Atlantic*, December 5, 2014. https://www.theatlantic.com/health/archive/2014/12/the-rolling-stone-fiasco-is-terrible-news-for-rape-survivors/383483/.

Kidd, Celeste, Amanda Schmitt, Sandra Muller, Jessica Cantlon, Adama Iwu, Wendy Walsh, Gabrielle Eubank, Lindsay Meyer, Lindsey Reynolds, Tarana Burke, Terry Crews, and Ashley Judd, "What Still Needs to be Done to Break the Silence Surrounding Sexual Harassment, *Time*, December 11, 2018, http://time.com/5475966/silence-breakers-2018/.

Kilgorus Circus Maximus. "Bill Cosby: Sleeping Beauty." July 17, 2015. https://kilgoriuscircusmaximus.wordpress.com/tag/bill-cosby/.

Kim, Kyle, Christina Littlefield, and Melissa Etehad. "Bill Cosby: A 50-Year Chronicle of Accusations and Accomplishments." *Los Angeles Times*, June 17, 2017. http://www.latimes.com/entertainment/la-et-bill-cosby-timeline-htmlstory.html.

Kipnis, Laura. "What We Lose When Sex Is All about Danger." *The Cut*. https://www.thecut.com/2017/03/laura-kipnis-unwanted-advances-excerpt.html.

Kirby, Jen. "Bill Cosby's Retrial May Be the First Real Test of the Power of #MeToo." *Vox*, April 9, 2018. https://www.vox.com/2018/4/9/17139824/bill-cosby-retrial-sex-assault-metoo.

———. "Cosby Defense Attorneys Used Personal Attacks to Try to Discredit Witnesses." *Vox*, April 13, 2018. https://www.vox.com/2018/4/13/17234172/bill-cosby-trial-accusers-janice-dickinson-testimony.

———. "Cosby Defense Lawyers: Andrea Constand is a 'Con Artist.'" *Vox*, April 10, 2018. https://www.vox.com/2018/4/10/17219730/bill-cosby-constand-defense-opening-statement-trial.

Kircher, Madison Malone. "Internet Trolls Can't Stop Arguing with Sarah Nyberg's Twitter Bot." *New York Magazine*, October 7, 2016. http://nymag.com/selectall/2016/10/sarah-nybergs-arguing-twitter-bot-exposes-trolls.html.

Kirk, Thomas James "TJ," III. "Feminism & Rape: Belief without Evidence." YouTube, December 13, 2014. https://www.youtube.com/watch?v=YhxYw9t_XMc.

Kodjak, Alison. "Experts Say There's Little Connection between Mental Health and Mass Shootings." *All Things Considered*. National Public Radio, February 23, 2018. https://www.npr.org/2018/02/23/588374658/experts-say-theres-little-connection-between-mental-health-and-mass-shootings.

Koss, Mary P., Christine A. Gidycz, and Nadine Wisniewski. "The Scope of Rape: Incidence and Prevalence of Sexual Aggression and Victimization in a National Sample of Higher Education Students." *Journal of Consulting and Clinical Psychology* 55, no. 2 (1987): 162–70.

Kotkin, Minna J. "How the Legal World Built a Wall of Silence around Workplace Sexual Harassment." *Washington Post*, October 20, 2017. https://www.washingtonpost.com/outlook/how-the-legal-world-built-a-wall-of-silence-around-workplace-sexual-harassment/2017/10/20/ac1f41dc-b2b1-11e7-9e58-e6288544af98_story.html?utm_term=.c37867127452.

LaMotte, Sandee. "How #MeToo Could Move from Social Campaign to Social Change." CNN, November 9, 2017. https://www.cnn.com/2017/10/30/health/metoo-legacy/index.html.

Landler, Mark. "Trump, Saying 'Mere Allegation' Ruins Lives, Appears to Doubt #MeToo Movement." *New York Times*, February 10, 2018. https://www.nytimes.com/2018/02/10/us/politics/trump-porter-me-too-movement.html.

Lapin, Tamar. "Trump Jr. Compares Christine Blasey Ford to Jussie Smollett in Oscar 'Hoax' Category." *New York Post*, February 24, 2019. https://nypost.com/2019/02/24/trump-jr-compares-christine-blasey-ford-to-jussie-smollett-in-oscar-hoax-category/.

"Larry Nassar's Letter Elicits Gasps in a Packed Courtroom." CBS News, January 25, 2018. https://www.cbsnews.com/news/larry-nassar-letter-elicits-gasps-in-packed-courtroom/.

Lavelle, Daniel. "From 'Slimeball Comey' to 'Crooked Hillary,' Why Trump Loves to Brand his Enemies." *Guardian*, April 17, 2018. https://www.theguardian.com/us-news/shortcuts/2018/apr/17/presidents-nicknames-slimeball-comey-former-fbi-director.

Lavigne, Paula. "Lawyers, Status, Public Backlash Aid College Athletes Accused of Crimes." ESPN, June 15, 2015. http://espn.go.com/espn/otl/story/_/id/13065247/college-athletes-major-programs-benefit-confluence-factors-somes-avoid-criminal-charges.

Lee, Cynthia. *Murder and the Reasonable Man: Passion and Fear in the Criminal Justice System*. New York: New York University Press, 2007.

Lee, Dami. "Emoji Are Showing Up in Court Cases Exponentially, and Courts Aren't Prepared." *The Verge*, February 18, 2019. https://www.theverge.com/2019/2/18/18225231/emoji-emoticon-court-case-reference.

Lee, Dave. "The Tactics of a Russian Troll Farm." BBC News, February 16, 2018.

Lens, Kim M. E., Anthony Pemberton, Karen Brans, Johen Braeken, Stephen Bogaerts, and Esmah Lahlah, "Delivering a Victim Impact Statement: Emotionally Effective or Counter-Productive?," *European Journal of Criminology* 12 (2015), 17–34.

Lepore, Jill. "The Rise of the Victims'-Rights Movement." *New Yorker*, May 21, 2018. https://www.newyorker.com/magazine/2018/05/21/the-rise-of-the-victims-rights-movement.

Levine, Ethan Czuy. "Sexual Scripts and Criminal Statutes: Gender Restrictions, Spousal Allowances, and Victim Accountability after Rape Law Reform." *Violence Against Women* 23, no. 3 (2017): 324.

Levitt, Peggy, and Sally Merry. "Vernacularization on the Ground: Local Uses of Global Women's Rights in Peru, China, India and the United States." *Global Networks* 9, no. 4 (2009): 441–61.

Lewinsky, Monica. "Emerging from 'the House of Gaslight' in the Age of #MeToo." *Vanity Fair*, February 25, 2018. https://www.vanityfair.com/news/2018/02/monica-lewinsky-in-the-age-of-metoo.

Lieberman, J. D., D. Koetzle, and M. Sakiyama. "Police Departments' Use of Facebook: Patterns and Policy Issues." *Criminology and Penology* 16, no. 4 (2013): 442.

Lily News. "The Bill Cosby Trial Touches on Common Rape Myths." April 23, 2018. https://www.thelily.com/the-bill-cosby-trial-touches-on-common-rape-myths/.

Lininger, Tom. "Is It Wrong to Sue for Rape?" *Duke Law Journal* 57 (2008): 1557–640.

Linker, Maureen. "Considering Online News Comments: Are We Really So Irrational and Hate Filled?" *Social Epistemology Review and Reply Collective* 3, no. 12 (2014): 1–10.

Linskey, Annie. "Ethnicity Not a Factor in Elizabeth Warren's Rise in Law. *Boston Globe*, September 1, 2018. https://www.bostonglobe.com/news/nation/2018/09/01/did-claiming-native-american-heritage-actually-help-elizabeth-warren-get-ahead-but-complicated/wUZZcrKKEOUv5Spnb7IO0K/story.html.

Lipstick Alley. "'Thot' Things Thread." Started by jeansaprincess, August 15, 2015. https://www.lipstickalley.com/threads/thot-things-thread.911948/.

Lisak, David, Lori Gardinier, Sarah C. Nicksa, and Ashley M. Cote. "False Allegations of Sexual Assault: An Analysis of Ten Years of Reported Cases." *Violence Against Women* 16, no. 1 (2010): 1319.

Livingstone, Josephine. "The Task Ahead for Feminism." *New Republic*, November 17, 2017. https://newrepublic.com/article/145850/task-ahead-feminism.

Livsey, Anna. "Liam Neeson Says Harassment Allegations Are Now 'A Witch-Hunt.'" *Guardian*, January 13, 2018. https://www.theguardian.com/film/2018/jan/13/liam-neeson-says-harassment-allegations-have-become-a-witch-hunt.

Loewen, Kim. "Rejecting the Purity Myth: Reforming Rape Shield Laws in the Age of Social Media." *UCLA Women's Law Journal* 22, no. 2 (2015): 154.

Loftus, Elizabeth F. *Eyewitness Testimony*. Cambridge: Harvard University Press, 1996.

Lopez, German. "The Rise of Rage in Social Media Politics, in One Chart." *Vox*, July 18, 2018. https://www.vox.com/policy-and-politics/2018/7/18/17588120/trump-politics-anger-facebook-pew.

———. "Voters Recall Judge Who Sentenced Brock Turner to 6 Months in Jail for Sexual Assault." *Vox*, June 6, 2018. https://www.vox.com/policy-and-politics/2018/6/6/17433576/judge-aaron-persky-recall-brock-turner-results.

Luther, Jessica. "'I'm Broken': The Duke Lacrosse Rape Accuser, 10 Years Later: A Decade after Crystal Magnum Accused Duke Lacrosse Players of Raping Her, She Tells Her Story from Inside Prison." Vocativ.com, March 10, 2016. http://www.vocativ.com/295731/im-broken-the-duke-lacrosse-rape-accuser-10-years-later/.

———. "The Jameis Winston Rape Lawsuit Has Some Damaging New Information." *Vice Sports*, April 17, 2015. https://sports.vice.com/en_us/article/wn33gm/the-jameis-winston-rape-lawsuit-has-some-damaging-new-information.

Lynch, Jeffrey, dir. *The Simpsons*. Season 6, episode 9, "Homer Badman." Original air date November 27, 1994, on FOX.

"Lynching in America: Confronting the Legacy of Racial Terror." Equal Justice Initiative. https://lynchinginamerica.eji.org.

Maas, Megan, Heather McCauley, Amy E. Bonomi, and S. Gisela Leija. "'I Was Grabbed by My Pussy and Its #NotOkay': A Twitter Backlash against Donald Trump's Degrading Commentary." *Violence Against Women* 24, no. 14 (2018): 3.

MacKinnon, Catharine A. *Butterfly Politics*. Cambridge: Harvard University Press, 2017.

———. "#MeToo Has Done What the Law Could Not." Opinion. *New York Times*, February 4, 2018. https://www.nytimes.com/2018/02/04/opinion/metoo-law-legal-system.html.

———. "Rape, Genocide, and Women's Human Rights." *Harvard Women's Law Journal* 17, no. 5 (1994): 5.

Mahler, Jonathan. "For Many Women, Trump's 'Locker Room Talk' Brings Memories of Abuse." *New York Times*, October 10, 2016. https://www.nytimes.com/2016/10/11/us/politics/sexual-assault-survivor-reaction.html.

Makela, Mark. "Transcript: Donald Trump's Taped Comments about Women." *New York Times*, October 8, 2016. https://www.nytimes.com/2016/10/08/us/donald-trump-tape-transcript.html.

Malala Fund. https://www.malala.org/malalas-story?g=1&utm_expid=.rFt8T4goQvu3waedVYhuNA.1&utm_referrer=https%3A%2F%2Fwww.google.com%2F.

Malkin, Michelle. "Beware the Rape Allegation Bandwagon." *National Review*, October 18, 2017. https://www.nationalreview.com/2017/10/metoo-may-exaggerate-prevalence-sex-crimes/.

Malone, Noreen. "Sexual-Harassment Claims against a 'She-E.O.'" *The Cut*. https://www.thecut.com/2017/03/thinx-employee-accuses-miki-agrawal-of-sexual-harassment.html.

Manderson, Desmond. "Trust Us Justice: *24*, Popular Culture, and the Law." Chapter 1 in *Imagining Legality: Where Law Meets Popular Culture*, edited by Austin Sarat. Birmingham: University of Alabama Press, 2014.

Manne, Kate. "Brett Kavanaugh and America's 'Himpathy' Reckoning." *New York Times*, Opinion, September 26, 2018. https://www.nytimes.com/2018/09/26/opinion/brett-kavanaugh-hearing-himpathy.html.

Martineau, Kim. "Crowdsourced Family Tree Yields New Insights about Humanity." *Columbia News*, March 1, 2018. https://news.columbia.edu/news/crowdsourced-family-tree-yields-new-insights-about-humanity.

Marwick, Alice. "Ethnographic and Qualitative Research on Twitter." In *Twitter and Society*, edited by Katrin Weller, Axel Bruns, Jean Burgess, Merja Mahrt, and Cornelius Puschmann. New York: Peter Lang AG, 2013.

Marwick, Alice, and danah boyd. "I Tweet Honestly, I Tweet Passionately: Twitter Users, Context Collapse, and the Imagined Audience." *New Media and Society* 13(1) (2011): 114–33.

Masur, Jonathan S., and Eric A. Posner. "Toward a Pigouvian State." *University of Pennsylvania Law Review* 164 (2015): 93.

Matthews, Dylan. "Michael Cohen's Hush Money Payments to Stormy Daniels and Karen McDougal, Explained." *Vox*, August 21, 2018. https://www.vox.com/2018/8/21/17765348/.

Matthews, Natalie. "This New App Could've Prevented My Friend's Rape." *Elle*, April 17, 2014. https://www.elle.com/culture/tech/a10/kitestring-app-safety-apps-women/.

Maxi, Levi. "False Flags in Cyberspace: Targeting Public Opinion and Political Will." *Cipher Brief*, March 6, 2018. https://www.thecipherbrief.com/false-flags-cyberspace-targeting-public-opinion-political-will.

McArdle, Mairead. "Wave of Bomb Threats Targets Prominent Democrats." *National Review*, October 24, 2018. https://www.nationalreview.com/news/bomb-threats-target-prominent-democrats-nationwide/.

McCann, Hannah. "Big Reputations: Who Has the Power to Speak #MeToo." *Australian Humanities Review* 63 (2018): 185–89.

McCann, Michael. "The Unbearable Lightness of Rights: On Sociolegal Inquiry in the Global Era." *Law and Society Review* 18, no. 2 (2014).

McCarthy, Andrew C. "On Hush Money, the President's Best Defense Is Lack of Criminal Intent." *National Review*, August 25, 2018. https://www.nationalreview.com/2018/08/trump-cohen-hush-money-president-had-lack-of-criminal-intent/.

McCaskill, Nolan D. "Trump Credits Social Media for his Election." Politico.com, October 20, 2017. https://www.politico.com/story/2017/10/20/trump-social-media-election-244009.

McClellan, Frank M., Augustus A. White III, Ramon L. Jiminez, and Sherin Fahmy. "Do Poor People Sue Doctors More Frequently? Confronting Unconscious Bias and the Role of Cultural Competency." *Clinical Orthopaedics and Related Research* 470 (2012): 1393–97.

McDonnell-Parry, Amelia. "*Making a Murderer* One Year Later: Everything You Need to Know." *Rolling Stone*, December 16, 2016. http://www.rollingstone.com/culture/news/making-a-murderer-one-year-later-everything-to-know-w455262.

McDonough, Katie. "This Was Always Going to Hurt." *Splinter*, October 13, 2017. https://splinternews.com/this-was-always-going-to-hurt-1819434482.

McEvoy, Fiona J. "Social Bots are Ruining the Internet for the Rest of Us." *Venture Beat*, December 5, 2017. https://venturebeat.com/2017/12/05/social-bots-are-ruining-the-internet-for-the-rest-of-us/.

McGowan, Rose. Tweet, October 8, 2017, 2:27 p.m. https://twitter.com/rosemcgowan/status/917139398101106689?lang=en.

McGuire, Danielle L. *At the Dark End of the Street: Black Women, Rape, and Resistance—A New History of the Civil Rights Movement from Rosa Parks to the Rise of Black Power*. New York: Random House, 2011.

McLaughlin, Elliott. "Janay Rice: Ray Rice was 'Terrified' after Hitting Me." CNN.com, December 1, 2014. https://www.cnn.com/2014/12/01/us/ray-rice-wife-janay-today-show/index.html.

McMahon, Sarah, and Lawrence G. Farmer, "An Updated Measure for Assessing Subtle Rape Myths." *Social Work Research* 35 (2012): 71–81.

Mears, Daniel P. *American Criminal Justice Policy: An Evaluation Approach to Increasing Accountability and Effectiveness.* New York: Cambridge University Press, 2011.

Megarry, Jessica. "Online Incivility or Sexual Harassment? Conceptualising Women's Experiences in the Digital Age." *Women's Studies International Forum* 47 (2014): 46, 49–50.

Mendlow, Gabriel Seltzer. "Is Tort Law a Form of Institutionalized Revenge?" *Florida State Law Review* 39 (2011): 129, 132, 134.

MenEngage Alliance, UN Women, UNPFA. "Men, Masculinities, and Changing Power." United Nations Population Fund, 2014. https://www.unfpa.org/resources/men-masculinities-and-changing-power.

Merkin, Daphne. "Publicly, We Say #MeToo. Privately, We Have Misgivings." *New York Times*, January 5, 2018. https://www.nytimes.com/2018/01/05/opinion/golden-globes-metoo.html.

Merlan, Anna. "*Rolling Stone* Partially Retracts UVA Story over "Discrepancies.'" *Jezebel*, December 5, 2014. http://jezebel.com/rolling-stone-partially-retracts-uva-story-over-discrep-1667329573.

Messner, Michael A. *Politics of Masculinities: Men in Movements.* Lanham, MD: Rowman & Littlefield, 2000.

"The #MeToo Movement and Les Moonves." National Public Radio, August 5, 2018. https://www.npr.org/2018/08/05/635748549/the-metoo-movement-and-les-moonves.

Michigan Automotive News. "Uber Will No Longer Force Victims of Sexual Assault into Private Arbitration." MLive.com, May 15, 2018. https://www.mlive.com/auto/index.ssf/2018/05/uber_will_no_longer_force_arbi.html.

Miller, Mike. "Child Molesters, Human Rights Abusers and Maybe Harvey Weinstein: What It Takes to have the Queen Revoke Your Honorary Title." *People*, October 26, 2017. http://people.com/movies/child-molesters-human-rights-abusers-and-maybe-harvey-weinstein-what-it-takes-to-have-the-queen-revoke-your-honorary-title/.

Miller, Susan. "Stanford Sex Assault Survivor Named a Woman of the Year." *USA Today*, November 2, 2016. https://www.usatoday.com/story/news/nation/2016/11/01/stanford-sex-assault-survivor-named-woman-year/93145144/.

Mitchell, Jerry. "Bombshell Quote Missing from Emmett Till Tape. So, Did Caroline Bryant Donham Really Recant?, *Mississippi Clarion Ledger*, August 21, 2018, https://www.clarionledger.com/story/news/2018/08/21/emmett-till-carolyn-bryant-donham-recant-quote-missing/1017876002/.

Mitchell, Thomas A. "We're Only Fooling Ourselves: A Critical Analysis of the Biases Inherent in the Legal System's Treatment of Rape Victims." *Buffalo Journal of Gender, Law and Social Policy* 18 (2010): 98–100.

Mock, Brentin. "How Our Fear of 'Wilding' Colored the Central Park Five Case." *Grist*, July 8, 2014. https://grist.org/cities/how-our-fear-of-wilding-colored-the-central-park-five-case/.

"The Model Stalking Code Revisited: Responding to the New Realities of Stalking." National Center for Victims of Crime. http://victimsofcrime.org/docs/default-source/src/model-stalking-code.pdf?sfvrsn=12.

Moore, Sally. "'Rape Is a Crime Not of Lust, but Power,' Argues Susan Brownmiller." *People Archive*, November 10, 1975. https://people.com/archive/rape-is-a-crime-not-of-lust-but-power-argues-susan-brownmiller-vol-4-no-19/.

Moore, Sarah E. H. "Tracing the Life of a Crime Category: The Shifting Meaning of 'Date Rape.'" *Feminist Media Studies* 11 (2011): 456.

Morag-Levine, Noga. "Facts, Formalism, and the Brandeis Brief: The Origins of a Myth." *University of Illinois Law Review* (2013): 60.

Morgan, Phoebe A. "Risking Relationships: Understanding the Litigation Choices of Sexually Harassed Women." *Law and Society Review* 33 (1999): 67–68.

Muddiman, Ashley, and Natalie (Talia) Jomini Stroud. "10 Things We Learned by Analyzing 9 Million Comments from the *New York Times*." University of Texas at Austin Center for Media Engagement, June 21, 2016. https://mediaengagement.org/research/10-things-we-learned-by-analyzing-9-million-comments-from-the-new-york-times/.

Murray, Melissa. "Inequality's Frontiers." *Yale Law Journal Forum* 122 (February 21, 2013). https://www.yalelawjournal.org/forum/inequalitys-frontiers#footnote12.

Mustian, Jim and Michael R. Sisak, "Despite #MeToo, Rape Cases Still Confound Police," *US News*, December 28, 2018, https://www.usnews.com/news/best-states/michigan/articles/2018-12-27/despite-metoo-rape-cases-still-confound-police.

NBC15 Staff. "*Making a Murder*'s [Sic] Steven Avery Wins Appeal." WMTV-NBC15, February 27, 2019. https://www.nbc15.com/content/news/Making-a-Murders-Steven-Avery-wins-appeal-506452641.html.

Neff, Blake. "CNN's New Rape Documentary Relies on Myths, Not Facts." *Daily Caller*, March 19, 2015. http://dailycaller.com/2015/03/19/cnns-new-rape-documentary-relies-on-myths-not-facts/.

———. "UVA Jackie May Have Just Been Caught in Another Big Lie." *Daily Caller*, May 19, 2016. http://dailycaller.com/2016/05/19/uva-jackie-email-liar-new-evidence-lawsuit/.

Neuman, Scott. "Lawyers for Larry Nassar Say He Was Assaulted in Federal Prison." NPR, July 26, 2018. https://www.npr.org/2018/07/26/632564447/lawyers-for-larry-nassar-say-he-was-assaulted-in-federal-prison.

North, Anna. "What Happened to the Creator of the 'Shitty Media Men' List Shows Why the List Was Needed." *Vox*, January 11, 2018. https://www.vox.com/2018/1/11/16878316/shitty-media-men-list-katie-roiphe-moira-donegan.

Not Alone: The First White House Task Force to Protect Students from Sexual Assault. April 2004. Citing speech by Vice President Joe Biden, January 22, 2014. Formerly available at https://www.notalone.gov/assets/report.pdf.

Obasogie, Osagie K., and Zachary Newman. "Black Lives Matter and Respectability Politics in Local News Accounts of Officer-Involved Civilian Deaths: An Early Empirical Assessment." *Wisconsin Law Review* 2016, no. 3 (2016): 543.

Ohlheiser, Abby. "How #MeToo Really Was Different, according to Data." *Washington Post*, January 22, 2018. https://www.washingtonpost.com/news/the-intersect/wp/2018/01/22/how-metoo-really-was-different-according-to-data/?utm_term=.b88662a4a5f1.

Olivo, Natalie. "NY Bill Would Deny Tax Credits over Sexual Harassment." *Law360*, October 16, 2017. https://www.law360.com/articles/974896/ny-bill-would-deny-tax-credits-over-sexual-harassment.

Olorunnipa, Toluse. "How Trump Story on Cohen's Hush-Money Payments Shifted over Time." *Bloomberg*, August 24, 2018. https://www.bloomberg.com/news/articles/2018-08-24/how-trump-story-on-cohen-s-hush-money-payments-shifted-over-time.

Oppenheim, Maya. "Steve Bannon Warns Trump the 'Anti-Patriarchy Movement' Will Be Bigger than the Tea Party." *Independent*, February 12, 2018. http://www.independent.co.uk/news/world/americas/us-politics/steve-bannon-trump-tea-party-anti-patriarchy-movement-times-up-bloomberg-breitbart-news-a8206426.html.

Orchowski, L. M., A. S. Untied, and Christine A. Gidycz. "Factors Associated with College Women's Labeling of Sexual Victimization." *Violence and Victims* 28, no. 6 (2013): 940–58.

Ouellette, Laurie. "Real Justice: Law and Order on Reality Television." Chapter 4 in *Imagining Legality: Where Law Meets Popular Culture*, edited by Austin Sarat. Birmingham: University of Alabama Press, 2014.

Panariello, Lauren. "Apps That Help Prevent Rape." *Cosmopolitan*, August 22, 2012. https://www.cosmopolitan.com/lifestyle/advice/g2170/apps-that-help-prevent-rape/.

Panos, Maggie. "7 Important Things that Happened after the Events in *The Keepers*." Popsugar.com, July 28, 2017. https://www.popsugar.com/entertainment/Keepers-Update-43576120.

Patten, Dominic. "Imprisoned Bill Cosby Gets 2019 Trial Date for 1974 Playboy Mansion Assault Case." Deadline.com, November 13, 2018. https://deadline.com/2018/11/bill-cosby-playboy-mansion-assault-trial-date-los-angeles-judy-huth-1202501230/.

Patton, Stacey. "Why #MeToo Needs to Talk About Predatory White Women." *Dame*, October 23, 2018. https://www.damemagazine.com/2018/10/23/why-metoo-needs-to-talk-about-predatory-white-women/.

Pauly, Madison. "Why the 'Doctrine of Chances' Means Bill Cosby's Trial Will Be Different This Time." *Mother Jones*, April 5, 2018. https://www.motherjones.com/media/2018/04/why-the-doctrine-of-chances-means-bill-cosbys-trial-will-be-different-this-time/

Pearson, Patricia. *When She Was Bad: Violent Women and the Myth of Innocence*. New York: Penguin, 1998.

"Percentage of U.S. Population with a Social Media Profile from 2008 to 2018." Statista.com, August 17, 2018. https://www.statista.com/statistics/273476/percentage-of-us-population-with-a-social-network-profile/.

Pérez, Emma. *The Decolonial Imaginary: Writing Chicanas into History*. Bloomington: Indiana University Press, 1999.

Pérez-Peña, Richard, and Kate Taylor. "Fight against Sexual Assaults Holds Colleges to Account." *New York Times*, May 3, 2014. https://www.nytimes.com/2014/05/04/us/fight-against-sex-crimes-holds-colleges-to-account.html.

Pfister, Manuel. "The Great University of Virginia (UVA) Rape Hoax, Jackie Coakley, *Rolling Stone* and Sabrina Rubin Erdely." *The Single Dude's Guide to Life & Travel*, April 7, 2015. http://www.singledudetravel.com/2015/04/the-great-university-of-virginia-uva-rape-hoax-jackie-coakley-rolling-stone-and-sabrina-rubin-erdely/.

Pitofsky, Marina. "In Spain, Sexual Assault Legislation Says 'Yes Means Yes.'" *USA Today*, July 18, 2018. https://www.usatoday.com/story/news/world/2018/07/18/spain-sexual-assault-legislation-yes-means-yes/796773002/.

Planty, Michael G., Lynn Langton, Christopher Krebs, Marcus Berzofsky, and Hope Smiley-McDonald. *Female Victims of Sexual Violence 1994–2010*. Bureau of Justice Statistics (2013). https://www.bjs.gov/index.cfm?ty=pbdetail&iid=4594.

"Polaroid of Robed Bill Cosby before Alleged Dickinson Rape." TMZ, November 21, 2014. http://www.tmz.com/2014/11/21/janice-dickinson-bill-cosby-rape-robe-pictures/?adid=TMZ_Search_Results.

Pracher, Maria. "The Marital Rape Exemption: A Violation of a Woman's Right of Privacy." *Golden Gate University Law Review* 11, no. 3 (1981): 728.

Press, Alex. "It's Time to Weaponize the 'Whisper Network.'" *Vox*, October 17, 2017. https://www.vox.com/first-person/2017/10/16/16482800/harvey-weinstein-sexual-harassment-workplace.

Provine, Doris Marie. *Unequal Under Law: Race in the War on Drugs*. Chicago: University of Chicago Press, 2007.

Quilantan, Bianca. "U. of Pennsylvania Revokes Honorary Degrees to Steve Wynn and Bill Cosby." *Chronicle of Higher Education*, February 1, 2018. https://www.chronicle.com/article/U-of-Pennsylvania-Revokes/242415.

"Race and Wrongful Convictions." The Innocence Project, June 24, 2010. https://www.innocenceproject.org/race-and-wrongful-convictions/.

Raisman, Aly. "Rachael Denhollander." *Time Magazine* 100 Most Influential People of 2018. http://time.com/collection/most-influential-people-2018/5217581/rachael-denhollander/.

Reagle Jr., Joseph M. *Reading the Comments: Likers, Haters, and Manipulators at the Bottom of the Web*. Boston: Massachusetts Institute of Technology Press, 2015.

Reddit. The Red Pill. https://www.reddit.com/r/TheRedPill/.

Renkl, Margaret. "The Raw Power of #MeToo." Opinion. *New York Times*, October 19, 2017. https://www.nytimes.com/2017/10/19/opinion/the-raw-power-of-metoo.html.

Rentschler, Carrie A. "Rape Culture and the Feminist Politics of Social Media." *Girlhood Studies* 7, no. 1 (2014): 65–82.

"Revenge Porn Laws by State." FindLaw. https://criminal.findlaw.com/criminal-charges/revenge-porn-laws-by-state.html.

Richards, Kimberley. "Attorney Chris Darden to Stop Representing Nipsey Hussle's Accused Killer," *The Huffington Post*, May 10, 2019, https://www.huffpost.com/entry/chris-darden-nipsey-hussle-attorney-withdraw-eric-holder_n_5cd5e87de4b0796a95dc05d6.

Richer, Alanna Durkin. "Attorneys Make Final Pitch to Jurors in *Rolling Stone* Trial." Associated Press, November 2, 2016. https://apnews.com/38f01c70406b43d68b60b6b7690302ab.

Ridgeway, Cecilia L. *Framed by Gender: How Gender Inequality Persists in the Modern World.* London: Oxford University Press, 2011.

Robson, Peter, Guy Osborn, and Steve Greenfield. "The Impact of Film and Television on Perceptions of Law and Justice: Towards a Realisable Methodology." Chapter 46 in *Law, Culture and Visual Studies*, edited by Anne Wagner and Richard K. Sherwin. New York: Springer, 2014.

Rodino-Colocino, Michelle. "Me Too, #MeToo: Countering Cruelty with Empathy," *Communication and Critical/Cultural Studies* 15, 2018: 96–100.

Roebuck, Jeremy, and Laura McCrystal. "Cosby Accuser Constand Remains an Enigma." *Philadelphia Inquirer*, January 3, 2016. http://www.philly.com/philly/news/20160103_Cosby_accuser_Constand_remains_an_enigma.html.

Rogers, Richard. "Debanalizing Twitter: The Transformation of an Object of Study." Foreword in *Twitter and Society*, edited by Katrin Weller, Axel Bruns, Jean Burgess, Merja Mahrt, and Cornelius Puschmann. New York: Peter Lang AG, 2013.

Roiphe, Katie. "The Other Whisper Network: How Twitter Feminism Is Bad for Women." *Harper's*, August 22, 2018. https://harpers.org/archive/2018/03/the-other-whisper-network-2/.

Ronner, Amy D. "The Cassandra Curse: The Stereotype of the Female Liar Resurfaces in Jones v. Clinton." *University of California, Davis Law Review* 31 (1997–1998): 137.

Roose, Kevin. "Debunking 5 (More) Viral Rumors about Kavanaugh's Accusers." *New York Times*, September 26, 2018. https://www.nytimes.com/2018/09/26/us/politics/kavanaugh-fact-check.html.

Rose, Amber. "I'm Done with People Asking Me about 'My Brand' of Feminism." *Marie Claire*, September 28, 2017. https://www.marieclaire.com/celebrity/a12479685/amber-rose-slut-walk-essay/.

Rosenbaum, Claudia. "Bill Cosby's Jury Says #MeToo and Race Weren't Factors in His Guilty Verdict." BuzzFeedNews.com, April 30, 2018. https://www.buzzfeed.com/claudiarosenbaum/bill-cosby-jury-speaks-out?utm_term=.ogXQjqaAqR#.vhPJDVnqVX.

Rosin, Hanna. "Trolls Are Outing UVA's 'Jackie.' That's *Rolling Stone*'s Fault Too." *Slate*, December 8, 2014. http://www.slate.com/blogs/xx_factor/2014/12/08/doxxing_jackie_the_vile_and_dangerous_threats_of_charles_johnson_and_other.html.

Ross, Chuck. "UVA Dean Defamed in *Rolling Stone* Article Takes On Major Feminist Organization." *Daily Caller*, June 11, 2016. http://dailycaller.com/2016/06/11/uva-dean-defamed-in-rolling-stone-article-takes-on-major-feminist-organization/.

Ross, Jasmine N., and Nicole M. Coleman. "Gold Digger or Video Girl: The Salience of an Emerging Hip-Hop Sexual Script." *Culture, Health & Sexuality: An International Journal for Research, Prevention, and Care* 13, no. 2 (2011): 158.

Rubenfeld, Jed. "The Riddle of Rape-by-Deception and the Myth of Sexual Autonomy." *Yale Law Journal* 122 (2013): 1372, 1392.

Rumney, Philip N. S. "False Allegations of Rape." *Cambridge Law Journal* 65 (2006): 130.

Russell, Yvette. "Woman's Voice/Law's Logos: The Rape Trial and the Limits of Liberal Reform." *Australian Feminist Law Journal* 42, no. 2 (2016): 275–76.

Ryan, Joan. *Little Girls in Pretty Boxes: The Making and Breaking of Elite Gymnasts and Figure Skaters*. New York: Grand Central, 1996.
Ryzik, Melena. "Weinstein in Handcuffs Is a 'Start to Justice' for His Accusers." *New York Times,* May 25, 2018. https://www.nytimes.com/2018/05/25/nyregion/metoo-accusers-harvey-weinstein.html.
Salter, Michael. "Justice and Revenge in Online Counter-Publics: Emerging Responses to Sexual Violence in the Age of Social Media." *Crime, Media, Culture* 9, no. 3 (2013): 225, 234.
Samuelson, Kate. "Harvey Weinstein Arrested on Charges of Rape, Sex Abuse and More." *Time,* May 25, 2018. http://time.com/5291392/harvey-weinstein-arrested/.
Sanday, Peggy Reeves. *A Woman Scorned: Acquaintance Rape on Trial*. New York: Doubleday, 1996.
Sandlin, Jennifer A., Jennie Stearns, Julie Garlin Maudlin, and Jake Burdick. "'Now I Ain't Sayin' She a Gold Digger': Wal-Mart Shoppers, Welfare Queens, and Other Gendered Stereotypes of Poor Women in the Big Curriculum of Consumption." *Cultural Studies* 11, no. 5 (2011): 466.
Savitsky, Sasha, and Leora Arnowitz. "Cosby Guilty: Jury Rules Comedian Sexually Assaulted Andrea Constand." Fox News, April 26, 2018. http://www.foxnews.com/entertainment/2018/04/26/cosby-guilty-jury-rules-comedian-sexually-assaulted-andrea-constand.html.
Schow, Ashe. "19 Harvard Law Professors Pen Letter Denouncing 'The Hunting Ground.'" *Washington Examiner,* November 11, 2015. https://www.washingtonexaminer.com/19-harvard-law-professors-pen-letter-denouncing-the-hunting-ground.
Schulz, Kathryn. "Dead Certainty." *New Yorker,* January 25, 2016. https://www.newyorker.com/magazine/2016/01/25/dead-certainty.
"The Scottsboro Accusers." PBS. http://www.pbs.org/wgbh/americanexperience/features/scottsboro-ruby-bates-and-victoria-price/.
Scully, Diana, and Joseph Marolla. "'Riding the Bull at Gilley's': Convicted Rapists Describe the Rewards of Rape." *Social Problems* 32, no. 3 (1985): 253.
Seligman, Kathryn, and Jordan Jaffe. "When Does an Anonymous Tip Provide Reasonable Suspicion for a Stop and Frisk?" First District Appellate Project. http://www.fdap.org/downloads/articles_and_outlines/anonymous_tips.pdf.
Severson, Kim. "Asia Argento, a #MeToo Leader, Made a Deal with Her Own Accuser." *New York Times,* August 19, 2018. https://www.nytimes.com/2018/08/19/us/asia-argento-assault-jimmy-bennett.html.
Shafrir, Doree. "What to Do with 'Shitty Media Men'?" BuzzFeedNews.com, October 12, 2017. https://www.buzzfeednews.com/article/doree/what-to-do-with-shitty-media-men#.raZYroJL6.
Sheley, Erin. "A Broken Windows Theory of Sexual Assault Enforcement." *Journal of Law and Criminology* 108, no. 3 (2017): 455–510.
———. "Victim Impact Statements and Expressive Punishment in the Age of Social Media." *Wake Forest Law Review* 52 (2017): 157.
Sherwin, Richard K. "Introductory Essay." In *Popular Culture and Law,* edited by Richard K. Sherwin. Aldershot, England: Ashgate, 2006.
Silbey, Susan S. "After Legal Consciousness." *Annual Review of Law and Social Science* 1 (2005): 323–68.
Silverstein, Jason. "#MeToo Movement Could Turn Women into 'Snowflakes' and Make Men Resent Them, Condoleezza Rice Says." *Newsweek,* January 14, 2018. http://www.newsweek.com/metoo-movement-women-snowflakes-condoleezza-rice-780939.
Simpson, Mark. "Respectability Is the New Closet." *Guardian,* June 2, 2009. https://www.theguardian.com/commentisfree/2009/jun/02/gay-stonewall-respectability-closet.
Sisario, Ben. "*Rolling Stone* Faces Revived Lawsuit over Campus Rape Article." *New York Times,* September 19, 2017. https://www.nytimes.com/2017/09/19/business/

media/rolling-stone-virginia-lawsuit.html.
Sjoberg, Laura. *Women as Wartime Rapists: Beyond Sensation and Stereotyping*. New York: New York University Press, 2016.
Sjoberg, Laura, and Caron E. Gentry, eds. *Mothers, Monsters, Whores: Women's Violence in Global Politics*. London: Zed Books, 2007.
Slovis, Michael, dir. *Law & Order: Special Victims Unit*. Season 16, episode 18, "Devastating Story." Original air date April 1, 2015, on NBC.
Smart, Carol. *Feminism and the Power of Law*. London: Routledge, 1989.
Smith, Fiona. "Privilege is Invisible to Those Who Have It: Engaging Men in Workplace Equality." *Guardian*, June 7, 2016. https://www.theguardian.com/sustainable-business/2016/jun/08/workplace-gender-equality-invisible-privilege.
Smith, Kyle. "Feminists Seize the Moment for Sisterly Revenge." *National Review*, February 5, 2018. https://www.nationalreview.com/2018/02/katie-roiphe-harpers-essay-common-sense/.
"Social Media." Merriam-Webster.com, August 17, 2018. https://www.merriam-webster.com/dictionary/social%20media.
Solberg, Lauren. "Data Mining on Facebook: A Free Space for Researchers or an IRB Nightmare?" *University of Illinois Journal of Law, Technology & Policy* 2 (2010): 311.
Somaiya, Ravi. "*Rolling Stone* Article on Rape at the University of Virginia Failed All the Basics, Report Says." *New York Times*, April 5, 2015. https://www.nytimes.com/2015/04/06/business/media/rolling-stone-retracts-article-on-rape-at-university-of-virginia.html.
Sommer, Will, and Kelly Weill. "Trump Allies Insist Bomb Threats against Clinton, Obama, CNN Are 'Pure BS,' a 'False Flag.'" *Daily Beast*, October 24, 2018. https://www.thedailybeast.com/pro-trump-media-insists-bomb-threats-against-clinton-obama-cnn-are-pure-bs-a-false-flag.
Spiesel, Christina O. "Trial by Ordeal: CSI and the Rule of Law." Chapter 37 *Law, Culture and Visual Studies*, edited by Anne Wagner and Richard K. Sherwin. New York: Springer, 2014.
St. Félix, Doreen. "The Rush of Seeing Harvey Weinstein's Perp Walk." *New Yorker*, May 25, 2018. https://www.newyorker.com/culture/annals-of-appearances/the-rush-of-feeling-seeing-harvey-weinsteins-perp-walk-arrest.
"Stanford Professor Speaks Out on Arrest of Suspect in White Powder Threat." Bay City News, NBC, March 1, 2018. https://www.nbcbayarea.com/news/local/Stanford-Professor-Speaks-Out-on-Arrest-of-Man-Suspected-in-White-Powder-Threat-475607163.html.
Stannow, Lovisa. "No One Deserves to be Raped—Not Even Larry Nassar." *Los Angeles Times*, January 28, 2018. http://www.latimes.com/opinion/opinion-la/la-ol-stannow-larry-nassar-prison-rape-20180128-story.html.
"Statistics on Perpetrators of Child Sexual Abuse." National Center for Victims of Crime. http://victimsofcrime.org/media/reporting-on-child-sexual-abuse/statistics-on-perpetrators-of-csa.
"Steelers QB Wants Written Apology." ESPN.com, September 16, 2009. http://sports.espn.go.com/nfl/news/story?id=4414936.
Stefan, Susan. "The Protection Racket: Rape Trauma Syndrome, Psychiatric Labeling, and Law." *Northwestern University Law Review* 88 (1994): 1328.
Steinberg, David E. "Zealous Officers and Neutral Magistrates: The Rhetoric of the Fourth Amendment." *Creighton Law Review* 43 (2010): 1023–24.
Stemple, Lara, and Ilan H. Meyer. "Sexual Victimization by Women Is More Common than Previously Known." *Scientific American*, October 10, 2017. https://www.scientificamerican.com/article/sexual-victimization-by-women-is-more-common-than-previously-known/.
Stephens, Dionne P., and Layli D. Phillips. "Freaks, Gold Diggers, Divas, and Dykes: The Sociohistorical Development of Adolescent African American Women's Sexual Scripts." *Sexuality and Culture* 7, no. 1 (2003): 11, 12.

Stolberg, Sheryl Gay, and Nicholas Fandos. "Brett Kavanaugh and Christine Blasey Ford Duel with Tears and Fury." *New York Times,* September 27, 2018. https://www.nytimes.com/2018/09/27/us/politics/brett-kavanaugh-confirmation-hearings.html.

Stracqualursi, Veronica. "Woman Admits Accusations against Broward County Sheriff are 'Fake.'" CNN, March 23, 2018. https://www.cnn.com/2018/03/23/politics/florida-sheriff-hoax-videos/index.html.

Street-Porter, Janet. "Harvey Weinstein's PR Machine Means That the Battle for Justice Is Far From Over." *Independent,* May 25, 2018. https://www.independent.co.uk/voices/harvey-weinstein-arrested-bail-me-too-pr-bill-cosby-a8369341.html.

Suk, Jeannie. "'The Look in His Eyes': The Story of Rusk and Rape Reform." Chapter 5 in *Criminal Law Stories*, edited by Robert Weisberg and Donna Coker. New York: Foundation Press, 2012.

Sundell, Allison. "Brock Turner's Mug Shot Next to Definition of Rape in Textbook." *USA Today*, September 14, 2017. https://www.usatoday.com/story/news/nation/2017/09/14/brock-turners-mug-shot-next-definition-rape-textbook/666857001/.

Sunstein, Cass R. *#Republic: Divided Democracy in the Age of Social Media*. Princeton: Princeton University Press, 2017.

Swaine, Jon. "FBI Asked to Investigate Suspected Double Hoax against Mueller." *Guardian,* October 30, 2018. https://www.theguardian.com/us-news/2018/oct/30/robert-mueller-fbi-hoax.

Swartout, Kevin M., Mary P. Koss, and Jacquelyn W. White et al. "Trajectory Analysis of the Campus Serial Rape Assumption." *JAMA Pediatrics* 169, no. 12 (2015): 1148–54.

Tambe, Ashwini. "Reckoning with the Silences of #MeToo." *Feminist Studies* 44, no. 1 (2018): 199.

Taslitz, Andrew E. *Rape and the Culture of the Courtroom*. New York: New York University Press, 1999.

"Tawana Brawley Rape Hoax Leads to Defamation Damage Payout 26 Years Late." Black Voices. *Huffington Post,* August 5, 2013, https://www.huffingtonpost.com/2013/08/05/tawana-brawley-hoax_n_3709058.html.

Taylor, M. Yvonne. "Why #MeToo Can Be for Men, Too." *Houston Chronicle,* October 16, 2017. https://www.houstonchronicle.com/local/gray-matters/article/Why-Me-Too-can-be-for-men-too-12281653.php.

Tenzer, Leslie Y. Garfield. "#MeToo, Statutory Rape Laws and the Persistence of Gender Stereotypes." Paper, Pace University School of Law, February 8, 2018. https://ssrn.com/abstract=3120348 or http://dx.doi.org/10.2139/ssrn.3120348.

Theisen, Lauren. "Larry Nassar Sentenced to 40 to 175 Years in Prison." Deadspin.com (blog), January 24, 2018. https://deadspin.com/larry-nassar-sentenced-to-40-to-175-years-in-prison-1822355055#replies.

Theixos, Helena. "Feminist Perspectives on the Apology of Louis CK and the #MeToo and #TimesUp Movements," *Media Watch* 9, 2018, 267–277.

Thomas, Kimberly. "Interpersonal Power in the Criminal System." *American Criminal Law Review* 50 (2013): 270.

Thompson, Monica. "Life after Rape: A Chance to Speak?" *Sexual and Relationship Therapy* 15, no. 4 (2000): 325–43.

Thuma, Emily L. *All Our Trials: Prisons, Policing, and the Feminist Fight to End Violence,* Urbana, Chicago, and Springfield: University of Illinois Press, 2019.

Tiger, Rebecca. "Celebrity Gossip Blogs and the Interactive Construction of Addiction." *New Media and Society* 17 (2013): 343–44.

The Times Editorial Board, "Rape Bill in Response to Brock Turner Case Shows Headlines Trump Thinking in Criminal Justice," *Los Angeles Times*, July 21, 2016, https://www.latimes.com/opinion/editorials/la-ed-rape-sentence-bill-20160630-snap-story.html.

TIME'S UP website. https://www.timesupnow.com.

"Tom Hanks Says No Way Back for Harvey Weinstein." BBC News, October 19, 2017. http://www.bbc.com/news/entertainment-arts-41678196.

Toplosky, Joshua. "The End of Twitter." *New Yorker*, January 29, 2016. https://www.newyorker.com/tech/elements/the-end-of-twitter.

Trabka, Laura. "Natalie Portman Gives Shout-Out to Ingham County Judge Aquilina on 'Saturday Night Live.'" *Lansing State Journal*, February 5, 2018. https://www.lansingstatejournal.com/story/entertainment/2018/02/05/natalie-portman-judge-aquilina/306358002/.

Tracy, Carol E., and Charlene Whitman. "Rape and Sexual Assault in the Legal System." *AEquitas Women's Law Project* (2013): 19.

Tracy, Marc. "Jameis Winston and Woman Who Accused Him of Rape Settle Lawsuits." *New York Times*, December 15, 2016. https://www.nytimes.com/2016/12/15/sports/football/jameis-winston-erica-kinsman-lawsuit.html.

Traister, Rebecca. *Good and Mad: The Revolutionary Power of Women's Anger*. New York: Simon & Schuster, 2018.

Tran, Marc. "Combatting Gender Privilege and Recognizing a Woman's Right to Privacy in Public Spaces: Arguments to Criminalize Catcalling and Creepshots." *Hastings Women's Law Journal* 26 (2015): 185.

Truesdell, Jeff, and Nicole Weisensee Egan. "Who Is Andrea Constand, Bill Cosby's Accuser?" People.com, June 13, 2017. https://www.imdb.com/news/ni61172968.

Tuerkheimer, Deborah. "Incredible Women: Sexual Violence and the Credibility Discount." *University of Pennsylvania Law Review* 166 (2017): 9, 16.

———. "Sex without Consent," *Yale Law Journal Online* 123 (2013): 352.

Ubell, Rose Mary Lynn. "Myths and Misogyny: The Legal Response to Sexual Assault." Melanie Randall, Supervisor. Western University Master of Studies in Law Research Papers Repository 4, January 2018.

U.S. Press and Publishing. "'Jackie' Testifies: *Rolling Stone* Story was 'What I Believed to Be True at the Time.'" *Guardian*, October 24, 2016. https://www.theguardian.com/media/2016/oct/24/rolling-stone-defamation-trial-uva-jackie-testifies.

Vagianos, Alanna. "The Rape Kit Backlog Shows Exactly How We Regard Women in this Country." *Huffington Post*, April 13, 2018. https://www.huffingtonpost.com/entry/the-rape-kit-backlog-shows-exactly-how-we-regard-women-in-this-country_us_5acfb5e1e4b016a07e9a8c65.

Valenti, Jessica. "In Rape Tragedies, the Shame Is Ours." *The Nation*, April 17, 2013. https://www.thenation.com/article/173911/rape-tragedies-shame- ours#.

Victor, Daniel. "Brock Turner Wanted Only 'Outercourse,' Lawyer Argues in Appeal." *New York Times*, July 26, 2018. https://www.nytimes.com/2018/07/26/us/brock-turner-victim-outercourse-appeal.html.

———. "*Making a Murderer* Left Out Crucial Facts, Prosecutor Says." *New York Times*, January 5, 2016. https://www.nytimes.com/2016/01/05/arts/television/ken-kratz-making-a-murderer.html?_r=0.

Visser, Nick. "Christine Blasey Ford Can't Return Home Due to 'Unending' Threats, Lawyers Say." *Huffington Post*, October 8, 2018. https://www.huffingtonpost.com/entry/christine-blasey-ford-home-unending-threats_us_5bbaa112e4b0876eda9f3317.

Vitiello, Michael. "Brock Turner: Sorting through the Noise," *University of the Pacific Law Review* 49, no. 3 (2018): 631–59.

Wade, Lisa. "Rape on Campus: Athletes, Status and the Sexual Assault Crisis." *Salon*, March 12, 2017. https://www.salon.com/2017/03/12/rape-on-campus-athletes-status-and-the-sexual-assault-crisis_partner/.

Wagner, Laura. "FSU Pays $950,000 to Woman Who Accused Jameis Winston of Sexual Assault." National Public Radio, January 25, 2016. https://www.npr.org/sections/thetwo-way/2016/01/25/464332250/fsu-pays-950-000-to-woman-who-accused-jameis-winston-of-sexual-assault.

Waterhouse-Watson, Deb. "(Un)Reasonable Doubt: A 'Narrative Immunity' for Footballers against Sexual Assault Allegations." *M/C Journal* 14, no. 11 (2011). http://www.journal .media-culture.org.au/index.php/mcjournal/article/viewArticle/337.

WebMD. "Date Rape Drugs." https://www.webmd.com/mental-health/addiction/date-rape-drugs.

Weiss, Bari. "The Limits of 'Believe All Women.'" Opinion. *New York Times*, November 28, 2017. https://www.nytimes.com/2017/11/28/opinion/metoo-sexual-harassment-believe-women.html?_r=0.

Weiss, Karen G., and Corey J. Colyer. "Roofies, Mickies and Cautionary Tales: Examining the Persistence of the 'Date-Rape Drug' Crime Narrative." *Deviant Behavior* 31, no. 4 (2010): 348–79.

Weiss, Suzannah. "#MeToo Has Made Me See Anyone Is Capable of Sexual Abuse—Including Me." *Establishment*, February 1, 2018. https://theestablishment.co/metoo-has-made-me-see-anyone-is-capable-of-sexual-abuse-including-me-6455f93309a9.

Weller, Sheila. "How Author Timothy Tyson Found the Woman at the Center of the Emmett Till Case." *Vanity Fair*, January 26, 2017. https://www.vanityfair.com/news/2017/01/how-author-timothy-tyson-found-the-woman-at-the-center-of-the-emmett-till-case?mbid=social_twitter.

Wemple, Erik. "The Full Demise of *Rolling Stone*'s Rape Story." *Washington Post*, December 11, 2014. https://www.washingtonpost.com/blogs/erik-wemple/wp/2014/12/11/the-full-demise-of-rolling-stones-rape-story/?utm_term=.1618c5f9f331.

Wesolowski, James J. "Indicia of Consent? A Proposal for Change to the Common Law Rule Admitting Evidence of Rape Victim's Character for Chastity." *Loyola University Chicago Law Journal* 7 (1976): 118.

West, Kanye. "Gold Digger." MetroLyrics, 2003. http://www.metrolyrics.com/gold-digger-lyrics-kanye-west.html.

Whitewater Special Report. *Washington Post*, 1998. https://www.washingtonpost.com/wp-srv/politics/special/whitewater/timeline.htm.

"Why One Dictionary Made 'Complicit' Its Word of the Year." *All Things Considered*. National Public Radio, November 20, 2017. https://www.npr.org/2017/11/30/567572975/why-one-dictionary-made-complicit-its-word-of-the-year.

Wiggins, Jennifer. "Rape, Racism, and the Law." *Harvard Women's Law Journal* 6 (1983): 127.

Williams, Joseph P. "Courts Considered Trump's Twitter in Ruling." *US News and World Report*, June 12, 2017. https://www.usnews.com/news/national-news/articles/2017-06-12/donald-trumps-statements-on-twitter-cited-in-courts-decision-to-upholds-block-on-travel-ban.

Williams, Mary Elizabeth. "'Don't Read the Comments': The Trolls, Racists and Abusers Won—Reasonable Online Feedback Is a Thing of the Distant Past." Salon.com, September 11, 2015. https://www.salon.com/2015/09/11/dont_read_the_comments_the_trolls_racists_and_abusers_won_reasonable_online_feedback_is_a_thing_of_the_distant_past/.

Williams, Sherri. "Digital Defense: Black Feminists Resist Violence with Hashtag Activism." *Feminist Media Studies* 15, no. 2 (2015): 341–44.

Willingham, Kamilah. "To the Harvard 19: Do Better." Medium.com, March 24, 2016. https://medium.com/@kamily/to-the-harvard-law-19-do-better-1053794288f2.

Wilson, Jason. "Crisis Actors, Deep State, False Flag: The Rise of Conspiracy Theory Code Words." *Guardian*, February 21, 2018. https://www.theguardian.com/us-news/2018/feb/21/crisis-actors-deep-state-false-flag-the-rise-of-conspiracy-theory-code-words.

Wilstein, Matt. "TBT: When Mark Halperin Dismissed Sexual Assault Allegations against Trump." *Daily Beast*, October 26, 2017. https://www.thedailybeast.com/when-mark-halperin-dismissed-sexual-assault-allegations-against-trump.

Withers, Bethany P. "Without Consequence: When Professional Athletes Are Violent Off the Field." *Harvard Journal of Sports & Entertainment Law* 6, no. 2 (2015): 373–411.

Wolf, Richard. "As Trump Travel Ban (Finally) Reaches Supreme Court, His Talk and Tweets Are Center Stage." *USA Today*, April 24, 2018. https://www.usatoday.com/story/news/politics/2018/04/24/trump-travel-ban-supreme-court-campaign-promises-tweets/543952002/.

———. "Manafort Trial: Why 'Reasonable Doubt' is Hard to Define in Courtrooms." *USA Today*, August 17, 2018. https://www.usatoday.com/story/news/politics/2018/08/17/reasonable-doubt-standard-manafort-trial-difficult-define/1017821002/.

Wolfinger, Emily. "'But It's Already Public, Right?': The Ethics of Using Online Data." *Data Driven Journalism*, November 25, 2016. http://datadrivenjournalism.net/news_and_analysis/but_its_already_public_right_the_ethics_of_using_online_data.

Woloch, Nancy. *A Class By Herself: Protective Laws for Women Workers, 1890s–1990s*. Princeton, NJ: Princeton University Press, 2017.

Wootson, Cleeve R., Jr. "The Judge in the Infamous Brock Turner Case Finally Explains His Decision a Year Later." *Washington Post*, July 2, 2017. https://www.washingtonpost.com/news/grade-point/wp/2017/07/02/the-judge-in-the-infamous-brock-turner-case-finally-explains-his-decision-a-year-later/?utm_term=.c74ddb8e8fbf.

World Health Organization. "Addressing Violence against Sex Workers." http://www.who.int/hiv/pub/sti/sex_worker_implementation/swit_chpt2.pdf.

Xu, Victor. "Brock Turner Sentenced to Six Months in County Jail, Three Years Probation." *Stanford Daily*, June 2, 2016. https://www.stanforddaily.com/2016/06/02/brock-turner-sentenced-to-six-months-in-county-jail-three-years-probation/.

Yin, Karen. "Capitalizing for Equality." *Conscious Style Guide*, February 22, 2017. https://consciousstyleguide.com/capitalizing-for-equality/.

Young, Damon. "The Stanford Sexual Assault Case: A White Privilege Cake with Vanilla Frosting on Top." *Guardian*, June 9, 2016. https://www.theguardian.com/society/2016/jun/09/standford-rape-case-white-privilege-brock-turner.

Yung, Corey Rayburn. "Concealing Campus Sexual Assault: An Empirical Examination." *Psychology, Public Policy, and Law* 21, no. 1 (2015): 6.

———. "One of These Laws Is Not Like the Others: Why the Federal Sex Offender Registration and Notification Act Raises New Constitutional Questions." *Harvard Journal on Legislation* 46 (2009): 372–73.

———. "Rape Law Fundamentals." *Yale Journal of Law and Feminism* 27, no. 1 (2015): 16.

Zacharek, Stephanie. "What Men—and Women—Can Learn from Joe Biden's 'Inappropriate Touching,'" *Time*, April 25, 2019, http://time.com/5578143/biden-inappropriate-touching/.

Zacharek, Stephanie, Eliana Dockterman, and Haley Sweetland Edwards. "The Silence Breakers." *Time*, December 2017. http://time.com/time-person-of-the-year-2017-silence-breakers/.

Zeitchik, Steven. "Prosecutors Say Bill Cosby Engaged in a Pattern of Sexually Abusive Behavior." *Los Angeles Times*, December 13, 2016. http://www.latimes.com/nation/la-na-bill-cosby-accusers-20161213-story.html.

Zimmer, Ben. "'Casting Couch': The Origins of a Pernicious Hollywood Cliché." *Atlantic*, October 16, 2017. https://www.theatlantic.com/entertainment/archive/2017/10/casting-couch-the-origins-of-a-pernicious-hollywood-cliche/543000/.

Index

About the Author

Francine Banner is associate professor of sociology at the University of Michigan—Dearborn. Prior to becoming a professor, she practiced law in New York City. This is her first book.